THE LAST DAYS OF OLD BEIJING

Life in the Vanishing Backstreets of a City Transformed

MICHAEL MEYER

WALKER & COMPANY
NEW YORK

Maps on pages viii and ix designed by Gary J. Antonetti, Ortelius Design, Inc. Map on
page x designed by Frances Feng; adapted by Gary J. Antonetti, Ortelius Design, Inc.
Photographs on pages xii, 40, 41, 240, 307, and 317 courtesy of Theodore Wright.
Map on page 47 from *Conservation Plan for the Historic City of Beijing and Imperial City
of Beijing* (Beijing Municipal Planning Commission, ed.). Photographs on pages 14,
311, 313, 315, 324, and 326 courtesy of Mark Leong. Maps on page 149 designed by
Gary J. Antonetti, Ortelius Design, Inc., adapted from *Chengji*, by Wang Jun. Photograph on page 196 courtesy of Zhang Jinqi. Drawing on page 283 from *The Collected
Works of Liang Sicheng*. Photograph on page 319 courtesy of SOHO. Every effort has
been made to locate the copyright holders of historic photographs in the book. All
other images are courtesy of the author.

Published by Walker Publishing Company, Inc., New York

All papers used by Walker & Company are natural, recyclable products made
from wood grown in well-managed forests. The manufacturing processes con-
form to the environmental regulations of the country of origin.

LIBRARY OF CONGRESS CATALOGING-IN-PUBLICATION DATA

Meyer, Michael
The last days of old Beijing : the life in the backstreets of a changing city / Michael
Meyer.—1st U.S. ed.
p. cm.
Includes bibliographical references.
ISBN-13: 978-0-8027-1652-1 (hardcover)
ISBN-10: 0-8027-1652-0 (hardcover)
1. Beijing (China)—Social life and customs. 2. Alleys—China—Beijing. 3. Streets—
China—Beijing—History. 4. Urban renewal—China—Beijing. I. Title.
DS795.7.A2 M46 2008
951'.156—dc22
2008015546

Visit Walker & Company's Web site at www.walkerbooks.com

First published by Walker & Company in 2008
This paperback edition published in 2009

Paperback ISBN-10: 0-8027-1750-0
ISBN-13: 978-0-8027-1750-4

1 3 5 7 9 10 8 6 4 2

Designed by Rachel Reiss

Typeset by Westchester Book Group
Printed in the United States of America by Quebecor World Fairfield

Praise for *The Last Days of Old Beijing*

"Michael Meyer's voracious curiosity has led him deep, deep into a vanishing world that other visitors and foreign correspondents almost all see only from a taxi window. He comes at it with a wide knowledge of history, a thirst for people's life stories, a novelist's ability to evoke a social universe, and an Arctic explorer's willingness to live through a sub-zero winter with little heat and the nearest communal toilet far down a snowy lane."
—**Adam Hochschild, author of**
King Leopold's Ghost **and** *Bury the Chains*

"Meyer's record of the dying ways of a city is an impressive feat. And while the phenomenon may be most extreme there, it's not just Beijing's problem. In a way, we're all living on New American Culture Street." —***New York Times Book Review***

"Impressive . . . one of the book's main attractions is its intense local focus, conveying the daily rhythms of life in his neighborhood . . . [Meyer's] greatest strength is in depicting how such changes affect, for better or worse, the widow next door and the other memorable characters who populate this evocative tale." —***Newsweek***

"Part memoir, part history, part travelogue and part call to action, journalist Meyer's elegant first book yearns for old Beijing and mourns the loss of an older way of life . . . Meyer's powerful book is to Beijing what Jane Jacobs's *The Death and Life of Great American Cities* was to New York City."
—***Publishers Weekly*** **(starred review)**

"Nimbly told . . . Through his skillful weaving of his professional experiences with his intimate encounters with neighbors, *The Last Days of Old Beijing* is as much a chronicle of the physical transformation of the city as it is a tribute to the inhabitants of his beloved hutong." —***San Francisco Chronicle***

"A substantive, smart book." —**Maureen Corrigan, *Fresh Air***

"A delightfully observed view of a vast part of Chinese society that barely was glimpsed during the recent Olympics, yet is fading away."
—***Minneapolis Star Tribune***

"Striking for the unsentimental pictures [it] paint[s] of the urban poor, whose homes and way of life are being eradicated to make room for malls and highrises . . . The local characters who share this intimate environment with him— some young, some old, most without resources to live elsewhere—give Mr. Meyer's portrait its flesh tones . . . But his history of land development in Beijing, from the time of the Italian Jesuit Matteo Ricci to Mao to the present, and of attempts in Hanoi, Havana and other Communist cities to preserve their own sense of place, are just as compelling (and sad) to read." —***New York Times* Travel**

"Michael Meyer eloquently portrays the madness of the city during this period."
—*Los Angeles Times*

"A spiritedness shines through among his earthy neighbors, even in the face of what Mr. Meyer calls "the Hand", which, visiting always at night, paints the Chinese character for "destroy" on houses that are to be razed."   —*Economist*

"Like Peter Hessler's *River Town*, it is a haunting portrait of the interaction between change and changelessness in China . . . his book reads like a love letter to the hutongs and to Old Beijing itself, a snapshot snatched before the scene disappears forever . . . Meyer beautifully dissects the tensions between tradition and modernity in the minds of the Chinese people and examines the identity crisis that still persists, for Beijing, and for China."   —*Slate*

"Not just an excellent, loving paean to a neighborhood imperiled by Beijing's Olympic-era makeover, but one of the best portraits of any city in the throes of modernization."   —*Far Eastern Economic Review*

"[A] warmhearted memoir."   —*Boston Globe*

"A mixture of romanticism and Chinese pragmatism and an attractive profile of a city in ceaseless change."   —*Chicago Tribune*

"The hutongs emerge as a Chinese version of the kind of urbanism advocated by Jane Jacobs 40 years ago when, against the brutal makeover of New York pushed through by the city's 'master builder' Robert Moses, she spoke up for mixed-use communities, pedestrian- and bicycle- rather than car-focused, whose dynamism sprang from their diversity and density."   —*New Statesman*

"To show us what this threatened neighborhood is like, Meyer takes us into his life, masterfully describing the seasons, his home and courtyard, and his students and their parents . . . All library collections that aim for a complete overview of China must add this unusual title."   —*Library Journal* (starred review)

"He writes vividly about both the spartan and sensuous sides of hutong living, with the pleasures outweighing the privations . . . 'The charm of a culture is its individuality,' states Feng Jicai, a preservationist whom Meyer interviews. 'The boredom of a culture is similarity.' It's an insight that resonates far beyond booming Beijing."
—*Houston Chronicle*

"A wistful, charming paean to a community and way of life that is soon to be swept away in the name of progress."   —*Booklist*

For Mom and Pop

Contents

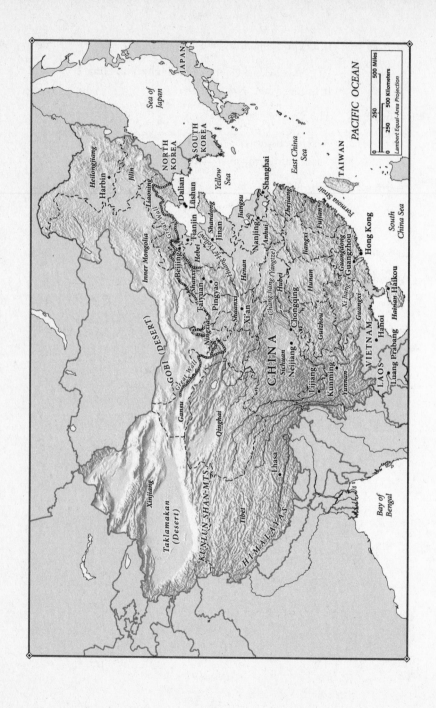

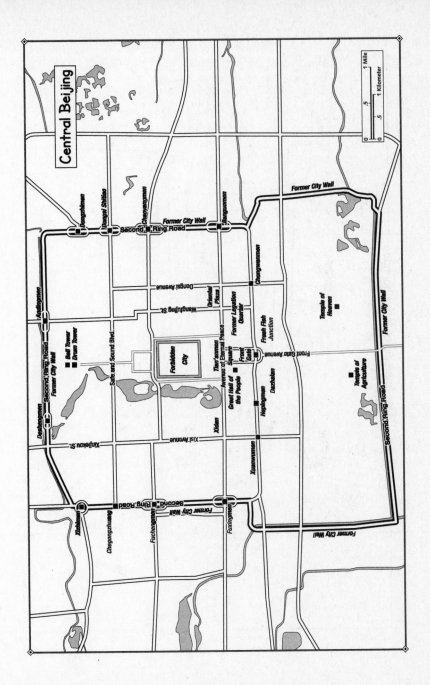

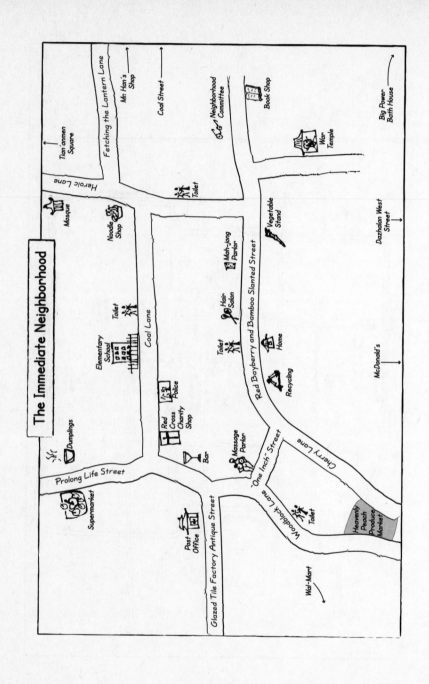

The Immediate Neighborhood

By "new Beijing," I meant we want to have a new humanism in Beijing, a new humanistic city. But the local officials and planners took this slogan literally. They think "new Beijing" means destroy old Beijing and build a new Beijing.

—Li Xiguang, journalism professor and author of the English slogan for the city's successful bid to host the 2008 Summer Games: "New Beijing, Great Olympics."

FRONT GATE AVENUE WILL BECOME FRONT GATE HEAVENLY STREET

At the end of this year, old Beijing residents' lingering memory of the five archways, electric trolley, and teahouse opera stages will return to Front Gate Avenue. After renovations, the street will change its name to Heavenly Street and restore the late-Qing dynasty and early Republican-era architecture, recalling the appearance of the ancient capital, and display its grand historical culture, while combining the traditional and modern in a newly built pedestrian shopping mall.

—Beijing Evening News, May 9, 2007

Our courtyard's entrance corridor.

CHAPTER I

THROUGH THE FRONT GATE

THE WIDOW OPENS my door without knocking. A trail of Flying Horse–brand cigarette smoke enters behind her. An old cotton cap hides coarse, mortar-colored hair, brushed back from her brow to reveal a gold loop in each ear. She wears a fleece vest and forearm mufflers that match the vermilion and crimson wood beams of our courtyard home. When I picture my neighbor the Widow, I see these colors—dull whites and grays, lustrous yellows, imperial reds—and smell ashes and age. She is the shade and scent of our *hutong*,* one of the lanes that lattice the heart of Beijing. The Widow has lived in this neighborhood for most of her eighty years. She can't imagine moving to the glassy high-rise landscape that encroaches from all sides. She often declares she will never leave. The Widow, like most *hutong* residents, will not have a choice.

"Little Plumblossom! Listen, you have to eat before class." I stand before her in a T-shirt and boxer shorts. The Widow scrapes the ends of a pair of chopsticks and places them in my hand. "Eat, Little Plumblossom!" She uses an endearment short for my Chinese name. I call her *da niang*, a term of respect for an elderly woman.

The Widow extends a steaming bowl of dumplings with two hands. Her eyes squint from the cigarette smoke curling up her sallow cheeks. She stuffed the dumplings with pork and chives, my favorite. "You know," she says, "it's too hard to cook for one person, so you have to eat these."

---

*胡同. Pronounced "who-TONG." *Hutong* is both the singular and plural romanization of the word. Chinese characters and the translations for place names appear in the appendix.

I always do what the Widow says. Although seven of us inhabit the five rooms of this courtyard, everyone knows that we are living in her home, even if she doesn't own it. The Widow has tenure. In 1962, the municipal housing bureau assigned her to the south-facing room opposite mine. In sixty-five square feet, she raised two children and a granddaughter. Their photos, and one of her as a radiant young woman with high cheekbones and a pressed gray dress, fill a single frame that hangs on her wall. The room has an exposed cement floor, a bureau made from walnut, two metal folding chairs at a card table, and a twin bed. She keeps the color television tuned to Channel 11, the Beijing opera station. Crashing gongs and plaintive wails fill our courtyard from sunrise until after dark.

The Widow lights another Flying Horse. The robin's-egg-blue package is decorated with a drawing of a horse leaping skyward, away from a horizon of petrochemical plants and smokestacks. It is the cheapest brand sold on our *hutong*, and tastes it.

"You should wake up earlier," she scolds. "I already went to Heavenly Peach market." It is seven o'clock in the morning. Our neighborhood's compact blend of housing and shops means the *hutong* is always open for business, and business is always nearby. In the morning, residents crowd the open-air bazaar, where farmers from outside Beijing sell fresh meat and produce. "I put the pot on the flame for the dumplings, then left," she says. "When I got back from Heavenly Peach with the ingredients, the water was already boiling."

The Widow watches me drink the salty broth. I thank her. She cocks her head and says, "What?" She is going deaf. By way of good-bye, she grunts, "Uh!" before stepping over our courtyard's wooden threshold and turning left. The four courtyards in this former mansion are each shared by multiple tenants. Our rooms are tucked in the back corner, farthest from the entrance gate. The Widow shuffles over the corridor's uneven earth and flagstones, running both hands along the gray brick walls for support. The women's latrine is opposite our front gate on the *hutong*, narrow enough that she can cross in a few unassisted strides.

The men's bathroom is farther away, and so with the Widow gone and my neighbors still asleep, I undo the padlock on the rotted door of a closet-size annex and pour a plastic bottle filled with the previous night's piss down the drain. I grab a towel off the outdoor line, snap it free of dust, and stick my head under the cold-water tap, shampooing quickly and rinsing with a coffee mug filled with frigid water. I scrub my face and under my arms, saving the rest of my skin for the Big Power Bathhouse, a few lanes away.

It is a typical morning in a typical Beijing *hutong*. The only thing exceptional is the weather, which is neither sweltering nor frigid, and the air unpolluted. "Tiger Autumn" arrives between summer and fall, bringing bracing mornings and warm afternoons. When I reach up to put the towel back on the line, the view shows a cloudless blue sky over serried rows of gray-tiled rooftops that crest between tufts of green leaves. A wind gust showers the courtyard in dust.

In its original state, a tea table and persimmon tree could have fit in the courtyard's open space. But over the decades, the cement slab has shrunk from an added bedroom, a kitchen sheltering a propane range, and clotheslines that web the air. When it rains, umbrellas have to be opened on the lane. In the courtyard, I must stoop to the Widow's height.

Inside my house, I tower over her. The north wall of my home is made of windows that stretch from waist high to the eaves, fifteen feet above. The door lock is a weak dead bolt, engaged only when I'm sleeping, because people wander in throughout the day. It is a very public life, lived in two rooms. Although the $100 monthly rent is a fraction of what a Beijing apartment with heat and plumbing costs, the Widow still thinks I'm wasting money. She lives in a single room, after all, as does the married couple in the adjoining room. They migrated from China's northeast to find work in the capital. We share a wall and a landlord, who divided his family's half of the courtyard into two spaces. Like the Widow, his mother was assigned to reside here. Unlike the Widow, he prefers living in a modern apartment and moved after his mother died, retaining the home's "usage rights," which are transferable and allow him to sell or rent his toehold in the neighborhood.

My living room holds a bookshelf, small couch, chair, tea table, and a desk. The floor's polished marble tiles are always cool and damp. The whitewashed straw-and-mud walls glow from sunlight or the uncovered bulb dangling from above. The other room's crimson-painted planks creak underfoot. It is furnished with a bureau, a platform bed that could sleep four adults, and a mineral-water heater. I spoon instant Nescafé coffee into a cup, switch off the computer, and turn on the water, avoiding a repeat of the morning when I blew the courtyard's fuses. That's why my unplugged refrigerator now stores underwear.

Because they did not own the home outright, the Widow and others put little of their meager salaries into its upkeep. Since the 1950s, that responsibility has fallen to the Municipal Bureau of Land Resources and Housing Administration. It holds the property rights of the majority of Beijing's vernacular architecture, the single-story courtyards that line the *hutong*. Decades of subsidized rents, budgetary shortfalls, overcrowding, and neglected maintenance have eroded the houses, built with perishable materials such as wood and earthen bricks. As the homes rot, they are condemned in lots by the municipal government and auctioned to developers who raze the neighborhood, erasing not only the homes and *hutong*, but also their unique pattern of life.

Hutong is derived from the Mongolian word for "water well," or "a path between tents," or from a Chinese word that described the narrow passageways that served as firebreaks in Kublai Khan's thirteenth-century capital. Marco Polo marveled that "the whole interior of the city is laid out in squares like a chessboard with such masterly precision that no description can do justice to it."

As the city grew, so did its number of lanes. Byways were cut to link parallel *hutong*, as some ran east-to-west for a mile without crossing. In 1949, a survey recorded more than seven thousand *hutong*. Shaded by rows of leaning locust trees, many were too narrow for vehicles to enter. The network of backstreets connected neighborhoods of walled courtyards and also formed an elongated public marketplace, where itinerant peddlers and performers worked door-to-door. In a period of the late 1990s, an average of six hundred lanes were destroyed each year. In 2005, the state-run media reported that only thirteen hundred *hutong* remained.

Given the vagaries of Beijing's urban-planning history, there is no consensus on the exact figure of extant lanes. Some tallies include only streets with *hutong* in their formal name, while others count all narrow streets and alleys, including the many added after the Communists expanded the capital after 1949. It is indisputable that beginning in 1990, Beijing's courtyard-lined *hutong* have systematically been razed under a municipal redevelopment plan. From its start until 2003, the government admits to evicting over five hundred thousand residents from the city center. Beijing's remaining traditional neighborhoods exist under the constant threat of obliteration.

Settled over eight centuries ago, Dazhalan—Big Fence—is the city's most venerable community. The name dates to the fifteenth century, when wicker gates on either end of the area's *hutong* were clasped shut at night to deter thieves from preying upon the many shops that formed the capital's prosperous commercial district. After a succession of seventeenth-century imperial edicts banned hotels, restaurants, teahouses, and theaters—and, eventually, all ethnic Han Chinese—from inside the imperial confines, businesses migrated through Qianmen (Front Gate) to the other side of the city wall. Dazhalan became the capital's entertainment, artisan, and antique district. Beijing specialties such as roast duck, acrobatics, and opera flourished here. Some lanes filled with silversmiths, silk embroiderers, and calligraphers; others with stages, brothels, and opium dens.

Things are tamer today, though officials view the neighborhood as an eyesore whose decay belies efforts to beautify the capital before it hosts the 2008 Summer Olympics, whose winning bid's Chinese slogan promised "New Beijing, New Olympics." Located at Beijing's core, Dazhalan's land is valuable to developers and visible to tourists. The parliamentary Great Hall of the People and Tian'anmen Square border the neighborhood's north, while its eastern boundary is drawn by the road connecting the Front Gate's towers to the Temple of Heaven.

Dazhalan is both the name of a popular pedestrian-only lane, and the surrounding neighborhood. Like Beijing—"northern capital"—the area is known by its Chinese name in English. Dazhalan's 114 *hutong* hold nearly fifteen hundred businesses, seven temples, and three thousand homes. Most are single-story courtyards that have gradually rotted across the twentieth century. It is Beijing's—if not the world's—densest urban environment. Equal in size to Vatican City (population 557), Dazhalan's half square mile contains some 57,000 residents, including one foreigner.

On the day I moved to Dazhalan, the Widow fixed her brown eyes on mine and explained the courtyard's only rule: "Public is public; private is private!"

Once over the threshold and into the *hutong*, life becomes all public. On my stoop, a group of old women pin red armbands to their sleeves that say PATROL in characters. "Little Plumblossom, have you eaten?" they ask in greeting. Officially, the women are volunteers on neighborhood watch. The Widow will not join them. "They just sit around and gossip all day," she says.

Grandmothers push prams filled with vegetables from Heavenly Peach market. The bells of black steel Flying Pigeon bicycles warn to make way. A five-year-old watches her pet chicken peck at the puddles on the lane's pockmarked asphalt. A caged mynah bird mimics the call of a vendor walking with an armful of morning newspapers. A man in a smock spreads a blanket on the ground and arranges dental bridges in neat rows upon it, bellowing, "Tooth repair!" Recycler Wang uses a cast-iron scale to weigh a satchel of empty mineral-water bottles. Their collector disagrees with the measurement and pesters him to step aside so she can adjust the sliding bar. They squint at the notch and agree he was right. He pays her and throws the burlap bag onto his flatbed truck. He exhales sharply when I ask, "How's business?" Recycler Wang fights over pennies all day.

On the lane, we are penned in by an unbroken row of buildings, without open space. Aside from painted gates, courtyard homes show only gray walls. The aesthetic is planned monotony, unlike the variety of facades seen in Europe's ancient capitals, which project their distinctiveness. "Just as our blessed God has arranged our own members so that the most beautiful are in positions most exposed to view and the more unpleasant are hidden," wrote the Italian Renaissance architect Palladio, "we too when building should place the most important and prestigious parts in full view and the less beautiful in locations concealed as far from our eyes as possible." A Beijing courtyard home, in contrast, turns its face inward, hiding its most attractive features behind gates and walls.

The run-down mansion where I live shows traces of its former owner's wealth. The heavy double-wooden doors retain coats of lacquer, though the painted couplet has been rubbed away. Unknown hands chipped off the guardian lions carved atop the twin rectangular stones anchoring the doorframe. Lotuses and clouds painted in bright primary colors fade on the lintel. Rusting hooks that once held halyards to raise red lanterns poke out from weeds growing in the furrows of the tiled roof.

Like all courtyards, the house is one story tall. Imperial Beijing had a low skyline that rippled outward from the heights of the Forbidden City. Using the city's former English name, the British attaché recorded that in 1865 Lord Stanley sneered, "Peking's a giant failure, isn't it? Not a two-storied house in the whole place, eh?" The disrespect was mutual. In the eighteenth century, the emperor Kangxi, when looking at drawings of European houses, remarked, "Undoubtedly this Europe must be a very small and pitiful country; since the inhabitants cannot find ground enough to spread out their towns, but are obliged to live up thus in the air."

According to the Widow, the best thing about living in a courtyard home is that it keeps one's feet on the ground, which is healthier than living in a high-rise apartment. The concept is called *jie diqi* in Chinese, "to be connected to the earth's energy." The Widow once demonstrated by gently tapping her foot on our gate's granite step, wooden threshold, and surrounding muddy lane. At every touch, she repeated *connected*.

Beijing is so flat and geometric that when people say how to go from place to place, they often substitute the cardinal directions for *left* and *right*, *forward* and *back*. Most of the city's *hutong* form a rigid grid, but Dazhalan's lanes were built outside the Front Gate, beyond the reach of imperial codes. Nowhere in Beijing exists such a variety of *hutong*, which include the city's shortest (ten yards) and narrowest (fifteen inches). Others bend and double back on themselves, then dead-end.

I live on Red Bayberry and Bamboo Slanted Street, a lane that runs eight hundred yards diagonally through the neighborhood, tracing the route of a former canal filled in by settlers. The *hutong* is wide enough for a single car to navigate, though doing so often requires moving parked bicycles to the gutterless edges.

Hutong names evoke a bygone era. Originally Red Bayberry and Bamboo was named after a matchmaker who arranged marriages on the lane. After the custom was deemed a relic of feudalism, municipal authorities swapped her name (*yang*) and profession (*mei*) for homophones that mean Red Bayberry (*yangmei*), then added bamboo (*zhu*). The name reflects the apothecaries who worked here, and the craftsmen who sold whistles carved from bamboo to attach to pigeon's pinion feathers. Red Bayberry and Bamboo is bordered by Glazed Tile Factory, a lane named for the kilns that once fired roof tiles for imperial palaces and temples. It connects to Coal Lane, which supplied fuel to the kilns, and Whisk Broom Lane, which made the tools to sweep up the ash.

The men's latrine is a few minutes' walk from my door, a route I have timed flat. My walk passes the vegetable seller arranging a pyramid of cabbages, the hairstylist massaging the temples of a customer, and the open doorway from which spills the clack of gamblers' mah-jongg tiles. Red Bayberry and Bamboo Slanted Street's architecture is a time line of Beijing's last century, a procession of red wooden gates, two-story beaux arts masonry, Soviet-inspired concrete storefronts, and patchy redbrick lean-tos. Separately, none of the fragile buildings are masterpieces. Together, they are the backdrop to a vanishing way of life.

Inside the public toilet, a placard warns NO SPITTING, NO SMOKING, NO COARSE LANGUAGE, NO MISSING THE HOLE. Four slits in the floor face one another, without dividers. A squatting man hacks up a wad of phlegm. Another, wearing pajamas, lights a cigarette. Into his cell phone, a guy shouts a common Beijing vulgarity: *"Shabi!"* He listens to the response and again barks, "Stupid cunt!" I fish a wad of tissue from my back pocket and squat over the hole. No one makes eye contact.

A child runs in, wearing the school-issued yellow baseball cap whose printed characters announce SAFETY. The hat makes kids visible to cars. *Hutong* traffic is mostly bicycles and the occasional mule cart, but rules are rules. A backpack weighs the boy down, and he struggles to keep balance while lowering his pants. He crouches, looks up, rises, makes a small bow, and yells, "Good morning, Teacher Plumblossom!"

CHAPTER 2

BECOMING TEACHER PLUMBLOSSOM

I FIRST CAME to China a decade before, as a Peace Corps volunteer. I had hoped the Peace Corps would send me to Latin America, as I was majoring in education at the University of Wisconsin earning credentials to teach Spanish and English. In the mornings, I taught ninth-graders at a high school, then sped past Madison's fuming Oscar Mayer plant to instruct an afternoon class of forty-two sixth-graders.

Student teaching did not pay a salary, so after school I worked as a relay operator, a telephone bridge between the deaf and hearing. Wearing a headset, I sat before a monitor and transcribed the hearing person's voice, then read back the deaf caller's typed response. Punctuation was omitted; *qq* represented a question mark, and *ga*—go ahead—indicated the other person could respond: *hello sara (happy) do you want to have dinner with me qq ga*. Relay operators were a phone line, forbidden to speak directly to the parties. I just narrated and said "go ahead." The job was a voyeur's dream, but a bad one. While trying to keep one chapter ahead in my students' assigned novel, I would pause to read a female caller's typed words aloud to a man, such as, "Baby my husband gone I want you now—*go ahead.*"

One spring morning, while the ninth-graders attended an assembly titled "We're All in the Same Gang," I lay flat on the cold classroom floor. My right eye had lost its vision. "Stress," the school nurse said, and shrugged. I stared up at the drop ceiling and saw, written on a panel in neatly penciled strokes, MR. MEYER IS A CHUMP! Down the hall, a phone rang.

The Peace Corps offered a placement in China, Mongolia, or Vladivostok. I didn't speak Chinese. I couldn't use chopsticks. But China had always intrigued me; I once stopped at a campus travel agent and asked how much a ticket there cost. She quoted a large sum and gave a look that suggested I start digging.

The Peace Corps said I could leave three weeks after graduation. They would express-mail the forms that night. I met the package at the airport. As I clawed through the envelope's contents—the Volunteer Assignment Description, the medical clearance forms and eyeglass order kits, the Privacy Act Release and visa application—it became real. Go ahead, the package said, and the words resonated as never before: go ahead, go ahead, go ahead.

In 1995, the Peace Corps remained politically suspect in China, so our group of fifteen teachers was repainted as "U.S.-China Friendship Volunteers." I was touched up, too. In Chinese, my English surname sounds like the characters that describe a boy auctioned off by his parents in the marketplace: *mai'er*, "sold son." During Peace Corps training, my first Chinese teacher laughed low and renamed me with characters that mean Heroic Eastern Plumblossom. Chinese people often snicker when they hear it. I prefer Sold Son.

The Peace Corps worked in China's southwestern Sichuan province. I was posted to a city named Neijiang (Inner River), located on a bend of the Tuo River. The town was considered a backwater, known for its sugarcane and heroin trade, the latter documented in a book by a local muckraker titled *The Battle Between Virtue and Vice in the Heavenly Kingdom*.

For two years, I trained English teachers at a technical institute located on a bluff across from town, accessed by a skiff that ferried people, vegetables, and livestock. Every morning the squeals of pigs outside my window woke me. I didn't have a cell phone or Internet access. Contact home was through letters written on onionskin stationery and mailed in envelopes bearing stamps affixed with fish glue. I ate meals at dirt-floor restaurants on a muddy strip that was the campus's main lane. At its busiest, my weekly schedule held eight hours of classes, taught to lively and intelligent students in their early twenties. I played basketball, read novels, and learned Chinese. The eight hundred yuan ($100) monthly salary was sufficient; aside from spicy meals and Five Star beer, there wasn't much to buy. I was never in a rush to do anything because there wasn't much pressing to be done. I stopped wearing a watch. Time was measured by seasons and the school year.

After finishing my term as a U.S.-China Friendship Volunteer in 1997, I moved to Beijing to teach English. Following two years in the countryside, Beijing felt cosmopolitan. It also looked unlike any other Chinese city. Here, the center was not a hollow cavern of wide boulevards and monolithic apartment blocks, but a chain of central lakes surrounded by a compact mixture of architecture built on a human scale. A *hutong* is often as wide as its bordering courtyard's walls are tall. Sichuan was terraced farms and open spaces, topped by a perpetual haze that choked out the sun. Beijing had a flat layout, open sky, and a climate that reminded me of my Minnesota home. Here, I also met my future wife. For me, Beijing was simply love at first sight.

Even though I am drawn to them the way climbers are to mountains, I was raised to distrust cities. Like my mother's childhood Detroit, they could be abandoned by industry and divided by class. Like my father's Los Angeles, they could pave freeways over orange groves and sprawl amorphously. Like Minneapolis, where I grew up, they could force you to watch major league baseball indoors. I lived outside the city on a dead-end dirt road that ran through a stand of elm and birch trees. Our back-yard post fence had no one to keep out but the rows of corn, extending for acres. Today the road is paved, the trees have been thinned to decorate office parking lots, and the cornfields are tracts of homes a teacher's salary cannot afford.

A similar trend accelerated in China. I returned to my former Peace Corps town every couple of years, but on the final trip the cabdriver turned and said, "Are you sure you lived here? Your directions got us lost!" I recognized nothing. A bridge had replaced the ferry; new roads ran along the river's bluff; the training institute had been upgraded to a college. I got out of the cab and stood in the misty dark, until a voice called, "Professor Plumblossom?" It was the postman. He led me down new sidewalks to the white-tiled building I used to live in. Built a decade before, and in fine shape, it was slated for destruction. A new guesthouse would replace it.

The former campus—where I had spent two of the happiest years of my life—had been erased.

Once my eyes adjusted from that shock, I saw that the changes were for the better. I am not a sentimentalist; no one should have to live in poverty, no matter how picturesque. The new campus featured modern classrooms, heated dormitories, expanded fitness areas, and safer, paved roads. The school had the funds to hire foreign teachers and no longer depended on volunteers.

In 2001, the capital's Olympic-bid slogan called for a "New Beijing," but the city's makeover had already been under way when I arrived in 1997. Shopping malls, high-rise apartments, and roads replaced the *hutong*, destroying landmarks both historical and personal. It was common to arrive at a favorite restaurant, open-air market, and even neighborhood to find that it had been torn down in the weeks since your last visit. Where had the people who had lived and worked there gone? Beyond, "away from here," no one could say.

To an American, New Beijing looked familiar. The city's first Starbucks opened in 1998. Nine years later, nearly sixty of the coffee shops operated in town, along with nearly two hundred McDonald's, an equal number of KFCs, dozens of Pizza Huts, and a Hooters. As a thousand new drivers pulled their cars onto the ever-widening streets each day, a headline in a Beijing newspaper boasted BICYCLE KINGDOM RULES NO MORE! Suburbs mushroomed, as did golf courses (eleven) and ski resorts (twelve).

In 2003, I taught at a school located in Beijing's sprawling outskirts that expats dubbed "villa land" for its tracts of luxury, detached homes. My commute from downtown snaked past a strip mall holding a Domino's Pizza and gated developments named Château Regalia, Dynasty Garden, and Yosemite. Staring half-awake through the school-bus windows as students argued over whose provincial nanny was dumber, I dreaded passing the building site for Merlin Champagne Town. Its billboards showed a gathering of plump Caucasians toasting with flutes of bubbly beside the English caption "Here's to champagne, the drink divine that makes all our troubles seem far away." I hated those people. Everything seemed far away in villa land, especially Beijing and its troubles, which at the time included severe acute respiratory syndrome (SARS), an epidemic that froze almost all activity, except construction. On the ride back into the historic city center, my school bus passed under a bridge decorated with a digital clock that counted down to the start of the 2008 Summer Olympics. One day I saw 165,456,718; the next, 165,369,211. The seconds ticked away.

I started to think about moving into a *hutong* that spring of 2003, when I met Mr. Yang. Reflecting its crowded, linked traditional architecture, Beijing's social network moves sideways. I was talking in a bar about writing an article on the city's disappearing heritage when a woman at a neighboring table overheard and wrote down the number of a friend whose courtyard home was being razed. Later that week, Mr. Yang waited for me at a subway stop on the west side of town.

Beijing's traffic overpasses and subway stations bear the names of the city-wall gates they replaced. We met at the one formerly reserved for the passage of coal shipments. "That KFC is where Marquis Wu Ding's palace used to be," Mr. Yang said. He was in his early thirties, with a round face and cropped black hair. He spoke Chinese with a slight stutter that disappeared when he talked about being evicted. "My courtyard stands—stood—alongside the Duke of Guangning's Palace. Now it's called Financial Street."

The area was a corridor of department stores, high-rise banks, and tree-less squares whose signs warned KEEP OFF THE GRASS. A sculpture of brick walls surrounding a seedling evoked a home it had replaced.

"My parents bought our courtyard in 1945," Mr. Yang said, "but after Liberation in 1949, they were afraid of being labeled capitalists, so they subdivided the rooms and sold them, as well. During the Cultural Revolution, two thirds of the courtyard's rooms were divided again, and cadres and workers moved in. My parents clung to one room."

They lived there until the character that means "raze"— 拆 (*chai*)—appeared on their home's gray exterior walls. It was brushed on condemned homes in ghostly white strokes and circled: 拆. Mr. Yang had never seen someone paint the symbol, and neither had I. It just appeared overnight, like a gang tag, or the work of a specter. The Hand.

"We were told we had to move," Mr. Yang continued. "In the beginning of forced relocations, residents were offered new apartments on the outskirts of town as compensation. But then people began resisting, not wanting to trade their homes and neighborhoods for a life in a high-rise far

Chai—raze—is daubed in white paint on the walls of condemned homes.

away. So cash began being offered instead. The sums are fair, 8,020 yuan [about $1,000] per square meter. But that's only if you actually receive it."

Mr. Yang produced a pen and drew on the back of a napkin. "In practice, it's difficult due to corruption. In theory, an evaluator is supposed to assess the property's value and act as mediator between residents and developers." He traced a triangle. "But the evaluator is in league with the developers, leaving people, really, against the two of them and the coming high-rises."

The napkin was a swirl of lines, figures, and ink-blotted scribbles. Mr. Yang's sketch of his home lay buried beneath them.

Despite offers of compensation, and the substandard living conditions, Mr. Yang did not want to move. He grew up in the house and knew the area's history. He was part of it, he said. Connected. One day, he wanted his child to know these things, too.

"But to resist is useless. There's no social network anymore," he said. "You have three groups in these old *hutong* neighborhoods: natives, people moved in during the Cultural Revolution, and those resettled since then by their work units. It's too hard to get everyone to agree. The middle class is still being formed and afraid to stand up, lest they lose what they've gained. Then there are the demolition crews. They're from the countryside and have no connection with the city. They're just doing their job. Then there are the city planners and developers, who lack a spiritual connection with Beijing and see the city as something to shape, rather than preserve."

Mr. Yang couldn't bear to watch the workers destroy his house. "They're not delicate, like you would be," he said. "They're just brutal." His jovial face fell. "It wasn't just a building. It was me. It was my family. Our spirit. My grandmother died of cancer, and last year one day after she had gone, I felt an immense sadness, like something was wrong. I walked over to the house, only to find they had knocked down the kitchen. Suddenly I remembered the last time she cooked for us." His eyes began to moisten. "She raised all of us, you see, and her best dish was meatballs. I just kept thinking of the last time she cooked those for us, with all of us home, and her laughing and talking. We were filled with such hope that perhaps somehow she would cheat death and be as healthy as she looked then. But she died. And so did our home."

Tears ran down his pale cheeks. "I'm sorry. I did this once before, in front of my girlfriend. She told me I was strange."

We walked to the rubble, past office towers named Investment Plaza and Corporate Square. I closed and opened my eyes, remarking that if I had just arrived, it would be hard to guess what city I was in. Mr. Yang laughed. "No, you would look around and see how ugly it is. That's how you would know you could only be in Beijing."

A Ritz-Carlton hotel was planned for his former *hutong*. "There is still one family living there, and one of my old rooms," he said. "My friend has a GPS, so he came over and recorded the coordinates of the house. Now I can take my kid back one day and stand in the hotel lobby and say, 'I grew up here.'"

He peeled back a layer of tin sheeting painted blue. We ducked into a landscape of shattered brick and bone-colored characters commanding 拆. The windows of Mr. Yang's room had been smashed. He carefully brushed the shards from the wooden sill.

The neighboring family refused to move. Their water had been shut off, though no one could say by whom; the Hand, again. The vegetable market had moved out of the area, making life even more hardscrabble. The father introduced himself as an ethnic Manchu. His ancestors had lived in the house while serving China's last emperors as imperial guards known as banner men.

"Now they expect me to go to a one-bedroom apartment in the suburbs?" he said. As the father criticized the government, his son made a face. He wanted to accept the money, the new apartment, the new life. "Why are you telling them this?" he finally blurted in a rising voice. "Do you think this brings you glory?"

Their argument carried to the other side of the wall, where the demolition squad bunked, waiting. You could still hear their voices on the lane, as a line of men in dark business suits strolled past. They cradled the neighborhood's future in rolled-up sheets, gesturing upward at buildings only they could see.

"A town is a tool," wrote Le Corbusier. In 1929's *The City of To-morrow and Its Planning*, the French architect advocated plowing under the jumble of narrow, winding streets at the heart of European towns to build wide roads that increased traffic circulation. "A home is a machine."

I picked up the book by chance, then couldn't put it down. The arguments against his ideas sounded familiar. Le Corbusier dismissed those who saw medieval living conditions as cultural heritage. "The Committee for the Preservation of Old Paris is hard at work," he wrote. "When it comes to a question of demolishing rotten old houses full of tuberculosis and demoralizing, you hear them cry, 'What about the iron-work, what about the beautiful old wrought-iron-work?' It may happen that the wife of one of these gentlemen has been doing a little 'slumming,' and has seen, and never forgotten, some delightful piece of iron-work in an old house which has now become a slum; climbing some tottering old staircase on her errand of mercy."

Le Corbusier continued, "Of course, these lovers of the past who are so busy writing for the papers and directing public opinion will tell you, if you ask them, that they live in such-and-such a quarter, in a new building with lifts, etc., or in some wonderful little house hidden deep in a garden."

The most strident *hutong* defenders I had met were historians and tourists. Neither lived in the lanes themselves, and both were drawn to the tangible architecture and its details, including beautiful old wrought-iron-work. Although I lamented Beijing's disappearing heritage, I had always lived in an apartment. Le Corbusier's complaint sounded like a challenge.

What did I really know about the *hutong*? Were they worth preserving? There wasn't much time to find out.

I spent a year learning to read Chinese at Tsinghua University, using Beijing urban-planning histories as texts. On a local Web site, I found a courtyard for rent, but before I moved in, the home was marked with ⊕. The landlord, in the helpful, horizontal Beijing way, passed me on to an acquaintance.

I moved to Red Bayberry and Bamboo Slanted Street on August 8, 2005. By coincidence, it was sixty-eight years to the day that the Japanese army marched past Dazhalan and through the Front Gate to occupy the city, and also exactly three years before the start of the Summer Olympics. The Japanese impact upon the neighborhood had proved ephemeral. What the games would do, no one could say. The Widow advised me to sign a short-term lease. The Hand could come at any moment and wipe it all away.

I wanted to live in the *hutong* as I had in the countryside a decade before, with unhurried days in a community where I played a role. One of Dazhalan's three elementary schools was a five-minute walk from my door, on the *hutong* that ran parallel to Red Bayberry and Bamboo Slanted Street. I knew from the Peace Corps that working at a school would define me in the eyes of the community, transforming me from the Foreigner into Teacher Plumblossom. People would know what I did, where I did it, and that I would be around for a while, and not just passing through.

Beijing's schools are wrapped in walls that keep strangers out, and students in. When I first approached Coal Lane Elementary, the security guards refused to open the school's high, wrought-iron gate. I returned with a résumé typed in Chinese, which a guard reluctantly accepted. A week later, the principal returned my phone messages and invited me inside.

A foreigner had never taught at the school, she said. In fact, she didn't have permission to hire one. Even if she could, funds weren't available. A day's work at the international school paid what Coal Lane's teachers earned in a month.

I was there to volunteer, I explained. My expenses were minimal, and I didn't want all of the obligations of paid work, such as having to attend the daily after-school staff meetings.

The principal laughed. She had never heard of a school with a volunteer teacher. By taking on a volunteer—moreover, a foreigner—Coal Lane Elementary would be setting a precedent. Principals didn't take risks, they managed them. They advanced through the bureaucracy by maintaining the status quo. "We'll have to get permission," she said.

I gave her photocopies of my passport, visa, teaching licenses, degrees, recommendation letters, and their Chinese translations.

A month later, in the autumn of 2005, I began teaching English at Coal Lane Elementary. Grade Four's students were divided into three classrooms. The blackboards were decorated with chalked drawings of the Olympic mascots, the five-colored rings, the slogan "One World, One Dream," and Chinese song lyrics that went:

> The Olympics will be held in 2008
> Our civic virtue environment must be great!
> Spitting everywhere is really terrible
> Littering trash is also unbearable
> To get a "thumbs-up" from foreign guests,
> Beijing's environment depends on us!

After standing for the national anthem each morning, the class was supposed to update the number of days until the start of the games. Only Class One kept the correct count. Class Three was a day or two ahead, then behind. Time had completely stopped in Class Two, where no one bothered to continue the countdown. In Class Two, there were always 996 days until the Olympics.

It was a pleasant illusion. The classroom walls held no clocks, and the view out their windows looked just as timeless. Waves of sloping, tiled rooftops washed toward the school, whose four stories made it the neighborhood's tallest building. From our classroom, students could point out my courtyard, the bookstore, the police station, and the green ceramic tiles of the mosque's pagoda-shaped minaret. We could see the flying eaves of the Front Gate and the row of red flags fluttering atop the Great Hall of the People. One day I challenged the kids to count all the trees they could see. No one finished. Poplar, cottonwood, and pine edged the lanes; courtyards

The view from Class Two.

hid persimmon, jujube, plum, cherry, haw, and walnut. Even in early autumn, the sea below was a blend of gray and green.

The wider view revealed that we lived on an ever-shrinking island. Modern office towers and apartments built on razed *hutong* squeezed our neighborhood from all sides. I pointed to the pair of golden arches shining in the distance, and the kids shouted, "McDonald's!" By the end of the school year, we could see a Wal-Mart, too.

CHAPTER 3

MOCKY & ME

MOCKY IS A naughty monkey. His friends Ken and Ann are humans. They often visit an orangutan named Uncle Booky, who explains grammar on his blackboard. Together, they teach English to Beijing's elementary students. My students love Mocky. He and his pals are more fun than the characters in their previous textbook series, the student Ma Nan and the teacher Miss Zhang. Those primers could have been titled *Hectoring English*. A typical dialogue went:

"You're late again, Ma Nan."

"I'm sorry, Miss Zhang."

"When do you get up every morning?"

"At seven."

"Get up earlier. Don't be late next time."

Beijing students begin studying English in Grade One. Every child is enrolled in three forty-five-minute lessons each week until the end of elementary school, at Grade Six. Much of Mocky's instruction is automated, reducing the teacher's role to leading students through recitations of the dialogues, animated on a disc included with the text. Although Mocky speaks slowly, he sounds as if he's inhaled some bad helium. Like my students, I followed the subtitles.

Mocky's voice grated on Miss Zhu. She planned her own lessons. Unlike Coal Lane Elementary's other English teacher, she spoke the language well and used it throughout her instruction. After the lesson ended, however, she preferred speaking to me in Chinese. English was a tool she used for work.

When Miss Zhu was fifteen, she failed the high school entrance exam, shutting her out of the system that led to college. Her father suggested she enlist to become a police officer.

"I passed a police station and looked inside," she said. "I saw a lot of heavy people sitting at desks filled with jars of tea and papers. I didn't know what I wanted, but I knew what I didn't want."

She enrolled in technical school to become a teacher. "I was lazy and just did what they assigned me to do. My English was comparatively good, so that's what they trained me in. When I graduated at age eighteen, they assigned me to this school. That was seven years ago."

Miss Zhu was Coal Lane Elementary's youngest teacher. She was also, according to students and faculty, the school beauty, a label she rejected with practiced modesty. Although born and raised in Beijing, she lacked a northerner's broad frame and ruddy complexion. She had a narrow waist, slight build, and buttery skin. She plucked her eyebrows, shunned makeup, and tied back her long, brown-tinted hair. While many teachers came to school dressed in the same rumpled tracksuit, Miss Zhu wore jeans and a different sweater every day.

Her grandparents had raised her in a nearby *hutong*. She lived close to the school, in a neighborhood that had recently been separated from Dazhalan by an eight-lane boulevard. Its pedestrian overpasses were adorned with red and yellow plastic symbols that formed $F = GM_1M_2/R^2$ and $E = MC^2$. Her house, like mine, was the type known as a "big, messy courtyard" (*dazayuan*). The erstwhile merchant's mansion had been subdivided to lodge forty-three families, none of whom she considered friends, and several— such as the folks with a yapping Pekingese—she found annoying. Her single room had been assigned to a relative decades before, when the government counted housing as a basic right, rather than an asset. The relative moved to an apartment, and she took over the subsidized rent of thirty yuan ($3.75) a month. Her monthly salary paid eighteen hundred yuan ($225), a figure below Beijing's per capita average and equal to what Recycler Wang earned. The school, however, provided basic health insurance and job security.

Even as personal restrictions were loosening and the economy provided choices that most people had never before enjoyed, Miss Zhu retained her Beijing-bred fatalism, the feeling that an unseen hand steered her life. I said she was fortunate to be assigned a job near an assigned house. "It wasn't my decision," she said with a shrug. "It just was."

Miss Zhu taught grades one, two, four, and five. The principal assigned us to "learn from each other." For the next two years, we would be coteachers.

A onetime visit to a school can give the impression that the building is filled with well-behaved whiz kids. While in the Peace Corps, I often visited teacher trainees at work in the field. Their Potemkin classrooms displayed neat rows of groomed children whose answers were—surprise!—correct.

Coal Lane Elementary, in contrast, felt unscripted and natural. Students shouted wrong answers, talked over each other, and laughed like the kids they were. They lived in *hutong* homes around the school and filed into the classroom bowing unwashed heads. Most boys had crew cuts, while the girls' long hair was held in place by a scaffolding of scrunchies. Their classrooms' walls were painted waist high in a seasick green. The white upper half was decorated with only a plastic Chinese flag and a typed list titled "Ten Actions That Show Civic Virtue and Decorum for the Olympics." Love the motherland, for starters.

The teachers had names that recalled a previous era: Red Army, Powerful East, Construct China. The children's own monikers exhibited the wishes of a new generation: Wealth of a Dragon, Inspired by Culture and Literature, A Seed That Grows Strong. One girl, whose divorced mother was a fashion designer, was named To Be at One with the Dust of the World, after a Buddhist saying. She was the only student who also had an English name. She called herself Cher.

A chart posted to the wall listed the children's names, and an evaluation of their:

Height (Above, Average, Below)
Weight (Above, Average, Below)
Lung capacity (Above, Average, Below)
Eyesight (Nearsighted, Normal, Farsighted)
Evidence of pinkeye (Yes, No, Perhaps)
Cavities (Yes, No)
Gum disease (Hard gums, Normal, Spongy)
Anemia (Yes, No)

Nutrition level (Muscular body, Normal, Soft)
Overall development (Great, Average, Poor)

In Class One, the development of four out of twenty-four students was judged "above average." The rest of the kids were "fat," "stunted," and "backward." There appeared to be a correlation between physical development and English ability. The worse a child's health, the better her English.

Our best student was Mao Mao, a plump girl with long, tangled hair who played the flute and asked questions in Chinese like "How do you say *mallard* in English? How do you say *forklift*? What about *hippopotamus*, and *giraffe*?" In Chinese, the nouns were *green-head duck*, *fork truck*, *river horse*, and *long-necked deer*. Mao Mao thought English was illogical.

When Miss Zhu called for volunteers to read, Little Liu always put her hand up first. She wanted to have accent-free pronunciation by the time she entered high school. At the beginning of Grade Four, Little Liu was nine. She wore thick glasses that hung crooked due to the blue patch covering her left eye. It was there to strengthen the right one, which she pinched into a squint. Four scrunchies pulled her black hair straight up from her scalp. Little Liu looked like an exclamation point.

She led the class through a recitation of the day's lesson, which began with Mocky exploring career options. He faced a choice of farmer, doctor, nurse, pilot, and dancer. After injuring himself while attempting to juggle, Mocky found a newfound respect for veterinarians. That's what he wanted to be.

The kids seemed older than their years, as if their adult clothes were hanging in the wardrobe, waiting to be filled. I had them write a sentence about their future profession. Little Liu gravely read, "When I grow up, I want to be a doctor, because I can heal the wounded and suckle the dying. Although my eye is very hurt, but I still want to continue to act collectively and give service."

A classmate yelled, "When I grow up, I want to be a foreigner!"

Other students selected nurse, vet, and teacher. An argument started over what the best job would be. Astronaut! Fireman! Tour guide! Soldier! Driver! No one wanted to be a government official.

Miss Zhu asked the students to describe what their parents did for a living. Mocky's vocabulary list didn't include those jobs. We fielded questions like: "How do you say *service worker* in English?"

"How do you say *cell phone repairman?*"

"How do you say *hairdresser?*"

"How do you say *unemployed?*"

On the blackboard, I translated *fried-food cook, road repairman, clothing saleswoman, accountant, bookseller,* and—for Cher—*fashion designer.* Little Liu pointed at a classmate and said in Chinese, "His father is a prisoner!"

Miss Zhu whispered to me, "He tried to rob a bank."

The boy slumped in his seat. Next to him, a girl with rosy cheeks named Wu Wu froze when I asked what her parents did. She didn't understand. Another child said, in a helpful tone, "Don't pay attention to her, Mr. Plumblossom. She's stupid."

As school instilled an obeisance to authority, students were exceedingly respectful of their teachers, announcing, "Reporting!" and bowing upon entering the classroom. When it came to relations among each other, however, it was everyone for himself. The kids formed tight cliques that substituted for the siblings the One-Child Policy denied them from having. They were encouraged to tattle on each other under a *Kapo* system run by student officers appointed by the homeroom teacher. One student was responsible for collecting homework and reporting truants. Another led a row of students through the outside morning exercises, fingering those who weren't executing the deep knee bends and wrist twists. One child supervised the cleaning of the classroom. Another listened for foul language. One student took charge of the daily ten minutes of eye exercises that were said to improve vision. On the blackboard, he chalked the name of any laggard who didn't massage his ocular sockets with enthusiasm.

I stopped the lesson and lectured in Chinese that because everyone had to learn English from the same textbook—regardless of his or her proficiency—the top students should help, not berate, their confused peers. Wu Wu, the silent, rosy-cheeked girl I defended, looked up and announced, in a cheerful voice, "No, it's true, Mr. Plumblossom. I am stupid."

Wu Wu lived on a *hutong* in a two-story cement box of a building neighbored by ramshackle houses with sloping tiled roofs. When courtyard homes rot to collapse, simple structures made from rudimentary materials often replace them. As a result, the *hutong* loses its homogeneous appearance. The intangible community fabric remains, but to an outsider, the neighborhood looks fragmented and blighted.

Wu Wu's parents were picture framers. They used the bottom level of the building as their workshop and slept upstairs. Their *hutong* was lined with framers, continuing a Dazhalan tradition where merchants set up shop next to their kin. "I know all these people," her father said, motioning down the lane. "We come from the same village in Zhejiang province."

Wu Wu contorted her body in embarrassment when I accepted her father's offer to stay for dinner. As I related what happened in class, she swatted my arm. I had asked other teachers about her abilities, and their uniform response was "Wu Wu is dumb." The only paperwork on the child's attributes was the chart that recorded physical fitness. It informed that Wu Wu's teeth had plaque.

"The school doesn't listen to me when I complain about how they treat her," her father said, "so I've stopped calling. It's good that she goes and learns to write characters and do math. I know she's not that smart. But that doesn't mean she's useless. I'm not that smart, either."

He unrolled a delicate painting on rice paper and mounted it onto a silk scroll with brushstrokes of glue. Wu Wu sat motionless, studying his movements. He talked as he worked. "I make a good living. Life is better here than back home." His goal was simple: stay in Beijing another day. If the Hand painted 拆 on the walls of this *hutong*, he would look for space on another lane. Going back to the village, he insisted, was unimaginable. "We moved here. This is the capital of China. Of course she should go to school here," he said, thrusting his chin at his daughter. "She'll have so many more opportunities. Who knows what she'll end up doing?"

I asked Wu Wu what she wanted to be when she grew up.

In Chinese, she said seriously, "I do not want to be an English teacher."

The principal could not say who had stamped the red chop that approved my working at Coal Lane Elementary. Decisions were made by the unseen. One morning, I was woken by the buzz of a chain saw. A man in a flimsy helmet felled the healthy cottonwood that was one of two trees shading Red Bayberry and Bamboo Slanted Street. There was no open space for the tree to fall, so the man worked his way down the trunk, lopping off sections.

I asked, "Why are you cutting down that tree?"

"Because it's my job," he responded.

The Widow stood at our gate watching, mute.

Recycler Wang looked at my incredulous face and explained, "The man is cutting down the tree." He turned to weigh a pile of scrap paper. Time to get back to work.

Beijing's warmest November in fifty years didn't change the fact that as ever, the city's central heating system was switched on. Our classroom sweltered until the first week of December, when the outside temperature dropped from forty-five to fifteen degrees. As the classroom was packed with twenty-five hyperactive bodies, steam still fogged the windows. Miss Zhu did what people were doing all across the city: she opened the panes to bleed away the nonadjustable heat.

It was a waste I wished I could pipe into my house, which, so refreshingly cool in summertime, had become an icy tomb. I started coming to school even on days I didn't teach. The electric heater that I thought would warm me through winter instead overloaded the fuse box. From the darkness came the Widow's scowled "Moron!" She walked into my room without knocking, complained about her opera program shutting off, then had her attention diverted by the heater's packaging, a thick cardboard box. "That has value," she advised. Recycler Wang paid 1.5 yuan ($.19) for it, enough for a bottle of Yanjing. I was so cold, the lukewarm beer felt like hot chocolate going down.

The Widow was toasty because her room's cast-iron stove constantly glowed from a "coal honeycomb," a puck-size briquette punctured with sixteen holes. I would not burn coal. It smelled terrible and blanketed the neighborhood with a sulfuric haze. I also didn't trust the stuff. The red propaganda banners hanging in the *hutong* had changed their yellow-character slogan from CREATE A HARMONIOUS COMMUNITY, REGISTER YOUR DOG to AVOID COAL POISONING. One morning, mummified under three levels of blankets, I awoke to frantic knocking.

"You didn't come to class!" Miss Zhu exhaled. "The principal told me to come and check on you. We thought you had been asphyxiated!" The previous winter, one of our students had also overslept. "Her mom taught dance class. The children loved her. There was a leak in the family's stove, and the room wasn't ventilated properly. Our student woke up the next morning, but her parents would not, no matter how hard she shook them."

Miss Zhu surveyed my room. "You don't even burn coal! Aren't you cold?"

Maps are a mystery to Mocky, and the students empathized. No globes or maps were posted in the school, or inside the Chinese textbooks. In the day's lesson, Mocky stared at a map and looked for the supermarket, the movie theater, and the public toilet. Our neighborhood had those, but not a swimming pool or a park, as Mocky's did. His friends Ken and Ann headed for the zoo. "I don't like zoos," Mocky cried fearfully. "I want to go home."

The kids lived amidst fifty-seven thousand people, plus tourists—including foreigners—who came to Dazhalan for its cheap hostels and less than salubrious nightlife. That didn't faze the students one bit. Instead, they were terrified of ghosts.

"They only come out at night," said a wide-eyed Little Liu. "They have a white body that you can see through. If they come for you, you can't defend yourself. It's useless. They take you away."

"Where do they take you to?"

"To where they live."

"What happens next?"

"You never come back. Never. You never see your friends or parents or family again. Not even after they die. Never." She shivered theatrically.

I put down the textbook. "Did you know that when Beijing had an emperor, Vegetable Market Junction used to be the execution ground where they chopped off criminals' heads?"

Little Liu and the rows of children widened their eyes. "That's really close! That's in our neighborhood!"

"One night, a pharmacist heard a rap at his shop's door. He heard a man's voice beg for pain medicine. The pharmacist opened the door and saw . . . a man holding his severed head in his hands!"

Shrieks filled the room. I closed the door. The kids demanded another story, like the one about the fox spirit that lived in the Front Gate that would change into human form at midnight, just as the city wall was being barricaded. He would wait for a tipsy person to pass through, invite him to sit down and share a drink, and then he would revert to his ethereal form and . . . steal the man away!

More screams. "*Aiya!* Where would he take the people?"

I didn't know. Where did they think?

"Maybe out to the suburbs," reasoned Little Liu.

That is where, after all, people snatched from the *hutong* usually ended up.

I showed the students a map of Beijing and asked where the zoo was. Silence. Our neighborhood? No one spoke. How about the chain of lakes at the center of town? Out of seventy-five students, three had been to them. Cher said, correctly, that they were two miles from Dazhalan. The other kids guessed thirty, and two hundred.

While the kids could, at age nine, slay me at math problems and memorization, their sense of geography, of space, was shaped by the *hutong*. Miss Zhu grew up with the same mentality; in her entire life, she had never explored the area around the lakes. They were for tourists. In my eyes, the neighborhood was one of the most unique urban spaces on the planet, and vanishing before us. To them, it was just *home*; emotional, not physical. When the kids drew a picture of their house, the image never depicted a gray wall with red, double wooden doors anchored by twin carved stones, and topped by a sloping roof that needed weeding. Instead, copying cartoons, they colored a smiling sun shining over green grass and stick people who lived in a two-story square with a single door, two windows, and a triangle top. The stick people's eyes were lines, not circles. Everything else looked foreign.

Our students could navigate the neighborhood's maze of lanes blindfolded. They knew where to buy fresh milk, and what store had the coolest yo-yo. They knew that the hair salons were a front for prostitution—"That's where the bad women work," a boy said, pointing it out to me, while a girl, when walking past the lottery-ticket office, shook her head and sighed, "Men wasting good money!"

Seeing the neighborhood abstractly was a bigger challenge. What Miss Zhu and I had planned as a weeklong project ended up taking three. None of the students had drawn a map before. The classroom's cutthroat atmosphere lessened as students with better English relied on those who could draw, or those—such as Wu Wu—who knew the location of the neighborhood's landmarks in relation to one another. The kids plotted the supermarket, bookstore, barber, butcher, pet store, post office, mosque, mah-jongg parlor, museum, bank, bar, hairdresser, hotel, Heavenly Peach produce market, restaurants, public toilets, and nine trees. No two maps looked alike, and all were unmistakably kid-drawn, not aided by the hands of parents who feared their child was average.

The principal visited our class for the first time. She praised Miss Zhu for hanging the students' work on the walls. That, she said, wasn't a bad precedent at all. She stayed to listen to the students explain their drawings.

Mao Mao read, "I go to school at half past seven every day. If you are at Three Wells *hutong*, go straight, then turn right at the toilet, and then go past the shop and the restaurant, and then turn left again. You can find our school. Our school is between the police station and toilet. I never go to the police station."

When Officer Li called to say he wanted me in his office immediately, I had seventy-five hand-drawn maps that showed the way.

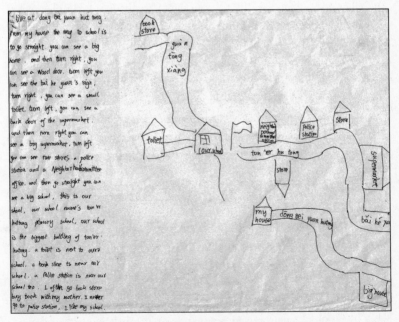

Our neighborhood, as drawn by a Grade Four student. Coal Lane Elementary is located next to the flag, at center.

• • •

Being summoned by the cops felt like getting pulled away from the pub by your mom. You weren't misbehaving, but suddenly there was reason to wonder.

Officer Li didn't look like a typical Beijing cop. He was thin and fit, with thick hair parted neatly to the right. His face was unlined and unworried. Yet like any Beijing police officer, he could have been between twenty and forty years old. They never seemed to age.

Officer Li had introduced himself a week after I moved to Red Bayberry and Bamboo Slanted Street. He called to express his concern about my choice of housing. The door to the courtyard was easy to open, as it was protected by just a small padlock when no one was home. I assured him there was nothing valuable inside my rooms. He laughed knowingly. I was, after all, a foreigner. Then he remembered that I was a teacher, which made me not only harmless, but a bit pitiful. Still, he said, it wasn't a good idea to reside in the *hutong*. No other foreigners lived permanently in Dazhalan. I should move. "It's for your safety," he had said. His plea meant that I was an unwanted responsibility.

We reached a compromise. The two of us would consider my courtyard a "study room," and not a registered residence. Yet I needed his red stamp on the palm-size housing registration receipt that Beijing required of all foreigners. I had been kicked out of apartments for not having it, once being given only two hours to pack my things or face a hefty fine or deportation.

Officer Li was sympathetic. Beijing's bureaucracy had not caught up to the city's reality. Hurdles still existed for a person living outside the system, without a "work unit" or sponsoring institution, such as a university, that would speed these matters along. They provided an identity that could be classified. Officer Li admired the "spirit of volunteerism" in general and had heard I was researching local history, but it bothered him that I chose a small school in what he considered a run-down neighborhood. He did not live here, but in another district of the city.

Beijing's residents do not divide themselves by an allegiance to a team, or by social markers such as school districts. During introductions, no one asks what high school a person went to; that doesn't reveal class or background, since kids often test into places outside their neighborhood. Instead, people ask which administrative district a person grew up in. Dazhalan was located in Xuanwu District, the southwest corner of downtown Beijing. Its name connoted history and poverty, both evinced in its crumbling *hutong*. Xuanwu was also known as a district populated by migrant workers.

Locals called them *waidi* (outsiders), and the word was usually a slur, as in, *waidi* crowded the city, *waidi* spoke nonstandard dialects, *waidi* were foulmouthed and ill-mannered. The natives—*bendi*—saw themselves as a cut above. In Beijing, the other side of the tracks was any place migrants called home.

Officer Li had suggested that I teach at another school, where the students weren't the children of migrants and their English teachers held university degrees. The school was located outside our neighborhood, between stacks of indistinguishable apartments. When we drove there down an eight-lane road clogged with cars, Officer Li made an illegal left turn, sparing us the traffic jam. Beijing was a different city when you had power. The school had an electric accordion gate, not a creaking wrought-iron one, and its Olympic countdown ticked down the days on a digital clock. The basketball rims were not parallel to each other and hidden behind the twigs of persimmon trees, as at Coal Lane Elementary. A clock hung on the wall of each classroom.

The principal offered a work visa, salary, and an apartment on a treeless street. No shops or restaurants lined the road, only light posts from which closed-circuit security cameras scanned rows of honking cars. The apartment building was fenced and entered past a teenaged guard manning a swing-arm gate. The view from the apartment's squat windows showed a beltway. New residential areas like this were what pushed me toward the *hutong*. As we idled in a traffic jam that even he could not avoid, Officer Li said he understood my decision, which he knew was final. His tone, however, suggested it was not. I suspected Officer Li would usher me from the neighborhood yet.

The Olympics intervened. Beijing announced that 35 percent of its population would be competent in basic spoken English by the start of the games, including six thousand police officers.

The police studied from a textbook titled *Olympic Security English*. In dialogues named "Dissuading Foreigners from Excessive Drinking" and "How to Stop Illegal News Coverage," the lessons presented such pattern drills as "I'm afraid we'll have to *detain you temporarily.*"

Politeness was stressed:

come to our office
Would you be able to _____?
Excuse me, would you _____?
Sorry to trouble you, could you _____?
Do me a favor and _____, will you?

As was protecting the honor of local women:

Please don't_____.
> be too familiar with the girl
> be so rude to that lady
> take too many liberties with the waitress
> take pictures
> take photographs
> do that

But so was directness:

Don't _____.
> pretend to be innocent
> try to fool us
> play any tricks

The two hundred pages of *Olympic Security English* taught officers how to break up press coverage of a Falun Gong demonstration, send home a teenager caught out after curfew, interrogate a heroin addict, and crack an antiques smuggling ring.

The foreign characters in the textbook's dialogues said things like "So what if I'm drunk! Waitress! I want a girl to drink with me!" and "You will never convict me" (a soccer hooligan promised that, after braining a fan with a stadium seat). The other baddies were Muslims, such as "Mohammed Ali." In Lesson Fifteen, a burglar was apprehended in a tourist's Beijing hotel room. The Chinese officer asked why he was there.

FOREIGNER: Because my family was killed when the U.S. bombed Afghanistan. I became homeless and I hate Americans.

POLICE: We feel sympathy for your misfortune. But your behavior to deliberately hurt an innocent American is against our law, and you disrupted our social order, especially during the Olympic Games. You caused a disturbance and damaged the reputation of our country, so you should shoulder the criminal responsibilities.

FOREIGNER: I didn't consider that much. And I didn't intend to make trouble for China.

POLICE: You must tell all that you did. Don't make any trouble for yourself.

FOREIGNER: Yes, ma'am.

Officer Li was an eager learner. He took me out to dumplings and asked me to teach him every English swear word because "I want to know when a foreigner is calling me a bad name." As the rounds of beers kept coming, and customers at other tables turned to stare, I compared Officer Li to body parts, told him what to do with himself, and appraised his mother. He nodded happily and asked for more.

After Officer Li called me at Coal Lane Elementary sounding solemn, I handed Mocky to Miss Zhu, who was affixing a stamp shaped like a red flag onto exemplary homework. Officer Li waited for me in his office. He looked concerned. He motioned for me to sit at his desk and left the small room. The narrow space had unadorned, whitewashed cement walls. My claustrophobia mounted. Officer Li was up to something.

He returned, flanked by two female officers. "Thank you for coming," he said sternly, closing the door. He turned his chair to face mine. In Chinese, he explained, "This is about *heka*."

The final word meant nothing to me. Who was He Ka? What did she say? I thought, *This is not going to end well.*

Officer Li continued, "He Ka is giving us big problems." He pointed to his nose, and over his shoulder at the two women. Their pursed lips made a sympathetic *ohhh* sound. He Ka was really a mess.

Officer Li extracted a crisp sheet of unlined paper from his desk drawer. He offered it to me with two hands. "We need to translate this story for our Christmas *heka*."

Click. *Greeting card*. I relaxed. In typed Chinese, the title of the paper's paragraphs said, "The Legend of the Christmas Stockings."

"We want to print the story in English on our Christmas cards," Officer Li explained.

As a kid, I hung a stocking over the fireplace on Christmas Eve because it would get filled with chocolate. I didn't know the tradition's origin. According to the police's investigation—printed from the Internet—it began because once there was a widower who had three beautiful daughters whose dowry he could not pay. They hung their washed stockings above the fireplace. St. Nicholas stopped by and filled them with gold. The daughters were sold off into marriage, and their father died in peace. The end.

The three officers leaned over my shoulder after I finished typing. "What does this mean, here? 'Once upon a time.'"

Living abroad makes the familiar new again. We repeated the phrase together until it sounded like a spell. Teacups were filled, cigarettes offered, and the red ink pad pulled from a drawer. "You really should stay in Dazhalan," Officer Li said, smiling. He suggested he stamp the residence registration receipt, allowing me to live legally in the courtyard. "It's a good thing you're interested in the neighborhood. It's filled with history." Officer Li looked at it every day, he said, but didn't see it at all.

CHAPTER 4

"Say Farewell to Dangerous Housing"

Beijing's heritage has vanished throughout the last century, as economic and political changes altered the city's appearance and lifestyle. Witnesses have long reported the twilight of the city's charms.

The capital "is giving way to everything that is new, and fighting a losing battle to retain all the traditions handed down by our forefathers," a local writer lamented in 1928. "It is more than likely that after a generation or two the social customs which have been stationary for so many centuries will be changed beyond recognition."

"The loss by vandalism and utter neglect has been proceeding at such a rate that, on repeated occasions, buildings and historical monuments have actually disappeared while the authors were still writing about them," reported the writers of 1935's *In Search of Old Peking*.* They predicted that the Temple of Heaven, where the emperor had formerly made annual sacrifices for prosperity and a bountiful harvest, "will be razed to the ground and converted into a municipal swimming-bath or a stadium, or some other equally utilitarian structure."

After fifteen years away, a Belgian journalist returned in 1962 to see China's capital under Communist rule. He wrote, "The first thing I did when I arrived in Peking was to look for Peking. It did not seem to be where I left it. Much of the beauty of ancient imperial Peking was gone, as was almost all its charm. It was a village, unsmiling, unshapely, and desperately

---

* The capital's English name officially changed from Peking to Beijing in 1975, following the adoption of a new standard to romanize Chinese characters.

self-assertive, the result, it seemed, of an experiment in modern slum planning. And grim, as all villages must have been at the very beginning, before age had given them beauty, and while they were still strictly, unmercifully utilitarian. Still, the biggest village ever."

The city's walls were pierced until they came down; social customs did change beyond recognition; the utter neglect of buildings proceeded rapidly. The "village" industrialized and grew into a municipality larger in area than Connecticut.

Still, vestiges of its past were visible. The Temple of Heaven was not razed to make way for a swimming pool, but converted to a public park and museum. Life was lived close to the ground and connected to community in *hutong* neighborhoods such as Dazhalan.

After translating for Officer Li, I walked home in the early-winter dusk from the police station. Adults I had never spoken to greeted me as "Teacher Plumblossom." Three of my students ran up to show off a new kite. They had tried flying it on Fetching the Lantern Lane, then Coal Lane, then Cherry Lane, but the utility lines kept interfering. A shopkeeper listening in asked, "It's five. Aren't you kids late for supper?" The kids moaned and took off for home. "Teacher Plumblossom, you should eat now, too," the shopkeeper added. "You should also cover the back of your neck. Don't catch a cold!"

I became a stranger when I wandered a few lanes away from Red Bayberry and Bamboo Slanted Street. The surrounding *hutong* could look foreign, as well. While I heard and witnessed the changes on my street—a tree being cut, a restaurant being remodeled—alterations to other neighborhoods were discovered after the fact. The sound of a sledgehammer does not travel far.

Hutong neighborhoods are located in the heart of Beijing, which once formed the imperial capital. Known as the Old City, the layout of its twenty-five square miles—an area slightly larger than Manhattan—resembled a series of interlocked boxes, centered by the Forbidden City. The emperor's palace was ringed by a wall marking the Imperial City, home to members of the court. Beyond that was a defensive wall that enclosed the *hutong* populated by commoners. A sixteenth-century project to add an additional ring of defenses stalled for lack of funds. Only the southern portion of the wall was completed, giving the Old City's perimeter a shape that resembled the character 凸 (*tu*). The upper square was called the Inner City, while the lower rectangle was known as the Outer City.

All of the capital's walls were pulled down during the twentieth century, erasing the Old City's distinctions. The sole remaining pair of gate towers is located at the nexus where the Inner and Outer Cities once met. An urn-shaped enceinte formerly linked the Front Gate's twin towers, but the brick enclosure was demolished for a boulevard that now runs east to west between the structures. The Front Gate's flying eaves and red, lacquered wood adorn the southern end of Tian'anmen Square, while the embrasures fronting the gray brick of the defensive arrow tower face Front Gate Avenue's *pailou*, a decorative arch that formerly marked the start of Beijing's streets. Like the city's walls, they had been pulled down to make way for traffic. Only four of the original hundreds of archways remain.

On a cold December night, I walked fifteen minutes east from my house and crossed Front Gate Avenue. The two-lane road runs south from Tian'anmen Square to the Temple of Heaven, a mile away. Front Gate Avenue divides the two administrative districts that form the lower rectangle of the Old City's 凸-shaped design. The west side of the street belongs to Xuanwu District, which includes Dazhalan. The east side marks the edge of Chongwen District, home to one of the capital's last unbroken *hutong* neighborhoods, arrayed around a lane named Fresh Fish Junction. I liked walking there because the area's *hutong* curved slightly, drawing you forward to see what was around the next bend. Although it was just steps from Dazhalan across Front Gate Avenue, Fresh Fish Junction's fate was in other hands.

BELIEVE THE PARTY AND GOVERNMENT. DON'T LISTEN TO RUMORS read a colorful poster pasted over the gray bricks of a courtyard home. A notice slapped onto the carved wooden doorway said SIGN THE MOVING CONTRACT IMMEDIATELY; IMMEDIATELY SELECT YOUR NEW HOUSE. CHOOSE A GOOD APARTMENT BUILDING AND WINDOWS THAT FACE THE SUN. The largest of the announcements promised FAIRNESS, OPENNESS, JUSTICE.

"The cops pulled her from that house this evening," said the old man standing behind the yellow police tape. We stared at a courtyard home whose front wall had been knocked away, exposing a furnished room. "She looked young, in her twenties. She was supposed to move out last week, but kept refusing. She was screaming and flailing." The old man flapped his arms. "They got the plastic cuffs on her and marched her out by her hair." He silently surveyed the timbers and shattered brick, then added, "A lot of us stood here and watched, but we didn't do anything."

The man was named Old Zhang. His white hair was cut close to his scalp, and the heaviest features on his gaunt frame were the eyelids and lips that pulled his face downward into an expression of sleepiness. A cataract clouded his right eye. His voice evinced a lifetime of smoking. He wore the navy serge jacket popular with his generation. Though retired, he had, at age seventy-three, begun teaching himself a foreign language.

"The police hit and kick her," he said in halting English. "Do you understand me?" We switched to Chinese and started to walk. Fresh Fish Junction usually bustled with residents and tourists eating duck or dumplings at the row of neon-illuminated restaurants, but tonight the only light came from a moon the color of Old Zhang's cataract.

He had moved to the neighborhood in the 1950s, after being assigned a room in a courtyard by his work unit, a transformer factory. He lived a few lanes from the eviction he had just silently witnessed. The following week, Old Zhang walked out his front gate to discover that, as he slept, the Hand had marked his house: 拆.

While the posters on Old Zhang's lane said BUILD A NEW BEIJING TO WEL-COME A NEW OLYMPICS, the fate of *hutong* neighborhoods such as Fresh Fish Junction had been decided before the city won the rights to host the games.

After 1956, Beijing's housing had largely been consolidated under government management, and rents had been lowered to the cost of a few packs of cigarettes. In the 1980s, as China transitioned to a market economy, housing also changed from being a welfare provision to a commodity. In 1983, Beijing's ten-year urban plan reversed course, saying that the capital would cease to be an industrial base and become a "political and cultural center" that should attract business investment and tourism.

For the first time, the city plan included designs for "old and dilapidated housing renewal." (In Chinese, the still ubiquitous phrase is *weifang gaizao*, appended to *weigai*.) Ninety-five percent of the twenty-nine neighborhoods targeted for renewal were located in Old City. The program was shelved, however, due to costs.

In the early nineties, Beijing announced it would bid to host the 2000 Summer Olympics. The 1983 urban plan was amended to say that by 2010, Beijing would have a new airport and train station, five beltways ("ring roads") around downtown, thirteen subway lines, increased green space, and new architecture that "maintained harmony" with heritage sites. The plan also said "the renovation of dilapidated houses in the Old City should be accelerated."

In April 1990, the municipal government formulated plans to improve twenty-two Old City *hutong* neighborhoods, home to one hundred thousand people. Under the Old and Dilapidated Housing Renewal (ODHR) program, the neighborhoods would be repaired in stages, under an "easy first, difficult later" strategy, beginning in less populated neighborhoods on the edge of the Old City and advancing toward those at its center. The communities outside the Front Gate—Dazhalan and Fresh Fish Junction—were marked for the program's fourth and final phase, to be completed by 2000, when the city hoped to host the Olympics.

Fiscal deficits of the late 1970s had caused China's central government to cease allocating resources for urban development. As a result, the responsibility of covering local expenses fell to municipal governments, which were given increased autonomy in designing and implementing economic policy, and spurring development.

In 1988, national policy was changed to allow local governments to raise resources through the property market. For the first time since the Communists came to power in 1949, land was commoditized. The state still owned the land, but its usage rights could be transferred. Municipalities or agents acting for them put a parcel of the land on the market; development companies bid for its rights; the winning bidder paid for its long-term lease, usually seventy years. The developer could build on the land or apportion it and sell parcels to other developers.

Property became the key to a city's growth. In the late 1990s, the municipal government of Beijing generated nearly 20 percent of its revenue from transferring land rights, an average of $361 million per year. In 1993, the city enlarged the ODHR program to 221 sites, affecting 986,300 people.

By 1995, the rights to nearly all of the Old City neighborhoods targeted under the ODHR program had been sold to developers. Most were a subsidiary of, or aligned with, a district government.

At the start of the ODHR program, Beijing's mayor had promised that residents would enjoy a higher standard of living. He did not specify where. After developers paid for the usage rights of a dilapidated neighborhood, they were free to "renew" it as they wanted, so long as residents were resettled. No stipulation was made for returning people to their original neighborhood, although the land-transfer fee would be reduced if at least 30 percent of the original community was rehoused on the site.

The ODHR program was launched as property prices skyrocketed and the housing market took root. Between 1990 and 1995, Beijing's twenty real estate companies increased to more than six hundred. The revised city plan announced the creation of a "Central Business District" and "Financial Street," though height restrictions in the city center increased scarcity.

Renovating single-story courtyards or building subsidized apartments on central Beijing real estate was far less profitable than adding commercial space. By law, if an evictee was resettled within twelve miles of his former

Prolong Life Street, our neighborhood's commercial center.

Tiantongyuan, a typical suburb where hutong residents have been resettled.
The new area is home to nearly two hundred thousand people.

home, the developer did not have to increase the amount of his or her housing subsidy. With an eye on profits, developers of ODHR sites bought the cheapest land available, located farthest from the city center. They built high-rise apartments known for their low quality. A ring of housing projects went up around Beijing, often in places lacking basic infrastructure such as hospitals, schools, markets, and public transportation.

While the majority of residents were eager to move out of shared, dilapidated courtyards into their own modern apartment, many did not want to be marooned in the far suburbs, away from their Old City neighborhood. A common saying went, "Hope for razing, fear razing"—*pan chai, pa chai.*

A program that began with intentions of beautifying Beijing and providing residents with standardized housing instead fueled government-sanctioned land speculation. If residents didn't want to move, they had little recourse. In the opaque "neighborhood renewal" process, the coalition between government officials and business elites was hard to see, let alone defeat. In their hands, communities were algorithms. The Hand painted a 拆 symbol at night and posted a notice announcing the redevelopment of a neighborhood, starting as soon as nine days hence. Speed was important, as it curtailed time for organizing opposition to the demolition.

A plaintiff complaining about resettlement could be laid off from the state-owned company that had transferred the housing rights to the district government or developer. The Neighborhood Committee—the lowest rung of the municipal government—was ordered to side with developers and not mediate disputed evictions. Although China permits class-action lawsuits, rulings against Party officials were rare. Cases, such as one filed by 10,356 evicted courtyard residents, were dismissed on procedural grounds. Kickbacks were common: by 1999, officials and developers had pocketed an estimated $15 billion off ODHR projects.

"The real estate market is now playing the strongest role in shaping the future aspect of old Beijing," warned a Tsinghua University architecture professor in 1997. "Even though that market is far from mature . . . The planning and development professions in Beijing currently have only a limited understanding of the potentially enormous impact renewal may have on the social and cultural aspects of the city's character."

The *hutong* disappeared. In the frenzy of ODHR-sanctioned clearances, heritage-protection bureaus could do little to stop the destruction. Developers "bought" entire neighborhoods, and everyone—even those holding full title, not just usage rights, to their homes—had to go. City officials said that 500,000 people were evicted from the center of town between 1991 and 2003, though unofficial estimates ran higher; one intrepid reporter tabulated that 572,000 people were forcibly moved between 1998 and 2001 alone—a number equivalent to the total population of Washington, D.C.

Beijing did not win the right to host the 2000 Summer Olympics, and the ODHR program had not cleared the Old City's dilapidated housing by then, as planned. District governments operated independently, at different speeds, and in competition with each other to attract investment. The demolition occurred in fits and starts. By the late 1990s, twenty-two of the East City district's forty-one blighted neighborhoods were still standing. The West City district had transferred the land rights to fifty-four parcels, only ten of which had been cleared. Xuanwu, home to Dazhalan, had finished razing and rebuilding only one of its sites, the Muslim neighborhood around the Ox Street mosque.

In 2001, Beijing was named the host city of the 2008 Olympics. The same year, the city overhauled compensation to those evicted under the ODHR program. Instead of being assigned to a new apartment, residents would be paid a minimum of 8,020 yuan (approximately $1,000) per square meter of living space. They could use the money as they wanted: to rent space in another courtyard, buy a used apartment, or move to a new one in suburbs such as Daxing, a three-to-five-hour roundtrip commute into town on public transportation. In 2007, the average price of a new apartment within the Fourth Ring Road—the forty-mile-long beltway that formed the outer boundary of property considered "centrally-located"—had reached 13,000 yuan ($1,700) a square meter. The 8,020 yuan settlement standard, however, remained unchanged from 2001.

Though neighborhoods such as Fresh Fish Junction and Dazhalan occupied valuable, central real estate, moving their large populations meant a developer would have to pay large resettlement fees. Overcrowding—the districts' disease—became their salvation and stalled demolition.

Still, the lanes fell. In 2004, I had watched the destruction of the neighborhood around Flower Market *hutong*, one-half mile to the east of Fresh Fish Junction. In under an hour, six workers making forty yuan ($5) a day dismantled a courtyard home with pickaxes and sledgehammers. On a white interior wall, an evicted tenant had written a poem in black ink: *Poor in the carefree city / there is no quarter / Prosperity is in the remote mountains / Where I know people who care.*

A year later, shopping malls and a Marriott Courtyard hotel occupied the site. The destruction proceeded from the edge of the ancient city toward its more populated center, like a wave cresting. Fresh Fish Junction, then Dazhalan, were next in its path.

"I don't want to leave this neighborhood," Old Zhang said as we walked down his *hutong*. People recognized him, and he stopped to chat with the women offering mandarin oranges from a cart, and a man selling cigarettes. "Can you lower the price a few cents?" Old Zhang asked. The man called him by his name and handed over a pack of discounted Pandas.

We walked slowly down Straw Mill Lane, named for the former warehouses that stored the mats that protected Beijing's earthen city wall from winter moisture, before it was bricked in the fifteenth century. Old Zhang paused before a notice pasted to a courtyard's wall that said:

After the last one hundred years of the elements and invasion of pests, the amount of dangerous housing has increased and the infrastructure has lagged behind city standards. This situation has captured the city government and Party's utmost attention.

Someone had used a black marker to scrawl 反 (*fan*; oppose) across the announcement. An adjoining poster contained the text of Municipal Regulation No. 87, which granted the city the power of eminent domain. A blade had scored the paper in long, straight cuts. The final set of posters listed the name of a *hutong*, followed by house numbers that would be razed, such as "West Grindstone Lane: 95, 97, 99, 101, 103, 104, 106, 108, 110, 114, 141, 145, 159, 165, 169, 175, 181, 197, 201, 205, 211, 219, 231, 237, 239, 241."

Old Zhang sidled up to the group of men scouring the list like students checking exam results. Their fingers traced a line from the street name to the figures. The roster included private homes whose gates had been fitted

Reading the eviction notices in Fresh Fish Junction.

with a small, blue metal plaque that said PROTECTED COURTYARD, cement buildings such as hotels and shops, and Old Zhang's house.

Framing the eviction notice were ads for relocation services—"We specialize in moving pianos!"—and real estate agencies. The cheapest of the new apartments was located in the far suburbs. It cost 3,000 yuan ($400) a square meter. Old Zhang was due to receive 8,020 yuan per square meter for his current house. But his space was small, and the apartments for sale were three times its size. He couldn't afford them.

Old Zhang said that Fresh Fish Junction's residents could buy a subsidized apartment, built by the development company. That would make his eviction payment the equivalent of scrip; the company would pay Old Zhang to leave his downtown home, and he would hand the money back to it for a faraway apartment that he didn't want.

"I don't know where I shall go," Old Zhang said in English. "I shall know later." He found his address on the posted eviction list. Typed columns displayed the names of his family, the number of rooms they occupied, their courtyard's total area, and the area they actually lived in. He would receive payment for the final figure, which subtracted storage space. "That's not correct," he said, jabbing the figure with his index finger.

A notice dated November 1, 2005, ordered residents to cease home improvements, new construction, and renting to outsiders. The notice of November 20 said residents had to move out by January 21. Two months seemed like short notice to evacuate, though I had seen other neighborhoods cleared within two weeks.

The developer wanted residents out quickly, and not collectively. One slogan said, LIVING IN THE FRONT GATE'S COURTYARDS IS ANCIENT HISTORY; MOVING TO AN APARTMENT MAKES YOU A GOOD NEIGHBOR. Another poster warned, EVERY FAMILY SHOULD FIGURE ITS OWN PROFIT. LISTENING TO RUMORED NEWS LEADS TO ENTRAPMENT.

If a family moved before December 30, it would receive, on top of its resettlement payment, a bonus of fifty-five thousand yuan ($7,333). Families that moved between December 31 and January 9 would receive a bonus of twenty-five hundred yuan ($333). Movers after that date received no additional payment.

Red banners decorated with white characters fluttered in the winter wind: THE CITY GOVERNMENT PROJECT REPAIRS THE ROAD FOR THE PEOPLE.

PROTECT THE ANCIENT CAPITAL'S CHARACTERISTIC APPEARANCE. BRING PROSPERITY FOR THE COMMONERS.

Old Zhang shook his head. He took my pen and in my notebook transcribed a poem:

> *You cannot predict the wind and clouds*
> *Dawn to dusk can bring disaster or fortune.*

In 2002, Fresh Fish Junction and Dazhalan were listed as two of the "Twenty-five Historic Areas in Old Beijing City," a protection plan authored by a committee of professors, architects, engineers, and ministry chairs that was approved by the Municipal City Planning Commission. The Twenty-five Historic Areas covered 17 percent (four square miles) of the Old City. When combined with already protected spaces—mostly former imperial parks and palaces—a total of 38 percent (nine square miles) of Old Beijing was marked as protected, leaving the rest open to destruction.

Only 1.9 square miles of the protected area was housing, two thirds of which was graded as dilapidated. The Twenty-five Historic Areas included 15,178 courtyard homes shared by 95,000 families—285,000 people. A third of them lived in a cell-size space that provided less than 100 square feet per person, well below the city's minimum per capita standard of 161 square feet.

"The living conditions of the conservation areas cannot be improved unless the population there is reduced," the plan recommended. "Therefore, depopulation is one of the goals as well as the key to the successful implementation of conservation planning." The projected population for the Twenty-five Historic Areas was 167,000. Forty-one percent—118,000—of the current population would be moved from the city's most venerable neighborhoods.

Forced relocations were among the capital's most sensitive topics, although many residents wanted out of cramped and crumbling courtyards. Even after the ODHR program was amended to pay cash settlements to residents, the process was so wracked by malfeasance that in 2003 the mu-

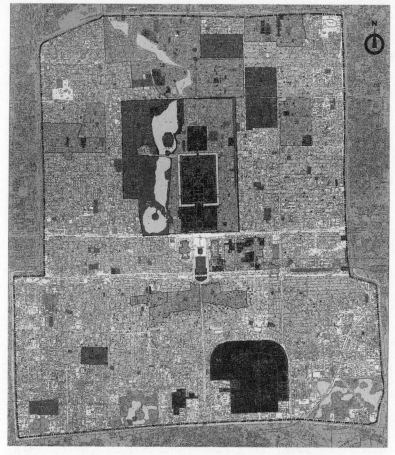

*A map showing the outline of the Old City and its "Twenty-five Historic Areas,"
which are shaded.*

nicipal government issued a rare criticism of its own policy. "The Beijing city government is demanding that all concerned work units correctly handle the development of the capital's construction, safeguard the specific rights of the people, and safeguard social responsibility," reported Xinhua, the state news agency. "The 'raze and removal' work has at times been too simple and attitudes too crude, some projects have been overhasty, and destruction and removal [of residents] has sometimes started before paperwork procedures are finished." The announcement came after several evictees attempted suicide through self-immolation on Tian'anmen Square.

Among residents' complaints was the lack of transparency: redevelopment plans were not made public. The Beijing City Planning Exhibition Center, located a few minutes' walk from Old Zhang's house near Fresh Fish Junction, displayed glossy posters of what had been built and showed a 3-D film that transported viewers into Future Beijing, where there was no traffic, residents could walk on the grass, and subway platforms included bench seating. Not on exhibit, however, was information on which neighborhoods would be razed next. After numerous visitor complaints, the center added a notice to its ticket window: THE EXHIBITS DO NOT CONCERN DEMOLITION. PLEASE BUY YOUR TICKETS WITH PRUDENCE. NO REFUNDS.

In the locked glass case of the Exhibition Center's gift shop, I came across the expensive, glossy book that listed the goals of the Twenty-five Historic Areas project:

1. Preserve traditional cityscape and *hutong* in general.
2. Keep historical authenticity and heritage intact.
3. Proceed with preservation work in a gradual and measured way.
4. Improve the infrastructure and living conditions of the local residents.
5. Encourage public participation.

In 2002, shortly after the inscription of the Twenty-five Historic Areas, notices papered one of the listed neighborhoods, named Nanchizi, located along the east moat of the Forbidden City in the center of Old Beijing. The district government announced that for Nanchizi to be preserved, it would have to be destroyed.

A letter to residents from the development company affiliated with the district government said, "Besides demolishing temporarily built houses, commercial two-story buildings will be erected in parts of Nanchizi to collect funds for the historic zone protection." Nine of Nanchizi's estimated nine hundred courtyard homes would be kept intact. The rest would be razed.

"This is all a real estate scam," a resident told a reporter. "They say our house is too old and falling apart, but they won't let us fix it up ourselves because they want the land. What's intolerable is that our centuries-old houses will be replaced with newly built ancient-style two-story buildings, which is a shame to the historic protection zone."

Given the gulf between the exchange value of the land and the actual value of decrepit houses, a developer could sell an "ancient-style" home on a downtown site such as Nanchizi for many times the fee it paid to evict former tenants.

Nanchizi's destruction was suspended in June 2002, after residents, preservationists, and local media voiced evictee complaints of unfair compensation. The United Nations Educational, Scientific, and Cultural Organization (UNESCO), which grants World Heritage status to cultural sites, raised its objections to the development on the grounds that Nanchizi served as a buffer zone around the World Heritage site of the Forbidden City. "The point of being a world cultural heritage site is to closely connect residents with local buildings and culture," a UNESCO official said. Its local representative announced, "We have expressed our concerns with the Beijing government and called for the end of the demolition to the Nanchizi area." UNESCO never received a formal reply. Six months after being halted, the demolition of Nanchizi resumed.

In August 2003, the East District government gave journalists a tour of Nanchizi after residents had been cleared from the land. An official said the neighborhood's renovation was a pilot project presented as a way to "protect Beijing's historic and cultural areas, and beautify the inner city."

The rebuilt Nanchizi had three hundred two-story apartments available for purchase by evicted families at a discounted price of forty-five hundred yuan ($600) a square meter. The neighborhood's per capita living space had been doubled, the official said, and the apartments included central heat and indoor plumbing. Before, one thousand people shared five public latrines. Thirty-one new courtyard homes would be built to resemble the ones they replaced. They would go on the market at $1 million, more than five times the compensation paid to former tenants.

If you remembered what it replaced, new development in Beijing initially appeared sterile. Some areas, such as the row of late-night restaurants on the city's remade Ghost Street, quickly regained the "human energy" (renqi) of their former selves. Other neighborhoods were indelibly altered. After its completion in 2005, Nanchizi was somewhere in between.

Critics called it a "fake antique" and said it lacked its former human energy, but considering what could have been built—had zoning restrictions and media coverage not intervened—things could have turned out worse. There were no high-rise apartments and no swing-arm gates blocking entrance to the gentrified lanes. The restored Pudu Temple rose above quiet, narrow streets lined with parked cars. Gone was the mixture of residences, shops, and street life that characterizes *hutong*. Nanchizi had been turned into a bedroom community at the heart of Beijing.

In the winter of 2005, the businesses on both sides of Front Gate Avenue were shuttered and their facades cloaked in metal sheets ten feet high. They displayed computer-generated drawings of the gray-brick, two-story buildings that were to come. In large characters, a slogan said PROTECT THE ANCIENT CITY'S APPEARANCE. In the drawing, the people strolling on the future, pedestrian-only Front Gate Avenue weren't Chinese, but white-skinned. The only depicted shop signs were for Pizza Hut and Starbucks.

Another slogan promised that the redevelopment of Front Gate Avenue and Fresh Fish Junction would RESTORE HISTORY'S CULTURAL PULSE. It did not say which period of history. Restoring Beijing to its past urban appearance meant selecting from eras that spanned eight centuries; visitors to Rome, for example, encounter a largely papal and Renaissance-era cityscape, built atop—or with—the rubble of the imperial capital. Judging by the old-fashioned trolley that ran down the center of the depicted Front Gate Avenue, the neighborhood would be remade to outwardly appear as it had in the 1920s. The intangible community fabric would be replaced by an open-air shopping center.

"If Front Gate Avenue forms a mall instead of being widened and reconstructed properly," cautioned a plan submitted by Tsinghua University's influential Urban Planning and Design Institute, "it shall cut the continuity of traffic and space, and lead to the blocking of the central axis."

That affected the capital's feng shui, the principle that once governed the construction of imperial Chinese cities. According to feng shui, a town's central axis should be unimpeded in the south due to the positive energy (yang) that flowed from that direction, and shielded in the north, to block out negative energy (yin) that originated there.

Beijing's central axis had already seen many of its nodes destroyed—the gates flanking the east and west sides of Tian'anmen Square, and the gate on the square itself, where Mao's mausoleum now squatted. Closing Front Gate Avenue to vehicle traffic would also require auxiliary roads to be sliced through the surrounding *hutong* neighborhoods.

"Building more roads only attracts more traffic and more congestion," warned a World Bank report urging the protection of Dazhalan. An urban planner whose scheme to construct a tunnel under Fresh Fish Junction had been rejected due to costs said, "The wider the road, the less 'human energy.'" She cited the new eight-lane boulevard on the area's southern edge. "It completely annihilated commerce there. It's really a highway. How can you build highways in the city center?" Additionally, the new streets bracketing Front Gate Avenue would destroy communities and architectural heritage.

The Hand drew them anyway.

The road through Fresh Fish Junction was not only affecting longtime residents such as Old Zhang, but also newcomers who owned businesses in the neighborhood.

The Liu family had migrated from their farm in central Shanxi province and opened a noodle restaurant whose interior held four tables. The mother greeted customers by name, remembered their usual order, and often sat down to chat. The father worked in the kitchen with their son, who had recently finished a tour in western Xinjiang province as a People's Liberation Army soldier. He was twenty-two and fretted about the matchmaking his mother had initiated back in their village to find him a wife.

The Lius' restaurant specialized in "knife-shaved" noodles (*daoxiao mian*), broad, thick pasta steeped in pork broth. Making knife-shaved noodles requires the cook to balance a board vertically against the inside of his forearm. A loaf-size lump of dough rests on the board. The cook uses a blade in his other hand to quickly scrape thick chunks of dough into a wok of boiling water. It is strenuous, hot work, but Soldier Liu retained his drill-ground physique. He didn't drink or smoke, and I never heard him swear. His usual customers did all three, with relish.

Soldier Liu often sat and tried to read aloud Mocky's latest misadventure from my students' textbook. He worked from sunup to ten o'clock at night and lived with his parents in a shared courtyard near the restaurant. "I like to study and would love to learn English," he said, "but I never have any time."

He didn't know where they would go after Fresh Fish Junction was destroyed. "We will stay in the city, that's for certain." His younger sister was back home, training to become a math teacher, and they were paying her tuition and saving money. "Our village is very backward and poor, and there's nothing to do there."

"Except find a wife," I said.

"No mistake!" He laughed. "I don't like Beijing girls. They're shallow." He studied Mocky kicking a soccer ball through a window, then told the page, "And they would never date a guy who makes knife-shaved noodles."

When their shop was razed, the Liu family would receive no compensation. They would lose their livelihood, but as they rented the space, only their landlord was entitled to a settlement. It seemed incongruous that Beijing's self-starting entrepreneurs were the ones that would suffer from a booming economy. Now all business owners would be scrambling to find new spaces. "Our location right now is really great," Soldier Liu said. "People walk by all day long, and we're the only noodle restaurant on the entire *hutong*."

Soldier Liu often crossed Front Gate Avenue to troll Dazhalan's lanes, but not one of the hundreds of storefronts showed a FOR RENT sign. The Lius would have to move out before they returned to their village to celebrate Spring Festival—Chinese New Year—in 2006.

For the evictions around Fresh Fish Junction, the district government initially employed persuasion, rather than force. The goal was to avoid confrontations such as the one Old Zhang had witnessed, when the woman had been pulled from her home. In early December, on the gray brick wall across from the Lius' restaurant, a government notice printed on yellow paper said:

CHERISH THE CHANCE; GRAB THE GOOD FORTUNE
SAY FAREWELL TO DANGEROUS HOUSING

You of course know that in our district there are many mixed courtyards, a high-density population, and lots of old and dangerous houses. Over the last decades of hardships, we on this old street all longed to leave dangerous housing as soon as possible. However, because of Front Gate district's architectural height restrictions and other reasons, many developers came here, took a look, shook their heads, and left. This not only broke everybody's heart, but it really pulled the heartstrings of the district government.

In recent years, through sit-down chats with residents and listening to their opinions, we came to understand that 95 percent of our district's residents desire—moreover, fervently want—an improved housing environment, and to say farewell to dangerous housing. To realize everyone's dream as soon as possible, the district government worked ceaselessly to make it happen.

Many years later, when you come back here and walk around, you will certainly say with pride, "My family once lived here, and to improve the area and protect the ancient capital's appearance, and contribute to New Beijing, New Olympics, we showed our collective strength!"

To realize this fifty-six-year-old dream, shouldn't we all cooperate with the district government? The excellent Party and government helps us, so don't we want to not miss this unbelievable chance?

That was the order: First the eviction notices were posted. Then, the houses of families who accepted the eviction payment were half-demolished, making them uninhabitable. Next, notices tried to convince the remaining holdouts to sign a settlement and leave. Finally, blue tin sheeting went up to conceal the flattening of the neighborhood.

In the rubble of a house near Old Zhang's, I picked up mail postmarked two days earlier. It was a circular for the New World shopping mall, which had replaced the *hutong* neighborhood just to the east. On the lane, a ring of men formed around a young woman. "You have to report the low compensation they are offering us!" one man yelled at her. "You journalists never write the truth! Pay attention to the common people!"

Destroyed houses at Fresh Fish Junction. The Hand spared the trees.

She was a reporter for the Beijing daily tabloid the *First* and had been assigned to write about the guildhalls—former guesthouses for itinerant scholars and merchants—that were being spared for display on the future open-air mall. The encounter had shaken her. "We're not allowed to report on the controversy over settlement payments," she told me as we walked away.

Her photographer shot pictures of courtyard exteriors, a woman wringing out hand-laundered sheets, a dirty white cat, and a child's chalked drawings of the Olympic mascots. The four-page spread that ran in the paper included these photos and a map of Fresh Fish Junction that did not show the planned road. Separated from their lively context, the images seemed to depict just another *hutong*, whose buildings and residents were disconnected and interchangeable with other shabby lanes.

The designation in 2002 of the Twenty-five Historic Areas occurred as Beijing began a $40 billion makeover to host the Olympics, adding new luster to a city whose economy was already surging as the capital of the fastest-growing economy in the world. Most Olympic events would be held at sites outside the Old City, meaning that no *hutong* would have to be torn down to construct a stadium. Those innovative structures—with nicknames such as the Bird's Nest and Water Cube—were going up in a district to the north, outside the Fourth Ring Road.

Old City neighborhoods were not immune from Olympic plans, however. A 2005 report authored by a leading government think tank titled the *Investigation of Urban Corners in Beijing* said, "In order to implement the mighty philosophy of 'New Beijing, New Olympics' in city planning, we cannot ignore and must solve the urban corner problem." The term was a euphemism for slum. The report's title page contained one photo. It wasn't of a courtyard home or *hutong*, but New York City's Chrysler Building.

The *Investigation* defined an "urban corner" (also called a "village in the city") as an area of high-density housing with narrow roads, little green space, and a "chaotic environment." For example, one unnamed *hutong* was lined with 167 beauty parlors, though only seven had hair styling equipment. The others dismissed the pretense and operated openly as "hand-job salons," charging two hundred yuan ($27) or less.

The *Investigation* tallied 343 urban corners that it said should be cleaned up before the Olympics. Some of the areas, such as Fresh Fish Junction and Dazhalan, were also among the Twenty-five Historic Areas the city had designated for protection.

The report described the neighborhoods in purely physical terms. The wood-framed homes of Fresh Fish Junction caught fire forty-eight times between 2000 and 2003; the *hutong* were not wide enough to accommodate fire engines. Houses were overcrowded, such as 275 West Grindstone Lane, home to twenty-two people. "Standing puddles form on the floors after it rains," the *Investigation* said, "and residents have installed braces for fear of the walls collapsing. Moreover, flies and mosquitoes buzz in and out freely." The cost of renovating buildings and installing sewage pipes would be astronomical, it warned. The neighborhood had 108 two-story wood-framed buildings and 2,440 courtyard homes—93 percent of which were substandard, and 47.5 percent outright dangerous.

The *Investigation* described the community through exacting statistics, not personal names or narratives. Nearly forty-two thousand people lived in Fresh Fish Junction. Many had migrated to Beijing, the report said, low-ering the neighborhood's "cultural level." Two thirds of the population had not continued past middle school. Criminal cases were on the rise; calls to the emergency operator at 110—Beijing's 911—increased an average of four hundred each month. The area's per capita monthly salary was a thou-sand yuan ($133), half the city norm.

Like Dazhalan, Fresh Fish Junction was a short walk south from Tian'an-men Square. "Foreigners absolutely view China through our capital," the report reminded. "The capital's appearance influences China's appearance. Urban corners represent our dark side."

The world couldn't arrive in Beijing for the games only to find a slum at its center. 拆!

One night at Soldier Liu's noodle restaurant, Old Zhang took my pen and grabbed a napkin. He sketched a stick figure with a frowning face whose arms were being pulled by two other stick figures. "This guy is the demoli-tion company," he explained. "This one is the construction company." The caption said, "I can only endure!" He quickly drew another that showed him bowing before a stick man. "If you are being demolished, you must kowtow to beg for a higher payment." A sly grin spread across his face. He was enjoying himself and took another napkin. The scene showed his sev-ered head on the ground between two players. "I get kicked between the government and the developers. They are on the same team. I am just the ball."

A second open letter to the neighborhood appeared on the wall across from the Lius' restaurant. Old Zhang said its tone was like an adult's when attempting to convince a child to finish a meal. The notice read, "Many people say that they don't want to move because their relations with neighbors are so tight. But now you only have to go to the settlement of-fice, sign the eviction agreement, and then you can choose an affordable apartment. Think about it: you and your family live in an old house, and now you finally have a chance to improve your living conditions. This is an extremely rare opportunity!"

The development company aligned with the district government was building apartment towers. "We should also warn you," the notice continued, "that this housing is reserved for our district's relocation." Other subsidized blocks in Beijing were under pressure to sell their vacant units to the public at market prices. "People in our district are already accepting settlements and clamoring to move out as early as possible into an affordable apartment. Therefore, you'll see that if you don't grab this chance, then other citizens will jump ahead of you, and then there will not be any good houses left for you. You and your family will lose out."

The site was in a comparatively good location, between the Second and Third Ring Roads in Beijing's southeast. I took a cab there and arrived at a vacant lot. The subsidized apartments earmarked for Fresh Fish Junction's evictees would not be finished for another year. Residents had to buy elsewhere, or to rent in the interim and put up money for homes that existed only on blueprints. It was standard practice in Beijing to buy an apartment before it was built, but just as common were the complaints over construction quality, management, and even the title-transfer process that followed.

The announcements posted overnight across from Soldier Liu's restaurant grew more beseeching as the eviction deadline approached. One printed on peach-colored paper argued:

> Winter is here, and to heat your home, you cause a fire hazard. In summer you hear the sound of raindrops, but then you fear your walls will collapse on your head. If someone is sick in your home, when it comes time to call an ambulance, it can't enter your narrow lane. For decades, some families have had three people living in a small, decrepit room. Then you see a new community with central heat and a private room for each family member, but here you are in the old house, burning coal honeycombs for heat, and sharing one water meter with several families. The migrant population keeps increasing around you, and so does crime. Residents just want to get out of here as soon as possible.

The poster added that by doing so "they make a tremendous contribution to the 2008 Olympic Games."

Old Zhang said, "I'm not moving."

On December 10, 2005, twenty days before the deadline to receive a bonus of fifty-five thousand yuan for moving, a green poster went up across from Soldier Liu's restaurant.

> The public notice of destruction due to the Front Gate district road project was posted on 11/21. Since then, with wide support of the masses, many citizens have grabbed the chance to move and netted the bonus. Presently 76.8 percent of residents have signed the agreement to move. However, certain citizens harbor the fantasy that if they put off moving, they can negotiate a much higher settlement. This kind of thinking is not only mistaken, it also impedes the government's project to fix the road to benefit the masses. To protect the project's smooth sailing and to protect the public's profit, we all have to support this policy. You cannot stand there with your mouth open, expecting to be fed. In other words, "Move early and receive profit, move late and you stand to lose."
>
> You still have twenty days. We earnestly give you this suggestion: don't lose the chance, you can't stop time! Don't listen to rumors, and don't listen to others' instigations, because when you suffer the loss, will those people accept responsibility? The time is already short, you have to grab the chance to sign the agreement, move from your house, and then enjoy fifty-five thousand yuan extra. This is a good policy, and accepting it is really the correct and sensible decision.

Old Zhang said, "I'm not moving."

He had been in and out of the relocation office, which was set up in the vacated #223 Middle School. You could walk right in and listen to the clerks calmly repeat, nearly verbatim, the notices posted around the neighborhood. The people there treated him politely, he said, but he thought their offered price was too low. With the bonus, Old Zhang stood to be paid 240,000 yuan ($32,000). "It's not enough to buy a house downtown, and if I move now, I would have to pay rent, anyway. I'm staying."

Fifteen days before the deadline, posters said that 83.9 percent of residents had accepted the settlement. The figure included one of the two other families that had shared Old Zhang's courtyard for decades. "They didn't tell me they were leaving," he said. "People don't work together like they used to."

Ten days before the deadline, 87.8 percent of the neighborhood had agreed to move, including the other family that lived in Old Zhang's courtyard. Now, he was alone.

On Christmas Day, the Liu family closed their noodle restaurant. "We're going back to our village for the New Year," Soldier Liu said. "After that, who knows?" The family was not sad or angry. This was Beijing, and that's just the way things went. The mother served me one last bowl of noodles in pork broth. "Add more black vinegar," she said. "It's made in our village. It's really the best." It was. As I ate, she wrote down their address in the countryside. We said good-bye.

Six days before the deadline, 92.9 percent of the residents had agreed to move. Three days later, the posted figure rose to 95 percent. Old Zhang would still not budge.

As I huddled over my electric heater at home, he sat at my desk, looking unaffected and hale. "I think my house won't be razed until April 2006," he said. That was four months away. "I only pay seventeen yuan [$2.26] a month for rent, because the house was provided by my work unit. I'll stay until the last possible minute and keep pestering them for a higher payment. I have nothing to lose."

The Widow walked in without knocking. She told me to add layers of clothing to my forearms, lest I catch pneumonia. I introduced her to Old Zhang, adding that his home was being destroyed. "Little Plumblossom," she said, "I am telling you, I will never move from here. Never! This courtyard is my home."

Fresh Fish Junction was now unlit and silent at night, making the empty lanes feel haunted. I wanted to see Old Zhang home. We left my house and biked down the brightly lit streets of Dazhalan, through clouds of steam billowing from restaurant kitchens. We dismounted at the rubble from the road being built to divert Front Gate Avenue's traffic.

Old Zhang motioned to my neighborhood. "These people," he said, "have no idea how their lives are about to change."

CHAPTER 5

WINTERTIME

IN CLASS TWO, Grade Four, there were still 996 days until the Olympics. School had become a timeless routine, and one with central heat. By January 2006, Miss Zhu and I had finished the lessons in our textbook, but regulations said that we couldn't begin teaching the next in the series until the following semester. We turned to the beginning, revisiting Mocky's attempts to juggle, Mocky buying a hat, and Mocky losing his nuts. (A kind squirrel returns them.)

When we weren't in class, I warmed myself over the office radiator and watched the *hutong* below. The other teachers thought there was nothing to see. Miss Zhu was the only one who lived in a courtyard home; the rest commuted from apartment blocks, some more than an hour away. They were afraid for their jobs, not the neighborhood. When a block of *hutong* was destroyed, its school was, too. The teachers' obligation to the work unit remained, however. Some were assigned new posts closer to home, some farther away; some were transferred to work under worse principals, and others better. They didn't know where they would be sent until the Education Bureau told them. Regardless, their seniority and comfort level were shattered. Teachers often asked me, "Do you know when our school will be razed?"

The kids stayed indoors for lunch during winter. In Western educational circles, it is said that observing children at play can reveal much about their personalities and abilities. I wondered what Miss Zhu saw when she watched our students play. "I see chaos," she said. "They sound like they're tearing down a house."

Coal Lane Elementary had no jigsaw puzzles or building blocks for the kids to manipulate. In the hallway they played *bao*, a game like pickle-in-the-middle in which a rubber ball is tossed between two players. They also kicked the Beijing version of a hacky sack, called a *jianzi*—a stack of washers with feathers glued in the hole. *Jianzi* was invented in Beijing at a *hutong* school that displayed a plaque announcing the fact. The rules for *jianzi* were simple: shout out the number of kicks before it hit the ground.

Miss Zhu was undefeated. She played the games during recess, and afterward the female students such as Little Liu and Mao Mao braided her hair. The male students challenged me to arm wrestle. The kids didn't have handheld video games, celebrity magazines, music players, cell phones, or even activity books with mazes. The most popular comic-book character was the Japanese hero Ultraman, and a well-worn copy of his adventures circulated in the room. Stickers were a valuable trading item. Miss Zhu didn't understand my appreciation, but she had never taught at a school where they banned the game of tag, or where kids waited for buses at stops plastered with ads for mortuaries and Kool cigarettes.

The school did not have a gymnasium, so the classroom was the largest indoor area the students played in each day. Mr. Han and his wife, the couple who lived beside me, had a seven-year-old son, but because their room was only seventy square feet, they wouldn't uproot him from their home in Manchuria, China's northeast. "There's no space here," Mr. Han said. "The quality of education is better, but at home he can run all over, and he has a lot of friends." Mr. Han's mother was watching the boy. Once a week, Mr. Han's wife called her son from the lane's "phone bar," where a row of cubicles provided discounted rates on long-distance calls. It was cheaper than using a cell phone, but provided little privacy.

Mr. Han's niece went to Coal Lane Elementary, and most days after class she ended up in my house, lying on her stomach surrounded by homework. Although she was old enough to be in Grade Three, she had started school late and squeezed into a Grade One desk. She asked me to teach her how to type in Chinese, because writing was hard.

Children begin learning characters through their romanized script (pinyin). In Chinese, I typed, "I like to eat panda bears." The niece recognized half the characters. She stared at the keyboard and pecked in *wo*, which the computer changed to 我, I. She concentrated on entering four more words, then selected the characters from the numbered list that popped up in a window. They made: 我住在北京. I live in Beijing.

Even at the end of a full semester, school was still a mystery to her. It took more time to decode her workbook's directions than to complete the activity. I read the directions aloud, and she repeated them. "So I'm supposed to draw a line to the sphere, the cylinder, the cube, and the square. Then I have to count the number of each piece and enter the total in these parentheses on this page. And then I circle the abnormal shapes . . ." I remembered first-grade math as pages of addition and subtraction problems. "That's for little kids," she said, laughing. "Can you repeat these instructions?"

In autumn, she had cut leaves from colored construction paper and taped them to my windows. Now they had been replaced by her patterned snowflakes. The girl liked the change of seasons because the *hutong*'s snacks changed from roasted yams to fried chestnuts and *tang hu lu*, red hawthorn berries stacked kebablike on a sharp stick and glazed with sugar syrup. Sometimes the berries hid hard kernels, or the syrup glued your teeth together, or the stick jabbed you in the gums. Other than that, she said, *tang hu lu* was delicious.

Winter was my favorite season in Beijing, despite that our breath froze even inside the house. Hot pot replaced summer's Korean cold noodles as comfort food. Hot pot is known as a Beijing cuisine, though it originated in Mongolia. Legend has it that centuries ago a camp of soldiers was un-expectedly called to battle. The cook, realizing that a meal had to be served—immediately—dispensed with the protocol of roasting meat over a fire and dumped the mutton into cauldrons of boiling water. The cook presented the dish to the general, hoping his head would be spared for the offense. The general liked it; it was delicious and different. "It's *boiled lamb*," at least one of his men must have grumbled. Nevertheless, the battle was fought, the Mongols won, and boiled lamb stayed on the menu.

Hot pot is a participatory cuisine, requiring its diners to dip chopstick-pinches of raw mutton and vegetables into a brazier of boiling water placed at the table's center. After the meat is cooked, you roll it around in a bowl of sesame paste and pickled garlic, then chase it with many beers. In winter, the steam coating the restaurant windows socks in diners, suspending them in a warm, timeless cloud.

The city's lakes froze in mid-December, the earliest that the ice had come in for a decade. The polar-bear swimmers chopped their hole on the south shore of Front Lake, but skating was difficult due to northern gusts that dumped dust and sand on the surface. Clearing a rink required several hands on whisk brooms, and avoiding the revelers on *pali*, sleds with metal runners propelled with short stakes.

I used to skate on Front Lake because it provided a clear view of the Drum and Bell towers, Beijing's former timekeepers. On its lakeshore, an old man who advertised himself as the Skate Sharpening King boasted that he had stayed open from 1937 through each of the eight winters that Japanese soldiers occupied the city. He was no match for developers, however. In the winter of 2005, his locale had been fenced off with panels of blue-painted tin shrouding the construction of an upscale restaurant. In a sense, the center of the Old City was reverting to its original form, when it was the playground of royalty and its acolytes.

Now the best skate sharpener worked across town at the rink inside Xidan's mall. The Hand had rubbed out the area—the sidewalk vendors, cluttered storefronts, and crowds—and replaced it with straight lines. Here a bank, there an office tower, here an underground shopping mall, there a widened intersection, and nowhere shade. Beijing's famous streets were ceasing to be destinations themselves, changing into viaducts between Point A and Mall B. Due to traffic, an errand such as skate sharpening that used to take a few minutes now took at least an hour.

Every season I played hockey with the same dozen Beijing natives. We only knew each other on the ice, for the month between Christmas and the Chinese New Year, whose beginning was determined by the lunar calendar. It was a different sort of Beijing camaraderie, free from the pressure to reciprocate favors.

After Front Lake began charging a higher fee to use its groomed rink—the ticket included a free coffee at the new Starbucks on the west shore—we moved our game to the Forbidden City's moat. Plywood painted vermilion to match the neighboring palace towers surrounded the rink on three sides. The stones separating the moat from Zhongshan Park formed the fourth barrier. The park filled at dawn with elderly doing exercises. Women rubbed their backs against the gnarled cypress trees. Old men paced while violently crossing their arms against their chest, belting out opera or phlegm-filled groans that went *Uhhh!* The quieter the surrounding environment, the noisier Beijingers behaved.

The day's rink conditions were chalked on a board: air temperature, wind direction, and ice thickness in the sun and shade. I laced up on a bench in the pavilion's courtyard. A steep wooden ramp provided a running start to the ice. The only advertisement on the rink's fence was a green banner whose white characters reminded OVERPOPULATION IS OUR NATION'S MOST PRESSING PROBLEM.

Not on the ice. No one else was here. In winter, Beijing's tourist crowds thinned, the skies were often clear and bright, and public spaces became personal ones. I liked to hike snow-covered paths at the Fragrant Hills and draw fortune sticks from the soothsayer at Tanzhe Temple, both of which emptied of people.

Once the elderly exercisers left, the only sounds on the Forbidden City moat were the scratches of my skates cutting into the ice. The sun rose over the palace walls, and at the top of every hour, the melody of "The East Is Red" chimed from the Ministry of Communication's clock tower, a mile away. I hung my scarf in the center of a goal as a target, dropped the puck, and began taking shots. I savored the routine; it was the most time I spent alone each day.

The men arrived, wearing hockey gloves, shin pads, and helmets. They set their tea-filled thermoses on the bench and lit cigarettes. Our games were speedy, loose, and fun. The men laughed out loud at their own mistakes. Unlike basketball, hockey is self-regulating; everyone has a stick, so hacking brings a reprisal. The only time we stopped play was when the puck flew over the boards, or someone wanted a smoke.

China invented many things, and the men claimed that hockey was one of them. Starting in the seventeenth century, when China was ruled by Manchu from the north, the imperial court held ice games on the central lakes every December. Soldiers from the Eight Banners—military units that lived inside the Imperial City—competed in a series of events on skates made by sliding a blade into a grooved shoe soul.

Hockey on the southwest corner of the Forbidden City moat.

The emperor watched from the shore on a sable-lined divan. The games began with a cannon shot, meant to demonstrate the safety of the ice, followed by two hundred banner men skating past for review. Soldiers divided into teams wearing yellow or red silk robes. Events included chasing after a ball made of feathers (hence the hockey claim), and drawing a bow and firing at a suspended orb while whizzing by at full speed. Acrobats performed on skates as "dancing dragon missiles." In the final event, soldiers donned pigskin shoes and attempted to stay upright as they slid down an ice slope three to four stories high.

That may not be enough to convince a Canadian of hockey's origin, but skating remained a popular Beijing pastime after the fall of the last emperor. "Skating on natural ice is an old recreation in North China and is much indulged in by children and grown-ups alike," reported the narrator of *The Adventures of Wu*, a collection of newspaper columns from 1939 to 1940 that ran in the English-language *Peking Chronicle*. The book is a gazetteer of pre-Communist *hutong* life. In its index, I randomly flipped to the letter *B*, for Beijing. The listed topics included:

> badger hunting;
> balancers, flagpole;
> bamboo, clappers;
> banner men, Manchu;
> bath, baby's third-day;
> bean curds, almond; stinky;
> bear show;
> Beating the Blind Tiger (game);
> bed, brick-stove (k'ang); God and Goddess of;
> beetle-cart man;
> Beginning of Winter;
> bell, dragon god of;
> bill-collecting devil;
> birds;
> boat, service on city moats;
> bread, steamed;
> bricks, for Peking city wall;
> bridge, for the dead; and dragon legend;
> brotherhood, sworn;
> brush, writing;
> buckwheat, cakes; husk pillows;
> Buddha;
> burials;
> butterflies.

Wu described the life, from cradle to wedlock, of a lower-middle-class *hutong* resident named Little Bald Head. Every year, he skated after the weather turned "so cold, even dogs and cats are frozen to death." His skates were made by mounting blades to squares of wood, then lashing the block to his shoes with leather bands. Back then, speed—not hockey—created a skater's reputation. Men would race along the city moat to where it met the Grand Canal in today's suburb of Tongzhou, twenty-six miles away, dodging the holes cut by ice-block sellers and fishermen. A skater would pur-

chase a souvenir to prove he had been there, then cover the distance back
to Beijing in ninety minutes.

But even in 1939, the last days of old Beijing felt near. The emperor had
encouraged ice sports, wrote the narrator of *The Adventures of Wu*, though
"skating and sledging are a fast vanishing sight from the frozen water-ways
of Peking and the last of them will probably be seen shortly."

While badger hunting, bear shows, the bill-collecting devil, and even
the Skate Sharpening King have disappeared from Beijing, ice-skating is a
tradition that lives on.

The public bathhouse survived, too. I biked back to the *hutong*, balancing
the hockey stick before me like a lance until I was halted by the motorcade
of black Audis that whooshed dignitaries past the Great Hall of the People
and Tian'anmen Square.

The sweat froze to my clothes before I reached home. I grabbed a
towel and shampoo and shivered on the walk down Red Bayberry and
Bamboo Slanted Street, then up a narrow alley lined with painted propaganda scenes exhibiting civic virtue. A wood house held an ax and
chased a globe with a forest for hair; a woman handed divorce papers to
her cheating husband; another woman lectured, "Eat your medicine!" to

*Hand-painted propaganda image off Red Bayberry and Bamboo Slanted Street.
During a clean-up campaign for the Olympics, such paintings were erased as unseemly.*

a man who had, according to the caption, neglected the cleanliness of his penis.

Beijing had spas that looked imported from a Las Vegas hotel, but the Big Power Bathhouse was not one of them. The entrance ticket cost ten yuan ($1.33), but only eight yuan if you bought twenty in advance. The attendant inked an X in one of my prepaid card's boxes, took my shoes and socks, and handed over a pair of plastic flip-flops. I locked my clothes in the changing room's wooden cabinet.

The shower rooms were segregated by sex. Four spigots lined either side of the white-tiled wall. They were not partitioned, just as in the latrine. The same etiquette was expected: bring your own supplies; first come, first served; stay in your own space.

The water was scalding, but its pressure didn't live up to Big Power's name. For a few extra yuan, a wiry old man in baby blue Jockey shorts exfoliated my body with a coarse mitten washcloth. When I hopped off his padded table, wads of peeled-off skin outlined where I had lain. "You're really dirty!" the man said. "I should charge you more since you are taller than Chinese!" I waited to enter the small sauna. An old man emerged, carrying an open twenty-ounce bottle of Yanjing beer. He padded to a spigot. As the cool water splashed through his white crew cut and down rolls of flesh, he chugged the bottle dry.

Big Power didn't have a hairdryer, so my head and towel often froze on the walk home. I stopped at the neighborhood Internet café to hang my towel over its radiator and check e-mail. The "café" was an undivided room holding rows of one hundred computers. At a cost of two yuan ($.27) an hour, they were usually full.

The median age of a Big Power customer looked about sixty-five, but the café's clientele was four decades younger. The female patrons were migrants who used a webcam and headset to chat with distant friends and relations. The men played online games such as *World of Warcraft* and *Counterstrike*. Cigarette smoke filled the café, along with the sounds of giggling girls, machine-gun blasts, a computerized voice proclaiming in English, "Terrorists win!" and the men's defeated howl of *Wo cao!*—Fuck me!

I typed the address of our district government's public-forum Web site, where residents could submit a question or suggestion. In early 2006, the site's index page showed 2,151 letters. I scrolled down; most of the subject lines included 拆. The letters asked, "Will we or won't we be razed?" (*Will*); "Is No. 56 cultural heritage or not?" (*Not*); and "Am I being cheated?" (*No*).

In a letter titled "Excuse Me, When Will Red Bayberry and Bamboo Slanted Street Be Demolished?" a man who identified himself as Mr. Jiang wrote:

"At present there are many rumors, and nonetheless we know that the government cannot not look out for us poor people, but everyone also really wants to know exactly when is the destruction? Thank you! Please respond!"

The unsigned reply appeared three days later:

"Jiang (Mr.): Hello! Your message to the district government has been received. Regarding the question of when Red Bayberry and Bamboo Slanted Street will be razed, Red Bayberry and Bamboo Slanted Street belongs to the Dazhalan Protected District. Presently, the scope of this district's razing is centered on Coal Street. It's estimated Red Bayberry and Bamboo Slanted Street will have to wait one or two years to be demolished."

Coal Street—not to be confused with Coal Lane, where the elementary school was located—was one of the north-south streets that bookended the neighborhood. Due to the closure of Front Gate Avenue to traffic, Coal Street was being remade to triple its width to seventy-five feet. The project took place three hundred yards from our front door, but we didn't hear the construction at our home, nor had the Widow ever seen it. Her daily shopping trip to Heavenly Peach market took her in the opposite direction.

Mr. Han and his wife crossed Coal Street every day to reach their shop, where they fixed cell phones and sold cigarettes. They passed the row of condemned homes and businesses, some of which displayed characters painted in protest by their evicted tenants, such as "The court has stepped aside on the issue of demolition and relocation. The demolition company has falsified agreements. It is difficult for the weak little people to survive."

To my neighbors, the road-widening project was an inconvenience, not something that would change their lives.

One morning I walked out to the latrine to find people standing before a row of white notices that had been pasted overnight to our home's exterior. "Destruction notice?" I asked.

Recycler Wang shook his head. "Fireworks."

The text declared an end to Beijing's twelve-year prohibition on lighting explosives inside the city during Spring Festival celebrations. In rescinding the ban, the government had agreed with petitioning residents that fireworks were cultural heritage. They were traditionally lit to ward off evil spirits and usher in the New Year. The poster announced that they could legally be bought and sold, but it was forbidden to light fireworks at "intersections, historical buildings, bus stops, military areas, government buildings, hospitals, kindergartens, forests, and gas stations."

Regardless, the city exploded on the eve of the Lunar New Year. A walk through the *hutong* became an exercise in dodging incoming fire. My students stood behind their fathers as they touched lit cigarettes to Happy Fat Twins, Diamond Flowers, Silver-Flowered Cherry Trees, and the Blizzard of Ten Thousand Flowers. Sparks showered down, Roman candles thumped upward, and the boom of M-80s called Pull Thunder's Tail resonated off courtyard exterior walls. A Butterfly King spinner buzzed my ear. A Cow Demon bounced off my bike spokes. The students whooped and demanded more. For the first time in their lives, the first night of Spring Festival felt like a festival, not just an occasion to eat too many dumplings and watch the televised variety show.

I biked to visit Old Zhang. This would be the last Lunar New Year he would spend in his house. Fresh Fish Junction was dark, and the only sounds came from the distant explosives. Old Zhang's gate was chained and padlocked from the inside. On the door he had chalked: OCCUPIED. I WILL CALL THE POLICE IF YOU ATTEMPT TO ENTER. YOU ASSUME ALL RESPONSIBILITY!

"That's to keep the vultures away," he said as he let me inside. "The recyclers pedal around on their flatbed bicycles, scanning for things with value." Some of the homes in the neighborhood had been boarded up and fenced with a green iron gate. "Those are buildings that will be protected. Maybe they will be museums. Maybe they will be restored as courtyards for millionaires. Who can say?"

Inside, his son and daughter-in-law worked over a wok, sizzling on the propane-fueled burner. Old Zhang's grandson, in Grade Three, ignored the televised pageant and frowned over a vocabulary workbook. No kids—nor anyone else—remained on the lane. In Chinese, he asked me, "How do I pronounce *badminton racquet* in English?"

Old Zhang's living room held a bed, a sofa, a desk, and bureau, upon which he laid a flat, cloth sack. It was already toasty inside, due to the glowing coal honeycombs, and our faces flushed after we finished the first round of bamboo wine he had saved for the evening. The annual variety show paused from its singing and acrobatic performances to announce that China would send a pair of pandas to Taiwan as a gesture of friendship. The program's five hundred million viewers could pick the animals' names by choosing from a list and sending a text message via cell phone.

"Who says we can't vote?" Old Zhang laughed.

The deadline for moving from the neighborhood had passed, and the demolition office said only 5 percent of residents remained. Old Zhang admitted that he was in the minority and could be criticized for stubbornness. "But what am I afraid of?" he asked. "I will be seventy-four years old. I am not an illegal element. I have no regrets. If I wanted money, I would have moved before. This is not about money, this is about justice. I just want to be able to live somewhere inside the Third Ring Road."

He poured another shot of bamboo wine. "It will all be decided soon. Now it's the New Year. Cheers, Little Plumblossom."

Bowls of food filled the table. The television was shut off, leaving only the distant sound of popping fireworks. Old Zhang opened the cloth sack. He delicately withdrew a framed, black-and-white portrait of an old woman. He folded the bag carefully, and with two hands straightened the picture so it faced the steaming dishes. "This is my wife."

"She loved Spring Festival. She could stuff dumplings all day, really." Old Zhang lit sticks of incense beside the picture. Before we began, he held an empty bowl that his son filled with food. "Get a big piece of tofu," Old Zhang said. "She loves daughter-in-law's braised tofu." His son added blood sausage, pea pods, broccoli, and diced pork. "We'll give her some dumplings later."

Old Zhang placed the bowl before the picture. It showed an unsmiling, lined face with black, combed-back hair. He stood silent with his eyes closed, then sat down looking refreshed, as if the trance had been broken.

"She died last year," he said. "After they announced the road project, she worried all the time. Our grandson goes to a very good elementary school near here, and he was living with us. She couldn't stop worrying about what was going to happen to our house, to his education. She became neurotic."

Old Zhang's son waited a moment, then spoke to me. "You have to understand something very clearly. The problem isn't that the city is developing. That's a good thing. And the problem isn't that the government is bad. The government is actually very good. We are all patriotic here. The problem is that the entire process isn't transparent. The only ones with eyes are the district government and its development company."

Old Zhang turned to his wife, staring mutely from the frame. "I just wanted her to have one more New Year here."

Daughter-in-law and grandson stared into their bowls. "Eat more!" she suddenly urged. Old Zhang filled the shot glasses and handed his son and me a Panda cigarette. He ran his hand through his white crew cut, puffed in silence, wiped a drop that leaked from the eye with the cataract, then stood to add dumplings to his wife's brimming bowl.

We ate and watched television until Unity and Wholeness were announced as the winners of the name-the-panda election. (Taiwan's government would initially refuse the animals.) At midnight, Beijing erupted in fireworks to welcome the Year of the Dog.

"Will it be an auspicious year?" Old Zhang wondered aloud as he opened more bottles of beer. "I don't care, as long as I don't have to move to the outskirts." We toasted to that.

The fireworks continued until three in the morning, which is about when my cell phone stopped whirring with short text messages and rhymes from friends wishing "Happy New Year." Our courtyard was illuminated all night, as the Widow and her son, daughter-in-law, and granddaughter played mah-jongg and ate dumplings. The Widow opened my door to deliver a big, steaming bowl.

The blasts started again at eight A.M. By that time, the *hutong* looked as if a parade had passed through. Exploded red tissue paper piled against the base of the courtyard walls. Red lanterns hung from some gates; ours displayed a red Chinese flag. Before they returned to the northeast to see their son, Mr. Han and his wife taped a red cardboard 福 (*fu*; prosperity) character upside down on our courtyard's entrance and pasted the door gods and vertical couplets on either side of our rooms' entrance to summon protection and fortune in the coming year.

The doors also held a notice from the Neighborhood Committee that reminded "our friends, the broad masses of migrants in Beijing's labor, commerce, and service sectors" to register for their Temporary Residence Permit when they returned to the capital after the holiday. "Let's make a joint effort," the notice concluded, "and grasp hands to work as one to build a beautiful homeland for Beijing's overall development and the 2008 Olympics."

Spring Festival is a period of packed train stations and overbooked flights, but the *hutong* emptied. The contribution of migrant workers to the neighborhood economy became noticeable by their absence. Most shops and restaurants closed, along with all but a few of the stalls at the Heavenly Peach market. The only snack stop that remained open on Prolong Life Street was owned by one of my student's parents. They fried up oily pork pot-stickers and *jianbing*, a pancake of grilled flour batter, scallions, and an egg wrapped around a fried dough cracker seasoned with hot sauce. A *jianbing* is the Egg McMuffin of Beijing street food. The two-week holiday was an unhealthy time for me.

My students plumped up on kebabs of candied hawthorn berries, White Rabbit taffy, cut sugarcane, and *yuanxiao* dumplings, a traditional snack made from sweet, gummy rice flour. They stopped by to declare how much money their red envelopes from relatives contained. Any amount was great, but a big payday was more than one hundred yuan ($13). Yo-yos were the must-have item of early 2006. A Blazing Teens yo-yo cost two yuan at Coal Lane's toy shop; a butterfly-style King of Warriors was five.

The kids also spent their money at temple fair, the New Year's winter carnival. The neighborhood hosted Beijing's first, some four hundred years before. According to a pamphlet issued by the district government, the fair had survived through two dynasties, the warlord and republican eras, Japanese occupation and revival of New China, only to be shut down in 1963 "due to historical reasons." A Taoist temple no longer existed on the street where the fair was held, but the government restored the festivities in 2001. It was inscribed on the list of the district's "intangible cultural heritage." The movement to protect these customs—which included indigenous snacks, shadow puppets, and singing and painting styles—had formed after Beijing was announced as the Olympic host. The temple fair was reborn as "a bright incarnation of 'New Beijing, New Olympics' and serves the 2008 games." The slogan could be invoked to protect tradition, too.

The fair was held on South New China Avenue, which formed the neighborhood's western border. Area traffic was rerouted, and booths lined both sides of the road. For my students, the weeklong fair filled their days. They saw costumed dancers parade as lions and dragons; walked through the legs of stilt walkers; watched magicians; gasped at acrobats balancing pots on their foreheads; had their faces painted like an opera singer's; ate roasted chicken hearts on a stick; painted their names on rice paper; tossed beanbags at cans of almond milk for prizes; and bought tiered pinwheels made from hollow bamboo.

Temple fairs had enjoyed a renaissance across Beijing and were held in *hutong* neighborhoods, temples, or former imperial sites, not in suburban high-rises. Some were elaborate carnivals; the largest, at the Altar of Earth park, featured an ice slide, butterfly topiary, haunted house, Skateboard Daredevils performance, and a snake lady, who languidly reclined onstage draped in serpents.

My landlord stopped by the house with a gift from our local fair. "It's a lunar day calendar!" he announced before I opened the bag.

Like a flip-chart *Farmers' Almanac*, each postcard-size page alerted the reader to the day's auspicious and inauspicious signs. The day was broken into twelve two-hour blocks, each marked with a symbol: "Five to seven P.M. is lucky; seven to nine P.M. is unlucky." The calendar also interpreted omens. A dream about drinking was a good thing. The day bode well for people born in the Year of the Horse, but Rats should stay indoors. The God of Unborn Children faced the bed, to the east.

The landlord interpreted the symbols in the slurpy voice that makes old Beijing men sound as if they are sucking on a lozenge. He had bushy, black eyebrows and a vise-grip handshake. In the past, I had never had much luck with Beijing landlords; the relationships were decidedly one-sided, and petty. But this one lent me history books and clipped newspaper articles that he thought I would enjoy. He halted when he saw my interest deepen in the calendar.

"Little Plumblossom, you understand this is just a superstition, right?

This is from the old society, before Liberation. When the emperor fell, Beijing switched to the solar calendar. We still use the solar calendar now."

Not always. Regardless of the below-freezing temperatures, the city's skating rinks closed on *li chun*, the date the lunar calendar decreed as the Beginning of Spring. Older people—including the Widow, and those from rural areas, such as Recycler Wang—knew the other twenty-three "spells," fortnight-long periods describing the weather based on the sun's longitude. The traditional calendar began and ended not on an arbitrary date in the dead of winter, but at the start of the cycle of rebirth. After the Beginning of Spring came the spell called Rain Water, then the Awakening of Insects, and the Vernal Equinox—one I looked forward to. It was still a month away, at the end of March.

The neighborhood eyed another measure of time, the countdown clock to the games. My landlord dismissed the piles of dirt and brick rubble from the widening of nearby Coal Street. "They will not demolish this lane, or this house," he said. "They cannot. It's protected." He repeated the word to make sure I understood. "Protected."

I asked by whom.

"By them. By whoever protects things." He arched his furry eyebrows, tapped my shoulder, and announced, "Hey, it's a good day for bathing, woodcutting, and hunting! Avoid weddings and funerals. Look! Look, the calendar says so, right here."

He tore away the day's page and narrated with certainty what tomorrow would bring.

CHAPTER 6

A BRIEF HISTORY OF 拆 PART ONE:
Traces of Pre-Beijing

FIRST, THE LAND belonged to dragons. Humans called it the Bitter Sea Waste. They led a hardscrabble existence in the hills around the briny marshland ruled by a dragon tribe. One day, a prince named Nezha put on his red jacket and short pants and challenged the Dragon King to battle. They fought nine times a day for nine days. Nezha finally subdued the Dragon King and sealed him and his wife in a large lake capped by a white pagoda. The water ebbed to reveal rich soil. Humans moved onto the plain and built houses and markets. The Dragon Palace was pulled down. To protect his father from dragon reprisals, Nezha cut off his own flesh, signaling detachment from his family. After he died, the gods transformed him into a deity with a lotus-flower body and eight arms.

The area prospered under the protection of Nezha, but still the dragons plotted revenge. When the emperor decided to build his northern capital here, his minister of works begged off the job. "The dragons lie in wait," he said fearfully. The emperor turned to two of his military advisers and asked, "Which of you will go?"

Both men traveled to the region, surveyed the terrain, slept in a hostel, and despised one another. They agreed to split up. In ten days, they would sit back-to-back and draw their designs for the capital.

Though they were apart, the men each heard a child's voice saying, "Copy me, and you'll do fine." Both saw a boy wearing a red jacket and short pants who was impossible to overtake. When the men sped up, so did the child. When they slowed down, the child did, too. The boy did not have eight arms, but the next time the men saw him, they noticed he wore a cape with a lotus-leaf edge. Eight strips of silk dangled from beneath his shoulders. Again, they heard him say, "Copy me, and you'll do fine."

At noon on the tenth day, the military advisers sat back-to-back at two tables in an empty square. The weapons for this duel were paper, brushes, and inkstones. They began drawing their plans for the emperor's capital. Both finished just before sunset. Each man looked at the other's design. The plans were identical.

The city would be shaped like Nezha, its protector. The Front Gate represented his brain, and the city's other gates his arms and feet, placed symmetrically around a square perimeter. Lesser gates represented Nezha's head, ears, and mouth. The Imperial City formed his viscera. Based on their width, the lanes were his arteries, veins, and capillaries. *Hutong* carried the lifeblood of Beijing.

Given current developments, it's fitting that the capital's founding legend features a battle over land, a forced eviction, the razing of buildings, and a planning competition in which both designers copied another's idea, yet each craved the glory. Unable to share credit, one of the emperor's advisers stormed off and became a monk. The other defended the capital from the dragon tribe, but not before they stole most of the city's sweet water. That is why, the story holds, most Beijing wells are brackish to this day.

That's one of the few remaining clues to the city's origins. Peking Man is missing. The bones of one of mankind's earliest ancestors—*Homo erectus*—who lived one-half million years ago, were discovered in 1923, and lost on December 7, 1941. The Chinese director of the nation's geological survey transferred the yellowed remains for safekeeping to the American president of the Rockefeller-funded Peking Union hospital. The president handed the fossils to the commander of the embassy's marine detachment. He placed the unmarked package on a coast-bound train for evacuation by sea. Japanese captors looted the train for ammunition. "Perhaps they found the remains and just threw them away, like canned foods," the commander later imagined.

A rumor floated that the Japanese soldiers used the bones to make soup. Another story said that the relics made it onto the American ship, which was grounded by her crew to avoid capture, repaired by the Japanese—and sunk by a U.S. submarine on its first voyage for the other side. After the Second World War, an Australian businessman claimed to have buried the fossils in a Tasmanian rain forest and demanded a $2 million ransom. That proved untrue; where Peking Man went remains unknown.

In the basement of Beijing's ritziest shopping mall is what a sign promises to be the "first Paleolithic site unearthed within the downtown area of a capital city worldwide." The mall, named Oriental Plaza, has a footprint that is half the size of the Forbidden City's. At five and a half football fields long, Oriental Plaza is located on the Avenue of Eternal Peace—the city's main thoroughfare that runs past Tian'anmen Square—and the Wangfujing pedestrian-only commercial street. When I visited the Paleolithic Museum, the young docent led me into a single room, centered by a patch of soil. The docent pointed at a mannequin of a rugged man in a loincloth, leaning on a stick. "Even twenty-five thousand years ago," she said with practiced enthusiasm, "people liked shopping here!"

The museum was the result of a battle, whose details were absent from its captioned plaques. Planned by the Hong Kong billionaire developer Li Kai-shing and approved in the early 1990s. Oriental Plaza was to stand on a site then occupied by the world's largest McDonald's, as well as twenty-five hundred families living in *hutong*.

The mall would be the biggest in Asia, and, two and a half times taller than the hundred-foot height restriction on buildings in Beijing's historic center. (The rule had already been flouted numerous times, including by the wing of the Beijing Hotel that neighbored the proposed site.) The State Council, the national organ that controls land, shelved the project in 1994 after prominent architects and historians protested its impact on the city's heritage.

A scaled-down plan was approved, and then, in April 1995, it was revealed that after the mayor and his associates had evicted residents—including several prominent civil war veterans—from the site, they received $37 million in kickbacks. The development was tabled again.

In 1996, plans were approved that scaled down the height of Oriental Plaza's office towers. "It is still a monster," said a member of the Ancient Architecture Commission. "If Mr. Li [Kai-shing] does not want to be the archenemy of the entire Chinese people, he should stop it now and redeem himself."

The project continued. Residents were evicted, and *hutong* razed. In December 1996, excavators unearthed bone tools, burned objects, stone artifacts, and animal fossils—the remains of a Paleolithic settlement. Construction halted, and new debates erupted over the importance of preserving the past or developing for the future. Opponents of Oriental Plaza seized the discovery, advocating that a museum, not a mall, be built around the site. In the meantime, the sacked mayor was sentenced to sixteen years in prison.

In autumn of 1997, construction restarted after a museum was promised inside the mall. The People's Republic's fiftieth anniversary was less than two years away. Some twenty thousand workers completed the complex's exterior in time to be a backdrop for 1999's national parade.

Oriental Plaza has a Grand Hyatt hotel, fine jewelry shops such as Tiffany & Co., and car showrooms for Volkswagen and Lamborghini. The mall is usually crowded, even if few people carry shopping bags.

The Paleolithic Museum is housed in a single room in the mall's subbasement, between the subway entrance and the food court's Orange Julius. The docent and I stood before a painting of prehistoric people knocking rocks together by a river. At that time, she said, more than forty streams crossed this area, carrying sediment from the hills and filling the formerly marshy plain. The painted sky was a deep azure. "Way back then," the docent added, "there wasn't any air pollution."

Nor was there a "Beijing" for the first two millennia of its history. A settlement in the southwest of the city's present site first appeared in the written records of an era called the Western Zhou, from the eleventh through eighth centuries BC. On the other side of the world during this span, King David captured Jerusalem, the Olympic Games began, Homer composed the *Odyssey* and *Iliad*, and Rome was founded. Beijing, too, began, though as a small walled village called Ji, the Reeds.

By the Warring States period (fifth through third centuries BC), the Reeds enjoyed prosperity from producing rice, millet, fruit, and salt. After a neighboring fief absorbed it, the Reeds became Yanjing, the Capital of Swallows. In 221 BC, China's first emperor, Qin Shihuang, formed an empire by overthrowing Yan and other rival kingdoms. His capital was near modern Xi'an, in central China. Yanjing remained a capital of a northern prefecture, forming a strategic gateway between Han Chinese and the ethnic nomads outside the empire. Emperor Qin died and was placed in a tomb guarded by thousands of life-size terra-cotta warriors. Yanjing crumbled.

And then the city was reborn, this time as Youzhou, or Serene Prefecture. It rose during the Han dynasty (206 BC to AD 220) and grew larger than Yanjing. The empire's capital was elsewhere, but Youzhou became a border trading center and military garrison, on guard against incursions from northern tribes.

In cities with histories as long as Beijing's, the past can unexpectedly breach the surface of contemporary life. In 1998, the wheat fields around the apartment where I lived then in the city's northwest were being transformed into a high-tech research park. The farming village had been plowed over, and the walk to the school where I taught now traversed a field of open dirt. One morning, I came upon three pits ringed with clay-mottled soil. Two were rectangular, while one was shaped like a key. I imagined they were storage areas or bomb shelters—all that remained from the razed houses.

When I crossed the field later that day, a thin man stood at a pit's edge. The characters on his yellow mesh baseball cap spelled CULTURAL RELICS BUREAU. He smoked patiently as a crew of four cloth-shoed women scraped away at the soil. "I don't have much time," he said, motioning to a parked earthmover. "These will all be buried next week."

The man was an archaeologist with the bureau, which had been collecting the artifacts emerging from the soil. "I think these pits were burial places from a Han Dynasty settlement," he said. "We've gathered more than a thousand artifacts around here. They're two thousand years old. Pottery. Tools."

Soon they would be beneath cement foundations. The Hand couldn't wait. "Meibanfa," the archaeologist said. There was nothing he could do about it.

The next day, I brought my sixth-graders to watch his crew. The kids had heard the word tomb, stormed downstairs, and run to the site, chattering about treasure, mummies, and curses.

The archaeologist let them jump into the tombs cleared of artifacts. His team's equipment consisted of four hardware-store-variety shovels. He had a core sampler, a clipboard with scribbled notes and sketches, and a pack of fake Marlboros. The group had ridden in a tattered bread-box taxi to the site. The driver had run out of receipts. The archaeologist would not even be reimbursed for the fare.

He stuck a pole into the ground and pulled out a chunk of earth. "Nothing there." He paced once to the left and sank the pole again. He said there had not been any local opposition to developing the site because the farmers who had been cleared off the land would rather have new apartments than preserve antiquity. To hell with antiquity; let's see some future!

My students scooped up handfuls of loam, rubbed it onto their notebook pages, and imagined the rock they held was actually a fossilized tooth. Magpies squawked in the sky above them.

"Maybe China has too much history, so this isn't a big deal," a girl said.

"*Wa!*" a boy exclaimed. "I didn't know that history was all around us."

"History *is* us, moron," his friend replied.

We walked back to school on ground that echoed the past and would cover the future. The archaeologist said that the developer promised to build a museum to display the finds. It never did. The land is filled with identical rows of walk-up apartment buildings. They are made from cement and painted bone white—ossuaries for a later generation to exhume.

CHAPTER 7

THE *EVENING NEWS*

U NLIKE THE REST of Beijing, the *hutong* has no newsstands. Individual vendors sell papers. Their cry of *"WanBAO!"* (*Evening News!*) told the neighborhood it was around three P.M. I bought my copy from a woman who stood in front of the supermarket on Prolong Life Street, the busy market lane near the school. Half of her face was paralyzed, and the unwashed black hair that piled on her narrow shoulders gave her the otherworldly appearance of an oracle. She called me "Foreigner" to my face, even though the roast-duck vendor and grain seller at her back greeted me every day as "Teacher Plumblossom." Her hello was always the same: "Hey, Foreigner! I have your paper."

She sold the news from a wheeled wire cart. She started with a full basket a mile to the east, then yelped *"WanBAO!"* twice a minute as she walked through Fresh Fish Junction, past Old Zhang's *hutong*, over Front Gate Avenue, and across our neighborhood, ending here, where she would sell the rest of her stock by four o'clock.

Beijing had eight daily newspapers, but the *Evening News* was emperor. The tabloid usually contained at least 50 pages. Its record size was 208 pages, a tactic that backfired as vendors calculated they could make more selling it as scrap than as news.

The paper cost five *mao* ($.07), less than its competitors. With a circulation of 1.2 million, the *Evening News* controlled over half of the local market and had the top advertising revenue of any Chinese daily. Judging by its most ubiquitous ads, its readers were sexually frustrated, but in the market for a cell phone and a car. The paper was fattened by pullout supplements asking, "Why can't I have an orgasm? 75 percent of men can't satisfy their woman." Testimonials from women who had purchased the advertised "health powder" described its potency in breathless detail. "As he massaged my body, I thought, 'Heavens, is this my husband?' and then he entered my deepest part . . ." There was more, much more, and when I handed the paper to the Widow every day, I teased her to read the ads. "The print is too small!" she complained innocently.

For the leading paper of the capital of the world's rising economic power, the *Evening News* reminded me of the weekly community paper I grew up with in Minnesota, the one that posted the fishing forecast, high school sports results, and driving-under-the-influence arrests. The government controlled the *Evening News*, but this was no *Good News Daily*, like the other papers in its stable. The front page always ran stories based on announcements ("Register your dog or face a serious fine"; "Junk short-text message senders can be fined 30,000 yuan"; "Welcome the Olympics, stress civic virtue, establish a new wind"), but the inside was filled with crime and citizen misdeeds. Beijing looked very different on the pages of the *Evening News*.

I always flipped to the Police section first, where the headlines included "Girl lights gasoline on sleeping boyfriend"; "Forty prostitutes arrested at karaoke club"; "Five-year-old lies next to dead mother for nine hours, thinking she was asleep"; "Unlicensed sixteen-year-old clubgoer kills migrant with his Mercedes"; "Foreigner smashes taxi window in dispute over fare."

Like any big city, Beijing had its share of car crashes, overdoses, and suicides. The *Evening News*, keeping pace with the competition, ran photos of sheet-covered corpses lying on the pavement in pools of blood. Beijing had a tall-building problem—they provided a leaping-off point for young women and were a danger to window-cleaners. *Hutong* advocates never mentioned this in their defense, but it was true: people didn't die plunging from a courtyard home.

Guns were forbidden, but judging by the offenses, the city needed watermelon-knife control. A customer at a duck restaurant argued with staff over his bill's not being discounted, grabbed a knife, and stabbed six workers. A migrant knifed his boss over a pay dispute and chopped her body in pieces, hoping to transport it home to avoid detection. A foot-massage-parlor owner stabbed a customer to death after being sexually harassed. A recycler took a fatal cut to the gut after refusing to pay one yuan more to a customer selling cloth bags. A woman sliced up her mother-in-law's head over an argument about their eviction settlement. A migrant killed a prostitute in her underground room—no one opened his or her door to her screams—and used her bank card repeatedly at the same cash-withdrawal machine. The cops nabbed him there on the third day.

Beijing's inner-city residents were afraid of crime in the big, wide-open suburbs. It was safe in the *hutong*, where eyes were always on the street and everyone knew the neighbors. It was one more reason to not want to move to a high-rise. But a *hutong* was not immune from ill-temper and a knife. The paper reported that two neighboring shopkeepers who shared one electricity meter went at it after years of arguing over how to split the bill. One dead, three injured. It wasn't in our district, but in the East City. "That's different over there," the Widow insisted, though she couldn't say how.

In the *Evening News*, migrants were usually the bad guys, the perpetrators of the most violent crimes, as in the story of a thirty-one-year-old man from Henan province who commandeered a taxi and sped down Wangfujing pedestrian shopping street, killing three people and injuring six. "I wanted to retaliate against society and the rich," he told the judge. "I thought that now, out of ten city residents, nine are black-hearted." He regretted killing the taxi driver. "My revenge was not aimed at him. I just wanted to take his car, but he resisted and screamed at me, so the knife I had planned to turn on myself instead was used on him." He wanted to be wealthy, he said, but hadn't the means. The judge sentenced him to death. The sentence was carried out within days, by a pistol shot to the back of the head.

The saddest part of the paper, and one I studied every day despite knowing better, was the Missing Person ads. The photo of the disappeared was usually an ID headshot, in which the person sat wide-eyed and grim-faced. The description listed what the person was wearing, hairstyle, accent, and mental condition. Many of the vanished elderly were deaf, neurotic, or liked "to drink alcohol to excess." The children were walking to school or missing from other provinces. One day, the *Evening News* ran photos of seventeen kids, aged six to seventeen. Other notices asked to locate a migrant whose parent was sick back home. A man and woman who were mentally retarded ran off together. Gone, too: a neurotic woman aged fifty-four; a forty-nine-year-old with chronic depression; a fourteen-year-old girl with a ponytail wearing a tracksuit and athletic shoes. Where did they go?

None of the missing had disappeared from a *hutong*. Rather, they vanished from wide roads, high-rise complexes, and bus stops. Erasing a city's urban corners left only straight lines, hollow spaces, and nowhere to hide.

> Wang Lin, female, 33, dark-skinned, white collared shirt, blue jeans, white-and-black sneakers, green purse, went missing at noon on the 15th by the side of Beiyuan Road. Call Mr. Deng with information.

Miss Zhu felt that Wang Lin, and the ads' other missing women, ran away. "Maybe they had a bad boss, or a bad husband. Maybe they worked in a bad place." The men, she said, owed money. The kids were escaping broken homes. Look, she said, the ads seldom mentioned a reward, other than the tipster being promised "gratitude." In two years, the highest figure I saw was ten thousand yuan ($1,333), offered for the whereabouts of an eighty-two-year-old woman with Alzheimer's. In contrast, the ads for Missing Dogs regularly promised three thousand to five thousand yuan ($400 to $667) for the pet's safe return. It was a Beijing trait to place suspicion before trust, and to assume the worst of a person's motives before the best. Maybe Miss Zhu was right. But seeing the same photos appear from one week to the next was still depressing. She had a Beijing solution for that, too. "Don't pay attention to it. Turn to the next page."

It wasn't all blood and bad times in the *Beijing Evening News*. The crime section only took up one or two pages. The rest of the paper presented the contradictions of a city that was both small town and megacity. Peak traffic times filled sixteen hours of every day. A woman got her hand stuck in a latrine hole for an hour. Beijing GDP was at an all-time high. Ten ducks at a central lake fell dead from a virus. Migrant construction workers crowded public buses when they got off work. The world is giving us sixteen days during the Olympics, and we'll give the world five thousand years of history. A cat ate a bird worth $1,000, so the bird owner strangled the cat. Its eight-year-old owner looked at the empty food bowl and wept. Would cat-strangling be made illegal? A man took off his shoes and socks and aired them from an open bus window, offending passengers with the smell. A section of the Third Ring Road collapsed from a sinkhole. An uneven side-walk tripped a seventy-four-year-old granny. Vandals smashed four police cars' windows at the Coal Street road project. Gasoline reached its highest price ever, the equivalent of $2.57 a gallon. Residents of an apartment complex whose sunlight would be blocked by a neighboring project took to the streets and surrounded the workers. Where do courtyard residents shower? *We investigate*. The city would destroy 4.5 million square meters of buildings in 2006.

The weather column advised readers what to wear and eat and told how the next day would suit morning exercises, car washing, mountain climbing, visiting the beach, and airing out the house. Below the banner on the front page, the day's date was given according to the solar and lunar calendars.

It's true that the *Evening News* once ran as hard news an item from the American satirical paper the *Onion*. It reported that U.S. congressmen were demanding a new Capitol with a retractable roof, more concession stands, better sight lines, and expanded parking. Otherwise, Congress would relocate to a city like Memphis. In its correction, the *Evening News* wrote, "Some small American newspapers frequently fabricate offbeat news to trick people into noticing them with the aim of making money."

The paper also ran pages of international news, translated from, but not credited to, European and American wire services. It told readers what was in that week's *New Yorker* and other American magazines. A daily page of English lessons explained how a British pub was different from one in Bei-jing, misconceptions about applying for an American visa, and the mean-ing of words such as *eggnog* and sayings like "her clock is ticking."

I am addicted to newsprint anyhow, but when locals laughed at me for reading what they considered a rag, they were surprised to learn that American papers didn't have the same windows on foreign culture, no mat-ter how narrow. And in a city whose broadcast media, films, video games, and advertising imitated American forms, the *Evening News* was one of the last products that felt as if it was doing things its unique way, no matter how antiquated.

The section that drew the liveliest participation was the Courtyard pull-out that appeared on Sundays, in which contributors wrote essays remembering their demolished *hutong* or home. Historical essays revealed that Chairman Mao refused to have an indoor toilet installed in the courtyard of his Beijing compound, or that the novelist Lao She—the city's famous chronicler of *hutong* life—bought his courtyard with one hundred bolts of calico. The paper called for the submission of photos, and readers sent them in. Disputes over demolition settlements or complaints about life in high-rises would never make it into the state-run *Evening News*. But as Beijing had no *hutong* museum, the Courtyard section became a repository of memories, if not memorabilia.

The Widow showed me another use for the paper. "Run a soapy wet cloth over your windows," she said. "Then dry them with an unfolded page, like this." The glass sparkled. "Now, ball up the whole mess and bring it to Recycler Wang. He'll give you a cent or two for it."

As usual, she asked if I knew when our home would be marked for destruction. "We can be certain of something," she said. "Tomorrow, and the next day, and the day after that, there will be another *Evening News*."

CHAPTER 8

HIGH TIMES IN HAPPINESS CITY

MY LIVING ROOM'S wall of windows made a screen, on which I watched the Widow and Mr. Han and his wife come and go. Inside, the room was perfectly quiet. I didn't have a clock; time was measured by a rising pile of read books and a falling level of Nescafé granules. Emerging from the house brought the same enjoyably disorienting feeling as exiting a theater into direct sunlight. Everything looked otherworldly.

My students felt the same entering my room. "Your house really has a Western flavor!" they would gasp. "Your scarf sure looks different from ours! Do kids in America eat ice cream? Chocolate or strawberry? What time is it in San Francisco right now? Wait, let us figure it out. *Wa!* It's three thirty-four in the morning there! Aren't you sleepy?"

The Olympic countdown clock said 892 days to go, but my real time was marked by a text message from Miss Zhu. "I'm not sure when we start school again," she wrote. "They just send me a note telling me that our first meeting is the next day. That's how I know." The school's desk calendars showed only the current month, not the one that came before or after it. Time was the present, period.

When the message came, I reported for spring semester. Aside from explaining Mocky's exploits to the kids, my other duty was to pick up breakfast for the Grade Four teachers. They liked Prolong Life Street's steamed Sichuan dumplings and *shaobing*, a buckwheat roll holding a fried egg. A variety of the snack shaped like a pizza and sprinkled with roast beef had become a brief craze in the city, marketed as "the Tu national minority cake." But the teachers dismissed it as too oily. Dieting and weight control

was an unceasing discussion in the office, despite that most of the teachers
looked anemic. The music instructor wondered if American schools really
had a psychologist on staff. She thought that was a great idea. When I told
her that the psychologist served the students, not the teachers, her face
fell. "Teachers are the ones with problems. The students are just kids!"

Teachers had homework, too. The principal had assigned a 750-
character essay titled "Moral Errors Correction Plan." The music instructor
typed one that quoted the Education Bureau's "Teacher's Law" and "Elementary School Teacher's Morality Guidelines." "Love is the core of
teacher's virtue," she wrote. "Respect teachers, and love students." Her colleagues copied and pasted it onto their own blank document, made a few
changes, and handed it in. The essays were never returned or commented
upon at all.

The principal told me that because of Coal Street's widening project,
another elementary school in our neighborhood would be razed. Its staff
and students had been reassigned across the city. Coal Lane Elementary
would take on two instructors, and their two classes of students. One of the
teachers spoke English. "What's she like?" the principal repeated. "She's
very pretty."

Her eyes narrowed, and she added, "Teacher Plumblossom, do you know
when our school will be demolished?"

The classrooms looked as they had the day we left for Spring Festival vacation, three weeks before. The only changes to the building were the hallway's new framed portraits of Archimedes, Copernicus, Galileo, Newton,
Darwin, Nobel, Edison, and Curie. Also added was a poster from the nation's leader, "Central Secretary Hu Jintao," detailing the Eight Honors
and Eight Disgraces. The morality campaign listed the dos and don'ts of
achieving civic virtue. Loving the motherland was a do, harming the
motherland was a don't. Serving the people was good, separating yourself
from the people was bad.

Every semester started with a new activity. The previous term's focused
on smoking prevention and environmentalism. This time, the students
were given a pamphlet titled *Eight Honors and Eight Disgraces Nursery
Rhymes* and a checkbook-size ledger named the Red Neckscarf Passbook.
The neckscarf formed their uniform for the Young Pioneers, a patriotic
club in which children were enrolled nationwide.

The passbook recorded points earned for virtuous activities such as helping parents with housework, eating everything on one's plate, and visiting the Resistance Against Japan War Memorial Museum. Points were deducted for disgracing the school and the community, or violating school rules. The onus was on Not Messing Up, even once. Housework earned you two points, helping someone five, and writing an essay on morality netted eight. But any infraction set you back at least twenty points, all the way up to losing fifty for not assisting the community. *It is a disgrace to separate yourself from the people.*

Teachers had a new activity, as well. In the office, the women unpacked navy blue suits and white, collared shirts assigned by the Education Bureau. Every Monday morning, the teachers donned the outfit to wear during the weekly flag raising and playing of the national anthem. As with the passbook, compliance was enforced to a point. Most teachers changed back into their casual clothes when they reentered the school. The kids remained outside for morning exercises. They stood in place, kicked each leg, squatted, flapped their arms, rolled their head, and turned an imaginary faucet with their wrists.

The school's male teachers taught physical education. They had been handed new guidelines for the kids' fitness, which they began implementing with a series of higher-intensity activities to increase heart rates. I looked out the window and saw teams merrily grimacing through tug-of-war and drills in which they turned somersaults, ran around a cone, and hurdled a stack of mats. Our best English students were terrible at it. They flopped forward, exhaled dramatically, and sprawled like cats in a patch of sun.

Classes were canceled one early-spring morning for an assembly. The students cheered as Ronald McDonald bounded onto the outdoor stage. He urged them to embody the Olympic spirit, performed a dance to his company's "I'm Lovin' It!" commercial jingle, and handed out plastic toys and coupons for the restaurant's food.

At the rear of the playground, the two gym teachers watched with their arms crossed. "Hey, Plumblossom," one said. "Does McDonald's go into schools in America?"

McDonald's China menu did not offer salads or diet soda. *"Wo cao!"* the other teacher exhaled. "Fuck me! I'm trying to make these kids healthy, and now they'll just want to eat more junk."

Students and teachers pacing through morning exercises.
The schoolyard is the neighborhood's largest open space.

Ronald bounded off the stage to the children's cheers. He was due at another elementary school in an hour.

The weather warmed, which meant I could stop visiting our lane's hairdresser. She had a water heater and let me wash up during the cold months when the Big Power Bathhouse felt too far away. Mr. Han constructed a solution. On the roof of our shared kitchen, he placed a rubber bag filled with water and ran a hose from it to hang over the sink. On sunny days, the water heated to a tolerable degree. When I said that our shower was environmentally friendly, Mr. Han nodded. "More important, it's free."

As spring came, life moved back outdoors. Old men set their bamboo birdcages in a circle around them as they sat on low, folding wooden stools, playing Chinese chess. The round wooden pieces made a sharp snap when "eating" an opponent's piece. Officer Li had told me that winter had a higher domestic crime rate, which he theorized was because men sat around drinking rice liquor to stay warm. The typed-out police notice posted on the *hutong* that week said, "Three incidents of theft due to doors left unlocked."

One instance of vandalism did not make it into the official report. On a Front Gate Avenue billboard that covered the destruction of a building, a slogan promised:

再现古都　(The ancient capital reappears.)

When I crossed the street to visit Old Zhang in Fresh Fish Junction, I noticed that the propaganda had been altered. Someone had neatly excised part of the second character, so it read:

再见古都 (Farewell, ancient capital.)

By afternoon, the altered sign had been pulled down, as had all of the road's slogans.

The Hand worked on, peeling back the layers. It razed Soldier Liu's shaved-noodle restaurant, and masked the road-widening project at Fresh Fish Junction with blue tin sheeting. Old Zhang remained in his house, cheered by the news that the district government's Construction Committee had agreed to arbitrate the dispute over his moving compensation.

At the end of February 2006, its office held an hour-long summit, in which Old Zhang and the government-backed Heavenly Street Development Company presented their demands. A company officer explained its settlement offer of 211,302 yuan ($28,174). The figure included 186,016 yuan for Old Zhang's living area, and 25,286 yuan for his relocation, which would cover moving fees (464 yuan) and charges to transfer phone service (235 yuan), cable television (350 yuan), and transport an air conditioner (400 yuan).

"I can eat nothing but cabbage and radishes," Old Zhang told the arbitrator, "but that figure is still too low to buy a house inside the Third Ring Road. If I had moved before the deadline, I know I could have pocketed the fifty-five thousand yuan [$7,333] bonus. But even then, the money was not enough."

Old Zhang scoured his copy of the meeting's minutes. The cited eminent-domain laws were inviolable, but he disputed the developer's assessment of his living space. They calculated it at 23.194 square meters (250 square feet). Old Zhang underlined the figure and above it wrote "31.7" (341 square feet). The notes reported that he demanded six hundred thousand yuan ($80,000). On his copy, he wrote, "I did not say this."

A week later, he returned for another hearing. This time, he faced three people: one from the development company, and two from its affiliated demolition business. A cadre from the Neighborhood Committee filmed the proceedings. A police officer stood watch. Other residents sat in the back of the room, waiting to testify in their own cases. Old Zhang wore a blue serge "Mao suit" and black cloth shoes—the standard style of the seventy-three-year-old's generation, one that grew up rallying around Communism. The people he faced wore white-collar shirts and suit coats.

The developer restated its original offer of 211,302 yuan ($28,174). Old Zhang demanded 800,000 yuan ($106,667). He said that was the price of a modest, pre-owned two-bedroom apartment inside the Second Ring Road. The developer countered that Old Zhang had not vacated his residence by the posted deadline and was thus in violation of the law.

"I am not a bad person," he testified. "I may be retired, but I am not lazy. I study English all day so I can greet foreigners when they walk in the neighborhood. This gives them a good impression of Beijing. This is important for our city, as we will host the 2008 Olympics!"

The arbitrator smiled slightly.

Old Zhang said he grew up in Beijing and did nine years of rural labor during the Cultural Revolution after being branded a "landlord" because his family owned a house on a farm in a distant suburb. "This is not about money," he said. "I have a grandson who goes to school near here. I'm a widower, and I want to find a house where I can live with him and his parents as I grow old." He repeated the line about being able to survive on only cabbages and radishes.

Afterward, when he retold the story, I said he earned an A. He had employed every keyword that could activate sympathy: *Olympics, civic pride, English, grandson, extended family.* Old Zhang waved his hand dismissively: "Look, you speak plainly when you face your executioners."

The arbitrator asked Old Zhang, "What's the least amount of money you'll accept?"

"I think eight hundred thousand yuan is fair," he replied. "But we can talk about seven hundred thousand."

The arbitrator said that if the two parties could not come to an agreement within sixty days, either could file a lawsuit within three months, which would be heard by the district court. He handed Old Zhang a sheet that listed his options and protections under the national and city "Urban Housing Relocation Supervision Law."

Three weeks later, Old Zhang and his family were summoned to a different location, where a different arbitrator brokered the settlement. The two sides agreed that if he moved by April 15, Old Zhang would receive 580,000 yuan ($77,333). It was less than his requested 800,000 yuan, but nearly three times the developer's original offer. It was also far more than what he would have earned had he accepted the bonus payment for moving out at the end of December.

"I'm not happy to be leaving," Old Zhang said. "But I didn't have to pay rent somewhere else these last three months." He paused and wiped a drop away from his cataract-clouded eye. "My family found part of a shared courtyard for rent in another district, not far from here. I can still ride my bicycle to pick up my grandson after school. I will still enjoy the lifestyle that keeps both of my feet on the ground."

The rest of Beijing was moving up. "Live larger and higher, higher than you ever dreamed of being!" yelled the man selling apartments named Atlantic Place. "Rising, rising, above it all!" A chain of people circled the development's model at the Four Seasons Springtime Real Estate Fair, held at Beijing's World Trade Center. The four-day event drew two hundred thousand visitors, who paid five yuan ($.67) to enter. Inside, the competition for attention was unceasing. A Beijing opera singer in full makeup wailed before one booth, a magician pulled silk scarves from his sleeve in front of another. At Cowboy City's display, the hawkers wore cowboy hats and carried lariats; their villa model showed a detached redbrick house with a porch swing and white picket fence.

Each development's touts handed out thick brochures, which delighted the grandmothers, who gathered them up in bagfuls to sell as scrap. After an hour, my arm grew heavy and I found a spot of wall to sit against and sort through the load. I read ads for Apple Pie Apartment, Bobo Garden House, Latte Town, Match Box, Olive Garden, Starry Town III, and Yoyo. This year, there were no flyers for Merlin Champagne Town, but ones for Margarita Island.

These new projects were not displacing *hutong*. All were going up in the rising suburbs, a trend that gave Beijing residents China's second-longest average commute—nine miles—after Shanghai. Some four hundred government offices remained downtown, which led to increased traffic pressure on the Old City.

The new city plan called for more suburbs and satellite towns, and Beijingers moved farther and farther away, chasing cheaper homes. In early 2006, the average price for an apartment topped six thousand yuan ($800) per square meter (about $74 per square foot), but new developments inside the Third Ring Road ran as high as six times that. In the outskirts, the price fell to two thousand yuan ($267). There, a home could be closer to the Great Wall than the Forbidden City.

In the first five months of 2006, $6 billion was invested in Beijing's real estate market. According to the *Evening News*, 59 percent of apartment buyers were locals, and 37 percent came from other provinces. The tone implied that it was migrants—rich ones, for a change—that upped prices and spoiled the city for everyone else. Locals accounted for 38 percent of villa purchases, while 39 percent of buyers were from other parts of China, and 13 percent were foreigners, including Hong Kong and Taiwan residents. New laws establishing a capital gains tax and restricting multiple mortgages (no more than four per person) aimed to curb speculation. As Beijing's lower and middle classes faced a housing crunch, the government enacted a law ordering that 70 percent of each development had to be "affordable units," which were no larger than 90 square meters (968 square feet).

Still, in a city flush with cash and few places to park it, developers appealed to buyers' investment dreams. Homes could sit unoccupied as their values increased or be rented to newcomers. The ads for Cosmopolite studios said in Chinese, "Become a foreigner's landlord." At the Four Seasons Springtime Real Estate Fair, the only bubbles consumers saw were the ones being blown by the clown at the booth for Happiness City.

The housing craze was, like so many of Beijing's changes, the result of a revision of an outmoded policy. It began with a laconic sentence from the paramount leader Deng Xiaoping, who in 1980 said, "The construction industry can make money . . . urban residents may purchase dwellings and also build houses . . . Both new and old houses may be sold." A quarter century later, Beijing had thirty-five hundred registered developers, and in 2006, per capita housing space had risen to 344 square feet. That was equal to less than a quarter of a tennis court's area, but represented a fourfold increase since 1978, when overcrowding and a housing shortage led many families to share spaces, be it one apartment or a courtyard like mine.

At the founding of the People's Republic in 1949, 77 percent of Beijing's 1.2 million houses were owned privately. Government-managed housing gradually became the norm over the next decade, as the state seized property. Housing was not a commodity, but rather a worker's basic right, and rents were a fraction of one's salary. Miss Zhu paid thirty yuan ($3.75) a month for her family's assigned portion of a courtyard; Old Zhang paid seventeen, a sum that in contemporary Beijing barely covered a short cab ride, or a burger, fries, and soda at McDonald's.

By 1978, 90 percent of China's housing stock was government-run, either by a work unit that provided subsidized housing for employees—such as Old Zhang—or the local housing bureau that assigned space to citizens—such as the Widow. Though one unofficial estimate said as many as a third of Old City courtyard rooms were held privately, most Beijing residents were tenants of the state, whose budgetary shortfalls led to the neglect of basic maintenance. Due to low rent, a central location, and tight-knit community, many residents did not want to leave their decrepit homes.

According to the Old and Dilapidated Housing Renewal program, *hutong* were like a forest that had become so diseased only clear-cutting and reseeding could revive it. That was the strategy being implemented in the Twenty-five Historic Areas, such as Nanchizi, and now, Fresh Fish Junction. Areas razed under the ODHR program resulted in increased revenues for the district governments that sold rights to the land and also cleared hundreds of thousands of residents off municipal housing ledgers. By offering cash settlements that displaced residents would spend on housing, the city mortgaged its socialist policies for market ones. And the government still owned the earth—house purchasers were buying the physical building, but leasing for seventy years the land that it stood upon.

It was all placid waters, green grass, and a shining sky in the Four Seasons Springtime Real Estate Fair's brochures. The developments sold a lifestyle that featured covered garages, tee times, yoga classes, bilingual kindergartens, and "a shopping mall as close as less than a few steps." No rice liquor or roasted chicken feet were pictured, but rather red wine and cheese. The bookshelves didn't hold Confucius, but *The Da Vinci Code*.

Many developments explicitly invoked America, in names such as Portland Garden, Napa Valley, Dating Bright California, and Wilshire Boulevard. Also, Manhattan Garden, MoMA, Upper East Side, and Central Park. The booth for the New Yorker said its merits were "history and golf." Silo City used the preamble of the Declaration of Independence as its slogan: "Life, liberty, and the pursuit of happiness."

Buying a home did not mean independence from outside oversight, however. What the state used to administer was now handled by private management. Service companies supplied elevator attendants and security guards; even detached villas were part of a "development," rather than existing as single, private entities on a street, with services such as street cleaning provided by the city in exchange for tax revenue. According to a survey in the *Evening News*, only 6 percent of new homeowners were satisfied with the construction quality and management of their complex. Nearly half of respondents wanted increased government supervision of developers.

No matter their name, the new developments look interchangeable. A half dozen towers are usually arranged around an open center that holds not an expanse of grass to play on, but a shadeless, cement stage without benches. Commercial space is minimized for "safety." Migrants run small shops, after all. It is all very New Beijing, right down to the absence of bicycle parking. When I pedaled over to Park Avenue's showroom on a smoggy day, the security guard carried my bike away from its entrance, setting it next to a seedling planted along the sidewalk. The saleswoman asked if I would like to recharge in their oxygen bar.

A room at the Four Seasons Springtime Real Estate Fair displayed the prices of "secondhand" dwellings, including courtyards. A law passed in 2004 exempted buyers of old courtyards from preliminary property taxes, which encouraged their sale and their renovation by the new owners. A thirty-six-hundred-square-foot home by the central lakes was posted for

$525,000, but it was a complete fixer-upper. One in better condition re-tailed for $1 million.

Or, you could stroll to the next room and visit the booth of Cathay View, "Beijing's First Chinese Courtyard Residences." Its brochure promised:

THE PRIVACY OF A COURTYARD—LIFE IN A COURTYARD

Sauntering through the yard, listening to the sound of the rain in your pavilion, resting in the shade of the trees, life in a courtyard residence means being by yourself, being yourself, being free.

The 320 detached villas were built in the suburbs near the airport and international schools. A ten-foot wall laced with infrared motion detectors surrounded every home. Passage into each block required scanning an ID card on a sensor. Closed-circuit cameras monitored the lanes. The master bedroom had "emergency buttons" that summoned the complex's private security squad.

The developer hired the guild that worked on restoring the Forbidden City to paint scenes on the homes' gate beams and to fire the roof tiles. The cheapest model: $600,000 for twenty-nine hundred square feet. "Since I started working here," a saleswoman told me, "I realize how many rich people there are in Beijing."

She opened the gate to a model. "Chinese people don't like to live very isolated, but they want their privacy." She gestured to the high wall. "Here, you can still feel the space and enjoy the garden. After sunset, the family can sit outside and have a barbecue!"

Inside the home, a copy of *Motor Trend* and Bill Clinton's autobiography shared the shelves with calligraphy books. The wine cellar was stocked with Great Wall cabernet. The development's teahouse neighbored a base-ball diamond.

"If you put thirty percent down, the interest rate is five point five per-cent," the saleswoman said. "Our partner banks offer you a mortgage in Chinese yuan, Hong Kong dollars, Taiwan dollars, and U.S. dollars. But if it's your second mortgage, the rate is six point eleven." Not long after Cathay View's red-bereted gate guard saluted me onward, my cab passed a billboard that suggested USE WISDOM TO CREATE WEALTH.

The courtyard villa project was designed in part by an international firm that employed a friend of mine named Theodore "Duke" Wright. Duke grew up in a nineteenth-century Victorian house on San Francisco's Potrero Hill. His master's thesis at Columbia developed alternatives to high-rise housing demolition in New York City. After graduation, he worked for the city under Mayor Bloomberg on community participation in the design process. One day, he scrolled job postings on an Internet bulletin board. On a lark, he applied to a listing in China. That he didn't speak Chinese at the time was not a deterrent. He suspected that the firm would prefer that elements of its business remain obscure.

Duke had a mane of reddish brown hair, a large frame, and an easy laugh. He often looked bemused, and children flocked to him. After three years of work at two of the capital's largest architecture firms, the city still surprised him.

"There isn't really a housing development named Chocolate City," he once insisted. "That's the name of a Parliament album!" I showed him the project's advertisement in the *Evening News*.

Duke laughed. "That's genius. I should've thought of that."

He was on the front lines of Beijing's building boom. Though trained as an urban planner, he now handled a variety of tasks for the constant flow of projects pouring in. What was it like to be a midlevel architect in Beijing? It was being told to design a zero-nuisance glass-manufacturing plant for a second-tier city. "I drew a big box," Duke said when I asked what the factory would look like.

Another day, he sent a text message that read, "I am selling Chinese real estate with Thomas Hobbes quotes!"

I guessed, " 'Curiosity is the lust of the mind'?"

" 'Leisure is the mother of philosophy,' " he replied.

From a municipal planning meeting, he sent, "A man just walked into the room with a black eye and sunglasses. Update—he is the mayor." The official brought along his teenaged mistress, who noisily sucked a lollipop at dinner, while Duke kept pace with the mayor's whiskey-and-green-tea-cocktail toasts, topped off by a karaoke spree.

On a visit to his next project, he wrote, "The site includes: jail, oil processing plant, port, highway, several cement quarries, coal processing plant, car dealerships, food processing plants and something nobody can translate except for *poison*. Oh, and the planners I am with cannot read a map."

At one location, he discovered a giant hole. "They were mining something there before," he said. "The pit hadn't shown up on any of my reference materials. I suggested they build a Formula One racetrack at the bottom. I hope they know I was kidding."

Once, on a trip to meet a potential client, his boss asked Duke if he minded speaking in a British accent for the meeting's duration. The clients expected that the "foreign expert" coming to see them was from England.

I had known Duke since he had arrived in Beijing. "I feel like a sellout," he once said. "Developers are copying America in the most simplistic way you can imagine. The whole idea of planning is to care about people. They have to live in what you designed. You combine social needs, architecture, and economic conditions and find the best fit for people's needs. I really believe in that. But the city government doesn't. When it approves projects, it should be looking for an innovative solution, not an innovative idea."

Developers, he said, wanted designers to present a westernized plan that looked modernist. "The developer says, 'Give us a concept.' That could mean something like 'pocket parks.' It sounds good in English and makes them look smart. That's what developers want, period. They want the newest and hottest.

"When I first came to China in 2005," he continued, "I thought, 'Oh, this will be great, I'll have a chance to travel and spend a week at each site and talk to the current tenants about their needs.' After a while the sites began to look the same. It was just a big flat lot, already cleared of people and buildings."

An architect was often at a remove from a project's origin and completion. "The developer leases a parcel of land from the government," he explained. "All of this happens behind closed doors. We don't see any of this. The developer then comes to us with this enormous—think sixty square miles—parcel. They want us to do a plan for the entire thing, but what they're really concerned about is a two-square-mile section. That's the

A typical sign in a new neighborhood's park. The characters at lower right
mean "vending stands."

housing or offices they'll sell. The rest, they flip to other developers. The
market is so high that the minute you acquire any piece of land, you can
parlay it. A foreign real estate hedge fund will take it. Some chump operating out of New York who's never been to Beijing will put money in. Who
cares what's built on it?"

In the coastal city of Qingdao, he once presented a design in a competition for a holiday resort. His was modeled after the low-density cottage
community of Sea Ranch, on the northern California coast. "The panel
was a bunch of eighty-year-olds, city-elder types," he said. They did not ask

questions about water supply, energy consumption, waste removal, or impact on the shoreline. "The winning design was a huge crystal palace that rose from the water," Duke said. "That was the concept. A 'crystal palace.' The castle was linked to shore by a suspension bridge." He paused, then laughed. "It looked really good in the computer animation."

Unlike most white-collar expatriates, Duke lived in Old City housing, on the sixth floor of a walk-up whose sun porch faced the Bell Tower. There was enough good design happening in the city to keep him engaged, and he enjoyed his colleagues, and studying the language. Like most Beijing architects he had not been involved in comprehensive urban planning, but was limited to entering design competitions. "I am proud of a lot of my ideas," he said. "They just haven't won."

Duke did succeed with a plan for a small development of five hundred homes in a Beijing suburb near the Great Wall. "I snuck past the developers the idea of communities and mixed housing. No cul-de-sacs." Closed streets were an American export appearing in copycat designs in Beijing's new neighborhoods, reducing traffic circulation and community interaction. "I got something approved without cul-de-sacs," Duke said. "The streets have a shared green area at their center."

The project was under construction, but Duke, like most architects here, was not allowed to supervise at the site. The developer could do whatever it wanted, if it thought a change to the plan would sell. Duke exhaled. "There will probably end up being cul-de-sacs."

Duke didn't consider himself a functionary, nor a visionary. He said his work was a continual example of sensible planning being changed during development. Another side of the city's architecture was seen in its landmark buildings, such as the Olympic venues under construction, or the National Theater ("The Egg"), which was being completed next to the Great Hall of the People on the Avenue of Eternal Peace at the Old City's heart.

The Beijing architect Zhang Yonghe (Yung Ho Chang) dubbed these freestanding, unique, and sculptural designs Object Buildings. They were monuments, detached and contrasting with their surroundings. In his essay "City of Objects," Zhang wrote, "It used to be a Horizontal City where I grew up. From above, one saw nothing but a gray ocean of tiled roofs over mostly single-story brick houses, interrupted only by the green of the trees floating over the courtyards and the golden yellow from the City within the City."

In the 1950s, Beijing began adding Object Buildings. The first Object, Zhang wrote, was the Monument to the People's Heroes, the column in Tian'anmen Square. The first Object Building was the Minority Culture Palace, just west on the Avenue of Eternal Peace, one of the capital's Ten Greats, a project that constructed ten monumental buildings in 1959, the tenth anniversary of the founding of the People's Republic. Another of the Greats was designed by Zhang's father, Zhang Kaiji, who created the National Museum of Revolution and History, which borders the east side of Tian'anmen Square.

The Ten Greats, like all landmark architecture, do not look timeless, but rather precisely of their time. Their sandy stone or cream-tiled facades fulfilled a government diktat to combine the Chinese, Western, and Soviet aesthetic. The Great Hall of the People, for example, sits on a wide plinth (a traditional Chinese feature), has rows of marble columns (classical Western), and a flat roof over a mostly undecorated block (socialist utilitarianism).

Even in today's market-driven Beijing, the center's appearance is shaped by codes from this era. There is a mostly enforced height limit within the Second Ring Road, which loops the Old City on the footprint of the razed, formerly 凸-shaped wall. Thus, the capital has an inverted skyline, saddle-shaped and rising higher as it moves away from Tian'anmen Square. According to Zhang, rules governing floor-area ratio, building and greenery coverage, and a minimum setback of sixteen feet from the street mean that "there can be no other possibilities but a City of Objects. It is intentional and deliberate."

Thus, life in the City of Objects is defined by congestion, lack of public spaces, discontinuous neighborhoods, and an absence of public housing. Out go the *hutong*, in comes "singularity and verticality." In Beijing, I often saw billboards in front of building sites that promised marvels such as "the world's first flexible cable glass curtain wall," though never "an affordable, pleasant place to work and live."

In 1993, Zhang Yonghe founded China's first private architecture firm. I wanted to meet him because his candor was rare in a sector that masked itself in anonymity. City plans were not posted publicly, neighborhood demolition was reported after the fact, and municipal planning officials followed the Hand's script. Zhang, however, had once admitted to a reporter that his first internship in America had been disheartening. He worked for the San Francisco firm that designed Beijing's first joint-venture hotel, the Jianguo. The lead architect, Zhang said, was Chinese and had become "very practical. The Jianguo was a direct copy of the Palo Alto Holiday Inn."

Zhang's firm, Atelier FCJZ, is tucked beside the east gate of the Old Summer Palace, far from the downtown, high-rise offices of international firms. The single-story wood building has white walls, exposed timber beams, and a Double Fish Ping-Pong table on the inside. The landscaping features a loose-gravel sidewalk, vegetable garden, and a small café.

Zhang cleared a pile of design books off his small office's only other chair. Black bangs drew a straight line just above his eyebrows. His round face was framed by the sort of plastic glasses with narrow lenses that designers seem preternaturally drawn to.

"To give people a better place to live, offer them convenience, comfort, and so on—that's the reason I'm an architect," he said in fluent English. "New Beijing is not doing that, and that's the problem."

Born in 1956, Zhang was raised on Wet Nurse *hutong*, a central lane near the Forbidden City that once housed the imperial nannies. The courtyard in which he grew up was bulldozed. But the increasingly popular notion that *hutong* could only be saved by handing them over to tourism, making the Old City residents a sort of urban Amish, was not a solution he admired. "I don't want to see *hutong* converted into boutique hotels and shops. That's a dead museum." What was being lost he said, was "this community feeling. A lot of basic neighborhood functions are being sacrificed."

Looking to the government for a solution was also not feasible. "There are more people who believe in Marxism in Berkeley than there are in China," he said, smiling. "The government lost that battle. Now it's 'forget about politics.' If the government develops the economy, then everything else will be okay. Use that as an excuse, and nothing will get in the way."

When Zhang first went to the United States for study in 1981, he took a bus from San Francisco to Ball State, in Muncie, Indiana. "That was an interesting experience," he said. "Muncie was the quintessential Midwest American town. It had a dead town center ringed by suburbs."

Chinese architecture at the time remained in the matchbox mode of rows of six-story, rectangular buildings. By the time Zhang got to graduate school at the University of California–Berkeley, he said, "I was doing poetic, artsy-fartsy stuff. But after eight years of conceptual design, I was old enough to realize I wasn't getting anywhere. I had the urge to build buildings."

He moved back to China in 1993. In China, you could get things built, even after the compromises. "As an architect it is great to work here. There's room even for me to pursue my ideal."

Still, his time in the United States had made him too straightforward. "People got offended. I felt like we weren't getting anywhere." One of his first commissions came the Beijing way, by word of mouth.

Zhang's best-known design was 2002's Split House at the Commune at the Great Wall, a group of eleven detached homes, each by a different architect. Split House was made of tamped earth and laminated wood, reflecting the local ecology.

Zhang carved a niche in designing homes, classroom buildings, small museums, and a town hall. In 2005, he was named the first Chinese head of the Massachusetts Institute of Technology's Department of Architecture. His Chinese clients were, like him, a generation that missed a decade of school during the Cultural Revolution. Zhang spent that time reading smuggled books, and drawing. "We learned from uncertainty, and to make our own judgments. All this newly acquired wealth means people want to consume what they think is best. It's a consumer mentality, where possibilities remain open."

The Kempinski hotel group manages the Commune at the Great Wall as a luxury resort. A night in Zhang's Split House begins at $1,500. Reservations are a must.

I left Zhang's office and walked through the Old Summer Palace. The complex was designed, and destroyed, by Westerners. Jesuits drew up the baroque plans for the Manchu emperor Qianlong, who ruled in the same era as America's fight for independence from Britain. In 1860, Anglo-French forces looted the complex during the first Opium War. "You can scarcely imagine the beauty and magnificence of the places we burnt," the young British captain Charles Gordon wrote in a letter home. "It made one's heart sore to burn them; in fact, these places were so large, and we were so pressed for time, that we could not plunder them carefully. Quantities of gold ornaments were burnt, considered as brass. It was wretchedly demoralising work for an army. Everybody was wild for plunder." After the forces sailed back, Queen Victoria was presented with the first Pekingese dog ever seen in Great Britain. She named it Looty.

Gordon would later be immortalized at Khartoum. The Old Summer Palace lay in ruins for the next century; glazed roof tiles from the destroyed halls were used in 1890 to repair the Temple of Heaven. Now it is a Patriotic Education Base, where groups of schoolchildren and visitors can walk on the rubble—a column here, a pedestal there—and see the injustices China endured at the hands of foreigners, an era that ended, the plaques reminded, once the Communist Party took charge. In the late 1980s a French consortium of historians and architects helped reconstruct the palace's Ten-Thousand Flower Maze, made from shoulder-high walls and open to the public to navigate. The French team's contribution is not noted at the Old Summer Palace. But visitors do learn that the halls the French army destroyed had names like Belvedere, Tin Terrace, and Harmonious Wonder. They could be names of Beijing housing developments today.

I took a water taxi back into town. The covered skiff motored down the river once reserved for the imperial court when it journeyed from the Forbidden City to outlying palaces. The guide narrating the trip at last roused passengers by asking them to guess the cost of the quayside apartments we floated past. The shouted estimates escalated until reaching the correct figure: $1,000 per square foot.

The boat passed the zoo and docked behind the Exhibition Center, a 1950s gift from Moscow, whose spire is capped with a red star, an anachronistic design in contemporary Beijing. I walked beside a restored creek that ran through a typical new neighborhood, one where I lived before moving to the *hutong*.

The area felt regimented. Wide streets formed a grid with intersections every third of a mile. Security cameras scanned the open sight lines. The view looked straight: long, empty sidewalks; parallel rows of seedlings;

twenty-story apartment buildings. In the paved square at their centers, a trio of men banged on drums for a group of middle-aged women who waved scarves and hopped the mincing steps of the Rice Seedling Dance, an exercise routine.

I never saw the dance in the *hutong*, not because it was a relic from the 1960s, but because there was not enough open space to perform. Nor did the lanes buzz with swarms of three-wheel pedicabs that ferried the elderly through new neighborhoods, where public transportation stops were spaced far apart and away from the apartment entrance gates. An eight-foot-tall iron fence surrounded the complex's perimeter, leaving only one opening, patrolled by a guard. Apartment windows, even those on upper floors, were sheathed in bars for additional security. Entering the building required punching in a code; it took two keys to unlock a home's thick metal door.

Inside, sound-activated lights illuminated the building's stairwells. In addition to the dance's crashing cymbals, and pedicabs' bleating horns, new Beijing communities resounded with the echo of feet stomping away the shadows. When I first moved into the *hutong*, I reflexively pounded my foot on the pavement after dusk. The lane stayed silent and dark.

CHAPTER 9

PRESERVING A SENSE OF PLACE

IN FEBRUARY 2006, as a biting wind blew through the Forbidden City, an elderly American pinched the collar of her fur coat and said, in a Brahmin accent, "It's colder than charity."

We stood inside a corner of the palace being restored with some of her foundation's money. An emperor's Lodge of Retirement would open to the public in 2008, with the remaining work on twenty-three other buildings and four gardens completed by 2016.

The garden had been all but sealed off from the world before 1925, when the Forbidden City opened to the public as a museum. In his Beijing memoir, *The Years That Were Fat*, George Kates wrote that he spent weeks in the 1930s bribing a guard before gaining entrance. "We were told that it was so overgrown that it literally could no longer be shown." Once inside, having seen thick dust on bundles of orange cloth, and traceried doors without paper windows, peeling murals and disintegrating lacquer, he became, when contemplating the loss, "fatigued with a sense of almost personal evisceration."

I felt the same when seeing *hutong* communities crumble from neglect and pickaxes. They are as integral to Beijing's heritage as an imperial garden.

At the press conference announcing the extension of the partnership between the Palace Museum and New York–based World Monuments Fund, its president said, "In the field of historic preservation, we face many challenges. It can be difficult to establish priorities. It's rare to be given an opportunity, to be given a bold vision, and achieve it. Here, we have that opportunity."

Flashbulbs popped, agreements were signed, and a plaque was unveiled listing the underwriters of the $15 million project, including British American Tobacco (UK), the Tiffany & Co. Foundation, and the Freeman Foundation—begun by a founder of the American International Group insurance company. The press kit included color brochures and a CD filled with images. As the speeches continued, I balanced the folder's heavy stock in my palm, wondering how much Recycler Wang would pay for it. Enough for the small bag of nails a neighbor named Aunty Yang needed. She was—at that moment—perched on her courtyard's sloped roof, patching holes with tar paper and scrap wood. Aunty Yang was seventy.

Her courtyard home was intact, as no drop ceiling or additional windows had been added over the past century. The rotting wood trellises that separated rooms were among the most beautiful I had seen, though the interior had turned dark and smoky after decades of coal-fueled heating. Unfortunately for Aunty Yang and Beijing's other courtyard owners, her home—unlike the Forbidden City's gardens—did not have pavilion-topped rockeries, or China's four remaining trompe l'oeil silk murals.

In another corner of the Forbidden City, the Hong Kong–based China Heritage Fund was rebuilding the Palace of Established Happiness. "It's the biggest reconstruction of a Chinese palace in history," the organization's Alex Breel said. The building burned to the ground in 1923, the result of either a sparking film projector—the last emperor screened films here—or deliberate arson by pilfering eunuchs who feared the results of an ordered audit of its treasures.

"When we began work, all that was here were pediments," Breel said. "The Forbidden City is a living piece of architecture. It's been in a continuous process of rebuilding and design since it began in 1407."

The work site was saturated in color and texture: walls layered in the traditional rough mixture of clay, straw, and pig's blood; ocher beams; blue-glazed roof tiles; and jade-, orange-, and gold-painted designs. The finished product, however, would not be open to the public. Plans called for it to be used as a private reception area for VIPs.

The World Monuments Fund did not only finance the restoration of palace architecture. It had twenty sites on its Monuments Watch scattered across

China, a list that included small towns built with traditional architecture. I had visited one village, named Tuanshan, located in the country's far southwest in a region marked by magnificent stone bridges covered with flying-eave pavilions. The town's incomparable manors reflected the prosperous tin-mining era, a century ago. Under Communism, the private homes had been converted to public use. Now, they were being marketed as a tourist attraction.

Tuanshan was a living community of nine hundred people, a rare example of an entire town being deemed worthy of protection. In China, preserving the past usually meant resurrecting the dead—restoring imperial, uninhabited structures, or rebuilding them in an idealized form to put on display for paying customers. What's "old" looks new, because the wooden beams are freshly lacquered, the roof tiles unbroken, and the painted details vibrant for lack of grime. Restoration of Asian buildings has long followed this pattern, and thus structures do not display the romantic decay of Europe's stone monuments. Pulling down and rebuilding architecture made with perishable materials is cheaper, and more efficient, than repairing it. The result is that truly old artifacts—such as courtyard homes—evince the decrepitude of the past, instead of its glory. After all, the thinking holds, the old buildings that matter have been repainted or rebuilt.

The architect Zhang Yonghe, whose studio was located at the Old Summer Palace, said that one reason "people here don't understand the notion of preservation as Europeans do" is because western architecture is characterized by different eras and governments, whereas Chinese building materials and design remained largely unchanged over two thousand years. A highly visible and visited site such as a cathedral was a portal back to a specific time, and its attendant politics, arts, ethics, and economy. In Beijing, however, old buildings were seen as reminders of one pre-Liberation period: feudalism. "People don't differentiate between the old and the new," Zhang said.

Yet as Beijing evicted whole communities, it raced to repair structures that had until recently been derided as fossils of a backward regime and put to other uses as schools, offices, and barracks. Now the buildings could represent Chinese culture, and earn revenue. Between 2000 and 2003, the capital sank three billion yuan ($360 million) into the preservation of sites popular with tourists—an amount nearly equal to that spent nationally in the same period. Another six hundred million yuan ($72.6 million) was budgeted for heritage protection until 2008. The total investment equaled Beijing's heritage protection outlay "for several decades before 2000," according to *China Daily*.

The Drum and Bell towers underwent repairs, and the southernmost tower on the central axis was rebuilt on a smaller scale. Workers uncovered the Old City's Changpu Creek, and cleared warehouses that stored national parade decorations to build a pedestrian park. Nonconforming structures on the ancient commercial *hutong* Tobacco Pipe Slanted Street, near the Old City's Rear Lake, were pulled down, and West Drum Tower Boulevard was improved without the widening that would have destroyed its canopy of locust trees.

What merited preservation was a question of priorities, and perspective. No matter how fragile, it was easier to rally around a single structure than an entire neighborhood, and to raise or appropriate funds for its renovation. It was even harder to convince outsiders to protect intangible social patterns. They did not live them nor witness how even small fissures—a new road; the eviction of a few families—led to irreparable fractures. The Hand did not repair old communities. It tore them down.

Miss Zhu and I often walked east from school across the rubble of the Coal Street widening project to eat lunch at Langfang Second Lane. Its forty small restaurants formed the city's densest concentration of "old brand names" (*laozihao*). Some had been immortalized in the nineteenth-century *Poems on the Specialties in Beijing*.

Recently, the *Evening News* lamented that of the capital's six hundred famous local snacks, only one hundred were still being made. It said youths preferred the taste of pizza and KFC. Fair play to the youths: Beijing's snacks are often fried and dry, and not all are mouthwatering. Miss Zhu tied her hair back and leaned forward to slurp at a plate of sheep brain, but groaned when I sipped a bowl of *douzhi*, a sour green drink made from bean dregs.

Langfang Second Lane was located between Front Gate Avenue and Coal Street in a group of streets lined with *langfang*, distinctive two-story, gray brick buildings with wood-railed verandas. In the early fifteenth century, the first emperor of the Ming dynasty summoned tradesmen to set up shops in this part of Dazhalan. A later edict stated that merchants and artisans had to operate on the same street. Living near your guild offered mutual safety. The Langfang *hutong* came to be named for the products sold there. Western tourist maps from the turn of the twentieth century label them Lantern Street, Jade Street, Jewelry Street, Brass Street, and Silk Street. Private banks flourished, too, making the lanes the capital's antiques and financial center.

The area felt like an open-air museum. The lanes were too small for a car to enter. One alley formerly used by banks was only fifteen inches wide, so as to impede bandits. Another required a pedestrian to duck under a cement slab at its midpoint. With their blend of wood and brick, carved flowers, and peaked tiled roofs, the buildings here were among the neighborhood's most beautiful. Most, however, looked ready to collapse. Rotting wood and old signs make for romantic snapshots, yet this was life, not a postcard. "Hair salons" and shops selling pirated DVDs, cheap scroll paintings, and sex toys occupied most buildings. The small-stall restaurants operated according to old customs. They posted prices on a hand-painted sign—5.50 yuan ($.73) for a small bowl of intestines, say. You paid first, then took the square of pink tissue paper that was the receipt and lined up outside, until it was your turn at the black steel cauldron filled with *luzhu*, a thick, gamy tripe stew.

I often ate on the lane because it was rare in Beijing to find an eatery that had a staff with low turnover, and regular customers who recognized each other. Though it was also one *hutong* away from my house, I never ate at Dazhalan West Street's many restaurants. That was the domain of tourists, and the businesses there treated you like one, while their customers asked the same series of questions about your nationality, age, income, and ability to use chopsticks.

At Langfang Second Lane, I felt like a neighbor. My favorite restaurant specialized in *dalian huoshao*, a fried dumpling shaped like the rectangular bags sewn at each end formerly used to carry coins. The restaurant had operated since 1876. On a March morning in 2006, a notice was pasted to its wall: PROTECT THE CAPITAL'S ANCIENT APPEARANCE, WELCOME THE OLYMPICS!

When 拆 appeared next to every door on the lane, the public responded not with outrage for the loss of the buildings, but remorse over the closing of the "old brand names" restaurants.

A simmering cauldron of luzhu, *the gamy tripe stew.*

The lines for a seat began at opening time and stretched one hundred deep. They blended into one another, so you had to call out which type of food you were waiting for. An elderly man waiting behind me had brought his grandchildren so they could taste, for the first and last time, Feng's boiled tripe and Chen's stewed intestine at Langfang Second Lane, this special place. The walk to get here, the surrounding architecture, the street sounds and crowds—all were part of the dishes' flavor. It took some getting used to, the old man admitted, as his grandchildren stared wide-eyed at the bubbling cauldron.

While Beijing prepared to host the Summer Olympics, preservationists in Seoul, South Korea, attempted to save the traditional houses called *hanok*. Peter Bartholomew, a former Peace Corps volunteer who owned one, told the *South China Morning Post*, "The problem in Korea and across Asia is that people see no value in old buildings other than monumental structures like palaces and temples. New is, de facto, better than old and traditional. There's a prejudice that old homes are uncomfortable and obsolete. A growing sector of society is becoming concerned at the loss of their traditional architectural heritage. But it's almost too late."

In Russia, elderly tenants were evicted from Moscow's Ostozhenka neighborhood around Christ the Savior Cathedral so apartments costing $33,000 a square meter could be built with riverside views of the Kremlin. A skyscraper three times taller than St. Petersburg's tallest building, Peter and Paul Cathedral, was approved amidst debate over the damage the building would inflict on the old city center's skyline. "Without big companies coming," the governor told the *New York Times*, "without turning the city into a financial and economic center, we shall never have these resources, and the unique architectural heritage in the center of the city will be quietly falling apart before our eyes."

In Beijing, I asked a preservation activist to describe the lack of public participation in the city's planning. "It's like living under the emperor," Hua Xinmin said. The daughter of a renowned local architect, she had fought to save the courtyard home her family had owned since 1914. All that remained were photographs and the title documents she withdrew from a plastic folder and piled on the table between us. Now her former neighborhood held office buildings, and a Range Rover showroom standing apart on a thoroughfare.

Like other Beijing intellectuals with famous parents, Hua regularly spoke with atypical candor to the media. Privilege provided protection. As I flipped through a photo album that documented scores of courtyards pulled down over the years, Hua identified each in the voice one uses when speaking of the deceased. "That house was on Rice Market Lane," she said solemnly. "It was murdered. It had a life."

Hua compared her work to that of a firefighter's. She ran around Beijing shouting demolition crews down from protected structures and alerting the police. "It's as if we have terrorists from our own territory attacking our houses!"

The assault occurred worldwide throughout the last century, as historic cities modernized. "Between the years 1900 and 2000, nearly one quarter of the landmarks of Amsterdam were leveled by Amsterdammers," writes Anthony Tung in *Preserving the World's Great Cities*. "More than half of the indexed buildings of Islamic Cairo—one of the few intact medieval Muslim cities that had existed at the beginning of the century—were destroyed by Cairenes."

Singapore tore itself down. Athenians looted "all but a minute fraction" of their city's nineteenth-century design. Thousands of New York's buildings were razed by New Yorkers. Moscow knocked over its onion domes and bell towers. Despite that their city was spared from incendiary bombing during World War II, Kyoto's residents pulled down most of its wooden buildings afterward. "Romans demolished a third of Rome's historic structures." The Turks allowed Istanbul's Ottoman architecture to rot. Beginning in 1949, Beijing worried its Old City like a scab, scratching away the city wall, tearing off its *hutong*. So did the rest of China: of the three hundred walled cities that existed at the founding of the People's Republic, only four remained intact.

Paris destroyed its Les Halles market. In the mid-nineteenth century, the civil engineer Baron Georges-Eugène Haussmann performed drastic surgery on the medieval city center. He straightened its tangled lanes, tripling road width to 140 yards. Every new street took the place of six destroyed alleys. The novelist Paul LaFarge imagines the engineer thinking, "Ah, old city, old bitch. I'll spread your streets like a dancer's legs, and sow Haussmann in all your courtyards, your covered alleys, your dark places, dark no more."

The Beijing media often positively invoked Haussmann's reconfiguration of central Paris. Like the Hand, he, too, did not have to defend his plan to elected officials, an enfranchised public, and muckraking media. "It is no longer possible, as in Haussmann's day," wrote Le Corbusier in 1929, "to throw whole districts into confusion, drive out the tenants, and make a desert in the crowded heart of Paris over a space of three or even five years."

Haussmann's contemporary critics charged that his wide avenues formed artillery sight lines for Napoléon III's soldiers. A theory voiced in Beijing's lanes was that the government wanted the *hutong* razed so its central organs would no longer be surrounded by mazes of hiding places, as during 1989's Tian'anmen Square demonstrations. (Haussmann's boulevards did not prevent civil disorder. In 1871, a year after the roads were completed, the Paris Commune occupied the city for two months, until twenty thousand Communards were executed in a week, ending their tenure.)

Bulldozing six-lane roads through dilapidated neighborhoods does not mean a city will resemble Paris, however. Haussmann's roads were designed before the automotive age. His wide, plane-tree-lined sidewalks provide a means to experience that ancient pleasure of seeing a city on foot. The roadways remained in the public space, instead of forming a cavern of speeding traffic. Some of Beijing's new roads are so wide, it is common to see elderly pedestrians stranded halfway across after the light has changed. To his sidewalks, Haussmann drew in outdoor café seating, public bathrooms, and the distinctive painted iron uniform subway entrances and signboard holders.

The buildings along Paris's new boulevards were also integrated. Unlike Beijing's blocky mixture of unlinked architecture, Haussmann's structures' uniform height and materials formed a street wall of interlocking shops and homes, topped by slate, mansard roofs. They define the look of Paris today. When I once stayed in a Haussmann-designed apartment in the Latin Quarter, its Parisian owner motioned to the narrow alleys below and said, "The appearance of the past is still here. This building was designed so people of many economic classes would live together. Haussmann to me is simply the heart of Paris, and one still beating."

Yet at the completion of his project, Haussmann was sacked by Napoléon III in the face of public anger over the project's rising costs and allegations of graft. The projects were the first to use deficit financing to fund a city improvement scheme.

Beijing, like all Chinese cities, does not raise money through municipal bonds or by tax increases, but rather land-transfer fees in which wads of cash can be skimmed off as the deal passes through the levels of bureaucracy. In 2006, the capital's vice mayor—in charge of Olympic-venue construction projects and the final authority on city demolitions—was sacked and expelled from the Communist Party for corruption. The state press reported he "led a corrupt and perverted life, abused his power to grant contracts to favor his mistress, and earned huge amounts of money illegally."

Many urban historians note that Haussmann is rarely credited for adding enormous public parks to Paris. Some absolve Haussmann of his alleged crime, writing that no evidence shows that he gained personally from the redesign of Paris.

Is it true that on his deathbed he wished all his work undone? What's certain is that Haussmann, the expander, the widener, the man who advocated circulation in old quarters, the patron saint of 拆, died from congestion, in his lungs.

As some ancient cities tore themselves down, others safeguarded their attributes and maintained a unique sense of place. The historian Tung observes, "The preservation of great cities is ultimately the story of how different urban societies created environments of extraordinary meaning, were affected by their cityscapes through centuries of habitation, and came to realize that the loss of old buildings involved much more than just the visible destruction of ancient bricks and stones."

These cities also acted to finance neighborhood protection. In 1957, Amsterdam founded the Company for City Restoration. It improves historic houses in marginal areas threatened by redevelopment, then rents them back to the original tenants at a subsidized rate. It often targets corner buildings, which offer high visibility, as an advertisement for a block's beautification campaign. Neighboring building owners are allotted funds to paint facades and do minor repairs.

Similar city-funded initiatives renewed historic housing in Vienna and Paris's Marais neighborhood. Tung contrasts the fates of Paris and Beijing since 1900, when they were the "two largest works of unified urban artistry in the world." Paris is largely intact today, while Beijing is fractured. Why? "Did more contemporary Parisians share a sense of ownership of the beautiful construction because its loveliness was focused on the public realm? Did more of the beauty of Paris affect the daily life of more Parisians? And did more Parisians therefore feel the wound deeply and cry out when the visage of their lovely city began to be eroded?"

Yes. More important, the city's caretakers listened.

Each city is unique, however. Among other attributes, Paris and Beijing have different histories, economies, and functions. Beijing's Old City was not a collection of monuments; it was the monument, a symbol designed so the emperor could mediate between heaven and earth on behalf of agrarian society. That function had been rendered obsolete. Beijing's architecture was also built with more perishable materials than those used in Paris.

The cities also have dissimilar forms of government, and their citizens have different relationships to power. Residents, not officials, often started preservation movements, hastened by citizen participation in political and planning processes, and use of the media, petitions, and marches to gather support. Organizing opposition to the state is a crime in Beijing, where the government owns the land.

Thus, many preservation activists in the city limit their activities to surveying and photographing *hutong*, rather than rebuilding them. A program officer at Beijing's Ford Foundation office had never seen a grant application to do so. "We do not fund the renovation itself, but we can find ways to get all stakeholders to contribute," he told me. "Not just recording, but real intervention. Some of the private-house owners can repair theirs on their own, and our funding can help them along the way, summarize how that can be done properly, and disseminate the practice."

I had seen such a program in Lijiang, a town in southwest China. Lijiang was the capital of a former kingdom ruled by the Naxi, an ethnic group whose descendants formed the majority of its population. The city's Old Town was leveled in a 1996 earthquake. The reconstruction of its wooden houses and cobblestone lanes coincided with its designation as a World Heritage site. UNESCO certification is a double-edged sword; by attracting visitors, isolated spots cash in, altering the heritage under protection. I had first visited Lijiang before the quake and returned to a rebuilt city whose tourist economy was being fueled by the government's assertion that the region was the setting for Shangri-La in the novel *Lost Horizon*.

"There are twenty thousand residents of the Old Town, and each year five hundred thousand people come to visit," the chief of Lijiang's Old Town Management Committee told me. We paused in the central square to watch Han Chinese travelers join aged locals in a folk dance that involved a lot of one-legged hopping. "Tourists come with modern things to see a less-than-modern culture," she said, pointing to the video cameras and cell phones the tourists carried.

"We have to conserve while simultaneously modernizing," the chief continued. "If we don't raise the living standards of local people, they'll either move to new homes in the New Town or renovate cheaply and incorrectly."

With downtown real estate going for ten times of that in the freshly built suburbs, most locals had sold out. The ethnic Naxi owner of the Blue Moon Valley Hotel estimated that 95 percent of Lijiang's "folk style" inns were owned by Han Chinese from outside the city.

To prevent the erosion of the Old Town's character, the local government partnered with the Palo Alto, California–based Global Heritage Fund to restore native residents' homes, on the condition they wouldn't be converted into inns or shops.

Under the project, forty local homes had been restored, with plans for two hundred more under way. Architects from a Shanghai university were hired to draw Lijiang's first Master Conservation Plan. It did not recommend tearing down old houses to build new old-looking ones. It called for the removal of the cell phone tower shadowing the Old Town, as well as the destruction of modern concrete buildings, and restrictions on new construction.

The Global Heritage Fund's CEO said that the key to a preservation project is having an approved master plan prior to beginning work. An onsite leader is crucial. So is funding. "We are in many ways like a venture capitalist," he told me, "finding the right people, site, and timing—ensuring all investors keep investing and progress forward continues."

In the southeast city of Quanzhou, a team led by a University of Washington professor partnered with the municipal government to preserve the town's old canal-laced quarter, more than half of which had been slated for redevelopment before intervention. The project was unique in that it sought to codify community participation in the planning process.

In Beijing, that participation was limited to following eviction orders. *Hutong* residents such as Old Zhang often grumbled that they didn't have rights, but obligations. Both Lijiang and Quanzhou's old quarters are roughly the size of Dazhalan. The difference is that an estimated 90 percent of residents of those cities' heritage districts owned their homes. They are located in small towns, not the capital—Olympic host, corporate base, and the face of China, where the Hand rubbed out the persimmon trees, widened the roads, and penciled in rows of Object Buildings. This *hutong*?

Erase. Add a shopping center, fast-food outlets, 7-Eleven. Make it functional, make it like America. The bicycle is old, so make way for the car.
Irascible residents? *Erasable.*

Privation can preserve ancient cities, as I had seen in Havana, where buildings decayed but had not been pulled down to build shopping malls. A
moribund economy does not offer the temptation to trade heritage for instant money. Since the 1990s, Beijing had faced that allure as the national
economy soared and funded engineering projects that made the Great Wall
seem like a warm-up. The world's highest railroad ran to Lhasa, while the
largest dam blocked the Yangtze, submerging 127 towns, some of which
were seventeen centuries old. Shanghai opened the first magnetic levita-
tion train and was constructing the world's tallest building. The longest
canal was being carved to divert Yellow River water to the nation's north,
and a highway system to rival America's was being built. China launched
its first man into space.

I was curious how cities in neighboring Communist-governed countries
managed conservation in the transition from a planned to a market economy. Before Vietnam entered the World Trade Organization in 2007, I
traveled twice to its capital, Hanoi.

"The city government faces a choice," Le Van Lan told me in English.
"It can choose to preserve the Old Quarter for its population, or for
tourists." The seventy-year-old historian motioned to the flotsam of backpacker hotels, Internet cafés, and travel agents wedged between residences,
open-air noodle stands, and shopfronts. "Hanoi's preservation is aimed at
2010, when the city will celebrate the one-thousandth anniversary of its
founding. But if the Old Quarter is not protected, then we won't be attending Hanoi's birthday party. It will be its farewell party."

At four tenths of a square mile, the Old Quarter is smaller than
Dazhalan and has a population of sixty-six thousand. Both neighborhoods were built around commerce. Each of the Old Quarter's original
thirty-six lanes—today there are seventy-six—is named for the item sold
by the guilds who first settled in the area outside the palace in the thirteenth century. As we walked the narrow streets, Le translated their
names like a shopper ticking off a list: "Bamboo Market! Basket Market!

Sail Market!"—then on to brushes, bottles, rafts, salt, coffins, and worm clams.

As we walked, daylight was snuffed out by the five-story additions to the narrow traditional layout called a tube house. Historically, a home was taxed by the width of its ground-floor facade. Most of the Old Quarter's buildings evolved from a narrow storefront to an extension of housing stretching back 20 to 150 yards from the street. Now, residents reached for the sky. Land transactions used gold bars for payment, and a square meter in the Old Quarter cost five hundred grams' worth, Le said. "When people want to add rooms, they simply build up."

Regulations prevented structures from exceeding three stories, but the laws went unheeded. Also ignored, Le said, were government designs to thin the Old Quarter's density by moving some residents to the suburbs.

I told him that in Beijing, no one could avoid the Hand. "In Hanoi, we joke that there are three models of administration," Le said. "The first is that the government fears its people, as in the U.S. The second is that the people fear their government, as in China. Then there's Hanoi: the government and people fear one another and so go about their own business."

On Silver Street, a resident showed another model, in which government and residents worked together. His tube house was selected as a project site by a program funded by the Hanoi, Brussels, and Toulouse governments to restore Old Quarter homes to their original state. The structures could not be converted into a boutique hotel or café, leaving the community intact.

"The key to restoring the buildings of the Old Quarter is keeping the original people inside," said the project's French architect. "Four years ago, the government didn't think these homes were worth preserving. It's not that people here do not know how to preserve, but the idea of what deserves preservation is different than in the West, where we don't only want to restore tourist sites. Now people have a model to copy, and because Hanoi's Old Quarter is so important to tourism, the government and residents are paying attention to architectural heritage. It takes time, but people will understand."

The costs were significant. The yearlong restoration of one home cost seventy thousand euros ($90,000). Another tube house had been renovated and opened as a museum that explained its preservation. There, one can buy a series of self-guided explanatory maps titled "Architectural Walks in Hanoi." They were produced through a partnership between the Canadian embassy and Hanoi's Research Institute for Architecture. The maps are printed on heavy stock but narrow enough to fit into a back pocket. They explain a quarter's history, its architecture, religious buildings, markets, and battle sites. Dozens of exemplary homes are cited to hunt down and admire.

In Beijing, there was no such museum, and the most popular guide to the Old City is a pirated reproduction of a 1936 novelty map. It leads a visitor through a nostalgic recollection of razed landmarks, not the living, inhabited capital. The illustrations depict camels, temples, and pigtailed men smoking opium pipes. The map was drawn by Frank Dorn, a West Point graduate, language officer, and military attaché stationed in the city from 1934 to 1938. He lived in a courtyard home at East Zongbu *hutong*, with a chauffeur, cook, and gardener for whom he purchased a second wife, after the first one died. After the bombing of Pearl Harbor, Dorn became General Joseph Stilwell's senior aide-de-camp, serving in the China and Burma theaters. Like other "China hands," his military career froze in the anticommunist era of the 1950s, and he ended up advising Jimmy Stewart for a film about the Burmese front. None of this is noted on the map.

In an English-language classroom inside Hanoi's Old Quarter, I asked university-age students to describe their neighborhood. The board filled with *quaint, crowded, busy, uncomfortable, noisy, ancestral, venerable, collapsing.* Half the students wrote the word *slum*, or the Vietnamese equivalent, *mouse house.* And yet all of them expressed pride in it. "It's the harmonization between the old and the modern," one woman said. Another added, "The Old Quarter is a part of my childhood, that's why I love it." A man admitted, "I don't like to live in the Old Quarter, but I feel pride in living in it. If you live in a modern house, your house never appears on TV."

A city's collective nostalgia can form barriers to modernization, but can also preserve symbols of identity, such as San Francisco's cable cars. The cyclo is Hanoi's equivalent. The passengers in this bicycle rickshaw sit in a low-slung, open carriage in front of the handlebars. Its resurgence was the result of lobbying by an Old Quarter resident against government plans to ban them. "They said cyclos obstructed traffic," said the fifty-six-year-old founder of the No Worries cyclo company. "I argued that cyclos play an important part in preserving the spirit of old Hanoi. Cyclos are good for the Old Quarter; they're not noisy and bad for the environment, like mopeds."

The Old Quarter maintained its cuisine, as well. Hanoi's first KFC opened in 2006, yet every Old Quarter lane still looked as if it could be named Noodle Street. *Pho* is to Hanoi'ans what pizza is to Neapolitans. Diners cradled a ceramic bowl filled with rice noodles in a beef broth, mixed with locally grown herbs such as marjoram, amaranth, and basil.

The Old Quarter was celebrated in music, too. At his tube house, a local composer said, "The Old Quarter is not easy to explain. It's something flowing inside of me." His hands gestured at the air as he moved forward on the sofa. I asked if he could sing it.

As the piano boomed to life, the composer nodded violently. His long gray hair whipped behind him, his legs pumped, and his hands pounded on the keys. "This is a song I wrote called 'My Hanoi'an Childhood.'"

> *My childhood streets, my childhood roads. This is my Hanoi.*
> *Flower Market Street, Silk Street, is there some house there,*
> *   waiting for me?*
> *My song, my wind, blows the Red River's brown sails.*

After more verses, he returned to the couch, looking dazed. "Every culture has its own door to its spirit, to its tradition," he said with intensity. "The Old Quarter is a feeling. It's only a feeling. You have to see it. You have to live it. It's an organic connection."

Cui Jian, godfather of Chinese rock music, grew up in Beijing apartments. He didn't understand why Western reporters often compared him to Bruce Springsteen, bard of the busted factory town. "I don't relate to his songs at all," he told me. I wondered, why hadn't Beijing produced songs about the destruction of the *hutong*? "People here see that as a real estate transaction," Cui said. Who wants to sing about real estate?

On two trips to Luang Prabang, Laos, I saw an ancient capital threatened not by bulldozers, but tourists. Left to stagnate for decades after

Laos's capital was moved south to Vientiane, Luang Prabang showcased its neglect.

There were no Lao visitors inside the royal palace. Nor was there a king. I removed my shoes and slid in socks over teak floorboards past his majesty's elephant saddle and bric-a-brac tribute, including the moon rock from President Nixon. The captioned chronology ended there. No plaque informed anyone that in 1975, the king and queen, like thousands of their subjects on the losing side of the Communist revolution, were shipped to caves in the hinterland for "reeducation." They are thought to have died of malaria.

Uncomfortable facts are an anathema to tourism, an industry that sells escape—for the tourists. In Luang Prabang, escape was selling well. The palace, French colonial architecture, and saffron-robed Buddhist monks were Laos's version of Havana's Eisenhower-era autos. The town's main street was lined with two-story masonry buildings featuring tall windows, wood shutters, and creamy facades. After decades of scrubbing the country of symbols that didn't fit a people's dictatorship, relics of the old regime had crept back to Luang Prabang. The town's swank inns and eateries titled themselves in Romance languages: Villa Santi, L'Elephant. Uniformed schoolchildren shouted, *"Bonjour!"* Monks repaired the temples from which they were once evicted. Cafés served espresso and croissants at sidewalk tables. English was the lingua franca, the dollar the de facto currency. Spin the postcard stands, and you could smell the frangipani.

"Tourism is killing tourism!" Francis Engelmann's voice rose at the verb. Long vowels and exasperation accented the Frenchman's English. "If Luang Prabang's historical structures keep being converted to guesthouses, that also brings increased sewage, traffic, and activities connected to tourism. Traditional life will change. Luang Prabang will become a cultural Disneyland."

Engelmann was the project manager at La Maison du Patrimoine, Heritage House. The agency oversees the preservation of Luang Prabang, declared a World Heritage site by UNESCO in 1995. With his gray hair clipped close, sun-blushed cheeks, and a linen shirt hanging loose on a doughy frame, Engelmann looked comfortable in his post. I met him in his spartan office, where a lone window framed by exposed stone walls allowed in a moist breeze.

His workplace sat at a peninsula's end, overlooking the confluence of the Mekong and Khan rivers. The building used to be the Customs House, and in its renovated incarnation as Heritage House, it is again, with the agency's focus on preserving local customs eroded by French colonization, beginning in the mid-nineteenth century.

"We don't have a picture of the original palace," Engelmann lamented. "Not even one. After the French arrived, they wrote, 'The king is living in a shabby house.'"

Indochina's civil servants tore down the palace, which, like all of Luang Prabang's architecture, was built with wood. The French crafted the surviving compound from cement, imported from abroad. (This, too, failed to awe: "A tiny modest royal palace," wrote Graham Greene, on a 1954 visit. "The king is as poor as the state.")

"The French thought that everything made of wood is a slum," Engelmann said. "Today, people here agree. Luang Prabang is very poor, and you must understand the terrible inferiority complex that comes with poverty. Their only desire is to look modern."

Part of Engelmann's job was to convince residents otherwise. Funded by UNESCO, Heritage House worked in concert with the Laos Ministry of Culture to draft building regulations and help locals maintain the city's fabric when renovating homes and buildings. Staff architects—fifteen, all Lao—guided property owners through catalogs of native design, sketching plans for free. The exhibits were exhaustive: doors, windows, gardens, fences, gates. If it existed on a building, Heritage House had a photo, or sample. Can't find Bleached Pistachio at the local paint store? Using scrapings from century-old walls, the agency re-created the signature pastel pigments that tint the town.

Costs, however, fell to the builders, and many chose cheaper options. Others didn't have the patience for the long give-and-take involved in preserving a building. And if they chose to slather their home in poured concrete, Heritage House had no authority to stop them.

Luang Prabang property owners who committed to the preservation road usually did so to reopen as a guesthouse or café aimed at foreign tourists. Engelmann said the cycle was unsustainable: cash-strapped UNESCO was in the business of preservation, not bed-and-breakfast construction. The city, he said, was caught "between two unpleasant situations: it can die from neglect or be smothered by affection."

Thus far, the government had refused offers to build enormous resorts or towering high-rises. "But every month a new international group comes in and says an exception should be made, because the city deserves their project, which will create jobs."

The only statistic tourists often saw was the exchange rate, but Laos's six million residents lived with figures like these: daily per capita income of $4. One out of five children dies before age five. A quarter of the population has access to safe drinking water. More than half the population is illiterate, and over four fifths of villages suffer diarrhea and malaria. The average Lao dies at age fifty-four.

Outside of aromatherapy and a prix fixe menu, Luang Prabang provided few services. Nearly 20 percent of the country's GDP consisted of foreign aid. Navigating Luang Prabang's streets felt like swimming in alphabet soup, passing dozens of office nameplates for groups such as CARE, UNICEF, and WHO. Unlike neighboring Vietnam and China, Laos's Communist regime was not installed by popular revolt. Nor, despite continuing openness and reform, was the Party able to rest its mandate on economic development. Since the 1997 Asian financial crisis, no currency aside from Burma's had lost as much value as the Lao kip. Even the state-run Lao Airlines required U.S. dollars to purchase a ticket.

Luang Prabang was a union of unique neighborhoods, or *ban*. Each *ban*, named for the trade practiced there in imperial times, often included a Buddhist temple. A pond was central to each *ban*. In the past, the water functioned as fish farm, erosion-defender, and sewage treater—and drained to the Mekong via a series of channels running aside the pathways.

"Most visitors come to Luang Prabang and they leave retaining an image of a nice colonial city," Engelmann said. "They miss half of it. This is the exceptional value of Luang Prabang. Here, we have in one city, two cities. What is most precious here are the remains of the city before cement. It's like *Alice in Wonderland*: you have to cross through the mirror and enter another universe."

In Luang Prabang, the mirror is a redbrick alley. Each walkway cost Heritage House $4,000 to resurface. For tourists, a path was an invitation to step off the main streets into the town's traditional texture. For locals, the alleys patterned a dense network of home, garden, and water that recalled Luang Prabang's original design, one that since the fourteenth century had fused ecology with urbanism. The walk took me away from the rebuilt shopfronts and into a living world that reminded me of the *hutong*.

Engelmann had stayed long after work to chat, and the combination of a power outage and setting sun had us hurrying to conclude while light remained. He rustled through a stack of binders. They held an inventory of every structure and wetland within the city's protected zone. The project had taken five years and was ongoing—this, to record six hundred buildings and two hundred ponds in an area whose perimeter took an hour to walk. Flipping through the photos, Engelmann's face suggested that Luang Prabang's historic core was as small, yet elusive to capture, as the mosquito buzzing in his ear.

Perhaps Hanoi and Luang Prabang were more open to outsiders' preservation efforts because they had been colonial cities, and their distinctive centers blended local and foreign architecture. Their built heritage was largely constructed in cement, not wood, making it less expensive to repair. Maybe the privation, imposed by an external force, made the cities open to assistance. Lijiang rebuilt after an earthquake, Luang Prabang lost its status as national capital, and Hanoi had been through a half century of war. Beijing was the capital of the world's next superpower; its robust economy allowed it to manage its own fate and be selective about outside advice.

In 2004, Beijing's UNESCO office asked an American urban planner named David Westendorff to draft a proposal for minimizing damage to the social fabric of neighborhoods as the city prepared to host the Olympics. His internal memo urged UNESCO to pressure the International Olympic Committee (IOC) for support.

> The IOC has become the most influential of all "international organizations" in China. The IOC's authorization of Beijing to organize the 2008 Olympics is the psychological foundation stone for the recent and planned physical reconstruction and expansion of the city of Beijing . . . UNESCO's efforts in 2003 to engage the IOC in a discussion about the full implications of the 2008 Summer Games did not hit a responsive chord, or even elicit a promise

to look into the matter. With demolitions and relocations in central Beijing continuing, a stronger and more unified voice needs to be heard at the IOC.

Given the beautification campaigns that Olympic host cities have always undertook, and the IOC's difficulty in managing even its own affairs—think corrupt judges and imperfect drug testing—I was not surprised when Westendorff said his suggestions had not been enacted.

"Actually, I do believe that UNESCO made a real effort to push the agenda I suggested," he said. "As far as I can tell, the government never made a concrete contribution."

In 2005, UNESCO hosted a six-day open conference around the city titled "Beijing and Beijing: A Critical Dialogue." Its speakers included local and foreign preservationists, professors, artists, and real estate brokers—but no policy makers.

The Hand never sat for interviews or panel discussions. Beijing did not have a Haussmann, a person—or people—with names and faces and voices that said unabashedly, "This is what we're doing to the city, and here's why, and here's why you're going to appreciate it—if not now, then later."

Instead, these conferences were filled with people defining the problem, restating the problem, and agreeing that there was, in fact, a problem. A preservation activist named Ding Ai who lived at Nanchizi said, "If we continue to discuss urban preservation aloft in ivory towers, this is merely armchair strategizing. The chain of the real estate market is a vicious cycle, which will lead old Beijing to its death. If the existing chain cannot be broken, no armchair theorizing can save it from its fate."

My neighbors Mr. Han and his wife ran a shop on Langfang First Lane, one *hutong* over from the row of "old brand names" restaurants marked for destruction. His wife sold cigarettes, film, and batteries in the front of their narrow store, while Mr. Han fixed cell phones from a table at the back. "I drove a truck on a farm up in the northeast," he said, when I asked how he learned the trade. "There was nothing to do between routes, so one day I took apart my cell phone, then spent many nervous hours trying to get the thing back together. After I did, I took it apart again. I kept practicing. Now I can fix any kind."

When I stopped by to visit, his wife was usually sweeping the shop's front steps with a straw whisk broom. It was important to keep the entrance clean, she said. With all the foot traffic that passed by the store, a tidy appearance made you look trustworthy. Both of them always had washed hair, unblemished skin, and wore clean clothes. The couple worked in the shop together twelve hours a day, then came home to an even smaller room in our courtyard. Only a thin wall separated our spaces, and yet I never heard them argue or even raise their voices in annoyance to one another. The Widow adored them.

A year before, Mr. Han and his wife had left their six-year-old son with his grandparents and migrated from China's northeast. They had spent their life savings to open the store, which enjoyed a great location. Tourists and locals walked past from morning until night. The Hans were saving money and sending it home.

In spring 2006, the Hand painted 拆 on their shop. They had two weeks to leave.

Some of the "old brand names" restaurants tacked up signs that showed their new location. Chen's stewed intestine moved a couple hundred yards away, across the Coal Street road-widening project to Fetching the Lantern *hutong*. Feng's tripe moved a few yards across from its current location into a building that was not included in the lane's first phase of demolition.

By summer, it would open, along with the fried-dumplings restaurant and ten other famous eateries, in a food court built to appear old. It was located near Rear Lake, a touristy neighborhood far from Dazhalan.

Beijing tore down its constructed heritage and replaced it with look-alikes. The appearance lived on, if not the essence. After the city won its Olympics bid and began a flurry of face-lift designs, an official told the *Wall Street Journal*, "We think Las Vegas has special features. Fifty percent office buildings, twenty-five percent hotels and entertainment; good combination of life and leisure."

The capital did not need to copy or invent heritage like Vegas' themed casinos; the *hutong* and classic restaurants were wholly its own. But restoration was expensive, and, the Hand argued, foreign and domestic tourists were attracted to climate-controlled malls such as Oriental Plaza, not seedy lanes whose restaurants required patrons to line up outdoors, watch the free theater of daily life, and feel a sense of place—that they were some-where, not anywhere.

Mr. Han's landlord said he couldn't lease the shop for even an extra day or two past the eviction deadline. Mr. Han sold his glass display cases and shuttered the door. His wife carried her broom home. Because the Hans were renters, they received no compensation for being evicted.

The day they lost their jobs, I returned to giggles and singing in the courtyard. A dozen men squeezed around a table in Mr. Han's room, walled in by a ring of empty beer bottles. A pink-faced man put a new one in his mouth and yanked off the cap with his teeth.

Mr. Han said, "I'm celebrating because today, at least, I can say I have a job."

We clinked bottles. "Tomorrow?"

"When you're poor," Mr. Han said, "there is no tomorrow."

CHAPTER 10

SPRINGTIME

In April 2006, the postman pedaled his green bicycle down Red Bayberry and Bamboo Slanted Street. He walked into our courtyard and announced, "You've got mail!" The glossy flyer showed two young Chinese couples laden with goods, beneath the logo WAL-MART SUPERCENTER.

The American retailer's second Beijing store had opened in the *hutong* neighborhood that bordered Dazhalan's west. The new emporium faced the lane where Miss Zhu grew up. "My grandmother likes to shop at Wal-Mart," she said. "They have a moving ramp between floors, not an escalator, which many old people are afraid to use, because they've never been on one." Her grandmother also liked that, unlike in small stores on the lane, she did not have to bargain over prices. Shopping was no longer a series of exhausting arguments.

I wondered whether the store's opening portended a coming "expiration date," as the saying went, of her childhood home.

"Who can say?" Miss Zhu said as we walked through Wal-Mart's glass doors. "Do you know when the *hutong* will be razed?"

The store's entrance displayed posters of smiling employees, captioned DOING THE GOOD THINGS NEIGHBORS DO and HELPING TO MAKE A DIFFERENCE, RIGHT HERE AT HOME. The store's two levels were separated by three moving ramps, on which grandmothers balanced like surfers. The basement held electronics, clothes, and housewares. The top level was the neighborhood's largest grocery store. No more waiting for pineapple to come into season and appear on the flatbed tricycles trolling through the *hutong*. Now it could be enjoyed year-round, along with Granny Smith apples from Washington State and durian from Malaysia. The store sold dumplings, fresh seafood, sushi rolls, and chilled cans of Budweiser.

Wal-Mart also included a hair salon, an optometry center, and a bookshop that carried the *Evening News*. It was an entire *hutong*'s commerce housed under one roof, with central air and underground parking. As we pushed our way through the crowds to exit, a poster of smiling workers asserted WE LIVE HERE, TOO!

Wal-Mart did not sell the paper gold coins and "Bank of Heaven" currency on display outside in the lane. An itinerant saleswoman showed her wares there, on a blanket spread on the ground. Elderly shoppers clutching plastic Wal-Mart bags crowded around, sifting through paper cutouts of traditional clothing, fruits, and hot-pot braziers. The paper was for burning on Qingming, the holiday of "pure brightness," when people paid respects to the dead by sweeping tombs and sending necessities skyward to the departed via flame.

Miss Zhu wasn't buying. "That's just a superstition," she said. *Superstition* connoted backwardness, something only bumpkins and the uneducated believed. At school, teachers observed the holiday by instructing the students to make white paper flowers, then leading them to a park to hang them on a stela commemorating an early Communist Party martyr.

A cold, early-spring drizzle dissolved the kids' handiwork, but it was replaced by the next shift of students from another school, bearing the same tribute. That night, the sky cleared, and the *hutong* glowed from small piles of celestial currency, tended by the middle-aged and elderly. The Widow did not participate.

"Superstition?" I asked.

"I don't mourn anyone," she said.

"Your husband?"

"Ha!" she spat. "I don't even know if he's dead."

She walked out of my room and closed the door, leaving behind a cloud of smoke.

Ten dust storms enveloped Beijing in the spring of 2006. The worst dumped 330,000 tons of sand on the city. My home's windows and door were tucked under an eave, so the damage was minimal, but the noontime

sky looked like dusk, and you could see your footprints in the sand that
had been swept up from the Gobi Desert. It was Dust Bowl weather, the
kind that inspired Woody Guthrie to walk down the street of his Texas
town singing, "So Long, It's Been Good to Know Yuh." *This dusty old dust is
a-gettin' my home, and I got to be driftin' along.*

The *Evening News* showed pictures of pedestrians being blown over, and
smashed windows on a train caught in the gales. The weather page suggested readers "don't go outdoors, and drink a lot of water." In the box that
noted what activities the day's conditions favored, the paper advised, "Today it's not suitable to wash your car."

The municipal government promised that dust storms would not occur
during the Olympic Games and said the city's air quality was exacerbated
by loose soil at construction sites such as Fresh Fish Junction. After the
worst storm, the Chinese State Environmental Protection Agency reported that Beijing's air pollution index—gauging levels of sulfur dioxide,
nitrogen dioxide, and suspended particulates—had reached 500. A measurement of over 150 was considered dangerous enough that people
should remain indoors; 500 was so toxic the scale did not go any higher.
Beijing's air usually tasted noxious. Its daily average of suspended particulates was equivalent to the smoke of seventy cigarettes, double Los Angeles's figure.

The push for 2006's target of 238 "blue sky days" continued. The city
launched rocket shells and "cigarette-like sticks" containing silver iodide
into the sky. The effectiveness of these methods is debated, but soon after,
the heaviest rain of the season began, spattering my clothes with fat,
muddy droplets from above.

Outside of a few weeks in early summer and autumn, Beijing's weather is
unrelenting. After the dust storm, the annual kapok and catkin blizzard descended. Cottony tufts of willow and poplar seeds blanketed the city, ag-
gravating allergies. The *Evening News* reported that since 2001, only male
species of these trees had been planted, but one million female versions remained. They would be curbed from reproducing by injecting a growth in-
hibitor into their trunks.

As the government attempted to control nature, the school health officer came to the office to update the teachers' Reproductive Health Services card. The red booklet listed the birth date, race, and home address of

the teacher and her spouse. After a verbal consultation with her charge, the officer—she was also the school accountant—stamped one of two boxes that said PREGNANT or NOT PREGNANT.

The card contained instructions for which pill should be asked for at a pharmacy in case of suspected, and unwanted, conception. It also detailed a new law that said spouses who were both single children could have two kids, so long as the second child was born no sooner than four years after the first, and after the parents were age twenty-eight or older.

Miss Zhu qualified. She and her husband wanted a kid, and her grandparents craved their first grandchild. But she was living in less than ideal conditions in a shared courtyard. They owned an apartment in a southern suburb, but it was too far to commute to work, and she was under contract to the school. Changing jobs early meant paying an eight-thousand-yuan ($1,067) fee to the district, since it had subsidized her training. The same conditions applied to her husband. The health officer took Miss Zhu's card and pressed a red chop over NOT PREGNANT.

When I met the new English teacher, who had been transferred because her school was torn down to widen Coal Street, I expressed condolences.

"Why?" she said in contemptuous Chinese. "Isn't building a road a good thing?"

Miss Zhu whispered, "She's a Party member."

She also couldn't speak English very well. Mocky wasn't helping. The textbook focused on isolated vocabulary over complete sentences, asking the kids to touch a picture and say the word it described. The lessons didn't include any questions for students to answer or activities to complete. Every chapter included a section called "Let's Chant!" The new teacher opened her book and pointed at a picture of Mocky carrying a plate of greens. The chant went:

> We'll go and visit uncle,
> It's very, very far.
> We'll take some salad with us,
> And go there in a car.

The contents of the English textbooks were similar in design to the student's Chinese primers. Pre-reading questions were not provided, nor was there any guidance suggesting what strategies a child could use to read the material, or what information to extract. Like most Chinese texts, there was no index, and no ambiguity.

American textbooks often included—and teachers are trained to ask—six levels of questions, based on Bloom's Taxonomy, named for its creator, the education psychologist Benjamin Bloom. The difficulty of questions ascends from Knowledge (cues such as "tell, identify, list") to Comprehension ("contrast, extend, predict") to Application ("classify, solve, demonstrate") to Analysis ("analyze, connect, infer") to Synthesis ("rewrite, substitute, invent") and Evaluation ("convince, rank, assess").

The students' history text gave examples of non-Han Chinese leaders who strengthened the nation's unity by bringing Tibet peacefully into the fold during the Tang dynasty and repelling Mongolian invaders in the Qing. The single question at its end asked students to repeat, not analyze, the information: "Please say what you know about ancient and contemporary minority outstanding characters."

The reading textbook contained a chapter on cultural patrimony, explaining that China had thirty-one UNESCO-certified World Heritage sites. The single query after a section on the Great Wall asked, "Why do we say the Great Wall is a magnificent marvel of world history?" The passage about the terra-cotta warriors provided no question. End of chapter.

I took the English teachers to observe elementary classrooms at the International School of Beijing. All schools have their pluses and minuses, and the trip was meant to show different teaching methods, not promote them. But in the first class we watched, fifth-grade English-as-a-second-language, Coal Lane's teachers began scribbling notes as the students decoded a passage about oranges.

When the text began with a word the students didn't recognize, the teacher pointed to a poster that identified strategies to try before reaching for the dictionary, such as looking for parts of the word they knew, identifying prefixes and suffixes, and reading the entire sentence then making a guess based on context. The classroom wall held lists of learned vocabulary, and dozens of drafts of stories in sequence, showing progressive improvement.

Afterward, Miss Zhu said, "The teacher asked them so many questions—What is the main idea of the passage? Do you agree with the author? What might the next paragraph be about? She also made them speak in whole sentences, and the other students helped if the kid couldn't say it correctly."

Miss Zhu had been trained in a different approach. "The kids here are all so responsible," she said, watching students record their homework in a date book that parents had to sign each night. Lest the Potemkin classroom fool her into thinking that the international school's students were all pint-size Einsteins, I showed her a high school classroom that looked like a holding cell for offenders sentenced to adolescence. Among the inmates was my former student who had once turned in an essay that seriously argued the California Gold Rush had never occurred. (Miss Zhu frowned when I said it was wonderfully written, and earned an A.)

She saw enough she liked that when we returned to Coal Lane Elementary, she created a Word Wall of target vocabulary and posted simple classroom sentences she wanted kids to use such as "How do you say _____ in English?" She required students to begin keeping a running glossary of new words they learned—in sentences—and common syntax patterns. "I am only speaking English in class from now on," she told them. "And you need to answer in complete sentences. Don't be afraid to make mistakes. You have to make mistakes to learn."

The classroom did not have bookshelves, or any texts that students could read for fun. We visited Mr. Zhang's bookshop on the lane, but his tiny store did not have any English texts, aside from Mocky. I preferred to shop there, handing my money to a person I knew, and who knew me. But we were now left without a choice. We rode our bikes to Beijing Book Mansion.

Inside, a red cartoon dinosaur named Gogo bounced on a screen, singing in English, "Do you like doughnuts? Do you like burgers? Do you like sandwiches?"

"Yes, I do!" the subtitles prompted. But the audience missed their cue. Look at them ignoring Gogo: a seated bundle of green, hand-knit sweaters, black pigtails, and bowed heads. The kids pored over translations of Calvin and Hobbes, Japanese manga, and a Garfield English-Chinese dictionary, which contained no entry for lasagna, but one for tofu.

Book Mansion was overwhelming. China's largest bookstore occupied 172,000 square feet and carried 230,000 titles. Bestsellers included Chinese titles such as *I Was an American Police Officer*; *I'm Only Raising You for 18 Years*; *Chinese-Style Divorce*; and *Harvard Girl*, a memoir that revealed the parenting style that made her stand out from her Chinese classmates and gain acceptance to the school. That book was in its sixty-third printing.

Downstairs, *Monica's Story* lay between Bill and Hillary Clinton's autobiographies. A boxed set about Göring rubbed shoulders with *What's Behind Jewish Excellence?* Translated American titles ranged from the predictable—*The Da Vinci Code*, *The Atkins Diet*—to the surprising—Henry Rollins's *Get in the Van*, and a Woody Allen collection whose Chinese title promised *MENSA Whores*. An entire floor held English-learning materials. *Love English* taught pickup lines and pillow talk, including cultural hints such as " 'I'm bored' really means 'Do you want to have sex?' "

Outside, the view was pure New Beijing—bigger, flatter, wider, more. Cars and buses honked in stalled traffic, security guards told pedestrians to get off the grass at the neighboring square, and walking to the next store meant threading a treeless gauntlet of people shouting into cell phones, smoking cigarettes, and standing still in the sidewalk's center, where the crowd cursed and broke around them. Book Mansion was located near the former site of Democracy Wall, where in the late 1970s Beijing residents had posted demands for openness and reform. Now they could shop there.

Miss Zhu and I filled our basket with English picture dictionaries and storybooks to stock the classroom. Then we looked for texts for ourselves. On a shelf in the poetry section, the jacket photo of Wen Chu'an, the translator of Allen Ginsberg's *Howl*, showed a wan, fiftysomething man with a comb-over. Wen taught Beat Studies at Sichuan University. Once I called him to ask why, in an era of rampant consumerism, he translated Kerouac and Ginsberg.

"Because the impact of these beat editions on readers is great," he said. "Chinese young people can find something inspiring and encouraging in the beat lifestyle: the ardent love of freedom in action and speech, the firm stand against everything inhuman, the giving of priority to the spiritual life and denying the attitude that money-seeking is everything."

Each of his two Ginsberg titles had print runs of twenty thousand. *On the Road*, which was available for free online, sold an estimated thirty thousand. These figures were minuscule compared to sales of translated management guides like *The West Point Way of Leadership*.

"I believe there are pirate editions by unofficial private publishers," Mr. Wen continued. "So actually, the numbers are much more than that."

He didn't sound at all upset.

The school principal awarded the English teachers our own office. The janitor dusted off the Honors Room and moved in four desks. The trophy case remained. Gold-colored plaques lauded the school as a "Green Work Unit," a "Civilized Work Unit," and an "Outstanding Parents' Meeting Place."

On the day of parent-teacher conferences, the students arrived, picked up their desks, and carried them downstairs to the playground. The kids went home.

Their parents arrived and were directed to their child's desk. Rows of adults seated in tiny chairs faced the cement stage, where an Education Bureau official spoke into a microphone.

"According to a survey," she began, "seventy percent of Chinese parents blame school for their child's problems. In America, ninety-seven percent of parents say that the household, not school, is to blame."

When the teachers turned to me, I whispered that the statistic sounded made-up. They nodded conspiratorially. It was the tail end of dust-storm season, and the wind whipped the Chinese flag on the pole behind the official, sweeping her words into the bending fir trees. Some teachers began grading exercise books. I picked at the callus that came from writing with chalk. Other teachers closed their eyes, snapping to attention when the afternoon exercise music bleated from the loudspeakers. The secretary darted inside to turn it off. The official did not pause. Over the din, she shouted the challenges of raising a single child and the importance of respecting teachers. Parents, she said, should never, ever, ever, scapegoat a teacher for their child's shortcomings.

Miss Zhu leaned over and said, "Many parents took off work to come here today." The adults sat with bowed heads. Forty-five minutes later, at the speech's end, each picked up his or her child's desk and carried it to the classroom.

The parents again sat in rows. I saw my students, twenty-five years on. Miss Zhu and I explained what the kids were studying, praised their hard work, and urged parents to phone if they had any questions. Parents asked if they should spend money on expensive electronic learning aids, such as the kind advertised by a Canadian whose Chinese stage name was Da Shan. They were looking for a quick fix, something, anything, that would improve their child's English. The language would help them test into a better middle school, and college, and a better job, they said. The kids were nine and ten years old, and already the pressure was mounting.

A father with unruly hair and a snaggletooth waited for me in the hall with a concerned look. "My son tells me your elbow has been sore," he said. "That you can't write on the blackboard. You know, I'm an acupuncturist. We are on the same street. Come over and let me treat you."

Mr. Xie had lived in the shared courtyard his entire life. He commuted to his clinic, in an outlying district, but he kept a supply of fresh needles at home to treat his neighbors for free. "It's always interesting to find a new challenge," he said, examining the elbow. "I haven't felt something like this before." As he made quick jabs into my arm, his son pulled down texts from a wall of bookshelves and showed me his favorite historical novels by the popular writer Jin Yong. The school did not have a library, but Mr. Xie had accumulated an impressive heap of resources for his son. "He loves to read, and he loves to draw," Mr. Xie said. "I get him all the history books and classical Chinese texts I can find."

His wife stuffed me with oranges, tea, and then dinner. "I used to run a restaurant," she said. "When our son was born, I stopped to stay at home and raise him. It's not good for him to be alone, or to sit in a restaurant all day. He has to study."

My arm was numb, and as we waited for the needles to come out, Mr. Xie said that people assumed *hutong* dwellers were dumb. "Beijing people outside neighborhoods like this call us *chuanzi*." The old slang described a shiftless alley-dweller who idled the days away. "We're not dumb. We're just poor. That's not the same thing."

He opened a book that described the Source of Law Temple, situated in our district. "This is the Old City's temple with the longest history," he said. A discursive narrative followed, ending with "But the real reason to go there now is the lilacs are blossoming." And so they were. I sat and read in the temple's sunlit courtyard. My elbow no longer hurt when I held a book with that arm.

Like his son, Mr. Xie had attended Coal Lane Elementary. The school was founded in 1950 as a private institute named Solemn Honor Elementary, then was converted to a public school in 1956, named Religious Service Temple Elementary, due to its location on the *hutong* of the same name. The temple is now a mosque, and the *hutong*'s name was altered to Demonstrate Strength. The school moved again in 1957, when the name changed to West Canal Bank, as it was located on the water that ran outside the Imperial City wall. In 1974 the school was renamed Front Gate West Street Elementary and Middle School. The elementary school split off in 1981 and moved to Coal Lane.

It took months to assemble that paragraph, talking to people in the lanes like Mr. Xie. The principal didn't know the school's history; she was appointed by the Education Bureau and lived in another district. The school's office files didn't include a gazetteer. Historical texts told where famous people once lived in our neighborhood, but the story of homes, schools, and the life lived inside them went unrecorded.

Schools did not have mascots, and pride came from the top down. Following an Education Bureau directive, the principal and music teacher collaborated. After the parent conferences, each student was handed a freshly printed sheet of music for piano that said in Chinese:

COAL LANE ELEMENTARY SCHOOL ANTHEM

Fresh flowers blossom, green trees line up right
Coal Lane Elementary School bathes in sunlight.
Students read aloud together, and their song spreads far and near
Teachers and students are growing up together.
Diligent and civilized, healthy and driven

We are spreading our wings of idealism!
Honest and rule-bound, animated and united
We are eaglets spreading our wings, soaring free on the wind.
Chorus: Mother school, mother school, mother school's lessons
will be forever branded on our hearts.
The breeze blows, the national flag flutters
Coal Lane Elementary School bathes in the sunlight.
The gardener nurtures with love, the heartstrings of teachers and
students are tightly bound
Teachers and students are growing up together.
Motherland's builders, the people's hopes and dreams
We are spreading our wings of idealism.
The stars will point the way, the torches guide the voyage
We are eaglets spreading our wings, soaring free on the wind.
(Repeat chorus.)

The children sang the anthem with gusto, just as at the next playground assembly they belted out "Love Our China," which started:

Fifty-six stars, fifty-six flowers, it's all one family. Fifty-six races'
languages joyfully form one sentence: Love our China!
Chorus: Love our China, love our China, love our China, hey!

A drama troupe visited to teach the students how to "read aloud with expression." The lead performer was a strapping man who had the same half-dome hairline of Chairman Mao. He jutted out his chin and recited a poem whose climax was "Motherland! Motherland! My beloved motherland!" ·

I won a bet with Miss Zhu that in the next five minutes we would hear someone powerfully intone, "China has *five thousand* years of history."

The performers recited ancient poetry and played traditional instruments such as the stringed *pipa* and zither. The children stayed rapt, not budging when it began to drizzle. The PE teacher said, "I was afraid the students would think Ronald McDonald was more interesting."

That afternoon, when it was her turn to read the daily lunchtime story over the school loudspeaker, Little Liu—she of the eye patch and exclamation-point pigtail—made her voice sound like the midcareer per-formers'. Why did the police never age and officials always use the same ca-dence when giving speeches? More were being trained right behind them, beginning in elementary school.

In class, to everyone's delight, Little Liu read Mocky's dialogue dramati-cally. "I can *only* play in the *morning*," she said with a pained look. "I am *going*"—here she paused and stretched her hand to the horizon—"to visit Uncle *Booky* this afternoon." The students cheered.

At the end of April, the school presented a spongy yellow cake for my birthday, and the students sang the song in English and Chinese. The cake came with a yellow cardboard crown, which they jammed atop my head. Miss Zhu gave me a jar of Nescafé Gold instant coffee, and the kids pre-sented hand-drawn cards. When I blew out the candles, I didn't need to make a wish. I was thirty-four years old, and just happy to be here, while it all still was.

CHAPTER 11

A Brief History of 拆 Part Two:
The Rise and Fall of Imperial Beijing

O︎UTSIDE THE *HUTONG*, little remains of Beijing's earliest designs. The oldest extant structure stands in the southwest corner of the Old City. Built in 1083, the thirteen-story pagoda is shadowed by a factory smokestack that rises beside it. The pair of structures form a visual bracket of the city's past, as architectural forms transitioned from serving the palace to the proletariat. At its origin, however, Beijing was made for an emperor.

The pagoda was constructed during the city's first turn as an imperial capital. In AD 938, the northern Qidan people overran Youzhou, the military garrison located here. They made the town a secondary capital of their Liao (Boundless) dynasty. A palace sat at the center of a perimeter shielded by a thirty-foot wall, three miles long on each side. The name reverted to Yanjing, Capital of Swallows.

Another northern tribe, the Jurchen, conquered the city in 1153, re-naming it Zhongdu—Central Capital—the administrative center of the Jin (Golden) dynasty. After the new rulers evicted thirty thousand households from inside the city walls, many moved east, settling in the area of present Dazhalan. The city's walls were enlarged to a perimeter of thirty miles, punctured with twelve gates. The new emperor imprisoned a rival court in the temple that gave my neighborhood's Prolong Life Street its name. A captive there said his situation felt like "looking at the sky from the bottom of a well." Much of China's architectural heritage exists only in the mind, conjured by painted landscapes, or poetic descriptions. The temple was destroyed, but the saying is still used to describe seeing things with blinders on.

The Jurchen also proved shortsighted. They had invited Mongolian horsemen to assist them in advancing southward into China. After defeating those foes, the Mongolians turned on their hosts. Led by Genghis Khan, they conquered Zhongdu in 1215 "with glorious slaughter," the city falling to a barrage of flaming arrows. Every citizen was marked for death. When the siege was over, the capital's streets were slippery with melted flesh, and the landscape showed only vultures and ash.

In 1264, Genghis Khan's grandson Kublai Khan returned to the area and began construction of his capital. The Mongols' Yuan (Grandness) dynasty would become the largest land empire in history. Its dominions stretched north-south from present Moscow to Hanoi, and east-west from Seoul to outside Vienna. For the first time, the area of today's Beijing was the capital of all of China. The footprint of the khan's Dadu—Great Capital—forms much of the contemporary Old City.

To legitimize their rule in the eyes of their subjects, the Mongolians— even more than many Han Chinese emperors—adhered to an ancient book of Chinese city-planning codes set down in the *Record of Trades* (*kaogongji*) in the *Rites of the Zhou* (*zhou li*). The book specified a capital's layout, size, alignment, and functions. Everything had meaning. European cities grew organically as food production, transportation, and governance improved; a great city was one with a large population and economy. Chinese cites were planned from scratch as administrative centers; a great city was one with a high-ranking official. A capital did not primarily serve economic functions, but existed as a medium for the emperor to communicate with the universe through rites, balancing the harmony between the celestial and the earthly. The capital had to be fine-tuned and calibrated just so, allowing the Pole Star—the emperor— to remain fixed amidst the opposing and complementary forces of yin and yang.

Cities were laid out according to feng shui, omens determined by the earth's five elements. An ideal site was on level land near water, preferably slow-flowing, with many curves. The north should have mountains to block malicious winds and negative energy (yin), and the south should be open, as that was the direction of positive energy (yang). A central, south-oriented palace sat surrounded by a wall, outside of which would be another walled area holding connected, one-story housing. The symmetrical city wall had three gates on each side, leading to nine north-south and nine east-west trunk roads, with the north-south being the widest, allowing nine chariots to pass. The uniform roads ran in alignment with the cardinal directions. There were no open spaces or gathering places, as in Europe's great plazas and cathedrals. Markets operated outside the city wall to the inauspicious north.

The code invoked the Confucian principles of hierarchy and Taoist notions of balance. "Heaven and Earth are in perfect accord," it said, "where the four seasons come together, where the winds and rains gather, where the forces of yin and yang are harmonized."

Kublai Khan's Chinese planners situated his capital to the northeast of the destroyed Jurchen city, as it had better feng shui placed next to lakes they ordered dredged. The city's earthen wall was twenty-four miles square, but punctured by eleven gates, instead of the prescribed twelve. Planners subtracted one from the northern wall, so the palace would not be exposed to winds from that direction. The walls tapered as they rose and were whitewashed, to match the color of the Mongolians' tents, the robes they wore, and the horses they prized. Workers painted the city gates red, the color of gaiety.

No European capital compared to the Khan's. When Marco Polo arrived, he marveled at the palace, which "is the largest that was ever seen." He recorded that gilt and paintings of dragons and horsemen covered the interior walls and ceiling, "so that there is nothing to be seen anywhere but gold and pictures." The roof was colored scarlet, green, blue, and yellow, "so brilliantly varnished that it glitters like crystal and the sparkle of it can be seen from far away." The dining room seated six thousand men. The emperor's rear chambers held his treasure, and concubines.

Parkland stocked with stags, roebuck, and musk deer filled the space between the palace's inner and outer walls. Lapis lazuli covered the earth excavated to form a lake, and elephants dragged exotic trees from across the dominion to be planted there. During Lunar New Year's celebrations, five thousand elephants draped in silks paraded through the city, and one hundred thousand horses were presented as tribute.

There were too many houses to count, and a large population in the outskirts, including prostitutes. "They all live in the suburbs," Marco Polo reported, "and there are so many of them that no one could believe it. For I assure you that there are fully twenty thousand of them, all serving the needs of men for money."

The capital's streets were "so broad and straight that from the top of the wall above the one gate you can see along the whole length of the road to the gate opposite." Polo's description of the chessboard layout makes it seem the streets were uniform, though they actually varied from six horse paces across (a *hutong*), to twelve (a *huoxiang*, or side street), to twenty-four (an avenue). The *hutong* are to Beijing what the canals are to Venice, but the Venetian traveler didn't record the term.

Traces of the khan's capital can be seen around Beijing today. The Confucian Temple, Imperial College, White Pagoda Temple, and Altar to the God of Land and Grain are open to the public, while the Wanning Bridge carries traffic over the canal between the Drum Tower and Di'anmen intersection. Dongsi and Xisi avenues bracket the downtown. Restaurants and bars line the chain of lakes and north section of the Mongols' wall, part of a pleasant park with walking trails atop the earthen defense.

Dazhalan's lane of antique shops called Liulichang formerly held the kilns that fired ceramic roof tiles for palaces and temples. Connected to Red Bayberry and Bamboo Slanted Street and Coal Lane, it is one of four hundred *hutong* whose origin dates to the thirteenth century. One of the first written references to the word appears in a line of poetry from this era: "Fight one's way out of a bloody *hutong*." The term antedates *Beijing*, which wouldn't become the city's name until a century later.

In 1368, Chinese forces led by a former monk conquered the capital, driving the Mongolians out. The victor named his dynasty Ming (Brightness) and ruled from the southern city of Nanjing, on the Yangtze River. Fearing a return of the Mongols, he appointed a commander to fortify the former capital, done by building a new wall that shifted the city's grid five miles to the south, centered on the lakes. As it was no longer the imperial capital, the emperor renamed it Beiping, Northern Peace.

After he died, a Beiping-based nephew usurped the throne. Given his treacherous act, he opted to govern from the north. In 1403, he renamed himself Yongle, and the city Beijing—Northern Capital. The capital would not officially transfer from Nanjing until 1420. In the meantime, Yongle implemented secret designs to construct the world's grandest capital. At the time, England's Hampton Court had not been planned, a wooden palisade guarded Russia's Kremlin, and France's Versailles was a mere shooting lodge.

The Ming plan for Beijing used the foundations of the Mongols' capital, which had been based on ancient Chinese codes. The Grand Canal linked Beijing to the Yangtze, speeding the transport of material and men. Construction engaged more than three hundred thousand workers. The new city wall was thirty-five feet high and fifty-five feet wide at the bottom, tapering as it rose, and made with masonry instead of rammed earth. The wall was not a perfect square, as dictated by code, but had a dog-eared northwest corner to accommodate a small lake in its path. The city had nine gates, each guarded by twin defensive towers joined by a semicircular wall.

Planners enlarged the capital's grid from nine districts with 400 streets to thirty-six districts and 1,170 streets. Of these, 459 bore the name *hutong*. To suppress the defeated Mongols' "imperial air," Kublai Khan's former throne hall was razed and buried under the earth excavated to form a lake. At 230 feet, the resulting hill (today's Jingshan) would become the Old City's highest point. According to feng shui, the hill also shielded the palace from inauspicious northern winds.

The new palace contained 999.5 rooms, a number just below the one thousand rooms of heaven, which no man-made building could exceed. Its walls were not white, like the Mongolians', but a reddish purple. Beijing's polychromatic architecture reserved colors such as yellow for imperial roof tiles and green for temples. In Chinese cosmology, purple represented the Pole Star, which is how the emperor functioned, as a fixed medium that balanced the forces of the universe and the earth. In the Purple Forbidden City, as the palace was called in Chinese, his throne sat atop nine steps, symbolizing the nine layers of heaven. The emperor faced south, toward the positive energy that emanated from that direction.

In addition to its neatly planned interior, Beijing also featured a merchant quarter outside the Front Gate. Established by Yongle in 1403, it included stores, banks, hotels, teahouses, theaters, and brothels with male and female courtesans for hire. The streets of this Outer City had not been planned according to imperial codes and so were unique in their varying widths and diagonal courses. In 1422, the police complained that the many passageways allowed thieves to easily elude them at night. Yongle ordered fences—*zhalan*—erected at the *hutong* entrances, which were locked after dark. The lane named Fourth Veranda (Langfang Sitiao) had the biggest fence. Since "big" is *da* in Chinese, the name Dazhalan was born.

In 1603, an itinerant Jesuit from Italy named Matteo Ricci arrived, hoping for an audience with the emperor. He waited in vain for eight years. Before he died here, Ricci transliterated Chinese characters into the Roman alphabet for the first time. He called the city Pequim in Latin. In English, it was Peking.

The capital of the Ming dynasty was founded on treachery, and eventually it fell from betrayal. In 1644, the emperor dispatched a general to put down a rebellion being fomented by the Manchu, a people from China's northeast. When the general learned that a comrade had taken his favorite concubine, he permitted the enemy to stream through a Great Wall pass. The emperor hanged himself from a locust tree located outside the Forbidden City, which the Manchu overran.

Forgoing the tradition that a new dynasty razed all relics of the previous one, the founder of the Qing (Pure) dynasty retained Beijing's name, layout, and architecture. The new court enlarged the Forbidden City and added streets so the total increased to 2,077, of which 978 included *hutong* in their name. To foster relations with his Han Chinese subjects, the emperor ordered signs on buildings be posted in Chinese and Manchu script, prayers at rites read in both languages, and gate names altered to include the word *harmony* or *peace*, such as Tian'anmen—the Gate of Heavenly Peace.

Religious buildings were constructed to serve the city's diverse population, which reflected the empire's annexed domains. The Lama Temple catered to Mongols, mosques served migrants from western Xinjiang, and Tibet's Panchen Lama was given a palace beside the Forbidden City's west moat. Jesuit missionaries built a cathedral.

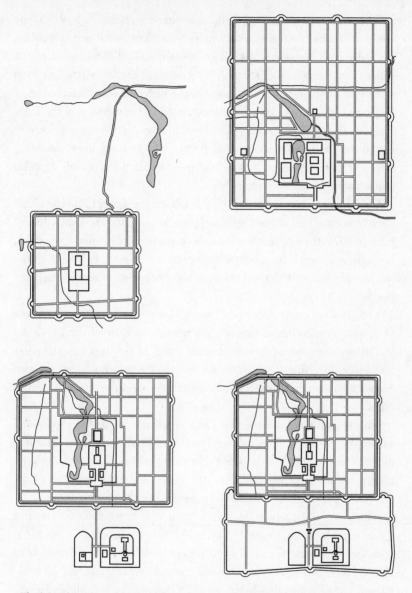

The shifting form of imperial Beijing. The Jin dynasty's capital (top left) was located southwest of the chain of lakes, whose feng shui properties were central to the Yuan dynasty capital (top right), shown at the same latitude. The Ming dynasty's capital (lower left) shifted south, and added the temples of Heaven and Agriculture to its outer limits. By the time the Qing dynasty (lower right) established its capital, the Old City's distinctive shape was in place, owing to a Ming project to build a second perimeter wall. Short of funds, only the bottom portion was completed.

The Manchu's inclusiveness did not extend to housing. In 1648, the emperor Shunzhi implemented Beijing's first compensated-eviction policy. He ordered all Han—save for select officials, and all monks—out of the Inner City, compensating for their lost courtyard homes by paying a fixed rate based on the number of rooms. For the next 250 years, the interior of Beijing was the domain of non-Chinese, restricted to members of the Eight Banners, the Manchu military-administrative system. One way to identify the former tenants of a courtyard home is to look for horse-mounting stones or coin-shaped hitches near its gate. Inside the city, only Manchu officials were permitted on horseback.

On English maps, the Inner City was labeled the Tartar City. The Outer City, or bottom half of the 凸-shaped plan, became known as the Chinese City. In 1671, the emperor Kangxi forbade theaters, teahouses, restaurants, brothels, and hotels from operating within the Inner City. Many moved just outside the wall to the Dazhalan and Fresh Fish Junction neighborhoods.

Kangxi was a contemporary of France's Louis XIV and Peter the Great of Russia. An avid outdoorsman, his reign, which began in 1654, was marked by the construction and beautification of Beijing's imperial parks and gardens, setting a precedent for his successors, who added the two Summer Palaces and developed the grounds around the chain of central lakes.

The Manchu architecture was Chinese in style, made from wood and susceptible to the weather, fire, and earthquakes. In 1679, a temblor leveled Beijing, killing four hundred thousand people. The Forbidden City caught fire the next year. Much of the imperial architecture seen in the city today is a reconstruction of older designs from before the disasters.

The Manchu dynasty, and its capital, rose to its apex under the emperor Qianlong, who reigned from 1736 to 1795, an era when the United Kingdom lost its American colonies and France was about to be taken over by Napoléon. Qianlong implemented a citywide renovation and commissioned its first comprehensive map, which recorded the outline of every building on every street.

Reprints of the map are sold in a heavy box covered in blue serge. Assembling its pieces—printed on five hundred sheets of paper—requires an

On this segment of the mid-eighteenth century Beijing map, Red Bayberry and Bamboo Slanted Street is the lowermost lane.

open space larger than my rooms or courtyard. When my living room filled with the squares detailing Dazhalan, the finished puzzle showed a *hutong* grid that matched, nearly identically, the contemporary satellite image snapped by Google Earth. In the mid-eighteenth century, on a similarly shaped Red Bayberry and Bamboo Slanted Street, a courtyard home stood where mine does today.

In the nineteenth century, Western powers pried Chinese cities open to trade. Beijing would not become an open port, like Tianjin or Shanghai, but was nonetheless sacked by Anglo-French forces in 1860 during the Second Opium War. While the armies did not remain in the capital, their incursion and the weakened Manchu court foreshadowed further destruction.

The capital had already fallen into disrepair, less than a century after Qianlong had created a masterpiece of urban design and refinement. "There is not a more squalid collection of houses in an Arab village or in the old City of Limerick," wrote a Western journalist in 1861. Describing the city's unpaved roads, he continued, "On a dry day their soft loam sends up a cloud of dust that puts your face and whiskers past the recognition of your most intimate friends. If it rains, you are knee-deep in mud." The roadbeds were high crowns bordered by sewage ditches filled with emptied bedpans and wastewater. Men drowned in the fetid black soup.

Returning after thirty years, an admiral commented in 1898 that Beijing was unchanged "except that it was thirty times dirtier, the smells thirty times more insufferable, and the roads thirty times the worse for wear." An American woman visiting in 1900 found the top of the city wall to be "a labyrinth of high weeds, whose sharp thorns played havoc with my pretty dress and best boots."

The Qing court's extravagant tastes emptied imperial coffers; funds earmarked for the navy were instead used to construct a marble pavilion shaped like a boat at the Summer Palace. In 1895, a traveler who had heard that the city wall's defensive towers held thousands of cannon discovered that the their mouths "are just black-and-white rings painted on boards, and the swindle—fortunately you do not know it then—is your whole visit to Peking in a nutshell. The place is a giant disappointment."

Soon, it would be in flames.

When the rebels that called themselves the Society of Righteous and Harmonious Fists besieged Beijing in June of 1900, their target wasn't the Forbidden City, but foreigners. Known as Boxers in English, the group had been defeated by imperial forces the year before. The regent Cixi, known as the Dowager Empress, had exiled or executed members of her court who had pressed for reforms. Now, she co-opted the Boxers to rid China of the foreigners she blamed for its woes. Paradoxically, the Boxers would hasten the end of imperial rule and the demise of old Beijing.

The Boxers believed themselves impervious to bullets and armed themselves with swords and lances. Press reports say they entered Beijing bearing torches, chanting, "Kill the foreign devils!" Trapped with foreigners behind the walls of church compounds and embassies were thousands of locals. Guilty by association, they bore the worst casualties. The *Times of*

London reported that on the streets outside the South Cathedral, "Awful sights were witnessed. Women and children hacked to pieces, men trussed like fowls, with noses and ears cut off and eyes gouged out."

On June 16, 1900, to punish the shop for doing business with foreigners, the rebels torched the Laodeji Western Medicine Shop in Dazhalan. The *Times of London* reported:

> Adjoining buildings took fire, the flames spread to the bookseller's street, and the most interesting street in China, filled with priceless scrolls, manuscripts, and printed books, was gutted from end to end. Fire licked up house after house, and soon the conflagration was the most disastrous ever known in China, reducing to ashes the richest part of Peking, the pearl and jewel shops, the silk and fur, the satin and embroidery stores, the great curio shops, the gold and silver shops, the melting houses, and nearly all that was of the highest value in the metropolis. Irreparable was the damage done.

The Front Gate, after the Boxer Rebellion.

Over four thousand stores and homes outside the Front Gate perished in the flames, including those on my *hutong*, and the adjoining lanes. The fire burned all day and all night, spreading to the Front Gate itself. "The great tiled roof with its upturned gables fell with a crash of falling worlds," said the *Times of London*, "while great volumes of smoke spread like a pall over the Imperial Palace foreboding the doom of the Imperial house. It was a sight never to be forgotten."

The bloodshed ended fifty-five days after it began when Western joint forces arrived in Beijing and routed the Boxers. The Dowager Empress and her court fled the Forbidden City. Disguised as peasants, they traveled by cart to central China. Beijing was at the mercy of the Eight Allied Army.

In August 1900, the joint Western forces divided the city into eight zones to be administered by a force from Austria, France, Germany, Great Britain, Italy, Japan, Russia, and the United States. The latter occupied Beijing's southwest corner near Dazhalan. The United States was simultaneously attempting to govern the spoils of its victory in the Spanish-American War. The situation in Cuba and Puerto Rico was stable, though American troops battled resistance forces in the Philippines.

At home, President McKinley faced a reelection campaign, under fire from anti-imperialists. The United States did not have any concessions in China and advocated an "open door" policy that disavowed colonies there in favor of a free market. Still, McKinley dispatched troops to protect American interests and speed the return of the Manchu court to stabilize the nation and prevent other nations from expanding their positions in China.

To head the American zone in Beijing, McKinley appointed Adna Chaffee, a bluff career soldier who had fought in the U.S. Civil War. As the first governor of Cuba after its American occupation, Chaffee had learned the importance of maintaining the public's goodwill and forbid his Beijing force of four thousand soldiers to loot or harass locals.

His infantry walked through a landscape of burned houses and pillaged shops. Dogs and pigs scavenged the ruins and corpses. The Americans lodged in the Temple of Agriculture and set up administrative headquarters in the Hunan guildhall, located on the southern edge of Dazhalan. They distributed six thousand small American flags, to identify buildings under their protection. A market reopened in September, providing jobs and filled by a good harvest. The Chinese Red Cross worked with the

Americans establishing public kitchens to feed the starving. The soldiers built latrines, so waste could be centrally collected, instead of tossed into ditches. They provided inoculations and started a campaign to eradicate public spitting.

Roads were graded, cleaned regularly, and lit at night—a first for Beijing. The Americans built a school for children. They closed gambling houses and opium dens, but kept the brothels open, providing medical checkups for prostitutes. Forces patrolled the streets at night to prevent looting. According to British and American journalists, the zone had stabilized to the point that houses emptied in the neighboring German-ruled quarter as people moved to the American side. The Germans themselves had to cross the boundary for food supplies. By October, the U.S. withdrew half its soldiers.

The American zone was unique among occupied areas for turning its courts over to the Chinese. Under order from Washington, D.C., Chaffee would not allow executions. In the spring of 1901, the *Times of London* reported, "Nine robbers arrested in the American section were beheaded yesterday. It is now stated that the execution was not due to General Chaffee's orders, but that the board of punishments received orders from the Chinese plenipotentiaries to carry out the Chinese law." Chaffee also refused to sanction the death penalty for a Boxer chief found guilty of killing fifty Chinese Christians. Again, the Chinese passed the sentence. Chaffee told Washington about reprisals of other occupying armies: "It is safe to say that where one real Boxer has been killed since the capture of Peking 50 harmless coolies or labourers on the farms, including not a few women and children, have been slain."

When rumors circulated about the Americans' departure, thirteen thousand of the zone's residents presented Chaffee with their signatures, written in calligraphy on slips of paper colored vermilion, rose, or yellow.

The accompanying petition began, "We, the people of the American section, consider ourselves fortunate to be protected under the glorious flag of the United States, a flag which has indeed secured us better protection than we ever had before. In addition to the commercial prosperity and individual privileges we have enjoyed since the arrival of the allied forces at Peking, we have been favored with many beneficial institutions, such as police station, charity house, Board of Health, vaccination, etc."

The Americans were given a silk umbrella, the traditional gift to a popular magistrate. An American officer told the *New York Times*, "I feel sure that this is the first time in the world's history that the invaded have begged the invaders to remain on their soil."

The courtesan Sai Jinhua, who worked in a Dazhalan brothel, counted among her lovers the German field marshal in command of the occupying forces. Fluent in German and English, Ms. Sai is said to have convinced him to implement a peace treaty that allowed the Dowager Empress and her court to return to Beijing. In May 1901, the Americans departed the capital, redeploying to Manila.

The West generally views the Boxer actions as a xenophobic killing spree, while Chinese historians honor it as a spontaneous proto-Communist uprising against a feudal regime and its appeasement of foreigners. The former headquarters of the American forces, the Hunan guildhall, now houses a Beijing opera museum and stage. The Americans' presence is not noted in the displays. The only evidence of their time in the city is found a short bike ride away, at the Temple of Agriculture, where the U.S. soldiers pitched camp. On a wall in one of its restored halls, an enlarged sepia photograph shows the Eight Allied Army generals. The men have trimmed mustaches, wear hats, and hold their spines as straight as the swords they lean upon. The caption's English translation identifies Chaffee as "commander-in-chief Joffee, American invading army."

The plaques do not mention the Boxers, noting only, "At the end of the Qing dynasty, the iron heels of foreign invaders treaded on China's territory. The Temple of Agriculture suffered serious calamity."

The temple's buildings were turned into a middle school in 1950, then converted to a public park in 1988. The New York–based World Monuments Fund, one of the groups currently at work in the Forbidden City, added the structure to its "watch list" of endangered architecture and contributed to its restoration. American Express sponsored the explanatory plaques.

Formerly, the emperor came to the temple's Hall of Jupiter to worship the God of Time. In Chinese, the word for *year* in terms of human life shares Jupiter's name. He was viewed as a wrathful deity, prayed to out of fear, rather than affection. The shrine to the God of Time now houses the city's Museum of Ancient Architecture. The forlorn exhibits show re-created models and photographs; the real artifacts have been destroyed.

The middle school was moved to a neighboring lot. Its baseball diamond borders the temple grounds. The field is a rarity in Beijing and was built to train future Olympians. A vermilion-colored wall runs along its first-base foul line, ivy veils the backstop, and a squad of ancient cypress trees patrols the outfield. Over its left-field wall, a display details the rites the emperor once performed here to appease the gods of the earth. After 2008, baseball will be dropped as an Olympic sport, so the field may be converted to a cricket pitch. I have only seen it occupied by magpies. Every time I walk the deserted temple grounds and see the field, I think: There is something very sad about an empty diamond.

CHAPTER 12

THE UNSLUMMING SLUM

MISS ZHU OFTEN told students, "Good news never exits the door, but bad news travels a thousand miles." While it was true that Beijing was being transformed in preparation for the Olympics, the Hand did more than raze *hutong*. "New Beijing," the official slogans promised, would host a "high-tech Olympics, humanitarian Olympics, and green Olympics."

"When people come from around the world to visit Beijing in 2008, they will find that the city looks like a beautiful garden with blue sky, clear water and vast areas of green land," a local newspaper reported in July 2001. "This is not feeding an illusion. Such imagination will come true because Beijing has decided to invest $12.2 billion before 2007 on environmental projects." Residents would be able to exercise outside in the morning without worries, the article said, because Beijing's air quality would reach international standards. Sandstorms would be eradicated by 2005.

Those predictions had not come to pass, though measures were attempted. The only aerial shot I had found of my neighborhood showed dozens of smokestacks sprouting from the *hutong* in 1978. Now they had been pulled down, and the seven hundred factories located in town would be relocated before the Olympics. The city converted public buses to environmentally friendly diesel and natural-gas engines.

The push to add green space across the city was evinced by new parks such as the long, leafy promenade inside the north Second Ring Road. Engineers mapped the capital's half million ancient trees and entered them into a digital database to be accessed by district governments when evaluating construction projects. When the demolition of a neighborhood retained 1,096 trees, the *Evening News* splashed the figure in a front-page headline. Now, the city's rubble was patterned with trees, outlining the destroyed *hutong*.

Beijing's urban plan at the time the games were awarded in 2001 had predicted a city population of fourteen million by 2040, a figure exceeded in 2003. The town's growth was often compared to that of a pancake, whose batter kept spreading in a concentric circle across the flat griddle of land. The plan said that Beijing would not have a million personal cars until 2010, a number also topped in 2003. By 2007, over three million vehicles clogged the streets, offsetting gains made to scrub the city's air. From our classroom's windows, the Western Hills infrequently appeared in the distance. Most days, the crescent of mountains ten miles north was cloaked in an eye-watering haze.

The media and schools lectured on the Olympic movement's history, the joy of cultural exchange, and the need to improve Beijing's "civic virtue." The bad traits to be eradicated included spitting, blocking subway riders from exiting the cars by pushing to board, delaying traffic by jaywalking, swearing constantly, never apologizing, never smiling, and treating foreigners better than people from the countryside. The *Evening News* ran a daily, illustrated feature that promoted good habits such as giving up a seat on public transport for an elderly or pregnant passenger. A front-page feature reminded readers that local slang for expressions such as "Excuse me" and "Sorry to trouble you" were actually part of the city's ancient culture. Also, the games would be smoke-free. Hospitals announced that they would, for the first time, ban the sale of cigarettes on their premises. A proposal to paint neighborhoods in one of the five Olympic ring colors was lambasted by the press and public, and withdrawn.

I woke one late-spring morning at six A.M. to the thuds of a sledgehammer. Wondering if the Hand had come calling, I opened my door to find four workers tearing up our cement courtyard. "They brought the new water meters," the Widow said.

To reduce residents' disputes over billing, the city was installing separate water and electric meters in shared courtyard homes. "Go back to bed," the Widow urged. "They said they would be finished by dark. Here, have these dumplings. I made too many." The workers respectfully set down their tools and passed the fragile bowl over the expanding hole, to my door. "I didn't know you would be coming this morning," the Widow apologized to the workers. "I'll make you all noodles for lunch."

The city announced any home could be wired for broadband Internet. At the Netcom Bureau, a helpful clerk said, "Of course we can install it in your courtyard! Unlimited access is one hundred and twenty yuan [$15] a month." On the machine that allowed customers to rate clerks' service, I rapidly tapped the key marked EXCELLENT as if it were the FIRE button on a video game. When the technician arrived the next day, he surveyed the *hutong*'s telephone pole and my rooms, tucked deep at the back of the courtyard. He ran the line over the sloping tiled rooftops and ended at my desk, sitting in a home that straddled the nineteenth and twenty-first centuries. We didn't have a toilet, but could get online.

Workmen refurbished our neighborhood's latrines with steel basins and flush pedals. While the older toilets were closed for repairs, I had to walk down Liulichang Antique Street to use a new-and-improved bathroom, with private stalls sealed by a locked door. After squatting, I raised my head to see, hanging at eye level:

Dong Da Hospital for Anus and Intestine Disease aimed its ad campaign at a captive audience. Another stall's door showed a cartoon elephant with a stethoscope pointing at a graphic checklist of worrisome symptoms. "Check yourself now!" it exhorted. The ads over the urinals showed an image of chicks hatching from eggs, and a poem titled "A Must-Read for Men":

> Too long a foreskin wrapped as bark
> The myriad forms and shapes
> Too much toil sets heaven askew
> Worms and germs upset and vex.

> Offensive odors swollen red
> Lengthy foreskin is the cause
> And if yours is so afflicted
> Dong Da Hospital has your fix.

> Korean-style circumcision
> Absent pain and absent wound
> Awkward maladies will vanish
> Lovers laugh and beam with bliss.

The hospital soon changed its English name to use the word *proctology*. The correction of translations was another Olympic campaign, aided by a South Carolinian named David Tool. Professor Tool had helped correct the English on more than fifty thousand signs in the capital and wasn't slowing down. He used American English, not British or Australian. So farewell to incorrect translations that conveyed truth, such as the highway exit sign that rendered the National Minorities theme park/human zoo as RACIST PARK. Farewell, too, to WC (toilet), *wicket* (ticket window), and *way out* (exit).

Correcting the English on menus and road signs and toning down nationalism on museum plaques didn't alter how residents understood and conceptualized the terms in Chinese. I liked seeing the language translated literally, which conveyed its economy and directness. Dazhalan shops retained their English translations, using *fake hair* instead of *toupee*, and *fake leg* for a prosthesis. *Vermicelli with shredded pork and peppers* remained *ants climbing trees*.

Dong Da Proctology Hospital's ode to circumcision still greeted me in unchanged Chinese. Outside in the *hutong*, the elderly bathroom attendant spat, and men with shirts rolled over their bellies swore at the television they had moved outside to watch the World Cup with a breakfast of beer. Beijing wanted its English to read and sound as standard as an airport announcement, as Mocky the monkey's. As Miss Zhu often said, when discussing recalcitrant students, "It's easy to alter rivers and mountains, but hard to change a person's nature."

In May, the spell called Grain Rains gave way to the Start of Summer. Cicadas droned unseen in the treetop framed by my windows. Mr. Han and his wife spent their days looking for a new storefront, as Soldier Liu searched for a stall in the neighborhood to open his family's knife-shaved-noodle restaurant. After moving away from Fresh Fish Junction, Old Zhang adjusted to his new shared courtyard home in the east of the Old City, meeting neighbors and marking space. He taught himself the difference between *alone* and *lonely* in English. He felt the latter.

They missed their old lives. Their homes and jobs gave them an accumulated rank in a fixed setting. How people regarded them raised their standing, and self-regard. That, not a building, is what formed their attachment to their former locales. Strip that away, and it took part of their selves along, too.

Outsiders often called *hutong* neighborhoods slums, but the neighborhood did not cause pathologies or problematic behavior. Our neighborhood was not a pit of despair; you heard laughter and lively talk and occasionally, tears and arguments, just like anywhere else. People treated each other with something I missed the minute I set foot outside the *hutong*: civility. Residents recognized each other, so there was no cursing or name-calling directed at anonymous faces, without repercussions. Cars could not blare the horn, cut you off, and motor away. In the lanes, belligerence was not a virtue, tolerance was. Strangers knew they were guests, not authorities.

I never saw drug sellers or passed-out drunks, as in the town's upscale-bar areas. People on Red Bayberry and Bamboo Slanted Street gambled at the mah-jongg parlors and drank. They also sat outside with their birds, played chess, tended potted plants and gardens flush with bean stalks and tomato vines, wiped their windows, repainted walls, swept their stoops, sold trash to Recycler Wang instead of tossing it on the street, and learned English to greet foreigners. I began teaching a weekly class at the Neighborhood Committee office, attended by retirees and shopkeepers who wanted to welcome Olympic visitors to the *hutong*, if it would still be standing in 2008.

When I moved in, Officer Li had been skeptical of the neighborhood's safety. In my first year, the area had one fire serious enough to appear in the pages of the *Evening News*. A man had placed a heating coil in a pot of water to boil it, went outside to the latrine, and came home to find flames billowing from his home. The coil's frayed cord had shorted. No one was injured, and the fire occurred not in a courtyard, but on the second story of a ramshackle concrete building built in the 1970s.

One murder was reported. A nationally known, sixty-three-year-old painter named Cai Yun was strangled in his studio off Liulichang Antique Street, a few hundred yards from my house. The incident also did not occur in a courtyard, but in a warren of walk-up apartments that had been built to improve the living conditions of former courtyard dwellers. The killers entered and left his studio undetected, the *Evening News* said. Within forty-eight hours, district police interviewed neighbors and passersby— eyes are always on a *hutong*—and tracked down three suspects in an outlying suburb. The lead suspect sold pancakes from a pushcart outside a new apartment compound. His shoes bore a stain of red oil paint matching that found in the artist's studio. He and his accomplices—one local and two migrants, the paper added—admitted their guilt. It was a robbery gone wrong.

One fire and one murder did not a slum make. Yet set in black type on an unspeaking white page, statistics told a different story, one of impending chaos. According to the *Investigation of Urban Corners in Beijing*, Dazhalan held so much commerce that oversight was impossible: 234 restaurants, 153 snack stalls, 121 hostels, 142 hair-salons-cum-massage-parlors, 22 book, audio, and video shops, and 28 internet cafés—packed among fifty-seven thousand residents in a half square mile.

That was one reason the city designated Dazhalan an "urban corner," its term for a slum. Other reasons included its population density, number of elderly and migrant residents, and decrepit housing, all of which exceeded levels in non-urban-corners.

In 1959, Herbert Gans wrote an article for the journal of the American Institute of Planners that described Boston's West End neighborhood as it was about to be destroyed in the name of renewal. It wasn't a slum, he said, but rather a "stable, low-rent area." If anything, it was "unslumming," as it continued to draw newcomers, had a dense social network, and displayed multiple uses: homes, inns, schools, and assorted businesses, instead of a single industry.

In her 1961 book, *The Death and Life of Great American Cities*, Jane Jacobs cited Gans's article and recycled the term *stable, low-rent area* to defend neighborhoods—such as Greenwich Village, where she lived—from bureaucrat planners, including Robert Moses, who was redrawing New York City at the time.

As parks commissioner and leader of the Triborough Bridge and Tunnel Authority, Moses was influenced by Le Corbusier's "City of To-morrow" ideas, which had never been implemented in France. Like Haussmann, Moses added open space to the city center, including Riverside and East River parks, and the Great Lawn and skating rink to Central Park. His tenure—lasting from the 1930s to 1960s—was also distinguished by forced evictions and obliterated neighborhoods cleared for expressways. He ordered bulldozers into Central Park at night to remove a playground and expand the Tavern on the Green parking lot. In Moses, Jacobs had the perfect villain to target her prose.

"Conventional planning approaches to slums and slum dwellers are thoroughly paternalistic," she wrote. "The trouble with paternalists is that they want to make impossibly profound changes, and they choose impossibly superficial means for doing so. To overcome slums, we must regard slum dwellers as people capable of understanding and acting upon their own self-interests, which they certainly are."

Razing such a neighborhood that was actually in recovery simply dispersed the problem, "adding its own tincture of extra hardship and disruption. Constructive and improving neighborhoods deserve encouragement rather than destruction."

An "unslumming slum" makes for better citizens, Jacobs argued. Lower-class people become middle-class and buy into the city's mores. Illiterates are transformed into the skilled and educated, and "greenhorns into competent citizens."

Substitute *migrant* for *greenhorn* and she could have been describing the way Dazhalan and Fresh Fish Junction transformed arrivals from outside the capital. As their prosperity rose, so did their acceptance and praise of the status quo. Their regional accents rounded to Mandarin, their dress and appearance changed, and they sent for family members to join them or hired more recent arrivals. It was the making of more Beijingers.

Regardless, a neighborhood such as ours was doomed, Jacobs wrote, "because no one is making a fortune out of it." Land values weren't being maximized, and to outsiders it looked chaotic and unsightly. "It is just providing a decent, animated place to live for people who are predominately of modest circumstances, and providing an unspectacular livelihood to the owners of many small enterprises. Thus the only people who object to destruction of an unslumming neighborhood . . . are those who have businesses there or who live there. If they try to explain to the uncomprehending experts that this is a good place and growing better, nobody pays attention. In every city, such protests are discounted as the howls of people of narrow vision standing in the way of progress and higher tax receipts."

The *hutong* served the same purposes as New York's sidewalks that Jacobs fought to preserve from Moses's drafting pencil. They provided safety, as multiple eyes of residents and business owners stayed focused on the street. They facilitated neighborhood contact, deepening the attachments people felt to one another and the area. They assimilated children through social rules between each other and adults, as opposed to allowing them to police themselves in unsupervised areas.

Kids want space in which to do that, however. Coal Lane Elementary locked its gates at four P.M., shutting students out of the cement yard and its basketball hoops. My students had never kicked a ball on a grass field. Instead, they played in the narrow lane, with adult eyes upon them. When I asked Miss Zhu what it was like being a teenager on her *hutong*, she considered for a moment and said, "My first kiss came in the back of a moving taxi." There, she had finally found privacy.

The Death and Life of Great American Cities advocated "fix the buildings, but leave the people." The book's Chinese translation was on sale at Book Mansion and other stores. It was not a threat. Beijing had no Haussmann, no Le Corbusier, no Moses, even. The Hand didn't have to listen to gadflies and theorists, or residents, at council meetings and public forums. The

Hand just erased and drew, erased and drew. When it was finished, it posted a notice that cleared the plan's final obstacle: people.

"We found a stall to work at," my neighbor Mr. Han said. "It's in the Muxiyuan market."

The cell phone market billed itself as Asia's largest. To enter was to step inside a labyrinth of low, glass cases holding cell phones and accessories. At first glance, each of the floors appeared to be selling the exact same thing. There were no uniformed personnel and no marked prices. The female vendors cracked sunflower seeds between their front teeth; the men played cards. A passing foreigner drew shouts of "Looka looka!" in English.

Stalls papered with lists of digits filled the ground floor. It was a market in numerology, buying and selling cell phone numbers. Despite the government's half-century effort to eradicate superstitions, many Chinese still put stock in auspicious numbers. The number four is pronounced *si*, which is a homonym for a character that means "death." Phone numbers containing fours are considered a bad omen, as are strings of digits that together portend doom, such as a one and nine (*yao jiu*), which could signify "need rescuing." Eight is the luckiest of numbers, something even the government could agree on, as it moved the start of the Olympics back two weeks (for more favorable weather, it said) to begin at 8:08:08 P.M. on 8/8/08. The stalls advertised eight-laden cell phone numbers for upwards of ten thousand yuan ($1,333). I asked a clerk how much she would pay for my number. It had no fours, but no eights or favorable pairings, either. She wasn't interested.

I found Mr. Han and his wife on the second floor, behind their counter. Their former shop had the advantages of constant pedestrian traffic of locals and tourists, plus a south-facing, sunny entrance and outdoor stoop that held a stool and the constant invitation to sweep away the dust. Lunch was a short walk away, at home.

Now Mr. Han and his wife endured at least an hour's commute to work, via a packed bus. They began leaving home at seven and returned haggard, at nine. Their new stall's display case held a dozen used phones. They couldn't sell smokes, film, or batteries here. Lunch came off a truck in white Styrofoam boxes: one serving of rice, one of an oily meat dish, five yuan (\$.67) each. An electric fan huffed behind them, but the air remained stifling.

"It's not as good as before," Mr. Han said. "The rent is a third of what we paid for the shop, but the profits are less than that. What else can we do? This is temporary. I'll keep looking for a storefront in our neighborhood."

Their counter was bordered by ones managed by fellow northeastern migrants, so at least, he said, everyone got along and looked out for each other.

I asked his wife if she missed their son. "You don't have to ask it," she said. "Of course. I always think of him. Look." She held up her cell phone display to show a picture of a smiling young boy with chubby cheeks who resembled her. "Ask the school what the rules are for enrolling a migrant next year. Maybe I could bring him here." She stared at her cell phone.

"Give him a call," I suggested.

She clucked her tongue. "It's too expensive. I talk to him here," she said, pointing at her head.

It was a gorgeous afternoon, the last days of the early June spell called Grain Buds, which, like autumn, shows Beijing at its most temperate. Peaches appeared in the lane's produce stalls, and cherries, too. I bought a bundle and carried them to Coal Lane Elementary.

"I have news for you," Miss Zhu said. "There is a rumor that our school will be demolished this summer. If the school expires," she said between bites, "then the neighborhood will expire, too."

She said posters had begun appearing in her grandparents' *hutong*, across from Wal-Mart. One said, WARMLY WELCOME THE OLYMPICS, BUILD A NEW BEIJING. DON'T LISTEN TO RUMORS, TRUST THE PARTY AND GOVERNMENT, said another. On the gray walls of nearby courtyard houses, the Hand had painted 拆.

"There's nothing to be done," Miss Zhu said. "We're just small potatoes. Teachers aren't good for anything. Time for class."

Little Liu handed me her blue exercise book. I opened it to read, *In 2008, Beijing Olympics games will be held in China. I am very happy. I take pride in being the descendant of Huangdi and Yandi.*

They were the mythical progenitors of the Han race. "What do they have to do with the Olympics?" I asked.

"Just keep reading!" she yelped, her exclamation-point ponytail stabbing the air.

We must protect the environment and take good care of public property. Welcome to 2008! One world, one dream.

"Very good, Little Liu."

"Is it perfect?" she said, using a new English word.

"It's not bad."

"I want a perfect!"

In the near distance, a flock of white birds dipped over the rooftops. "Hey, Little Liu, are those your father's birds?"

She strained to see with the one eye not covered by a patch. "I'm not sure. From far away, pigeons all look the same to me. I have to see them up close."

Little Liu lived in a neighboring *hutong* in a large courtyard I had seen photographed in books. The home once belonged to an opera singer. Now shared by four families, it was unique for an open central square, and the rooftop coop Little Liu's father built by erecting a frame of pipes and boards, then cementing the surface.

Little Liu and her parents lived in a single room, furnished with one bed, a vanity, and a stool. When I entered the first time, her mother bounded up from a nap and offered oranges and tea. "Her father and I moved here after the courtyards we grew up in were demolished," she said. "Little Liu was only one year old then.

"Do you know when this house will be razed?" she asked anxiously. "I hope it's not before she can take the middle school entrance exam."

Like those of all my students—save Cher's mother, who was a fashion designer—Little Liu's parents had never advanced past high school. Their efforts and hopes were directed at their daughter. The mother was unemployed. "I like that she comes home from school to me," she said. Little Liu's father had, after a year's search, found a job as a security guard at one of the souvenir shops bordering Tian'anmen Square.

"It's not bad," he said. "I work the night shift, which means I just sleep on a cot by the door. If I hear someone, I bang on the glass and go back to bed."

The idea of a security guard next to what had to be the world's highest concentration of surveillance made me smile. "The stuff in the shop isn't even worth that much," said Little Liu's father, laughing. "You know how Chinese are. It looks good if a guard is on duty. Shows power."

He was a stout man with a crew cut, rosy dumpling cheeks, and wire-rim glasses with thick lenses. "Little Liu got her eye troubles from me," he said. "Nothing else, I hope."

Little Liu clambered over the bed and held out her eyeglasses. We swapped pairs. The family blurred before me. "I can't see a thing!" Little Liu marveled in turn.

Only one item decorated the walls of their room. A wall calendar showed a profile of a pigeon. "That's a beauty," the father said, as if admiring a centerfold. He flipped to the next month, July. "So is this one." His wife grunted.

Little Liu and I followed him up a ladder welded to the frame of the house. The view showed sloping tiled rooftops in every direction. Little Liu bounded to the coop. Two birds sat in a small cage, isolated from the rest.

"That's the pigeon prison," she explained. "They were fighting. My dad got really mad."

"No, I didn't!" He laughed reflexively.

He unlocked a small hut, where he mixed the birds' feed of white and red sorghum, flaxseed, corn, and wheat. "The stuff they sell in packages is waste," he said. "The birds won't eat it. I buy my own grains and mix it myself. Pigeons fear diarrhea."

"I do, too." Little Liu giggled.

"Who likes it?" he asked. "Pigeons are the same as us. If they eat unclean food, they get the runs."

His unseen wife's voice echoed up from the courtyard. "I hate his birds! I can't hang the washing out, or they'll just crap all over it! He says it's just a hobby. Well, it's not a hobby! Chess is a hobby! Collecting coins is a hobby! This is, this is just disgusting!"

He smiled and continued, "Infection is also a problem. It's very easy for one bird to pass its sickness on to the next, even the common cold. When a pigeon gets a cold, I have to mix medicine and make it drink. That's not easy, I'll tell you."

The voice boomed from below, "He's going to give us all avian flu! That's your hobby for you!"

He made a what-can-I-do? look and shook his head. I admitted that I saw pigeons as rats with wings. Ducks were my favorite fowl, something I grew up around on lakes and marshes.

"*Ba!*" he said. "Ducks are good for roasting."

Raising pigeons was a *hutong* tradition. Tales from imperial times tell of pigeons being trained to fly to the emperor's granaries, swallow a few kernels, then flap home, where their keeper would induce them to regurgitate the stock. A few hundred sorties could yield enough rice for a meal. Like most hobbies, the practice was prohibited as a wasteful, bourgeois vice after the Communists took power. In 1956, the city rid itself of all crop-spoiling and disease-spreading vermin such as rats, mosquitoes, and birds. An editorial cartoon from a paper at the time shows children gleefully banging pots and waving red flags to prevent sparrows and other birds from landing. After exhausting themselves, they would plunge to Beijing's streets, dead.

Little Liu's father said that like most banned things in Beijing, the practice restored itself from the ground up, finally receiving government approval in the 1980s. His license was a piece of white paper with his photograph, sheathed in red plastic. The permit was stamped with a red chop that said BEIJING PIGEON RAISING ASSOCIATION.

Most of the city's *hutong* had at least one resident who tended a coop. Along with the cries of the newspaper vendor for the *Evening News* (*wan-BAO!*), the low, swooping sound made by whistles attached to the birds' pinion feathers signaled the end of the workday. At dusk, flocks flew swiftly in circles over the lanes.

I wondered if fears of avian flu had curtailed the pastime. "That's impossible," he said. "In fact, now that people have more money to spend, the hobby is becoming a sport."

He handed me a copy of a magazine titled *Sky Envoy*. The cover showed six pigeons in profile. "That one is named the Iron Lady," he said, fingering a bird that looked, to me, the same as the others. "Look at her eye. See how it's red with yellow in the center? That's really beautiful."

Sky Envoy's one hundred pages showed photo after photo of starting lines, race winners, and banquets. I counted a total of four women's faces in the magazine.

"It is a man's thing," he said. "But anyone can participate. Look." He flipped to an advertisement for the Beijing Europigeon Celebrity Auction. The page showed the faces of thirty Caucasian men. "Raising pigeons isn't just a *hutong* hobby, you see. There are carrier pigeon societies all over the world. Races, too. Can ducks race?"

He fished out flyers for upcoming competitions around Beijing. "The Victorious Flying Wings Challenge has a 1.42-million-yuan [$189,333] purse." The money would be doled out for finishers in speed and pathfinding races. I saw this is as legal way to indulge in gambling, albeit by feathered proxy. A top finisher could net sixty thousand yuan ($8,000). Another race had a purse five times that. "But the entry fee is twelve hundred yuan [$160] per bird," he said. "That's two months of my salary."

Champion stock sold for upward of thirty thousand yuan ($4,000). "All of my birds were gifts from friends, when they were small and couldn't fly. The mother of this one placed second out of one hundred and seventy in a race."

He stepped into the coop and carefully extracted the cooing animal. You could tell a good pigeon, he said, by its breast size, wing shape, and tail feathers. "Right now I'm just focusing on raising healthy birds," he said, stroking its breast. "I just like pigeons. When I wake, I come up here and see them. When I come home from work, I pay them a visit, too."

When released twice a day, the birds flew loops in formation. He didn't wave a red flag tied to a stalk of dried bamboo to lure other people's pigeons into his coop, though he knew of the Beijing sport in which prisoners of war were exchanged at peace summits. "If I take in a strange bird, it just proves he's a bad egg. I'm just increasing the risk of infection."

The birds came home when he placed bowls of feed on his platform's floor. "If one doesn't come back, then forget about it," he said. "It just proves it was a bad pigeon."

I ventured that, given his sixty birds, license, food-mixing skills, reading materials, and excitement when discussing pigeons, this was more than a hobby.

He laughed. "Look at me! My eyes are bad, I have to wear a brace on my back, I have no money. You say my daughter is smart, but I sure as hell am not. These pigeons are my sport, my school, my leisure, all in one. Fresh air, great space. Look at that view!"

From this height, we nearly had a bird's-eye perspective of the neighborhood. We followed the pigeons' wide circles above. The hobby's attraction revealed itself. Life in a *hutong* was cloistered, and the birds became an extension of their keeper, claiming an expanse of space in the sky.

"What will I do if our neighborhood is destroyed?" he repeated. "I don't know, look for a good school for Little Liu. Look for a place to rent. Look for a new job." He knew that pigeon keeping was a *hutong* hobby and banned from most new apartment complexes. "I'll tell you what. I would want to take these pigeons with me, that's for sure."

Their whistles hummed mournfully overhead. The pigeons whooshed in laps, free to fly anywhere, until, as always, they returned home.

The one correct classroom chalkboard said that 790 days remained until the Olympics. Class Two still held that 996 days remained, but time continued to flow around it. Beijing's late-June weather changes abruptly from tepid to saunalike as the spell named Minor Heat begins. The classrooms did not have air conditioners, only two wall-mounted electric fans. The jade-colored creeper vines crowded around the windows, and the kids loved to lean out and watch bees buzzing the leaves.

The rumor that the school would be destroyed over summer break never died. Teachers, then the principal, asked again whether I knew if it was true. The principal did have one announcement, however. Next year, the students would have the same teachers for Grade Five as they did for Grade Four. "It's not my idea, it's their decision. The Education Bureau sent a memo."

I agreed to return to teach the same students, if the school was still standing. The year had been unexpectedly rewarding, given past experiences. No one had asked me to sing a song. No one asked me to pose for a photograph. No one asked me to wear a school pin, sign an oath, or punch a clock. There were no mandatory meetings. Never having met a foreigner, let alone worked with or been taught by one, the school absorbed me by ignoring me. The kids loved to pull on my beard and arm hair, or to ask how I could possibly be left-handed, but after a few minutes, their yo-yos and *bao* ball proved more entertaining.

I arrived for the last day of school expecting a joyous morning watching kids clean out their desks, then saying good-bye as they skipped home unburdened by heavy backpacks. Instead, after their exams were finished and classrooms scrubbed, Miss Zhu said, "We all have to come to school next week, too."

"But the year is finished."

"The students have classes in the morning. We don't have to prepare lessons. They just listen to the loudspeaker."

For an hour each day, the announcement warned the kids not to sleep late, become lazy, litter, or touch garbage. The children turned their attention to the blackboard and copied their summer homework—pages of math, Chinese, science, and history exercises. Miss Zhu and I agreed that they should read a book for fun and find twenty new words for their personal dictionaries. For the next six weeks, neither of us wanted to correct anything.

Miss Zhu had homework, too. The Education Bureau required all of the district's English teachers to take a proficiency test at summer's end. "I have to memorize all of this," she said, lifting a phone-book-size text.

As the children stood in silent lines in the hallway, I congratulated them on graduating from Grade Four. I was proud, and looked forward to seeing them as fifth-graders. The other teachers stared. The children filed out with plump book bags knocking against the backs of their knees.

"It's summer!" I yelled to Miss Zhu in our office. "Let's go get beers at the lake."

She lifted her head off the desk. "Teachers have a meeting all afternoon."

That was the end of the school year at Coal Lane Elementary.

CHAPTER 13

SAVING THE OLD STREET

IN 2004, A group of the nation's leading intellectuals and preservationists wrote a letter to China's president and prime minister alerting them to the damage being done in Fresh Fish Junction and Dazhalan, which were on the list of Beijing's Twenty-five Historic Areas.

One of the letter's authors told a reporter that President Hu Jintao had written in its margins, "Take care to protect the old city and protect our cultural heritage. Everyone involved should give their support." Hu then ordered copies distributed to lower officials.

Yet the road-building and redevelopment projects that razed Fresh Fish Junction had been approved prior to the letter and petition. Now, in the summer of 2006, the destruction continued, rumors kept circulating, and life decisions were paralyzed by uncertainty. Mr. Han and his wife and Soldier Liu and his family became afraid to rent a shop or noodle restaurant in Dazhalan, since it could be razed months after building a customer base. Miss Zhu wasn't about to start a family without knowing the school's—and her job's—fate.

The group of intellectuals and preservationists again issued an appeal, this time to China's legislature, the National People's Congress. Their petition said that the destruction of Dazhalan would cause more harm to Beijing's heritage than the razing of the city wall.

One of the petition's signers was the novelist and painter Feng Jicai. He was unique in China for having undertaken a grassroots and very public, though mostly unsuccessful, Jane Jacobs–esque campaign to halt destruction in his hometown, a battle he recounted in the book *Saving the Old Street*. It is the only work of its kind in Chinese, much as his oral history of the Cultural Revolution, *Ten Years of Madness*, was distinguished by its frankness, as was *The Three-Inch Golden Lotus*, a novel about footbinding that he wrote during a term at the Iowa International Writing Program.

Feng lived in Tianjin, a port city fifty miles southeast of Beijing that was often chided as an ugly sibling—an Oakland to San Francisco, a St. Paul to Minneapolis. Unlike Beijing, in the nineteenth century the city had been carved into eight foreign concessions, each built in the style of its ruler. Because its port had forcibly been opened following the Opium Wars, a walk around pre-Communist Tianjin passed through a transplanted Belgium, then Russia, Italy, Austria, Japan, France, Britain, and Germany. Tianjin's "Chinese City" area contained tree-shaded neighborhoods of wooden homes and halls that had stood for six centuries. Just as Beijing razed its *hutong*, Tianjin pulled down its dilapidated native architecture, made from perishable materials. What remained of the city's foreign architecture—built from stone—was marked as protected.

Old Clothing Street ran through the heart of Tianjin's old quarter. It once sold materials used for funerals, but was redeveloped as a pedestrian mall that conjured Anywhere instead of a unique space. I strolled it alone. There were no crowds, no sidewalk vendors, only rows of shops selling Head & Shoulders shampoo and Three Smiles toothpaste. A tinny voice echoed. I followed the noise to find a bullhorn lying on the paving stones. The recording blared out a disembodied voice promising, "Insane reductions! Insane reductions! Insane reductions!"

Only one historic building remained. A guildhall built in 1917 for silk merchants that combined carved local brick with an upper pavilion fenced by Western-style wrought iron had been converted into a teahouse, empty when I entered. A waitress shrugged and said, "I wish Feng Jicai could have saved all the buildings, not just this one."

On the end of the street, a lipstick vendor said, "Of course we all wanted the entire street to be saved, but there was nothing to be done. It's none of our business, we can't interfere with government affairs. Even Feng

Jicai couldn't do it, and he really tried. Look at how ugly it is! Now it's not Chinese, it's not Western. It's just ugly."

"He really said that?" Feng asked me in his office, when we first met in 2003. "Well, he's right! It's such a shame. I tried," Feng said with a falling tone. "This was a very beautiful old street that had stood for six hundred years in the original city. There were over one hundred shops whose design reflected Tianjin's history, both a combination of Chinese and Western styles, elegant and lovely. Suddenly, one day the government announced it would be destroyed in twenty days. Everything is a race against time."

In his youth, Feng played basketball for the city team, and the sixty-one-year-old still looked hale enough to throw elbows on the court. With his mattress-size frame and an unkempt nest of black hair, he resembled a favorite, tolerant uncle and spoke in an earnest voice that matched what I had imagined from his stories. My favorite, *Winding Brook Way*, begins "For some reason I dislike neatly pruned trees. I prefer natural, gnarled trunks with sprawling branches and patchy, unkempt foliage. Take my hair for example. I hate to go to the barbershop and have it set and blow-dried so that it comes out looking like a shiny new black shoe."

A painter whose training was canceled by the Cultural Revolution, Feng estimated he wrote a million words during that time, concealing them in his bicycle rims or gluing them beneath the newsprint that papered his apartment walls. In the 1980s, he became one of China's first modern writers translated into English, rising to the fore of the "scar literature" movement, which described everyday life under Mao's political campaigns.

Feng's cramped office was in a redbrick walk-up apartment building. He decorated the room in Chinese Intellectual chic, with stacks of books teetering beside the tea table, relics and antique statues filling bookshelves, and his own ink-brush paintings and calligraphy hanging framed on the walls. A wooden plaque rescued from a razed temple read CROWN OF CULTURE.

"In the 1960s and '70s, we destroyed our culture angrily," he said. "In the 1980s to now, we're destroying our culture happily."

Feng unfolded his arms and gestured beyond the windowless walls. When plans for the destruction of Old Clothing Street were announced, "I stood on the street protesting after newspapers stopped printing my editorials," he said. "I used my own money to quickly organize volunteer photographers, outfitting them in red vests so everyone would know their work, and sent them out to snap every detail of the street: doorways, faces, lamps, street signs, carvings, every detail." The team also interviewed residents, recording their memories to caption the pictures.

"I want to let people know that these are not merely old houses," Feng told a local paper at the time. "They're vehicles for traditional culture. If you regard a city as having a spirit, you will respect it, safeguard it, and cherish it. If you regard it as only matter, you will use it excessively, transform it at will, and damage it without regret."

After two months of threats of destruction and reprieves for the street, Feng organized a fund-raising event at a local post office, signing a set of postcards depicting photographs of THE PRECIOUS REMAINS OF OLD CLOTHING STREET. When officials canceled one appearance, he moved to an outlying post office that hadn't yet heard of the ban. In two hours, he sold thirteen hundred sets of the cards.

Feng collected the street's photos and stories in a photo-album-size book titled *Remaining Flavor of the Old City*. He signed each copy, "This is our beloved city," and mailed it to every top municipal official.

"In the end," he said, "officials told me they would preserve six of the old buildings on the west side of the street. Then I left for France for two months, and they said, 'Feng is gone, so now we can proceed.'" When he returned, the street was leveled. Two thirds of a single building remained.

He hoped the narrative of his campaign—*Saving the Old Street*—would inspire preservationists in other cities to stand up and demand "protective transformation" of ancient neighborhoods instead of "developmental destruction."

I asked why the tension between old and new was manifested so brutally and finally in Chinese cities, with rapid clear-cutting the preferred method over selective thinning of buildings. "It's about time," Feng replied. "Speed. For the officials in charge, the faster they demolish old structures and begin new projects, the faster they can declare to those above them, 'Look what I've accomplished.' There are no paths to career advancement for 'Look what I saved,' because the focus is on economic development."

It was, he said, a conflict between current monetary profit over long-term cultural profit. Either choice carried a cost. Razing the neighborhood around Old Clothing Street cost less than 10 percent of the estimated price of restoration. The families moved out; the historic homes turned to rubble; the community vanished.

The process unfolded so rapidly, Feng continued, because of the lending market. "Developers front the costs for destruction of buildings, but they borrow this money from banks and have to move quickly to get projects completed so as to generate revenue to pay back their loans. The thinking goes, 'The faster the better.' " It also left residents and the increasingly bold media little time to organize resistance.

Feng was also outspoken on the need to protect Tianjin's colonial-era architecture, so unchanged that city streets often stood in for Shanghai in films set in the early-twentieth century. When I exited the train station in Tianjin the skyline looked more European than Chinese. Where were the Chinese buildings from the same era?

"Why has Tianjin preserved its legation buildings better than its Chinese ones from the same era?" Feng repeated with a slow chuckle. "The thinking goes that they are better looking, and more comfortable to live in. And who chooses to live in them? Officials." A broad smile creased his pillowy face. "Maybe what we should do is require officials to live in buildings we want to save."

In 2003, Feng turned his attention away from cities and to the countryside. He launched a decade-long project called "Saving Chinese Folk Cultural Heritage." It aimed to catalog village-level art, songs, legends, dress, and ways before they died off with their practitioners. Central to the project was enlisting school-age volunteers to do the recording, so they would learn the value of their local culture and differentiate it from the "modern and advanced" cities and products they saw on television, which, Feng said, "exaggerates the attraction of new products as a substitute for old things." It was a boundless cycle, with ever-newer things being produced and pitched through advertising.

Chinese had experienced a hard life until now, Feng said, and consumption—be it the latest cell phone or a new car—was a way to maintain face. He hoped his initiative would teach children that "the charm of a culture is its individuality. The boredom of a culture is similarity."

He authored a handbook for distribution to village schools that included a sample ethnography and survey forms to be returned to his office for collection into an encyclopedia.

"The government is good at protecting relics like the Great Wall or the Forbidden City," he said, "but we have to exercise our rights to protect our culture and what makes us unique. China is really diverse. In many places still, within a few kilometers, you can't see any uniform style of culture. Look, we're talking about a land with five thousand years of history, and only recently has it been transformed into a mutual culture. Now, globalization blurs the differences among human cultures more and more. In China, this process is being sped up due to entry into the World Trade Organization, and now the Olympics. There is pressure from above to reemphasize 'Chineseness,' but what is that? It's not relics, but our folk culture.

"Cities and villages want investment, so they turn to tourism. But often this form of development is haphazard instead of careful, and the result is a further vulgarization of Chinese culture. China wants UNESCO World Heritage sites the same way actors want Oscars, for the recognition. Often they don't do enough to protect the area.

"It's all disappearing so fast. Development in the West and China is not the same. In the West, it happened step-by-step, but not here, it's been a sudden opening. People want to change their lives now, they want things and convenience, and now they can afford to buy them. That's good. What is inexcusable is thoughtless destruction of architecture, communities overrun with tourists, and city planning by people who don't recognize beauty.

"Every minute, folk culture is being lost. In Tibet, traditional architecture is being pulled down to build concrete buildings. In Guizhou province, there are thirty-three ethnicities, but three hundred thousand people have migrated east to the coast for jobs. When they return, they laugh at their own culture, which they see as backward. They bring back technology and different customs. Last year in Gansu province we met a woman over eighty years old. She sang beautifully, she knew a ton of songs. We planned to go back to record her. But within a half year, she died. When we returned, her daughter told us that on her deathbed, she kept asking, 'Why aren't they here yet? When are they coming?' "

"History can not be brought back or restored," said Zhang Jinqi, a writer who lived near my house in Dazhalan. "History is always developing. A church next to a courtyard home, next to a 1920s brick building, next to a 1960s workers' dormitory, tells a story about the changes that happened on that street. Demolishing 'nonconforming' buildings and replacing them with 'fake antiques' destroys not just the buildings, but the entire story of that part of Beijing. Look, I can't just build a home according to the methods used to construct Lincoln's house, then say it's Lincoln's former residence. That's absurd."

I met Zhang wandering my lane with his camera, shooting every doorway, wall, street sign, and person he encountered. He entered the results on his Web site—memoryofchina.org—which posted submissions from photographers and essayists across the country, documenting urban and village architecture.

"In 2003, I wasn't working, and so started taking pictures of my *hutong*," he said. "I was really taken by how our neighborhood was always outside the imperial building codes. Because there were no strict specifications on design, the merchants and artists that lived here were free to express their wealth or creativity through eclectic architecture. I wanted to share the pictures with others, so I started the Web site."

Zhang was forty-three years old, and strangely for a Chinese man, he looked every day of it. He walked with a limp, caused by a steel rod that had been inserted in his leg after an accident. His entire body tilted right as a result—even the part in his frizzy black hair was off-center. When speaking to him, I involuntarily tilted my head, too. He looked frail, with bony arms and tobacco-stained teeth. His eyes were made sadder by the circles beneath them. All of this belied his extroverted, energetic personality.

He, his girlfriend, and their cat lived in two rooms of a courtyard, with no bathroom. He was self-employed, picking up money here and there from talks and articles. His first book was published in 2005, named *A Carnal History of the Eight Big Lanes*, a chronicle of Dazhalan's brothels and opium dens. Authors seldom make a living from writing in China. Agents are few, advances small, and accounting of sales for royalties is murky. Zhang didn't even own any copies of his book.

When I praised it, he shook his head. "The afterword is not bad. The version of my book that was published . . . changes were made," he said carefully. "Beijing's red-light-district history is not one that is 'officially' remembered, except for its eradication. I'm not saying that we should always remember ugly incidents, but we have to respect history."

One angle Zhang took when advocating the preservation of the neighborhood's architecture was that it retained evidence of the city's occupation from 1937 to 1945 by "Jap devils"—Zhang used the common Chinese term throughout the text. "The disappearance of relics from that time is happening across China," he said, "which has a serious effect on our understanding of history."

In the text, he explains, "I wanted to record and evince the loss of old Beijing . . . I also wrote this book because when looking for old pictures of Beijing, I discovered there are two kinds. One category of photographs are those taken by foreigners, which give the best account of old traditions. The other category is that taken by Chinese and foreigners of the Forbidden City, palaces and gardens. Seeing Beijing common people's everyday life through a Chinese person's eyes is extremely rare."

Still, Zhang groused that to get a book about a *hutong* published, one had to focus on former residences of famous people and old stories. There were no ethnographies or memoirs of life in a *hutong*, circa now. Publishers felt there was no market for that, he said. As a result, local booksellers' shelves displayed dozens of "Old Beijing" maps, tales, and photography texts that archived the past, giving the impression that the lanes had long been extinguished.

"The *hutong* should be celebrated," he said, "because of the person-to-person network of friends, neighbors, colleagues, classmates, and relatives, all interacting in this setting's stores, hostels, bathhouses, schools, and markets."

Zhang's family was from a village in neighboring Hebei province and rented his current courtyard home in 1947. He shuttled between the two locales from age twelve until moving permanently to Beijing when he was twenty. "The village is like the *hutong*," he said. "Everyone knows each other. If you have a wedding, everybody will come." He studied traditional medicine, but never went to university, and counted himself both an "old Beijinger" and a countrysider. His perspective reminded me of having "one foot in, one foot out," which the Tianjin writer and preservationist Feng Ji-cai said was necessary to understand a place—"If both feet are out, you might be gossiping about matters. If both feet are in, you might not be able to see the whole picture. One must have a sense of distance when talking about a place."

"I really admire Feng Jicai," Zhang said. "I've been going to Tianjin the last couple of months because there is a team of eleven preservationists there that contribute to the Web site. I grabbed Feng's books on trying to preserve the old street. It's a good model, showing the government and de-velopers exactly what's there, because you can persuade them not to de-molish it. We've been cataloging buildings accordingly, noting when they were built, by whom, who once worked there, and the current condition."

He likened this work to constructing a pharmacy. Once a building be-came "sick" and slated for destruction, a detailed survey of the structure's history could be "prescribed" to government officials. Zhang believed that no one in power would knowingly order the razing of heritage. "They are logical people who aren't trying to harm anyone," he said. He cited a law enacted in 2006 that forbade developers from using "terror tactics," such as shutting off heat, water, and electricity to force holdouts from their homes.

Yet most city officials were trained as civil engineers and appointed from outside the area they governed. During Beijing's Olympic bid, the Party-appointed mayor was from Jiangsu province and had majored at university in iron smelting. The government prioritized construction and modernization.

"Cadres just need proper information," Zhang argued. "They need to be reminded that when it comes to destroying our architectural heritage, a mistake can not be remedied."

That presumed one had access to decision makers. Zhang countered that every preservation success story he had heard in China resulted not from the courts, but the lobbying of cultural-heritage experts and profes-sors who bent the ear of officials, persuading them to intervene. It was the old Zhou Enlai End Run, a play credited to Chairman Mao's prime minis-ter, who, if official histories are correct, spent the decade during the Cultural Revolution making phone calls demanding the protection of temples, gardens, Buddhist cave sculptures, palaces, and select individuals.

Like Feng Jicai, Zhang felt he was finished writing books; the cataloging of heritage took all his time. "My first book was about the Eight Big *hutong*," he said, holding his hands parallel, with the palms facing in, before his stomach. "I just finished another book on Dazhalan's history, which covers one hundred and fourteen *hutong*." His hands moved farther apart, framing his body. "That just got me interested in the rest of Beijing's remaining neighborhoods." The space between his hands grew wider. "Then I wanted to know more about all of China." Now his arms were fully outstretched. "Next, I need to learn about all of the world's other cities and how they protect heritage!" His arms windmilled in the ashy air. He was reading the translation of Jane Jacobs's *The Death and Life of Great American Cities*.

Every Saturday morning, Zhang and a group of photographers chose a *hutong* and walked its length, recording and entering the buildings to interview residents. One excursion to Brick Pagoda Lane, in the Old City's west, took us past an example of cadre housing from the height of the Communist era. The five-story, pink-painted brick apartment buildings had peaked roofs and were centered on a large fir-shaded courtyard.

"We're going to the old houses," Zhang said. "This *hutong* dates from the Yuan dynasty. It's one of Beijing's original streets."

"You snob!" snapped the group's only female member. "This complex isn't part of Beijing history, too? *Hng!* When all the courtyard homes are gone, you'll have to protect this stuff that was built in the fifties!"

Zhang bowed his head rapidly. "I'm sorry, forgive me, forgive me." He laughed. "This building also has value." After we ascended the stairwell, he pointed excitedly. "Look at that!"

Blocked from sight at street level by a fresh brick wall, but visible from this height, was a moonscape where courtyard homes used to stand. Zhang aimed his camera. He wished aloud that he had taken a photo of the neighborhood before its destruction.

Farther on, he ducked through a nondescript gate into a former carriageway that led to a near-intact two-story home. As Zhang photographed the house and an assistant recorded audio, the grandmother living there explained that it was built in the early twentieth century as the residence of a Protestant minister.

It was an interesting find, and a good story, one that illustrated not only the home's provenance but also that of the nearby Gangwashi Church, which dated from an era when missionary activity reached its zenith and families such as Pearl Buck's settled across China. But was the story true?

Written proof of a Beijing building's history wasn't easy to find. In this case, Zhang could search for the origin of the church's founders and follow the trail from there, hoping it would lead to records in a U.S. church's archives. Zhang's research scope was so large, and his means so limited, that checking the accuracy of every tale he recorded wasn't feasible.

Locating records on a common courtyard home was an equal challenge. Given what he knew of the neighborhood and street's history, along with its exterior decoration, Zhang estimated that my home was built between 1910 and 1920. My landlord had no idea. The Widow guessed it was constructed a bit earlier, before the last emperor fell. No one, however, knew anything about its original residents.

People also disagreed on its address. In 1965, Beijing renumbered *hutong* homes to reflect their actual conditions, giving the divided portions of a larger dwelling a separate address. The small courtyard I shared with the Widow and others was labeled with its own numbered red plate, as were the former mansion's three other small courtyard spaces. Originally, however, the entire structure held one family and thus had one number. The rectification of addresses left traces of the original numbers on the blue plates still visible on the front of some homes. They were illegible on my street, however. That meant that the only resource was the memory of people who had lived there before 1965. Finding a consensus was difficult. After taking a day to think about it, the Widow averred that the house had been No. 76. Then Aunty Yang next door said the Widow was senile; the place used to be No. 72.

I related this to the Widow. "What does she know?" she protested. "I moved to Dazhalan in 1947. She wasn't here until 1958. *Ba!*"

I triangulated by asking old men across the street what their house numbers used to be. They agreed on a figure. I walked from the start of the lane, where I knew the first house number had begun, and counted doorways, assuming structures built after 1965 stood on the site of a former single home. I called my landlord again. He thought about it. I asked Aunty Yang if she had remembered a different address. I tested the Widow by asking her the dates of famous events she had lived through, relatives' birthdates, and the sum of a complicated math problem. At that, she said, "Disgusting!" and waved me away. "My memory is excellent!" she crowed. "I forget nothing."

After all the data was sorted, the Widow seemed correct. I took her word and dialed the historian Zhang. "The house used to be number seventy-six. I'm ready to go when you are."

Beijing's Municipal Archives requires a letter of introduction from a work unit or scholarly institute to enter. Zhang was my letter. "I know the director," he said as we got in a cab. "We're buddies."

I expected we would step inside a Forbidden City warehouse filled with wooden crates and musty scrolls, but the archives are housed in a nondescript white-tiled high-rise in the city's outlying southeast district. The ground floor was open to the public; Zhang didn't know what the other levels held. "Secrets," he guessed with a smile.

The open floor plan held rows of desks with reading lamps, live potted plants, and a single row of bookshelves. There weren't any computers. "How do we search for documents related to my house?"

Zhang nodded to the shelves labeled PRE-1949. "We pull out records catalogs and scan for your address."

We faced shelves holding two hundred ledgers. Each of their two hundred pages showed twenty entries scribbled in thick, complicated characters, the writing system replaced with simplified characters by the Communists in the 1950s to raise literacy. I had been taught to read simplified characters. My street's name had a few characters I recognized in either system, and so I took a bundle of ledgers to a table and squinted at their pages.

Two hours later, the archivist on staff quietly approached. He had white hair and wore a green cardigan sweater and glasses on a string around his neck. "Sorry to trouble you," he said. "Would you like to order a box lunch? We get food delivered for researchers so you don't have to stop."

"I want to stop."

"What are you looking for?"

"A title abstract, or even tax records for my house."

"Oh, you should be looking on that shelf over there."

Zhang found the correct ledger, and minutes later the archivist handed me a book the size of a large atlas, but as light as a weekday newspaper. The four hundred onionskin pages were inked black with delicate calligraphy.

"This is the oldest record we have," the archivist said. "It's the registration ledger from 1937. The Japs invaded after that, and we don't have any other documents."

The pages crinkled at every turn. I read the entries from No. 1 Red Bayberry and Bamboo Slanted Street. The excitement rose after every turned page, until I reached the entry for my house.

In May 1937, it was home to a family of five. Yu Dongpo, the father, was fifty-one. He was born in Yellow County, Shandong province. He was literate. He owned no firearms and was not a soldier. He was not disabled or afflicted. He believed in Buddhism. He rented the home from an unlisted landlord. His profession was selling "mixed goods."

Zhang whispered excitedly, "Yes! The front room of your house was a storefront. He sold his wares there!"

Mr. Yu's wife, Gao Shi, was forty-two, couldn't read, and came from the same county as her husband. That's all the register said about her. Their two sons were aged five and thirteen. The older one, named Hoping for Great Waves, was literate. Their eleven-year-old daughter, Native Morning Glow, was not.

"She didn't go to school," Zhang guessed. "She probably did housework or helped in the shop. The parents must have lived in the other front courtyard, and the kids in the back one. Maybe they had servants that lodged where your room is, since it's the one with the worst sunlight exposure."

Zhang returned to his research, and I sat at the table, turning the pages, strolling through the *hutong* seven decades before. It looked the same. Most addresses showed nine, twelve, twenty, even thirty-four people from different families living in a mixed courtyard. Residents worked an assortment of jobs, from the menial (water carrier, firewood seller) to the skilled tradesman (carpenter, barber, silversmith) to the white-collar (banker, teacher) and artisan (jade carver, calligrapher). There were Buddhists, Muslims, a Protestant, and atheists. Few were native to the city, the majority having migrated from Hebei, Shanxi, and Shandong provinces.

There was even a widow. At age thirty-four, she had nineteen- and sixteen-year-old sons. Her husband had been a soldier, though where he was lost, the page didn't say.

Like today, most of the lane's residents were tenants. The register repeatedly showed two landlord's names, one of which was Apricot Tree Nie.

A name like that was sure to have stuck in the Widow's memory, I
thought. But when I stepped outside of the archives and called to ask if she
had heard of Apricot Tree, she considered for a moment and said no. "He
owned a lot of the homes on our street," I urged her. "Maybe he was arrested or even killed in the 1950s?" No, she said, she would remember that.

"A lot of those fat landlords scurried when the Communists liberated
the city," she said. Mr. Yu and his family were gone when she moved in, as
well. Where to? As with so much of the neighborhood's history, no one
could say.

The archivist looked for tax records for my courtyard's storefront, but
only found an intricate hand-drawn rendering of every store and tea shop
on Liulichang Antique Street. The documents were priceless to me, I said.
He offered to photocopy them. I had never before met a civil servant as patient or polite.

The archivist began to walk to the machine, then stopped and turned,
as if remembering a restriction. "I'm sorry," he said. My heart sank, and I
regretted not tearing out the ledger page and absconding with it when I
had the chance. "I'm going to have to ask you to pay for the copier paper,"
he said, looking genuinely embarrassed. "The total is one yuan."

CHAPTER 14

A SUMMER OF RECYCLING

A T RED BAYBERRY and Bamboo Slanted Street's Neighborhood Committee office, the Elderly Services secretary handed me a Party organ called *Labor Afternoon News*. My photo appeared under the headline A WESTERN TEACHER HAS ARRIVED IN DAZHALAN. "This straw-haired, big-bearded foreigner is the district's English teacher, from America," the paper reported. "Slowly, the district's residents can't help but know that this Chinese-culture-lover has a Chinese name called Heroic Eastern Plumblossom, but neighbors call him Little Plumblossom for short."

The story heralded Little Plumblossom's spirit of volunteerism, and noted the praise of the fifty retired elderly residents who attended his free weekly language class. One pupil said, "This young foreigner is really humorous, studying English with him never makes me tired!"

The students were nothing if not enthusiastic. For two hours each week, they hunched over their textbooks and repeated sentences I read aloud in English. It was their first experience with the language; some had studied Russian when it was politically in fashion. Now, heeding the call of "Welcome the Olympics, Speak Civilized, and Usher in a New Wind," they said things like "My name is Wang Ping, welcome to our neighborhood!"

The woman sitting beside her said, "My name is Wang Ping, welcome to our neighborhood!"

"Wait," I said in Chinese. "Her name is Wang Ping. You should say your own name."

"I don't like my name." She frowned. "So I'll just use Wang Ping. *Ping* means 'peace.' That's a good name, don't you think, Little Plumblossom?"

The Neighborhood Committee is the lowest rung of the municipal government, and largely staffed by people who live in the community. Its Chinese name, *juweihui*, is also translated as Residential Committee. I shortened
it to NeighCom, as it was becoming a relic of the state-supervised past that
lent itself to Orwellian Newspeak.

I taught in the office's activity room, where a displayed poster listed
every aged person in the neighborhood, along with their affliction. Some
had rheumatism and needed help getting to the market. Others had de-
mentia and needed to be reminded who they were. I found the Widow's
name. The poster said she suffered from "loneliness." Once a week, Neigh-
Com sent someone over to see if she needed help mending anything, getting to the doctor, or just wanted to chat.

NeighCom also hosted movie nights and banquet lunches, organized
subsidized health checks and ultrasounds for the pregnant, and distributed
free condoms. They were available from a stand at the front of the office
across from a long desk where three clerks and a police officer faced them.
The box's design showed a white man kissing the neck of a smiling white
woman. The brand name said, in English and Chinese: CONDOM.

"Take some, Little Plumblossom!" a clerk urged. "Take as many boxes as
you usually use. Four or five, whatever."

NeighCom also gave me a debit card worth fifty yuan ($6.67) that I
could freely spend at the district's Chinese Red Cross donation station and
shop. "We give these to people as a form of welfare," a clerk said. "You can
use it, too."

For those on the dole in Beijing, subsidized goods included cooking oil,
toilet paper, toothpaste, flour, rice, and Red Star–brand *erguotou*, the city's
ubiquitous sorghum-based, 104-proof alcohol. "What about cigarettes?" I
asked the attendant. "No," he said. "We can't sell those. They're bad for
your health."

Our NeighCom was one of Beijing's originals, established in 1954. The
Dazhalan neighborhood had thirty-three altogether, keeping tabs on its
street area. Ours was responsible for eight hundred families totaling two
thousand people. NeighCom's staff worked for the government, but that
didn't mean they had all the answers. "Do you know when the neighborhood will be demolished?" the staff often asked me. "We don't know anything about that," one official said. "I live on this street, too, you know. We

find out when it's time to begin relocating people, including ourselves. We don't know much."

He lent me a text that was internally published as an official neighborhood history to be read by newly appointed cadres. The book was a gazetteer instead of a narrative, containing statistics of all stripes, from population through the decades to the number of trees, homes, factories, temples, schools, and "revolutionary martyrs." Dazhalan had three, though none were killed in the neighborhood. Two air force pilots died in plane crashes in 1968 and 1974, and a soldier was lost to a mountain landslide in 1977.

Residents were not quoted in the gazetteer, nor were photographs included. The dispassionate pages did not record the contributions of average citizens in the shaping of the neighborhood. Instead, the facts piled up. The time line began in 1267, with the establishment of the kilns that fired roof tiles for imperial structures. In 1403, the emperor Yongle established the merchant quarter. In 1671, Kangxi ordered all entertainment businesses out of the Inner City, and many moved out the Front Gate to Dazhalan.

The Boxer Rebellion and the fire that torched the neighborhood went unmentioned, as did the Japanese occupation. The time line skipped to 1949, when the People's Liberation Army arrived. In 1950, the district government participated in a "Resist America, Aid Korea" demonstration. Four million people attended the local temple fair in 1960. A hotel boiler exploded in 1962, injuring three. At the start of the Cultural Revolution in the summer of 1966, forty-two people labeled "bad elements" died; thirteen were beaten to death, and twenty-nine committed suicide. The 1976 earthquake, which killed more than three hundred thousand people, caused a smokestack at the Number Two Hostel to fall on a guest. He was the neighborhood's only fatality. The gazetteer did not comment how amazing that was, given the number of courtyard homes that could have— but did not—collapse. It continued two months later, to the passing of Chairman Mao. In 1978, the world's largest duck restaurant opened in the neighborhood.

The book held two entries concerning the 1989 demonstrations centered on Tian'anmen Square. "Four hundred people from our district joined the working team that was established to quell the riots and to protect the order of the capital," the first passage said. "The work team made three excursions to clear the barricades obstructing the roads to Front Gate and Pearl Market Junction, walked alongside the People's Liberation Army soldiers, offered rescue and aid to the injured, and sent food to the soldiers, etc."

The second entry was dated "Evening of June Fourth," when the military cleared the square: "Two hundred cadres from the district Party and government organs spared no effort to rescue five soldiers who were injured by bricks thrown by rioters when they waited for the People's Armed Police to show up."

On July 1, the district cadres "expressed sympathy and solicitude for the antiriot squads."

That's all the neighborhood's official history recorded of the event. The next entry notified the reader that a new district official was appointed on August 28.

My NeighCom coteacher was fifty years old and lived in two rooms he shared with his wife and ailing mother. I liked him immediately—wide eyes, unwashed hair flattened to the right, always smiling—but I didn't like entering his house. It was in a single-story cinder-block building erected in the 1950s as a dormitory for bank workers. Sunlight struggled through the single, narrow window, and his mother moaned from the bed below it. Stretching out a bony hand, she repeated in a strained voice, "Come here, come here, come here."

Like three other members of our class, her son walked with a pronounced limp. An infection had struck his spinal fluid as a child, and he had been hobbled ever since. People called him *canji*, disabled. His government-assigned job had placed him at an electric-meter factory. The bank's dormitory where he lived had belonged to his brother, who moved to the suburbs. He and his wife did not have a child, and when I asked why, he demurred, saying that they had been introduced when they were older. For him, it was love at first sight. Like most Beijing women of that age, she was attractive and dignified, proud of her cultured upbringing and disparaging of her current conditions. "This house is so bad," she apologized on my first visit. They were a couple for whom relocation to the suburbs would not have been a downgrade.

Except, he loved the neighborhood. He had grown up there, and as I sat on the back of his motorized pedicab, he slowly puttered through the lane, pointing out the buildings that had changed. "This used to be a famous literary teahouse . . . that used to be a temple to the fire spirit . . . this was a mansion . . . that house was the temple to the God of War. It's the only one left in Beijing."

He taught himself English, listening to shortwave Voice of America broadcasts, and soaking up any printed materials he could find. He spoke haltingly, but well, in a tone that made the language sound like a ballad.

I once spent two weeks on crutches in Beijing, mostly confined inside. Suddenly I saw high curbs, long distances between public transportation transfers, cabdrivers' impatience with passengers slow to board, and—everywhere—stairs. The *hutong* did not have any of those obstacles, which was another reason this man liked living on Red Bayberry and Bamboo Slanted Street.

"It's not so bad, having this leg," he said to me in Chinese. "During the Cultural Revolution, I didn't get sent to the countryside." Other teens during that decade were shipped out to perform menial labor and "learn from the peasants."

He had remained behind, in Dazhalan. "Since school was canceled, what did you do?" I wondered.

"For two years, we dug." He measured my face and added, "You know where the playground is at Coal Lane Elementary? I helped dig the neighborhood's largest bomb shelter there."

The area's first air-raid defenses were constructed in 1962 under the auspices of the Dazhalan People's Commune. The network of tunnels and 127 underground rooms could hold 2,090 people, according the gazetteer. In 1969, when relations with the Soviet Union reached a nadir and China's leaders maneuvered internally for power, orders were issued under the slogan "Dig deep tunnels, store grains, don't bow to hegemonism."

Between 1969 and 1971 in Dazhalan, a corvée labor force constructed nearly nineteen miles of anti-air-raid tunnels, reinforced with lime-mortared walls and ceilings, ranging from three to thirty feet wide, and six to twenty feet high. According to plans, the district's entire population could be housed underground. The shelter included freshwater wells, hospitals, kindergartens, barbershops, and cinemas. Nonetheless, older people in the neighborhood who remembered that time said they didn't like descending into Beijing's damp, moldy underground. "I felt like I was digging my grave," one man said.

Dazhalan was laced with *hutong* below its surface, as well. My mind drew a map of lanes running all the way—as local legend had it—to the far outskirts of the city. According to the Widow, if I made the right connections, one of these tunnels could take me to a hatch that opened into my house. "The trapdoor is under your bed," she said.

The door was nailed shut. On nights when I couldn't sleep, I closed my eyes and let my mind descend. Like so many aspects of the house and the neighborhood, the doors were everywhere—some open, some sealed. I kept turning handles and trying new routes.

After the Soviet bombers never arrived, the tunnels became converted into cold-storage cellars, pool halls, even hostels. In 1992, a portion of the tunnels opened to tourists. Steps led thirty feet down at Underground City, a section of shelters near Old Zhang's demolished home in Fresh Fish Junction.

A string of forty-watt bulbs dangled from the round tunnel's ceiling illuminating portraits of Marx, Engels, Lenin, and Stalin. The air was thick and clammy. The sound of voices directed me to the Underground City's exit, passing through a large room where women sat on couches sipping tea from mason jars. As I entered, they sprang up, grabbing cocoons from fish tanks and demonstrating how silk floss is spun into the comforters on sale in the shop. Built to shield Beijing residents from a foreign attack, the shelter now pandered to the invasion.

I ascended to the *hutong*, where thunderclouds darkened the sky. Bicycles piloted by riders in bright yellow and blue ponchos sliced through the forming puddles, filling the air with the sound of tearing paper. Water ran from the tile roofs, splashing onto the heads of two laughing children. My eyes adjusted to the light. Paper lanterns reflected red on the black, luminous asphalt. It was a lovely, delicate scene, and soon it would all disappear.

At the peak of summer, when the period the traditional calendar called Minor Heat transitioned to Major Heat, I did not feel as magnanimous toward life in the *hutong*. My rooms only had windows on the front wall, which meant the damp, ninety-degree air could not circulate. Dust and pollution clung to my sweaty skin, and the local restaurants' heavy, oily cuisine became unappetizing. Rumors circulated that the Hand had our lane within reach, and conversation centered on the rising cost of real estate, on being a victim. People talked about individual problems, not collective solutions. The tension and muggy air pressed down upon the neighborhood.

After school ended, and with it the structure work provided, I would wake at the four-thirty sunrise, listen to the Widow bang around in her kitchen, and think, *Another day.* Another cup of Nescafé, another baseball game on Internet radio, another bath in the sink. As I had agreed to instruct the same students for another year at Coal Lane Elementary, enjoyed teaching at NeighCom, and was researching Dazhalan's history, I didn't want to move from the *hutong* until the Hand forced it, which seemed forthcoming.

One predawn morning, a spider tickled my ear, and I reflexively crushed it, blearily waking to see that the dead brown insect was the size of my palm. I leaped up and staggered toward the tap, kicking over a row of empty Yanjing beer bottles, which plinked loudly on the stone floor. My dinner of braised fatty pork and twice-fried spicy green beans awoke within; I needed a toilet. I pawed at the wooden beams barricading our door and ran in minced, clenching steps down the dark lane. I didn't make it. As I kicked my boxers into the pit, part of me hoped that I would walk home and discover that on its walls the Hand had painted a bright white 拆.

The faded propaganda painted opposite the toilet said LONG LIVE THE PROLETARIAT. When the knife sharpener pedaled down the lane that afternoon, calling out, "Grind, grind, grind!" I thought, *You said it.*

Some days at dinnertime, I wandered Wal-Mart's aisles. The air-conditioning was frigid, and the deli served cold noodles and icy beer. I kept those trips, and the shameful hope for demolition, to myself. Like the weather, they would eventually cool.

Miss Zhu came over in the mornings to study for her English exam, while I pored over a pile of Beijing history books, none of which included an index or source notes. Just as I sighed when she asked, again, for a rule for employing such prepositions as *of* and *from*, she wearied of my questions about the same Chinese character. After a week, we started wordlessly tossing dictionaries at each other. I didn't care about the differences between *sit down, sit around,* and *sit tight* any more than she did about the minutiae of the capital's *hutong.* "You sure know a lot of useless information," she said.

I began to wonder. Who cared about poor people in Beijing, anyway? As a Peace Corps volunteer, I constantly heard incredulous Chinese ask what sort of nation sent its citizens overseas for two years, away from their family, to work with strangers. In Beijing, locals I met outside the *hutong* could not fathom why anyone would want to live there. After learning what I did, they would comment, "Who cares?"

That verdict was bluntly, and repeatedly, delivered by a Chinese middle-class man sitting outside the What? Bar, a small pub set in a three-hundred-year-old home on the west moat of the Forbidden City. The bartender was a friend who had migrated from the northeast as a teenager to play music. She let me pour my own beer from the tap, after which I would sit outside on the sidewalk under a canopy of locust trees, whose spindly trunks bore branches heavy with green leaves. The Zhongnanhai national leadership compound was a block away, and at night I liked to watch a 1980s black Cadillac El Dorado prowl in and out of the gate, wondering who rode within.

"Who cares about the *hutong?*" said the Chinese man outside the bar. He had never lived on a lane, but in China I was the foreigner, always, and could be dismissed with *You don't understand.*

"It's not the buildings that matter as much as the community."

"Who cares?"

"There's no transparency, no one knows how their life may change, and they can't sue—"

"No one cares." He waved a hand and spoke with the authority bestowed by brashness. "Those people should move out and open their eyes. This is 2006, not 1956." He nodded to his Buick minivan, parked on the sidewalk. His job was selling an American company's nutritional supplement. "The government is great. You can do whatever you want now, you can make money." He sipped his beer and said my neighbors were the shiftless and dumb.

The elderly students at NeighCom clucked their tongues when I recounted the story. "People like that are messing up our Beijing," a man said. "They are like the man in the ancient saying: 'I look back, and don't see the ancients; I look ahead and can't see the generations to come.'"

The students' determination to show their best faces to the world in 2008 never waned. They were embarrassed to tell people they were unemployed or laid-off, or retired even, and so we practiced "I am a grandmother!" as a reply to inquiries about their profession.

One afternoon, a row of rickshaw bicycles pedaled through our *hutong*, bearing German tourists, who pointed their camera lenses at decrepit doorways.

"Why do foreigners want to take pictures of a poor neighborhood?" the class asked. "Don't they want to go to the Forbidden City? Are they laughing at us?"

"I don't want to move," a woman said. "The house is bad, it's true. I'm used to it. We're all used to it. When foreigners come here, however, I feel ashamed. It looks really run-down."

"I want to show them pictures of what it used to look like when I was a little boy," a man with cropped white hair continued. "It was so clean then,

German tourists passing in front of my house on Red Bayberry and Bamboo Slanted Street.

in the 1950s. You can't imagine how great it was. We were so proud of our community."

"Aren't you proud of it now?"

"All these migrants have moved in, messing things up."

"You said it!" A woman nodded. "Beijing people used to be so polite. When you needed to get around someone, you would say, 'To the side!' and the person would move. Now it's all 'Uh!' and 'Watch the vehicle!' Disgusting! And the people don't even move over."

"Before the migrants, things were very civilized," a grandmother said. "They don't take care of the houses, and they spit everywhere. They can't even speak proper Mandarin."

The poor and weak picked on the poorer and weaker. Embarrassment from the gaze of someone imagined above them led to spite for those below. After ten minutes of migrant-baiting, I said, "I'm a migrant."

"No! You're a foreigner! That's different!"

"Where is the mayor from? Where are the national leaders from? They're migrants, too."

"Wrong! They're not who we're talking about. They don't make chaos in the neighborhood."

"The people who pay money to raze the *hutong* and invest in new real estate projects—you're saying these aren't Beijing people, but all outsiders?"

"That's not the same!" they repeated as a group. "Migrants aren't civilized. Their cultural level is low, they're bumpkins!"

Instead of cursing migrants, I said, they should empathize with them. After all, they were their neighbors. What was the use of putting on airs? When the demolition notices went up, they would all be equal before the Hand.

The classroom was silent for a moment. A man lifted his head and asked, "Little Plumblossom, do you know when our neighborhood will be destroyed?"

Recycler Wang always grinned toothily when I approached my front door. "Want to go outside town?" he asked one day. "Get in the truck. I have to bring these used tires to a friend."

He was from the Henan province countryside, a locale that drew especial ire from Beijing natives because it produced the majority of migrants from outside the region. Wang spoke in a thick accent that betrayed his origin. He hadn't come to the capital with the intention of becoming a resident. "Most of the trash recyclers in our neighborhood are from the same town as I am," he said. "We can't have a union, of course, but we help each other. In our eyes, frankly, we're just in Beijing because we need food. It's a better economy than our village. If it weren't, we would never leave."

He drove straight south, outside all five ring roads, past military institutes such as the Academy of Launch Vehicle Technology, and into a muddy landscape of crops.

"*Wo cao!*" he cursed. "Fuck me! They call that wheat? You should see the wheat in our village. It's already up to here." He pointed at his knee. "My parents are farmers, just like I was. We grow wheat, corn, and soybeans." He exhaled as the truck dodged a tractor crossing the road. "Am I proud of it? Farmers, what's there to say about them? We're just commoners. As long as we have food and a little money, we're content with our lot. It's not the same as being an official. One thousand yuan is a good salary at the start, but then you want fifteen hundred, then fifteen hundred is too low, so you want two thousand. Farmers just want pocket cash and food, and we're happy.

"Look, China's population is just too big, the density is too high, the government can't solve every problem. Actually, the government isn't bad at all, it's quite good to the farmers. Farmers don't pay taxes anymore—the first time in five thousand years of our nation's history. Farmers don't have to pay tuition for their children all the way up to middle school, now, too. Farmers also get basic health insurance that covers prevention and minor illnesses. Your country has a much smaller population, and you guys don't even have that!"

He swung the van onto a dirt road. "Actually, I know that in America, things are different. You can criticize the president all you want. Little Bush invades Iraq, why, even members of his own party will disagree in public."

We pulled into a cluster of redbrick homes arranged in rows on narrow lanes. It was like the *hutong*, only agrarian. A metal gate before each compound led to a dirt courtyard. Old tires filled this one. We added six more to the pile. "Can these be recycled?" I asked.

"Everything can be recycled," replied Recycler Wang.

"When you were little, did you dream of escaping the farm and becoming a recycler?"

He laughed. "When I was little, there was nothing to recycle."

On the drive back to the *hutong*, as the van exited wheat fields and passed under the ring-road overpasses, he said, "I'm thirty-nine, older than you, brother. My son is fifteen. He's back on the farm, going to middle school. I have two wishes for him. The first is that he doesn't become a farmer. It's too hard. The second is that he doesn't work in recycling. It's not easy, either. I learned this job from people who told me to come to Beijing. I don't want him to come here until he's educated. You see how people treat me. You live in a mixed courtyard, you work as a simple teacher. But when you come to China, you're completely protected by law. We're not the same, brother. If someone tells me to get lost, I have to get lost immediately. Frankly, you foreigners come to China and enjoy more rights than Chinese do."

We slowed in traffic. "I have no regrets," he said. "It's not a stable way of life, but that's life."

He pointed out a new BMW idling beside us at the stoplight. He corrected the sentence: "It's my life."

One night at ten o'clock, Recycler Wang told me to climb into his idling truck. The blue flatbed sagged on its axles under a heap of dismantled radiators, bundles of the *Evening News*, and sacks of bottles and cans. The cargo made a precarious pile, lashed with ropes.

"We're going to the dump," he said. His wife walked ahead, guiding the vehicle out of the *hutong*. Recycler Wang made it through without a scrape. "The police won't allow trucks like this inside the city. Part of the Olympics appearance campaign. The dump used to be inside the Second Ring Road, but every year since they won the bid, the government has pushed it farther and farther away. Now it's out past the Sixth Ring," twenty-five miles from our lane.

He took a winding route to reach the expressway out of town. "I know where the police checkpoints are."

His wife was stout and weather-beaten, with a tuft of frazzled hair. She criticized his driving the entire ride. On one tight corner, Wang swung the vehicle close to the curb. A clatter echoed behind us.

"What did you hit!" his wife howled.

I leaned out the window to see a formerly parked bicycle prone on the roadway.

"What did he hit!" she demanded.

"Nothing. Just the curb."

Recycler Wang leaned back, out of her view, and shot me a grin. The truck rumbled on until the city lights were replaced by the neon glow of karaoke clubs and bathhouses tucked off of poplar-lined service roads. Patrons at one club entered through a structure shaped like a massive Sphinx. Parking attendants covered black Audis' license plates with newspapers, a common practice at places where guests did not want their presence documented in photographs.

The truck turned right, followed an unlit dirt road, turned left, and picked up another dusty lane that ran alongside train tracks before terminating at a small gate adorned with a large poster that warned DO NOT RE-CYCLE THE FOLLOWING KINDS OF ITEMS, STOLEN ILLEGALLY! It showed pictures of manhole covers, storm-drain gates, fiber-optic cables, and electricity-pole conductors. No one was on duty to check the incoming loads.

The dump was not a landfill, but a Trash Village, where piles of sorted recyclables lined the dozen lanes. Families lived in small cinder-block structures beside the goods. The Plastic Bottles took up two entire lanes, while the Bottle Caps had Fan Blades and Paint Buckets as neighbors. Sink Basins lived next to Musical Instruments and Cardboard. One lane was the Beams from Courtyard Homes.

"These are the Bedsprings," Recycler Wang said as the truck's engine shuddered to a stop. "I'm going to start here, then drive to sell off each part of my load. You can wander around."

Each of the lanes framed an area the size of a football field. The rows were unlit, save for the bare sodium bulbs illuminating the scale before every shack. Recyclers bought refuse from individuals in the city, then trucked it out here after dark to sell it at a markup. Profit came from volume. Recycler Wang paid one fen ($.0013) per twelve-ounce plastic mineral-water bottle in town and received 1.5 fen ($.0020) for it here. If he bought a thousand bottles for $1.30, he could sell them for $2. The earned $.70 was the equivalent of a little over five yuan, the cost of a bowl of noodles.

Trash Village had a convenience store, clinic, and Henan restaurant, but no trees, no animals, and no children. The kids, Recycler Wang said, were back in Henan province with their grandparents and going to school. This work was their parents', and shifts began late, as recyclers trucked out the day's haul. The trash sorting's percussive crunches was broken only by the rumble of a passing train.

Recycler Wang squatted beside the scale at the Tin's, where a man squeezed a drop of acid on the metal, then touched an electric current to the surface, testing for conduction.

"This one isn't real," the man told Recycler Wang.

"*Wo cao!* Fuck me! Let me try, you didn't even touch the current to the acid!" When I returned an hour later, after calling on the Bicycle Frames, Bus Seats, and Cooking Oil Bottles, the two men were bickering over the integrity of a pile of vacuum-flask lids.

I walked to the Office Papers and waded into a pile that rose to my shoulders. One page showed the English and Chinese words *turn patties* followed by *vat, walk-in freezer, weekly customer count,* and *whipped butter pats.*

As Recycler Wang demanded a few pennies more for some congee cans, I read:

THE THREE RULES OF EQUIPMENT PURCHASING IN THE MCDONALD'S SYSTEM ARE:

1. You will not negotiate a more favorable price for your market.
2. You will not negotiate a more favorable price for your market.
3. You will not negotiate a more favorable price for your market.

Recycler Wang said, "That's how you make money. That guy I was just arguing with? Did you see his room there? The leather sofa and the big-screen TV? He started out just like me, with a three-wheeled flatbed bike in the city. Actually, I didn't even start with a bike. I used to carry the trash on my back to the dump. Then I got a bike, then a motorized one, now this used truck. That guy started in the eighties, a decade before me, and as society developed and created more trash, he was profiting right along with it. He kept saving his money and got out of my line. He paid a guy fifty thousand yuan [$6,667] to take over this spot. All he has to do is wait for the trash to come to him from all over the city. His volume is much higher than what I get in the *hutong*. You can earn at least two hundred thousand yuan [$26,667] in a year out here. That guy makes twice that. I want to work out here, brother. It's two in the morning, and I have to drive back, get some sleep, and be out on the lane at seven to start buying more trash. Now you know why I can't stand it when the grandmothers curse me when I don't offer them a few more cents for their junk. *Wo cao!* My profit margin is smaller than they can imagine."

He turned the truck's engine so it could warm. His wife was off haggling at the Pillows.

"Everything here gets sold on to the next place at another slight markup, where it's processed and passed on to the next stage." Recycler Wang didn't know where pillows went next. Paper went to the city of Baoding, newspapers to Shanxi and Shandong provinces, cardboard to a village in Hebei province, scrap metal to the town Tangshan. Bottles were loaded onto a train bound for Henan province. Each of the destinations was hundreds of miles away. As far as he was concerned, stores like Wal-Mart were great, because the products came in packaging that made him money.

His wife climbed into the truck, looking exhausted. She said flatly that she got a good price for the pillows. They didn't know how much money they made, despite penciling every transaction in a ledger. "We never really know," Recycler Wang said. "Some days you pay out more than you make, depending on the going rate we get out here."

Trash was a tradable commodity, a future, of sorts. As we turned onto the road leading home, a billboard for a new apartment complex named Braw City shone in our headlights. The English translation of its Chinese slogan said, "Future is here."

CHAPTER 15

PAST TENSE VS. FUTURE TENSE

I AM SO lucky to be eleven years old this year. Maybe you will ask me, why? Telling you a secret, when 2008 coming, I will be thirteen. It is the time for watching many races of Olympic Games, or to be a volunteer to serve for foreign children."

In August 2006, on the first day she was a fifth-grader, the girl who called herself Cher recited her entry for a citywide English-speaking contest whose theme was "The Olympic Games in My Heart." Cher stood before her classmates, who had carried their desks outside to the playground for the Start of the School Year Activity.

"What else do I like about the 2008 Olympic Games?" Cher asked. "For me, I hope I could taste the delicious food of all the world. I like Italian pizza, roast turkey, and many, many things. Beside roast duck, we will bring a lot of Beijing snacks to the world."

After all the rumors, Coal Lane Elementary had not been demolished. The principal did not know why. Miss Zhu and I entered the building to find it looking just as we had left it before summer break. The walls had not been painted, and the traces of our last lesson still shone in ghostly chalk on the blackboard. Our new classroom's three double windows faced north, giving a view of orange persimmons weighing down branches in courtyards, and a row of fluttering red flags atop the Great Hall of the People.

"The Beijing Olympic Games will be the best Chinese thing in the whole world!" Cher concluded. "I am proud of being Chinese. Wherever you are, do not forget our national culture forever, like calligraphy, painting, national instruments, traditional folk arts, and of course Chinese food. Nationality is the world."

The recording of the brassy national anthem began. Teachers and students stood. In salute to the national flag, the kids cocked their right fist beside their ear.

Little Liu mounted the stage. She wore her light blue eye patch. Her hair stood straight up in a single braid. When I closed my eyes, I heard an adult speaking. "Dearly beloved teachers, dearly beloved classmates," Little Liu intoned, "I am a colored ring of the Olympic logo. My name is Bei Bei!"

Bei Bei was one of the five Olympic mascots, called *fuwa*. Their English name had been Friendlies, until it was discovered that the word connoted a noncompetitive soccer match. It also was made up of *friend* and *lies*. Now the mascots were called *fuwa* in English, too. There were five animated *fuwa*, each colored a shade of the Olympic rings. The first character of the mascots' names—Bei Bei, Jing Jing, Huan Huan, Ying Ying, Ni Ni— spelled out "Beijing welcomes you" (*Beijing huanying ni*).

The *fuwa* saturated the capital like dust. They appeared as plush toys and on billboards, in the *Evening News*, and on the cards used to add credit to cell phones. The children had *fuwa* fever, but the adults wearied of them. At the NeighCom English class, the elderly students laughed when I said that three more *fuwa* should be added to represent Beijing's real cul-

The Olympic mascot named Jing Jing takes aim from a phone card.

ture: Ta Ta, Ma Ma, and De De. The first character of each of those names formed the common Beijing epithet "His mother!"

At school, the games were no joke. "This will be the first Olympics in China," Little Liu continued at the assembly. "Chinese people cannot wait to host the best Olympics ever. The games will convey we Beijing people's culture to the rest of the world. The games will reduce Beijing's population density and increase our quality of life. Under the guidance of *fuwa*, we will raise the education level of the people, while increasing our overall cultural level."

An instrumental version of "Footloose" boomed through the speakers. The Coal Lane Elementary dance team trotted out in pink pants and white-sparkle tank tops. As they smiled frozenly and went through their aerobics, their peers sat stone-faced. School assemblies had all the joy and spontaneity of a teeth cleaning.

The children stood, cocked their right fist, and pledged to a line of five students wearing colored paper crowns representing each *fuwa*, "We swear to advance our culture and make this the best Olympics ever!"

The children returned to their classrooms to watch a film that started with grainy black-and-white footage of Japanese soldiers stampeding Chinese positions. "The Communist Party resisted the invaders," a male narrator intoned. The people on the screen ran in the flickering, sped-up way that looked unnatural. The kids did not laugh. The film did not mention that the United States and other countries had also fought against Japan. At picture's end, the narrator summarized, "We won." It was the same vindicating verdict as after the Olympics site selection was announced: "We won."

I stabbed a chopstick into the plastic-sealed bundle of Grade Five textbooks. *Mocky, we meet again.*

"Who is the first man in the space?" Mocky asked incorrectly. "Do you know?"

"I don't know," the dialogue continued. "But I know about the first man from China in space. He is Yang Liwei."

Mocky looked at a picture of Yang, waving with a smile before a Chinese flag. "Wow, he is so great," the monkey said.

The Grade Four textbook focused on the past tense. In Grade Five, the kids would be introduced to the future tense. The entire school year fo-cused on the future tense: Beijing *will* host the best Olympics. Chinese cul-ture *will* attract the world deeply. We *will* win.

The morning had been filled with talk of nationalism and images of war, and now it was a relief to be sitting with Miss Zhu and the other Grade Five teachers over box lunches. School topics never carried over into con-versation. Instead, the women said things like:

"I bought an electric bike."

"An electric bike? How much?"

"Cheap!"

"No wonder you're so fat."

"No mistake! Are my clothes pretty? I bought them online."

"How much?"

"Cheap!"

"You can't find a husband wearing cheap clothes!"

"He won't look at her clothes if she's fat, that's for sure!

"Sell that electric bike and get some exercise."

With a pout, the bike buyer howled, "I don't want to!" *Wo buyao!*

When said in a high pitch, *wo buyao* became the talisman women in-voked to ward off untoward advances. The room filled with howls of laugh-ter and whinnying *wo buyao*s. It was good to be back at school.

Every year, the World Economic Forum hosted the China Business Summit at a five-star hotel. Government ministers took the stage to promise the as-sembled management of multinational corporations that China was re-forming, then the managers stepped up and affirmed they had seen it firsthand. The only people rolling their eyes were in the bullpen of free-lance writers hired to take notes at each session, then type them into press releases.

One day's pay would cover three months of my rent, however. I woke before dawn, washed my hair under the sink's cold-water tap, and put on the musty sport coat that hadn't been worn since the end of the last year's meetings.

At school, discourse was centered on the Olympics and China. The watchwords at the 2006 China Business Summit were *stability, smart growth, mutual respect,* and *innovation.* Here, *loyalty* referred to brands, not national flags. Just as the wealthy seldom talk about money, few people here used the word *profit.*

An attendee passionately complained, "We're deciding the tools before we do the baseline analysis!" I wrote it down. A man with surgeon's hands stood to agree: "We should focus on sequencing, rather than tools." I wrote that down, too. Transcribing the quotes reminded me, not pleasantly, of my former job typing and reading phone conversations between the deaf and hearing.

"You have to present solutions, not just define the problem."

"Take initiative and give employees ownership in the process."

"Think of the rights and responsibilities of the people in the surrounding community."

The foreign CEOs talked about *change* and *corporate governance,* while their support staff that actually lived in Beijing grumbled about *pollution* and *inefficiency.* In between sessions, the bosses said things like "Be transparent about costs, goals, and expected outcomes." The staff wondered if the vouchers provided for meals in the hotel would cover gin-and-tonics. (Go ahead!)

For the first time in the four summits I had attended, I heard foreigners express frustration with the slowing pace of reforms in China. A company president said that his firm had started in a Silicon Valley garage. It didn't need the shiny science parks that municipal governments kept building. The key to innovation, he said, was an open exchange of information feeding an independent stock market and private venture capitalists, strong patent-protection laws, and a willingness to fail. A Chinese entrepreneur said, "I'm tired of hearing that China lacks innovation. Just look at all the counterfeit products you can buy. That's a form of innovation. That spirit can be redirected."

My cell phone had recently received an unsolicited text message from a syndicate selling forged diplomas, and fake military license plates. Another message came from the Beijing chapter of the UFO society that had formed around a logging-commune worker I once visited in the far northeast. Unemployed when environmental regulations silenced his chain saw, he had become an income-generating tourist attraction after claiming to have impregnated an extraterrestrial. "After I had been abducted, the head alien wouldn't let me see her again," he said. "But the head alien told me, 'Know this: in sixty years, on a distant planet, an alien will give birth to a peasant.'" The man rode his notoriety out of the forest and into an apartment and university-cafeteria job in the provincial capital. The job covered his son's tuition. He was one of the most innovative people I had ever met.

The Business Summit didn't talk about case studies like that. This was Five Star China, where the plush carpet and baffled walls muted the weirdness outside.

When I returned to the *hutong*, Recycler Wang bought the notebooks filled with summit quotes. The Widow handed me a sweet yam steamed on her stove. She had taken her first delivery of coal from the salesman who pedaled it around the lanes on a flatbed bicycle, calling out, "Coal honeycombs! Coal honeycombs!"

"Autumn just started and you're thinking of winter?" I teased. "The traditional calendar says it's the spell named White Dew."

She swatted my arm. "Little Plumblossom, you moron! If I buy the coal now, they're each two cents cheaper than what they'll cost after the Descent of Frost!" That came at the end of October, a month away.

Mr. Han and his wife sat on their bed, wiped out from another day at the cell phone market.

"Why are you dressed like that?" he asked, handing me a bottle of Yanjing.

After I explained the day, Mr. Han said, "That's a good meeting. The economy keeps getting better."

Not for him personally, but Mr. Han was optimistic. He could repair cell phones, and everyone had one of those. If he could find the right location, his fortunes would improve. There was no returning home to the northeast. Admitting failure, he said, just wasn't imaginable. Sharing a rundown house in a *hutong*, separated from your young son and working a profitless job was failure enough.

The summer's heat and dust subsided. I carried a chair outside to the lane. Recycler Wang haggled with an elderly woman, an old vendor squatted next to a blanket filled with medicinal herbs, pumpkin vines reached for the second-story veranda on the house opposite our door, and the plump leaves of the cottonwood rustled in the wind. My students bounded by in pursuit of a chicken, then shifted their chase to a new poodle. The vegetable seller had rescued it from the side of a road after it had been tossed from a moving car. He bathed it in a soapy basin on the lane. A worried Chinese tourist asked me for the nearest latrine, then briskly waddled off, one hand pressed to his behind. A line of rickshaw bicycles pedaled past, bearing German tourists.

The Muslim restaurant next to the mosque put its tables back outside on the lane. An old man next door kept watch on the *hutong* from a stool he had placed next to his dozen potted mums and marigolds. He wore blue serge pants held up with a shoestring, while his body, from jowls to breasts to belly, sagged to resemble a mirthful Buddha. In one hand he held a wicker fan, in another a flyswatter made from a piece of window screen fastened to a bent coat hanger. Our daily discussion was limited to mutual silent nods as I picked up an order of hand-pulled pasta topped with caramelized garlic, sliced cold cucumber, and ripe tomatoes. The meal cost two yuan ($.27), which I untangled from the ball of currency and tissue-paper receipts that form nests in Beijing pockets.

That fall, I had visited the director of the China Architecture Association, whose office was on the eighth floor of a hulking high-rise in the west of Beijing. A secretary showed me upstairs. The elevator only reached the fourth floor. From there, she took me down a narrow, low-ceilinged hallway, climbed a staircase, walked down another hallway, then opened a door to a fire-exit stairway that led up to the office.

The route seemed an illustrative metaphor for modern Beijing planning and architecture, but the director shrugged and said that's just the way things were. He didn't have anything to say about *hutong*. He presented me with a heavy coffee-table book on the design history of courtyard homes. It was an academic subject, something from the past and already researched. He invited me to tour the Olympic stadiums, the National Theater, and the other new construction shaping Beijing's image for the twenty-first century. If a city is a collection of its residents' memories, then old Beijing would soon be found on a bookshelf and scattered in suburban high-rise apartments. Until the last *hutong* community or evictees perished, however, it lived on.

Migrants continued to move to Dazhalan, continuing a centuries-old cycle. The room opposite mine in the courtyard had been rented to a man from Shandong province who sold roasted yams, then to a young lawyer from Baoding city, and now to two nineteen-year-old girls from the northeast, working as waitresses. They came from a small town and had long dreamed of moving to Beijing.

The same determination held fast to Soldier Liu and his parents, who, ten months after the Hand wiped their shaved-noodle shop from Fresh Fish Junction, at last found a vacant space for rent in our neighborhood. The new restaurant, larger than their former one, was just off Dazhalan West Street, the *hutong* perpetually packed with foot traffic of locals and tourists. Soldier Liu and his father shaved slices of dough into a pot boiling on the lane, while his mother chatted up the diners inside.

The destruction of their old location had turned out to be a blessing, she said. The new space was a two-story box made of cement, but it allowed more seating downstairs and included a bigger kitchen, with a large room upstairs, where they lived. The increased customer volume more than covered the higher rent. Soldier Liu attended my English class at NeighCom, where the grandmothers adopted him as one of their own, despite his being a migrant. Miss Zhu and my other female coteachers said he was quite a catch, actually: handsome, fit, and polite. But Soldier Liu had still not warmed to Beijing girls. "They're not as beautiful as the girls in my village. Plus, the girls at home don't waste money on clothes."

The matchmaker hired to find him a bride had yet to locate a candidate in his hometown, but Soldier Liu was unhurried. He was twenty-three years old and could narrate what his life would be like at forty. The chapters went: Wife, Business, Child.

The setting could be here, on this lane, in this neighborhood, where he and his family had fit right in. Permanent patterns of life could coalesce around buildings made from impermanent materials. But Soldier Liu knew better than to plan around the Hand.

A measure of any great city is its potential for accidental discoveries, those places without entrance fees and tour guides that make you want to stay longer in hopes of finding the next one. Despite the advanced stage of the Old City's destruction, Beijing still held this attraction.

October brings two weeks of pure autumn, a spell named Cold Dew. It is weather that promotes wandering. After school, I got on my bike and pedaled east, across Front Gate Avenue into the former Legation Quarter, whose stone, Western-style buildings evoke the early-twentieth century. They have been preserved and adapted for new uses. The turreted entrance to the old Japanese embassy leads now to the Beijing Municipal Government offices. The old French post office has become a Sichuan restaurant. The pair of stone lions at the former French embassy gate guard the entrance to Cambodian prince Sihanouk's villa. The columned granite façade of Rockefeller's old Citibank houses the Beijing Police Museum.

You can walk right into the former offices of the Trans-Siberian Railway, since converted into apartments. The two-story building looks unlike any other in the capital, with wide wooden staircases, windows fitted with shut-

The Legation Quarter's tree-canopied East People's Diplomacy Lane,
running behind the former American embassy.

ters, and a garden in its yard. The entrance is across from another relic, a painted-over plaque behind an abandoned guardhouse that says USSR EMBASSY LANE. On another street is a sign, also brushed over, reading RUE HART, named for the British customs officer in 1900, when the Boxers laid siege to Beijing.

Some buildings are said to be haunted, such as the steeple-less church in the east of the Old City that—despite its valuable location—sits forlorn and fenced off. It was the former seat of the Catholic diocese, prior to the Communists' control of Beijing. When a developer known for remodeling old structures approached the church's leaseholder, the Religious Affairs Bureau, it told him they were keeping the building vacant until the Vatican renounced its recognition of Taiwan and restored ties with Beijing. Then, the building could revert back to the Holy See. Perhaps they could chase away the ghosts.

My bike's steel frame was so heavy that a normal kickstand couldn't support it. Instead, it backed onto a jacklike movable frame that lifted the back tire three inches into the air. The bike only had one speed, but even a slight elevation of the capital's flat grid resulted in a long coast. One day I cut west through the *hutong*, past Miss Zhu's grandfather sitting outside his home near Wal-Mart, and past the stela that marked the boundary of the former Jin dynasty capital. The ride took me down narrow, tree-canopied lanes that showed buildings in their original context.

If Beijing's historic structures are fitted with an explanatory plaque, the information notes the year it was built, its former use, and the year the relevant cultural bureau designated it as heritage. Every sign fronting a protected traditional-style home identifies it only as COURTYARD HOUSE. No narrative is provided to link the structures to the present, or with one another. The architecture forms a dotted line, whose blanks are often filled with guesswork, and misinterpretation. Once, at a UNESCO-sponsored training conference on the management of World Heritage sites, a Chinese mayor complained that tourists to his city didn't understand its history. I asked what he was doing to help. Had he printed interpretive signs and maps? Had he promoted restaurants that served local cuisine and shops selling locally made music and art? Had he outlined walks that would leave visitors with the feeling that they were in a unique place? "We hired more tour guides," the mayor said. "That's their job!"

One afternoon, I rode my bike north from Dazhalan, to the area of *hu-*

tong named West Fours. The courtyards here are a mixture of private mansions and shared tenements, though from the outside they all look tidy thanks to a gray paint job and streetlights that resemble antique gas lamps. Plaques on the ends of each lane detail its history and list the addresses of homes that are well maintained, or once housed a famous person. It does not cost much money or effort to remind residents and visitors that a neighborhood is unique.

Most of the city's architectural heritage, however, is unposted. The inhabitants hold the stories, as at the massive structure that lurks behind the White Pagoda temple in the west of the Old City. I had no idea that the pink, six-story building rising incongruously from the *hutong* was Beijing's last extant "urban commune." Its apartments were built without kitchens; residents ate from a central canteen. The building had recently been marked for demolition. A woman who had yet to move out said, while cooking over a propane-fueled stove installed in the hallway, "You can't even imagine what it was like forty years ago, when living here was a high honor. Now, no one wants to eat with their neighbors." She paused and added, "No one has to."

On a neighboring *hutong*, a gray-brick steeple poked up from behind sloping tiled rooftops. Several families lived in the converted church, constructed in the 1920s. One resident advised taking pictures now, as she had just received an eviction notice. I climbed up the smashed walls of a neighboring courtyard home for a better view of the church's roof. An unseen voice moaned in anguish. I called out, "Do you need help?" The only response was silence, broken by the sound of a distant jackhammer.

As Beijing was destroyed, it was also being constructed. That made its past difficult to decipher. The future was easier to assert. WE ARE BUILDING A NEW BEIJING promised a slogan posted in the lanes around the church and former urban commune. TOMORROW WILL BE EVEN BETTER. Even the weather was a fait accompli. Two years from the date the Olympics would begin, the government announced that the Opening Ceremony would not be disrupted by thunderstorms. "The possibility of rain on August eighth, 2008, is between thirty and forty percent," an official said. "If it does rain, it will most likely be only a drizzle."

CHAPTER 16

A Brief History of 拆 Part Three:
The Modernization of Republican Beijing

THEIR EXPLANATORY PLAQUES do not tell it, but the former Legation Quarter's Western-style buildings evince the first of many fractures to the capital's form following the Boxer Rebellion. The departure of American and other occupying forces in 1901, and the return of the Dowager Empress, did not mean that life resumed as before. The Boxers had not only destroyed much of Beijing, but also the city's entire concept.

In 1900, Boxers shelled and set fire to a Legation Quarter that had not been designed for defense. After the rebellion was squelched, the Manchu court agreed to enlarge the burned-out district, reserving it for the exclusive use of foreigners.

Envoys of Austria-Hungary, Italy, and France planned the eviction of Chinese living or operating businesses in the quarter, paying them a cash settlement for the vacated land. The process was fraught with mistrust: the foreigners questioned the veracity of property deeds, while the Chinese complained about the compensation standard.

In 1901, the foreigners razed government buildings and imperial-household shrines. Unbound to the building codes that had for five centuries given the capital the unified appearance of one-story wooden buildings that rolled like breakers from the Forbidden City, the foreigners built twelve embassies with masonry in each country's national style. "The result is interesting, even educative, but not by any way of looking at it architecturally harmonious," wrote a visitor. "The Belgian Legation shows you a tiny slice of Brussels, the Netherlands a morsel of Amsterdam; Italy grows homesick contemplating her broad façades of villaesque

stucco, while America echoes, faintly but with palpable intent, the pil-
lared and stepped and State-Departmental porticoes of Washington,
D.C." The French designed Beijing's tallest building, the Peking Hotel
(now the upscale Raffles Hotel), whose seven stories were served by the
city's first elevator. The Legation Quarter also featured Beijing's first
paved road.

Many evicted merchants moved outside the Front Gate to Dazhalan,
where the crafts economy thrived, as residents replaced the loot carried
off by foreign occupying forces. Torched in 1900 during the rebellion,
Dazhalan's shops again advertised cloisonné, diamonds, jade, pearls, silk
embroideries, and stolls. The neighborhood rebuilt in a hodgepodge of
styles including traditional wood-framed courtyards and two-story brick
buildings with verandas that gave the Langfang *hutong* their names. For
the first time, some lanes were covered in crushed stone, laid atop the layers of dust that had grown so high that many homes' entrances were
reached by steps leading down from the roadbed. One still stands on the
east end of Red Bayberry and Bamboo Slanted Street, a rare survivor of
the Boxer-era fire.

The Front Gate's burned arrow tower was rebuilt according to the design
of a German architect, who added white marble eyebrows over each embrasure, and balustrades around its base. It looked—and still looks—like an
unappetizing wedding cake. The gate had been reduced to an ornament,
regardless. Formerly, its iron gong was beaten slowly, at night, increasing in
rapidity as the gate was about to be sealed. Now, the doors always stayed
open, and the gong's clang gave way to steam whistles.

The Dowager Empress had forbidden a railroad to enter Beijing's walls.
For transport, the city relied on camels, mule carts, palanquins, and horses.
In 1888, one of her ministers had a small train installed in the Forbidden
City between her living quarters and a dining hall. The empress rode it, but
only if eunuchs pulled the cars. The steam-powered engine's clatter, she
feared, would disrupt the palace's feng shui.

After the Boxers were defeated, foreign engineers pierced Beijing's city
wall for the first time. The holes, warned feng shui practitioners, would
bleed the "imperial air" from the capital and reduce its power. The open-
ings were for drainage canals, and rails that brought trains into the city, to
a station constructed in 1911 beside the Front Gate.

The Front Gate after being rebuilt according to a design by the German architect Curt Rothkegel.

The structure that had once kept visitors out of Beijing now welcomed them, albeit with arched eyebrows.

Within a year, the eight-year-old emperor, Puyi, abdicated his throne. An uprising against Manchu soldiers in a southern Chinese city sparked a nationwide revolt, led by a doctor named Sun Yat-sen. In 1912, the Nationalist Party he chaired announced the founding of the Republic of China.

The last emperor was granted a lavish pension and permitted to live in the rear quarters of the Forbidden City. Its front courts, including the throne room, were renamed the Palace Museum. For the first time, commoners could tour Beijing's imperial monuments. The Altar to the God of Land and Grain became Central Park. The Ancestral Temple was converted to Peace Park. The fall of the emperor also toppled the city's economy, which had served the court, and the unemployment rate skyrocketed to 57 percent.

The republic's provisional government chose as its president a former Imperial Army general named Yuan Shikai. In 1915, the short, corpulent

Yuan—often photographed wearing a uniform resplendent in ribbons and medals—declared himself emperor. He lived in a two-story, Western-style villa made from masonry that he ordered built inside the Forbidden City. Although Yuan's claim was contested, and he was never officially enthroned, his short reign left lasting marks on the capital (aside from the villa, located inside the palace's west gate and now used by the army). Curiously for an "emperor," Yuan disregarded feng shui. He approved the dredging of Beijing's moats, planned the first new gate in the city wall—Hepingmen—to facilitate travel to his palace, and allowed a railroad to necklace the city's exterior by 1915. To the superstitious, Beijing was being strangled by train tracks. Yuan died the next year, of kidney failure.

The railroad that ran around the city wall had punctured the link between every remaining pair of its gate towers. In ancient cities, the destruction of one piece of architectural heritage makes it easier to justify the destruction of more. The whole has already been fractured; one transgression leads to another.

"Peking you simply would not be able to recognize except by its monuments," wrote a British journalist in 1916. "Macadamized roads, electric light, great open spaces, museums, modern buildings of all kinds, one or two of them on a scale that would not be out of place in Whitehall, motorcars (there are I think at least 200), motor cycles more numerous than we care for, and bicycles literally by the thousand. New roads are being driven through the city in many directions and the Imperial City wall is now pierced in a dozen places."

In 1920, a British author described telegraph lines webbing the formerly open sky, newspapers printed in English as well as Chinese, and "masses of ugly, foreign-style buildings dotted here and there over the city [that] mar the harmony of the general view." Already, she said, "we find the new mingling with the old. What remains of the older civilization, however, is so picturesque that to look back on the days when its illusions were still unbroken must always be a pleasure to whoever has felt that illusion."

The modernizations belied an era when the city smelled more like excrement than incense and camphor, women's foot-binding was fashionable, and the economy moribund. A 1917 Cook's travel guide advised travelers to obtain Mexican dollars at their Beijing office because its stability made it the money used throughout China. After the would-be emperor Yuan Shikai's death, China would not be united under a single currency until 1949.

Beijing was "boring, desiccated, dirty, dilatory, inconvenient, uneconomical, unhealthy, and devoid of amusement," declared a 1919 essay titled, "The New Life Beijing Residents Ought to Demand." It put forward twenty reforms that included schools, hospitals, old-age homes, and other institutions. It also demanded a public transportation system, so residents could "stop wasting time en route to where we are going, eating filthy street dust, consorting with oxen and horses, and dodging the wheels of automobiles." The author, Peking University library director Li Dazhao, wanted a trolley.

On May 4, 1919, thousands of students marched in Beijing in support of the New Culture Movement, which championed science, democracy, gender equality, and vernacular literature. The May Fourth Movement, as it is now known, also protested the concession of Chinese territory to Japan in the Treaty of Versailles that ended the First World War. The marchers called for a nation, instead of factional rule.

In 1921, Li Dazhao cofounded the Chinese Communist Party. One of the Party's early members, Mao Zedong, also worked in the university library, as a clerk.

That year, Beijing got its trolley. The unified nation would come later.

Sun Yat-sen, head of the Nationalist Party, which ruled the disjointed republic, called for a countrywide "reconstruction" to spur modernization. As China did not have an architecture school, or a glut of skilled tradesmen, foreigners were called upon to build. "The engineering societies of the world should make Dr. Sun their patron saint," said an American at the time, "because if he ever got in a position where he could put his plans into effect, there would be work for engineers in China for the next 1,000 years."

Chinese also studied abroad, many in America, which funded scholarships using money from the Boxer indemnity. Sun Yat-sen's son, Sun Ke, attended UCLA and Columbia. After he was put in charge of modernizing the southern port of Guangzhou (Canton), three of the city's six commissioners had graduated from American universities, where the nation's wide, paved roads designed for cars made a lasting impression. On their return, they ordered the pulling down of Guangzhou's eight-hundred-year-old wall. "The streets were cut through the maize [sic] of buildings with ruthless disregard of the protests of the house owners whose places happened to stand in the way," an engineer reported. "Only by forcing down this somewhat unpleasant medicine were the improvements made possible."

Across China, engineers toppled city walls and wood-framed, imperial-era architecture. Yet while multistory offices rose in commercial centers such as Shanghai, Beijing's walls absorbed and influenced Western architects to make traditional-looking buildings from permanent materials. The Canadian Henry Hussey and the American Henry Murphy both advocated an "adaptive architecture" that used modern engineering to construct buildings with traditional Chinese traits, including wide masonry foundations, lavish colors, and the sloping tiled roofs with eaves that curled toward the sky. Today, the Rockefeller Foundation–funded Peking Union (Xiehe) Hospital, and structures on the campuses of Peking University and Tsinghua University, are often mistaken as Chinese-drawn designs. No plaques explain their provenance.

Murphy disguised Peking University's water tower as a thirteen-story pagoda, while nearby classroom buildings look like traditional wooden halls, though built with concrete. At Tsinghua, modernizing Chinese rejected his native-appearing designs for ones resembling Western icons associated with democracy. Thus, with its dome atop a columned portico, Tsinghua's auditorium resembles something drawn by Palladio or Thomas Jefferson. Murphy based it on Columbia University's library.

Hussey tired of quarreling with clients and retired to a Beijing courtyard home. Murphy, however, enjoyed an elegant office on Shanghai's Bund. He became a top architectural adviser to the Nationalist government and helped design a new national capital complex outside Nanjing (Nanking). That plan was never realized. He also unsuccessfully lobbied to preserve that city's wall, arguing that cars could drive along its top.

Instead, Nanjing's dense, colorful lanes fell to wide boulevards, a process witnessed by Pearl Buck, living in the city. Her 1929 short story "The New

Road" imagined the construction from the perspective of a fifty-year-old grandfather named Lu Chen, who is given fifteen days to vacate his shop, without compensation.

"There is no money," a policeman tells him. "You are presenting this to the Republic."

Lu stays to watch the demolition team. "There was not one touch of sympathy in their faces. In this fashion they had already destroyed hundreds of shops and homes; and to them, he saw very clearly, he was only an old man and one more troublesome than others," writes Buck. When two workmen hacked at his copper cauldrons with pickaxes, Lu says suddenly, "My grandfather put those in . . . But he said nothing more while they took the tiles from the roof and the light began to seep down between the rafters. At last they took the rafters, and he sat there within four walls with the noonday sunshine beating on him . . . When evening came, he still sat there, his shop a heap of bricks and tiles and broken rafters about him. The two cauldrons stood up naked out of the ruins. People stared at him curiously but said nothing, and he sat on."

Lu moves outside the city and sits stunned and silent for months, while his son becomes an overseer of the road's workmen. "Why, these streets were made a thousand years ago," the son argues. "Are we never to have new ones?"

One day, Lu returns to the site of his destroyed neighborhood. Surprisingly, he cannot help admiring the finished road; it is grander than any he has seen, "a great wide sweep of emptiness, straight through the heart of the city . . . Not even emperors had made a road like this!" The story ends with Lu musing, "Had it taken this road to make his son a man? . . . This Revolution—this new road! Where did it lead?"

Beijing's *hutong* remained largely unchanged, physically and in spirit. The city still came to your door: merchants walked through lanes banging gongs, clappers, and castanets and lured customers by calling out rhymes for their products, such as a cake whose "oil is fragrant, the flour is white; throw it in the pot, it floats just right." A *hutong* dweller could watch a procession of professions, including barbers, china menders, lamplighters, herbalists, toy makers, florists, fortune-tellers, magicians, and bear baiters.

The old and new mingled in Dazhalan, where Packards drove down Front Gate Avenue, and trains pulled into the station, but most people still traveled on foot or by rickshaw. Like tracing paper, modern infrastructure was laid over a city economy still dominated by craftsmen, not industry. Many residents had depended on the imperial court for employment or business. A 1926 survey found that a quarter of the city's population was destitute, and nearly half were lower-middle-class.

At a time when New York was building skyscrapers such as the Empire State Building and was the workplace of Babe Ruth, Beijing still delivered water to homes by wheelbarrow and suffered bandit raids led by outlaws with names such as White Wolf. *White Wolf is coming!* The Nationalists kept a tenuous hold on the city, pestered by warlords who controlled China's northeast. Battles erupted in Beijing; a bomb was tossed from a biplane over the Temple of Heaven. It slightly injured a passerby. The Temple was unharmed.

The city, the author of a Chinese textbook warned, consisted of "high palaces and deep courtyards that might easily encourage an ambitious politician in dreams of destroying the Republic and restoring the empire."

A late-1920s snapshot of Front Gate Avenue, when automobiles joined rickshaws and trolley tracks.

1920s rickshaws run under the gated entrance to Dazhalan—Big Fence—the commercial hutong for which the neighborhood is named.

The Nationalists agreed. The government, now led by a southern general named Chiang Kai-shek, planted trees in the area outside the Gate of Heavenly Peace (Tian'anmen) to reduce the open space protesters regularly used to rally crowds. In 1928, Chiang declared Nanjing as China's new capital. Beijing was once again optimistically renamed Beiping, "Northern Peace."

Nationalists started a campaign to rid Beiping of its erstwhile decadence. *Hutong* and street names that invoked the imperial past were changed to modern-sounding monikers such as Sovereign Rights Lane and Unequal Treaties Boulevard. Street signs were posted to rectify maps and end the habit of lanes being identified by names coined by the neighborhood's residents. The government renamed Central Park to honor the deceased Sun Yat-sen, and painted its walls blue—the Nationalists' symbolic color—over the imperial vermilion. It ordered yellow roof tiles, which covered the emperor's palaces, stripped from buildings. It banned clothing fashions from the imperial era, and also the city's elaborate weddings and funerals.

The *New York Times* reported that residents "resent the determined effort to reduce this ancient capital to the status of a drab and modernized provincial city."

They also resented modernization that outmoded professions. Beiping's first trolley looped the Forbidden City, following the outline of the razed wall that had formed a buffer zone around it. (Known as the ring route, its name is one theory explaining why, today, Beijing's series of beltways begins with the Second Ring Road, instead of the First, which doesn't exist. Typically, there is no consensus.) By 1929, a resident could traverse the entire Old City on several trolley lines. In a depressed economy, the transport challenged the livelihood of the city's sixty thousand rickshaw pullers.

In October of that year, an estimated twenty-five thousand residents— mostly rickshaw pullers—marched through Beiping chanting, "Give every rickshaw man an extra fifty coppers a day!" When the procession came across trolleys, they smashed their windows with iron bars, yelling, "Down with the streetcar company!"

The violence was short-lived, and the trolleys continued running. Beiping's citizens were not cowed by the city's Nationalist government, however. Grievances were aired in public demonstrations by groups as diverse as Buddhist monks and vegetable sellers. In 1929, a coalition of merchants began a four-year battle to prevent their shops from being demolished for a road-widening project near Dazhalan.

"We are exhausted, as are our financial resources," a merchant named Li Mengji wrote to the city in February. "Our businesses have not been here for very long, but we have suffered many wars. Although we have been trying our best, the life of our businesses is still vulnerable as a thin thread . . . It is very hard for us to leave this land. Moving away from this place will put us in debt, hurt our property and the reputation of our businesses. We will also lose the relationship we have built up with our customers over the years. This will be a negative influence on society. We sincerely ask for your permission to allow us to keep our businesses."

The government responded, "All shops must move as soon as the project begins."

The dispute had not been resolved in October 1930, when the merchants, denied access to the road's planning documents, decried the government's lack of transparency. A sixty-eight-year-old named Qi Dekui sent the city a letter signed by representatives for more than one hundred merchant families.

"Although we are ignorant," Qi wrote, "there are some people who know a little bit more among us. The way we see it, if it is the government that needs this land, you have to provide detailed regulations regarding people's livelihood. You should distinguish the prices of the houses according to their quality and pay people when tearing them down so that people will not complain. In addition, the residents should also be informed beforehand. There is no rationality in your keeping silent about the project and all of a sudden deciding to force us to tear down our houses and evacuate the land."

The merchants worried that "some dishonest people will act as the middlemen, collect money and act as agents, making a profit in the process." Their homes were measured in secret, Qi reported. "We began asking around but have not been able to find out the truth."

A government representative sent to speak with Qi found him to be "very rude and could not be reasoned with. The other families, encouraged by his behavior, watched this and did not cooperate with the investigation."

The media did not report the dissent. A newspaper's editorial writer said that a "foreign friend" had disagreed with the project, because the Inner City wall was architecturally superb and should be protected. Another reporter decried the government's monopoly on information, making "residents trapped in a constantly defensive position."

The road was built two years later. Widened to ten lanes in the early twenty-first century, the street is now lined with a KFC, Starbucks, and our neighborhood's Wal-Mart.

In 1934, the Nationalists launched a plan to turn Beiping into a tourist attraction. The mayor lamented the destruction of most of the wall that had ringed the neighborhood around the Forbidden City, as well as damage to numerous city gate towers. The renovation program targeted imperial gardens and palaces, not courtyard homes. The city's grandest architecture could lure paying customers and leave them with a positive impression of China.

Foreigners living in Beiping during the 1930s had already fallen for its charms. "I cannot too highly commend leisurely residence in an ancient capital," wrote George Kates in *The Years That Were Fat*, his memoir of courtyard life. "Gently decaying palaces offer charming possibilities for rearrangement and simple dwelling; manners are markedly more sensitive and refined; and the simplest acts of daily living are performed more agreeably in such surroundings. Time is used elegantly, in courtly fashion, with a quite special knowledge that its luxury abides where others have departed."

Chinese intellectuals saw something else. The poet Xu Zhimo branded the former capital a "dead city." Another writer called it a "phantom city, thriving only in and for the past . . . observing obsolete customs, recalling old glories, and cultivating wistful airs." Beiping, a writer complained, "after all is only a place for foreign visitors to have fun in. How pathetic [that] it possesses only this tiny bit of an advantage."

Osbert Sitwell, another expatriate memoirist, found that the city "has none of the dreadful impersonal quality of the more recently designed quarter of a European capital; none of the coldness of the new Berlin, or of Haussmann's Paris: moreover, there is no lack of small streets, which are necessary, too, to the soul of a city."

A Chinese writer, complaining of Beiping's backwardness, said, "I dream of the prosperity of Paris, the grandeur of Berlin, the skyscrapers and speedy cars of London."

As the new capital, Nanjing, did not have a Legation Quarter, the embassies remained behind, a situation one British writer compared to Parliament convening in London while the representatives of foreign powers lived somewhere in the middle of Scotland, "with the additional disadvantage of slow train services and no long-distance telephones."

Life for the foreign population was dreamlike and idle. "Everyone agreed that Puritanism and Beiping didn't mix well," wrote a Belgian journalist. Expatriates could afford Mongolian ponies, polo competitions, daylong picnics, and personal rickshaw-pullers. "Life was an endless string of parties. Everything was cheap because labor was cheap. Beiping was simply heaven. Whether the Chinese thought so, too, was quite immaterial."

"Of a population of 1.3 million, many are unemployed," said a city report. "If they want to work they have no factories to go to, if they want to trade, there is no commerce to pursue . . . In one street, there might be several or even several dozens of households with no means of earning a living and nothing to do but sit and wait for the end."

They were the subjects of the 1936 novel *Camel Xiangzi*, written by Lao She, the pen name of Shu Sheyu. He grew up in a *hutong*, and his father, a Manchu banner man, was killed during the Boxer Rebellion. Also titled *Rickshaw* in early English translations, *Camel Xiangzi* is named for its protagonist, a Beiping rickshaw puller who lived in a shared courtyard home where "there wasn't a single flowering tree. Instead, the spring wind blew little pockmarks in the ice in the center of the courtyard first and then blew a fetid stench off the trash heap." Some of the house's children did not have clothes to wear, and their sooty faces were chilblained. "Dying must be the easiest, simplest thing there is because living was hell already."

The city's stunted economy sent Lao She on a peripatetic search for employment. He taught literature in cities across China, and for six years at

Rickshaw pullers and their upper-class fares.

London University's School of Oriental Studies. His best-loved works are set in his hometown, however, and filled with vivid descriptions of its native attractions, foods, dialect, and obscenities.

Camel Xiangzi tells a different tale, set in an impoverished city filled with betrayal and peopled by soldiers, thieves, and whores. The novel ends so devastatingly that—without telling the author—its first English translator rewrote the conclusion so that everyone lived happily ever after.

After its victory over Russia in 1905 for control of Port Arthur (Lüshun), Japan had expanded its toehold in China's northeast. In 1931 its invasion of the entire region was complete, and in 1934 Japan put Puyi on the throne as emperor of a puppet state named Manchukuo. In addition to controlling the mineral-rich area, Japan also had a base from which it could push south into China.

In July 1937, the initial reports announced that Chinese forces had routed the Japanese on the outskirts of Beiping. The lies covered terrible losses. When the truth emerged, "never have I seen such gloom settled over any people as settled over all the Chinese," wrote a member of the U.S. Embassy Marine Guard. "I felt terribly sorry for them, they had been so elated and after years of being humiliated by the Japanese, they thought the tide had turned and they had defeated them."

Captain John Seymour "Buzz" Letcher was a Virginian posted to Beiping in 1937 as the commander of a rifle company. With twenty officers and five hundred enlisted men, the embassy guard formed the Legation Quarter's largest force. Letcher was thirty-four years old, large-framed, with a doughy face topped by pale eyebrows and thinning hair. In photographs, his martial demeanor is apparent; he stands erect and expressionless. The unsmiling image does not reveal how deeply Letcher had fallen for Beiping's charms.

Even in its advancing decrepitude, the city's settings could still resemble something from a Pearl Buck novel: magnolia perfume, sticky opium smoke, rainbow silks and satins, turquoise and gold flashing upon slim ivory hands. Letcher enjoyed a dessert called Peking Dust, made from ground chestnuts and honey served inside "a wall of glacéed fruits all covered with whipped cream. Pretty good I can tell you."

Letcher was stationed in Beiping for two years, and his letters—which begin, "Dearest Mother"—give a rare glimpse of the city under Japanese control. Many Chinese intellectuals left; foreign memoirists, such as *The Years That Were Fat*'s author, suddenly distinguished themselves as nonlocal. "When the Japanese came, Kates ran an American flag up over his house," his *hutong* neighbor remembered decades later. "It was the biggest flag I ever saw. He lived here all those years like a Chinese. But when things got tough, he ran up the Stars and Stripes. I had no flag to run up."

In 1937, Captain Letcher visited the battlefield in the northern suburb of Nanyuan to find the bodies of horses and Chinese soldiers piled fifteen high. Many had been gunned down while they fled, tossing canteens and peeling off their gray uniforms. "I don't believe the soldiers are trained in anything except the most rudimentary things," he wrote. "The Chinese trenches were poorly sited, poor fields of fire, no bays or irregular turns to keep them from being enfiladed. Their communications are probably very poor, medical department is nothing . . . No airplanes or tanks . . . There can only be one outcome to this war, a Japanese victory."

On the Sunday morning of August 8, 1937, Letcher watched as the Japanese entered the city via Front Gate Avenue. "Following the tanks came the infantry marching in a column of four. We estimated their number to be about 1500. They were small and most of them were bandy-legged. They marched without trying to keep in step and made no effort to maintain an erect posture. Their khaki-colored woolen coats and trousers were ill-fitting and their puttees were made by wrapping long strips of woolen cloth around their legs. Their shoes were heavy and unpolished."

Posters were glued to walls around the city announcing that Kawabe Shozo was Beiping's military governor. He had commanded the Japanese forces at Nanyuan. Any Chinese who disobeyed his administration would be executed.

At the end of August, Letcher wrote that the city "appears to be quite normal now, stores shops etc. are all open. I believe the Japs are very anxious to keep things going here, so that they can get food and supplies for their armies and also collect taxes. They will never let go of Peking now." Letcher hoped to go snipe hunting on the grounds of the Summer Palace. In October, the racecourse reopened. Three months before, it had been a battlefield, but "to-day in the warm fall sunshine the crowd of Chinese and foreigners watched the races and bet on the ponies as if nothing had ever happened. The trenches have been filled up, the dead buried and not a trace of anything warlike remains."

He noted the surge in opium into the city to both subdue the population and increase revenues. By 1940, the occupiers had set up or licensed six hundred opium dens, many located in Dazhalan.

Japan planned Beiping to be a provincial capital, as well as a military and cultural center, with a population doubled to 2.5 million within twenty years. Its "New Beiping" plan opened the heart of the Old City to vehicle traffic. Engineers punched holes in the city wall to lay the broad boulevard, the Avenue of Eternal Peace, that still runs past Tian'anmen Square and the capital's most important government offices.

The Japanese built other roads inside the Old City, whose number of *hutong* had expanded to thirty-six hundred, according to a census. The occupying administration did not want Japanese to reside in the *hutong*, however. "In order to avoid Japanese and Chinese living in mixed housing, we will build a Japanese new city district," the plan said. "Traditional houses do not satisfy Japanese life demands, and repairing them is difficult." The district featured axial roads on a symmetrical grid, and its own airfield.

Still, the occupiers made use of the choicest imperial courtyards, Letcher wrote. "These old Manchu families after three centuries of living in China's best are now hard put to it because the Japanese are just taking their houses and land without any pretense of payment for it, but I don't think that they deserve any better fate because they are the ones who let China go to seed."

Japan's New Beiping plan pledged to "vigorously protect Chinese culture" and to repair the grounds of the Old Summer Palace, which had been looted by the Anglo-French armies. Budgetary restraints said otherwise. "If a lot of money isn't soon expended in repair work," Letcher wrote in 1939, "the Palaces will be in ruins and with Japan drawing every bit of money out of here the chances of such work being done are rather remote. So it is nice to have seen the city before too many changes take place."

The marines built a large rink shielded by a tent outside their embassy, on a corner of today's Tian'anmen Square. "Right now the only exercise I can get is ice skating," Letcher wrote in 1939, "and on many days the dust on the ice prevents it being skated on." He hated cocktail parties—"you see the same people again and again and it becomes boring"—and found the Westerners who hung around the Peking Club "rather ridiculous. Very small frogs in a very small pond acting like they were big frogs in an ocean." He preferred hunting pheasant outside the city. In February 1939, Letcher looked forward to attending Dazhalan's New Year's temple fair, noting, "I went last year several times."

Outside the Temple of Heaven, his tour guide "told us to look well at the street and the houses along it because he said that they had been changed none at all since they were built seven or eight hundred years ago and were an excellent example of how an old Chinese city street looked in the days of Kublai Khan. So we were seeing the street just as Marco Polo did except for the rickshaws which swarmed along it and the occasional Japanese army motor truck."

The scene impressed Letcher enough to indulge in some rare—if slight—hyperbole. It is doubtful the street's appearance had been unchanged since Marco Polo visited, but to Letcher it must have been a lovely illusion. Destitution can imbue cities with romance and nostalgia. Even after being stripped of its purpose and occupied by a hostile army, the city could still enchant. As he awaited his leave orders, Letcher wrote his mother, "If I had to live in a city, could never leave it for any reason, I would choose Peking of all the cities I've ever seen to live in."

CHAPTER 17

MISS ZHU REMEMBERS THE TREES

THE LAKES AND Forbidden City moat would not freeze in the winter of 2006. The calendar passed through the two-week spells named Major Snow, Winter Solstice, Minor Cold, and even Major Cold, but the outside temperature stayed tepid. The Lunar New Year's Spring Festival holiday arrived relatively late, in mid-February, but still the ice remained out. For the first time in the decade since I had moved to Beijing, the weather canceled hockey season.

I traveled to the United States to see family. The country was waging two wars, yet life proceeded as normal, except for the voice on the airport intercom announcing, "Threat Level Orange." Advertisements said Americans were plagued by an affliction called restless legs syndrome. My friends were settling down with kids and dogs, though they seemed to have reversed the monikers—a retriever called Jeff, a son named Ranger. *Chai* was a beverage, not an order to destroy. The air was clean, and my lungs expelled sticky souvenirs of Beijing's pollution. The book I carried from the courtyard released a musty smell when opened, transporting me back.

At a construction site I read the posted notices ordering the builder to prepare a Historic Resource Protection Plan and halt work should "human skeletal remains be encountered." The builder had to submit test results for on-site groundwater and hazardous materials, as well as a safety plan. There were noise restraints (no pile drivers, no rigs), and rules governing traffic rerouting. If the public had questions or objections to the project, it could attend a hearing scheduled at city hall. I wished America could export that transparency to China, along with open-stack libraries.

Life in the United States felt convenient, if lonely. Telephone and electric bills could be paid over the Internet, not by waiting in line at the bank. The mail was delivered at four, and the recycling picked up from the curb on Mondays. I didn't know by whom. Neighbors said "Hello." On a university campus, I often passed a couple that stood holding a sign protesting nuclear weapons. I never saw anyone approach them. America granted the freedom to be ignored.

When I returned to Beijing in late February, the police were looking for me. My cell phone rang as I took a taxi from the airport. "Some guy got in a fight on your *hutong*," Officer Li said. "He was Chinese, and when the cop interviewed him, he gave your Chinese name as his own. But we sorted it out. Everyone knows Heroic Eastern Plumblossom is a foreigner!"

At his post in front of my courtyard's gate, Recycler Wang nodded and asked if I had eaten, as if I had only been gone a few hours. My rooms' windows needed a good scrubbing with the *Evening News*. Aside from spiders, the only living things I had ever seen in my house weren't rats or cockroaches, but two slugs that occasionally appeared, as now, halfway up the bedroom wall.

They left a trail of slime. Flying Horse cigarette ash followed the Widow. She walked into the room without knocking and said, "You're back." After upbraiding me for wasting money on taking a cab, not the bus, from the airport, she puttered to the kitchen to prepare noodles topped with sesame paste. "Eat noodles, Little Plumblossom. Eat!" She watched me slurp, then took the empty bowl and left.

I asked Mr. Han why he was home in the afternoon. "We went to the northeast for Spring Festival to see our son," he said. "While we were gone, someone else rented our stall at the cell phone market." His wife did not want to return to Beijing, he said. Yet he believed 2007 would be the year their luck improved.

After returning from the United States, where I enjoyed privacy, heat, and indoor plumbing, the courtyard felt different. Now I was back in the cold, damp fishbowl, and again peeing in bottles at night because the Widow kept the door lashed with beams. The elderly students at the

NeighCom English class said that once people moved from their shared courtyards into apartments, they never went back. It was, they said with sorrow, as if a spell had been broken.

The warm winter allowed the road-building projects to speed up. A ribbon of empty blacktop ran through the heart of Fresh Fish Junction. A cement wall painted to resemble a wooden fence bordered the one-way, four-lane road.

The ruins of the neighborhood had been gated and blocked from the public. I slipped past the security guard to see, near Old Zhang's former home, newly built replicas of a shop and a bathhouse that had been destroyed. Old Zhang's home still stood, almost a year after he had been evicted. When I called him, he said, "The rumor is that the district government's developing company is having difficulty attracting investors to fund construction of a mall on that land. It's very controversial."

The new road through Fresh Fish Junction, just after its completion.

AK-47's art, painted on the wall of a destroyed Fresh Fish Junction home.

On the white walls of some half-destroyed courtyards, a bald head's profile shone in black. The artist signed his work *AK-47*. He began adding the heads—spray-painted in one fluid line—to destroyed *hutong* in the late 1990s, at a time when such graffiti had to be done anonymously for fear of punishment. He called the series "Dialogue," representing his conversation with the vanishing city. Like the mark of Zorro, the bald heads testified to existence, saying, "I was here. I saw this, too." As China's art market ascended, the artist stepped forward. His real name was Zhang Dali. He had since become famous and collected internationally. Now, a signed photograph of his work could fetch a sum higher than what developers gave the evictees from his canvases. That was the new Beijing.

I walked across Front Gate Avenue, past Mr. Han's former shop, shuttered, but still standing. The road project here had been finished, too. Bordering the east end of Red Bayberry and Bamboo Slanted Street, the improved Coal Street divided Dazhalan, but with less disruption than feared. The one-way road had only two lanes, and two dedicated bike lanes. Billboards along its eastern edge showed a cherub-faced hawker with an imperial-era cap, gown, and braided queue shouting out, in English only:

**Dashilar
Along the Forbidden City
600 Years
Legend Commerce**

The ad used the traditional local slang for Dazhalan, "Dashilar" (pronounced *DA-sure-LAR*). The accompanying computer graphic displayed modern courtyard homes planned for the area. Another pair of billboards showed a black-and-white photograph of the pedestrian street and said:

> **Mega Cheerful Business Travels Reserved
> Flourish of Legend Street Recurring
> All Brands Co-exist Harmoniously
> Ideal Ancient Streetscape for Tourists**

The neighborhood already had brands and classes coexisting harmoniously, from the *jianbing* (pancake) seller to the artists selling antiques, and the dozens of "old brand names" that had been evicted the previous year. In March 2007, their former buildings remained, vacant. The area still exhibited an ancient streetscape, though one not ideal to the Hand.

Another new billboard displayed an image of Buckingham Fountain, in Chicago's Grant Park. Was that the future of our *hutong*? The sign didn't say. It's doubtful that the Hand knew that the park's appearance resulted from citizen opposition to development. In the late-nineteenth century, mail-order pioneer Aaron Montgomery Ward fought several court battles with civic leaders who wanted to build on the vacant plot formed after Great Fire debris was plowed into Lake Michigan. Excepting the Art Institute, Ward successfully fought to preserve the park's open space, free to all.

Even after abandoning their chalkboard countdown, my students knew that the Olympics began in five hundred days. The first day of the second semester began with another assembly celebrating the milestone, with more oaths sworn to the games' mascots, the five cartoon characters collectively called the *fuwa*. Miss Zhu and four of her colleagues—each wearing a sweater the color of an Olympic ring—stood on the outdoor stage holding plush *fuwa* toys. They sang a tune issued to every elementary school by the Education Bureau, called "Beijing Smile."

> *Smile, smile, volunteers' smile*
> *Smile, smile, the friendliness of friends*
> *The lengthy smile twinkling on a face, sweat reflecting*
>   *the blue sky*
> *Gently asking in English, "How are you?"*
> *Come friends, friends come*
> *Volunteers' smile is Beijing's best name card*
> *Smile Beijing, with limitless genuine feelings*
> *Volunteers' smile is Beijing's best name card.*

The familiar twanging guitar of "Footloose" boomed in high treble, and in skipped the school dance line with frozen smiles. I asked Miss Zhu why the teachers' *fuwa* toys were still in their plastic bags. She gestured to the tobacco-colored air. "This dust storm will get them dirty," she said. "We'll have to use them for every assembly until the Olympics."

One of our best students moved, to attend a school in her home province. A child of migrant workers, she had been able to enroll at Coal Lane Elementary for the same three-hundred-yuan ($40) fee a local paid for a year's study. All students, however, had to take the middle school entrance examination where their identity card (*hukou*) was registered. The exam was more than a year away, but the mother worried her daughter wouldn't quickly adapt to a place where she had never lived and would therefore do badly on the exam.

In our textbook, Mocky was reading "The Emperor's New Clothes."

Miss Zhu asked students to rewrite the story from the perspective of the emperor. One boy's telling began, "My name is USA. I like watermelon. I like new clothes. I like steak sausages. I like XO. My country's name is Texas."

Miss Zhu and I were hanging up the kids' illustrated versions of the tale when an Education Bureau official entered our classroom. "You are a volunteer!" the woman said, pumping my hand in a limp shake. "Being a volunteer is really great! You're a real volunteer! You have volunteer spirit! You've really sunk in here!"

Not entirely. Miss Zhu had to attend a meeting in which the official would tick off directives while jabbing her pinkie into the opposite palm, for emphasis. I could skip the lecture. I walked downstairs to eat lunch at Soldier Liu's. Bunched before the school's black iron gate, the student brass band clanged out a halting version of "Auld Lang Syne." The bass drum thundered, and the trumpets began "Ode to Joy." Watching the kids' determination made me smile. As ever, it was good to be home.

Over a bowl of Soldier Liu's knife-shaved noodles, I asked him what living conditions his family had traded for life in the *hutong*. Was this environment better than what they had in the countryside? I doubted the positive response, repeatedly, until finally Soldier Liu wrote down their address in Shanxi province and said to go see for myself.

An overnight train deposited me before dawn in Pingyao, one of China's last remaining walled cities, located four hundred miles southwest of Beijing. The sun's face was beet red, as if it, too, were gagging on air pollution that made my eyes water. The bus to Soldier Liu's village bounced on a rutted road through flat, arid farmland. Dump trucks with sagging axles lumbered past, spilling coal from their beds. At the side of the road, a man with long, matted hair swept the black dust into neat piles beside a mound of discarded shoes. "He's nuts," a passenger explained.

At the village, Soldier Liu's sister waited at the arch that memorialized a Communist martyr. A smooth cement road led into town, comprising a grid of two dozen lanes, lined with high brick walls and doors that opened into homes set beside a private courtyard. It was a rural version of the *hutong*.

For the decoration of their home's interior courtyard wall, Soldier Liu's

The village outside of Pingyao, in central China, where Soldier Liu grew up.

mother had chosen tiles painted with a southern mountain range and lake. "She's never been there," his sister said. "She thinks the bright colors are pretty." The courtyard was tamped earth, and clean. A wall included a stone carved with the characters for Mount Tai, regarded as a Taoist shrine and believed to protect the house. The same talisman marked many Beijing *hutong* homes.

Soldier Liu's sister walked me through the large kitchen, three bedrooms, and up steps to the flat roof, which was used for spreading grains for drying. The older houses behind the Lius' were entered through wooden doors carved with auspicious rhyming couplets and anchored by decorative stones, as in the *hutong*.

"In fact, this has always been a prosperous village," his sister said. "Things have never been that bad here. It's just that people know they can make more money in the city." She was training in a neighboring town to become a math teacher. On our walk around her village, we had seen only one other person, a grandfather who greeted her by name. "I live at school," she said. "There's really nothing here anymore. Everyone except the elderly has moved to towns." The village was repopulated during Spring Festival, when residents reunited with family for the New Year. Working the land was a thing of the past. "We still have soybean crops here, but we hire laborers to do the planting and harvesting for us."

Soldier Liu's sister was cheerful and always smiling, but every time I praised an architectural detail or the surrounding environment, she cut me short. The village and their home was nothing compared to the city, she said.

"One day a few years back, my parents just decided to stop farming and start their own business. They went to an old landlord's mansion near here that's a tourist site and movie set. They opened a small noodle stand, and once they saved enough, they moved to Beijing. You met them at their first restaurant, the one that was destroyed."

They had never given up on Beijing, she said. In China, the urban economy was much more robust than the rural one, and countryside villages such as this were emptying, as the population shifted to cities.

Soldier Liu's sister said there was one big advantage to the village, however. "Of course my brother should marry a girl from here. They've known him his entire life, and what kind of a man he is. Also, they all think he's really handsome."

I looked down the empty lanes. "Where are the girls now?"

"Oh, they're in different cities, of course!"

The ten-hour bus ride back to Beijing passed village after village that, although it was spring, showed no one working the fields. The congestion was on the highway, where filled coal trucks and passenger buses ferried fresh loads of energy to the capital, which consumed all it could.

Miss Zhu stood on a pedestrian overpass, surveying her childhood neighborhood. The view was a before-and-after photo. On the right, the web of narrow lanes and courtyard houses. On the left, wide boulevards and high-rises whose signs announced Beijing's first Brooks Brothers, another Starbucks, and the Wal-Mart. The *hutong* opposite was plastered with yellow posters reminding residents not to listen to rumors, to trust the Party, and welcome a new Olympics.

The new road through Miss Zhu's neighborhood. Wal-Mart is located just to the left of the frame.

"It's not so tragic that the house I was raised in is being torn down," Miss Zhu said as we walked. "I don't recognize the neighborhood, anyway. It didn't look anything like this when I was little."

As a girl, she lived with her grandparents in a neighborhood that was a fifteen-minute walk west from my home and Coal Lane Elementary. Miss Zhu grew up on a lane named Tree of Heaven, a species that flourished in the area. The tree is also known in Chinese as stinking spring, for its blossoms' pungent aroma. In English, the tree is called Chinese sumac, or ghetto palm, due to its weedy ability to grow anywhere.

The tree is listed in the oldest extant Chinese dictionary. Its satiny yellow wood is commonly used to make dim-sum steamers, its large leaves to feed silkworms, and its roots—when mixed with fermented black beans and young boys' urine, according to an ancient medical text—cured mental illness. The tree is one of the last to emerge from winter dormancy, giving it the name spring tree, as well. That's how Miss Zhu thought of it, because like many Beijing natives, she looked forward to the season when its leaves were ready to be picked.

"They weren't green when they first blossomed," she said, pointing to the tree. "They were a little purple and a little red. I would climb up that one and pick the leaves, and my grandmother would fry them with eggs. It was so delicious! They tasted so fresh, almost like cilantro, but with a stronger aroma and texture."

A worker tore at her childhood home with a pickax, but she fixed her stare at the trees on the lane. "That one's a jujube. After they ripened, they would just fall to the ground. But the best-tasting ones needed to be beaten off the branches with a stick. Any old stick would do, we didn't have a special tool. Life was very practical then."

When people in Beijing recounted their memories, I reminded myself to not speak during the silence. Often, as now, Miss Zhu would say something that appeared headed in one direction, pause, not speak for a few minutes, then start again on another topic whose connection was obvious only to her.

"I knew everyone on these *hutong*," she said, still looking at the tree as the sound of her home's being smashed resonated behind us. "Everyone knew me. They would call me by my name when I ran around playing, and I knew their names, too, even if I couldn't say who lived at what address. There was some sort of factory opposite the lane. It was very small, but its business was terrible. I remember that it had an iron gate, and it was always closed. It was about as tall as my grandmother's house, also two stories, and the gate was always closed, and there was an open space in front of the recessed doorframe, and it became the favorite spot for old people to sit and chat all day."

An elderly woman ambled toward us. "Little Zhu! You're back. Have you eaten?"

"I've eaten, you?"

Acquaintances, even against a scene of their homes being destroyed around them, do not hug or shake hands. The two stood a foot apart and chatted about their families' respective health. The woman did not call me a foreigner or ask who I was or wonder where Miss Zhu's husband was. I was part of the landscape, nothing more. "We have to move next week," the woman said without emotion. "Don't want to, but have to. How are your grandparents?" The worker continued to swing his pickax. The woman walked to the latrine.

"I don't think of this as our house," Miss Zhu continued, watching the destruction. "The house he's demolishing now was rebuilt on the site of our old one. That house really had its own character. I've never found another

High-rise apartments replaced courtyard homes around Tree of Heaven Lane, where Miss Zhu grew up.

one like it. It was gray, with a peaked roof. The roof had a big space underneath it, and you could climb up there and walk around. Very interesting. The stairs were wood. When you walked on them, your feet made a *gezhi gezhi* sound. The bricks made a yin/yang pattern, placed vertically and horizontally so it looked like 凹 and 凸. Metal gutters ran down the sides. It was warm in winter and cold in summer, really great. Now it's all gone. What you're looking at now is all new brick. Before, aside from the outside walls, everything was old wood."

She paused and watched the worker smash through a section of wall. "It used to be all one yard, with no other houses or families sharing it. The government rented it to my grandparents. It used to be a Nationalist army officer's house. He left, obviously. I don't know who he was. Who can say where he went? There weren't these other little houses here, those used to be our own kitchen and bathroom."

She pointed to a pile of rubble. "My mother and father lived in that room for a time, after they just got married. When I was a little girl, the private bath was already gone, changed to someone else's home. We used the latrine."

"The house had two stories. I lived upstairs with my grandmother. There was a massive beam running along the roof seam, a big piece of wood. Very rough, like it was the trunk of an old tree. My grandmother enjoyed it when I walked on her back, and so I would hold on to the beam and step on her. I would say, 'No,' and she would say, 'What's no? Stand on me.' I said I didn't weigh enough to massage her back, and she said, 'You get up there.' I was afraid I would fall, so she said to grab on to the beam for balance."

Miss Zhu raised her arms above her head. "So I would hold on to the beam and take a step on her back, then slide my hands forward, then take another step. That made her happy. She made sounds."

Miss Zhu smiled, then went silent. She rubbed her hands. The pickax struck brick, releasing a cloud of dust.

"Now, at the root of it, this just isn't my house," she repeated, sounding unconvinced. "It's really ugly. Grandmother and grandfather of course weren't willing to move to the suburbs. Although, they don't have the strong feelings that you think they would. Right now they're doing okay. Sometimes my father has business near here, and my grandmother always says, 'Take me! Take me!' Because she can't go out on her own, she needs someone to watch her. Whenever we bring her somewhere, though, she says, 'I'll sit outside and wait for you.' She can sit for an hour in one place and look at everything. Last month, my mom got some opera tickets, and she invited a friend and my grandmother. Once they arrived at the theater, she said, 'You guys go see the opera. I'll just stroll around outside.'"

Miss Zhu's grandparents were living in her parents' apartment, in a high-rise twenty miles away, far from the *hutong* and its streaming scenes of life. "The building has a small yard, and sometimes she goes out there and sits, but for the most part they both stay inside all day. I think getting used to the new environment requires time. We're using their resettlement compensation to buy the apartment next door to my parents."

Miss Zhu handled negotiations with the developers. People in Beijing without power talk fast and loud, growing shriller the further they get pushed away. The developer's representative was downright somnambulant. "At first he offered three hundred and eighty thousand yuan [$50,667]. I went to his office three times. His attitude was great, actually.

You could raise whatever hardships you had. The important thing was not to suggest a price really over the top, like one and a half million. We don't have property rights here, as this was a public, subsidized residence. I talked to the same person every time. He spoke slowly, and calmly, really controlling his emotions and pace. He let me speak, then he spoke, then let me speak some more. He even brought me a glass of water! He gave us enough time to think things over. It took about a month. In the end, we agreed on seven hundred thousand yuan [$93,333]. It will pay for the new apartment, which is what matters. There will also be some money left over in case my grandparents get sick and have to be hospitalized."

The worker had dismantled the topmost walls and began hacking at the floor that separated levels. A New Year's decoration still hung in the stairwell, showing a boy's hands pressed together, supplicating for good fortune. Miss Zhu didn't want to grab it. "Let him do his job," she said, motioning to the man swinging the pickax.

"My grandfather misses sitting under that tree there after dinner with his pipe and talking to all his friends. My grandmother misses going to Wal-Mart," Miss Zhu said with a laugh. "She can't recognize Chinese characters, and she doesn't like to ride escalators. But things were easy to find at Wal-Mart because the packages are all displayed and she knew what labels to look for. It has that angled conveyor thing instead of an escalator. There used to be a supermarket across the lane, but that's already closed now. It just had a big flight of steps, so she needed to find someone to help her up them. Every time, 'Young fellow, lend a hand.' Most of the time she waited for me to take her shopping. She said it was embarrassing asking other people, so she would grab whatever package looked correct and hope it was soap for washing bowls and not clothes. At Wal-Mart she could do it on her own."

I took pictures of Miss Zhu in front of what remained of the lane and home, which had a 拆 symbol the size of her torso swabbed on its wall. "One day, I can show the photos to my child," she said. Becoming pregnant remained her utmost goal. Her grandmother wanted a baby to help raise. With the school's future still unresolved, she worried about planning a family: "Who can say what will happen?"

Office towers were replacing the surrounding lanes, which I counted among the prettiest in the city. The branches of mature locust trees cast

A tree-lined lane near Miss Zhu's home, where the Hand marked courtyards,
including this one, for destruction.

twisted shadows on residences' gray walls, and blossoming spring trees
peeked out from courtyards. The homes were in better condition than
those in Dazhalan, with still-legible couplets carved and painted black on
the vermilion gates: BENEVOLENCE SPRINGS FROM RIGHTEOUSNESS; VIRTUE
BRINGS HAPPINESS. A tin pattern, representing clouds, ornamented the base
of some doors. The decorations on brick lintels showed bats (symbolizing
wealth) and deer (indicating an official lived within). A pair of round,
drum-shaped stones anchoring the doorframe meant that the home once
belonged to an imperial military officer. Auspicious cranes, peonies, and
unicorns adorned the rectangular stones that fronted the former homes of
merchants and scholars.

In a few weeks, they would all be gone, like their former occupants who
were once the target of the faded propaganda still visible on the walls:
NEVER FORGET CLASS STRUGGLE!

Miss Zhu wasn't paying attention to these relics, however. After no reply came to my question about the meaning of a gate's decoration, I turned around to find her standing alone down the lane. She stared up, at the trees.

CHAPTER 18

"If Someone Is Sick and You Do Not Aid Him, It Is Your Fault, Not His"

In the spring of 2007, the *Evening News* ran daily updates on what the Chinese media dubbed the "nail house," located in the southwest city of Chongqing. A married couple refused to vacate the two-story building, for which they held full property—not just usage—rights. Two hundred and eighty neighboring homes had already been razed to make way for a shopping mall, the foundation for which had been dug out around the couple's building. *Nail house* was slang for a structure that tenants refused to vacate, but here it also described the scene: the couple's building balanced atop a spike of earth in the middle of a pit fifty-six feet deep.

The husband, a martial arts champion, stayed in the house, subsisting on supplies pulled up by rope. He raised a national flag and unfurled a banner that said THE LEGAL PRIVATE PROPERTY OF CITIZENS CANNOT BE VIOLATED. His forty-year-old firebrand of a wife granted a stream of interviews, telling the press, "I want to safeguard my dignity and lawful rights." The couple was not against moving, but as they had leased out the ground floor of the well-located building, they wanted a property of equal value in return.

Word of the impasse, and the dramatic image of the building's precarious plight, spread quickly with the aid of cell phones and the Internet. The standoff took place as the central government prepared to promulgate a national law—years in the drafting—that explicitly protected private property for the first time in the People's Republic's history.

In online forums, support for the brazen couple ran high, but wasn't unanimous. To settle the dispute, the developer offered them eighteen thousand yuan ($2,400) per square meter, more than double what evictees received in Beijing, and more than the amount received by the other buildings cleared for the construction. The couple accepted a settlement mediated by a local court that included funds for a new apartment and reimbursement of lost revenue for the leased space.

The *Evening News* printed a short sidebar to the announcement, titled HOW DO FOREIGN COUNTRIES HANDLE "NAIL HOUSES"? In the United States, it said, "Commercial development is helpless against holdouts."

Many evictees in Beijing believed the same. Seizure of homes and forced relocation would never happen in America, they said. Old Zhang, who had to leave Fresh Fish Junction, once fixed his cataract-clouded eye on mine and said, "In your country, the government cannot force people to move."

And yet, it can. The U.S. Constitution grants the federal government the power of eminent domain. The Fifth Amendment prohibits "double jeopardy," says a defendant may refuse to incriminate himself, cannot be deprived of "life, liberty, or property" without due process of law, "nor shall private property be taken for public use without just compensation."

According to this "Takings Clause," the government can seize land for specific purposes, if it pays its reasonable value. Some judges, such as Supreme Court justice Clarence Thomas, have interpreted the clause differently, saying it expressly limits "the power of government over the individual, no less than with every other liberty expressly enumerated in the amendment," as he wrote in his dissenting opinion to *Kelo v. New London*. The 2005 case pitted private property owners against the city of New London, Connecticut, which had created a private, nonprofit entity to plan a housing and parkland development that would include a $300 million pharmaceutical research campus for the Pfizer Corporation.

The case's nine plaintiffs held fifteen properties in the area zoned for development. Unlike the owners of one hundred other properties who accepted a settlement, the plaintiffs were unwilling to move. Some roots ran deep. One woman was born in her house in 1918 and lived there with her husband for sixty years.

At issue before the Supreme Court was whether a commercial development plan—unlike a transport project or the clearance of blighted housing—served a "public purpose." The court ruled five-to-four for the city, saying that promoting economic development is a traditional and long-accepted function of government. New London's planned development would create in excess of one thousand jobs, increase the tax base, and revitalize an economically distressed city, Justice Stevens wrote in the majority opinion.

In the dissenting opinion, Justice O'Connor wrote, "Petitioners are not hold-outs; they do not seek increased compensation, and none is opposed to new development in the area. Theirs is an objection in principle . . . While the government may take their homes to build a road or a railroad or to eliminate a property use that harms the public . . . it cannot take their property for the private use of other owners simply because the new owners may make more productive use of the property. The beneficiaries are likely to be those citizens with disproportionate influence and power in the political process, including large corporations and development firms . . . The government now has license to transfer property from those with fewer resources to those with more."

Justice Thomas wrote that the judgment "enables the Court to hold, against all common sense, that a costly urban-renewal project whose stated purpose is a vague promise of new jobs and increased tax revenue, but which is also suspiciously agreeable to the Pfizer Corporation, is for a 'public use.'" The losses, he said, would "fall disproportionally on poor communities," noting development projects of the 1950s and 1960s that destroyed neighborhoods with predominantly minority populations. "In cities across the country," Thomas wrote, "urban renewal came to be known as 'Negro removal.'"

And money could not cover all losses. "So-called 'urban renewal' programs provide some compensation for the properties they take," Thomas argued, "but no compensation is possible for the subjective value of these lands to the individuals displaced and the indignity inflicted by uprooting them from their homes."

In the majority opinion, Justice Stevens said that it was still a matter for states, not the federal government, to decide. "We emphasize that nothing in our opinion precludes any State from placing further restrictions on its exercise of the takings power," he wrote. "Indeed, many States already impose 'public use' requirements that are stricter than the federal baseline."

The backlash against the ruling was largely symbolic. The House of

Representatives inserted an amendment to the Department of Housing and Urban Development's budget that forbade it from using federal funds for condemnations apparently sanctioned by the *Kelo v. New London* ruling. In the 2006 congressional elections, ballot measures limiting eminent domain powers were approved in nine states, though in many cases city officials could still label areas as "blighted" and freely raze them, or state legislatures could override opposition with a three-fifths vote in each house.

Justice Souter, who was in the majority deciding for New London, owned a farmhouse in New Hampshire. The city government there received letters urging it (unsuccessfully) to seize the property and open a boutique hotel. The project, proponents argued, would create jobs and increase tax revenues.

Article Ten of China's Constitution stipulates, "The state may, in the public interest, requisition land for its use in accordance with the law . . . Land in cities is owned by the state."

Homes, on the other hand, belong to the owner, if he has the deed, or "property rights" (*chan quan*). If he holds only "usage rights" (*shiyong quan*), then the deed likely belongs to the municipal Housing Administration Bureau or a state-owned work unit.

Like the majority of *hutong* residents, Miss Zhu's grandparents and Old Zhang held usage rights for their homes, though the factory that once employed them held the property rights. The Widow was granted her rights through the Housing Administration. In principle, homeowners with full property rights, such as the nail-house couple, are entitled to a higher standard of compensation, since their housing costs (such as rent) have not been subsidized by the state.

Both types of rights are transferable. My landlord also held usage rights, which he could sell to a willing buyer. The landlord paid a pittance each month to the Housing Administration; he often said our house could never be razed, but if it was, he would miss the income it would have generated over the years, which would surpass any eviction settlement he might receive.

This tangled web of interests was one reason *hutong* neighborhoods continued to rot. Preserving an entire courtyard home in Beijing often required a buyer to negotiate a payment to individuals with usage rights and agencies with property rights. Each has the power to squelch the deal or demand a higher price. In addition, the state owns the land the house stands upon and can requisition it at any time. Contesting the ruling is tantamount to opposing the state; lawyers and plaintiffs have been jailed for it, and most Chinese lawyers shy away from representing evictees. Once the Hand paints 拆 on a home's wall, the only thing open to debate is compensation.

The property law enacted in the spring of 2007 says that adequate compensation must be paid for seized or damaged goods, including real estate. According to the state-run *China Daily*, the directive was drafted in response to—among other grievances—the travails of Beijing residents being evicted from their homes, or being cheated by developers when buying new apartments that were poorly constructed, or even mortgaged to others.

If enforced, the rule could alleviate the frustrations of evicted or swindled home owners by requiring a hearing to determine compensation. Yet because the state's powers of eminent domain remained inviolable, the new property law would not protect Beijing's historic neighborhoods any more than the U.S. Supreme Court could protect homes in New London, Connecticut.

Feng Jicai, the writer who had organized the grassroots effort to protect a Tianjin street, had insisted that preserving a neighborhood required citizen, not government, action. As coverage of the "nail house" and property law increased in spring 2007, I wondered what had become of Feng in the four years since our previous meeting. I dialed the digits listed after his name in my cell phone. Strangely in China for a public figure, his number had not changed.

"My office is now at Tianjin University," Feng said.

"What's the address?"

"Just come and ask around. You'll find me."

I boarded a train east, dreading a slog around a broad campus, inquiring if anyone had seen the affable, mattress-size man, who was, I imagined, stuck in a shared cramped office, and subsisting on a literature professor's salary.

At the school's gate, the first student I stopped said, "Oh, sure, I know where Professor Feng is." She led me to a modernist building whose gray brick facade evoked the colors of Tianjin's old lanes. An aerating pump bubbled in the shallow, goldfish-stocked pond. A weathered antique wooden gate was the courtyard's only other ornamentation. The day's calendar of events scrolled in red lights on an electronic bulletin board. A plaque announced, in Chinese and English, FENG JICAI RESEARCH INSTITUTE OF ARTS AND LITERATURE.

A secretary showed me into a large room with a thick, blue carpet that looked as if it had been vacuumed minutes before. The windows faced another pond. Live potted plants decorated the dust-free antique wood tables, and bookshelves overflowed with texts on ancient architecture and painting. Hanging on a wall was the carved plaque from a destroyed temple that I remembered from his former office, a cluttered room in a nondescript brick walk-up apartment. The plaque read CROWN OF CULTURE.

Feng entered, waved hello, and was intercepted by a reporter, followed by a female student holding a bouquet of sixty-five roses. "It's my sixty-fifth birthday today. I forgot all about it. Sorry to keep you waiting." He still looked like a messy bed—rumpled clothes and unkempt hair. A different secretary poured us cups of tea. Feng motioned for me to sit in a plush armchair covered with an antimacassar. The officious routine reminded me of visiting a government ministry.

The trappings had come after Feng had sparred with city officials and created the nationwide folk-heritage survey. It was ongoing, though underfunded. He had recently auctioned some of his own paintings to raise money, he said. In 2006, Tianjin University provided the funds for his institute and classroom building, where he taught classes on heritage protection. He had stopped writing novels. He hoped his graduate students would organize their own preservation teams and teach others. Time was running out.

"I'm not optimistic at all!" Feng said. "We're in a race of two speeds. One is the speed of our ability to rescue, the other is our pace of destruction. Our first speed must exceed the pace of the latter. If not, we'll lose everything.

"All of traditional Chinese culture faces a problem—from Dazhalan to countryside villages. After our survey, I estimated that there are about six thousand ancient villages. Temples, opera stages, wells, bridges—their form is still there. So is their intangible cultural heritage: customs, holidays, dances, food, and arts. This ancient villagescape is being destroyed, however. They are building homes that resemble those in Hong Kong. If they think Hong Kong is bad, they build them to resemble American homes, and if America isn't good enough, they copy Spanish models.

"The problem I discovered when doing the survey is that even if China's ancient villages don't seem to face a problem, given their outside appearance, when you actually enter a farmer's home, they don't own anything old. Everything is new. Everything authentic is gone. What are the reasons for this? There are three reasons."

Feng's tone indicated that he had enumerated them many times before. "One reason is the destruction of heritage during the Cultural Revolution. Another is that farmers were comparatively poor, so did not value and protect their old possessions. The hot antique market in cities is the third reason.

"Many of the homes no longer have any history inside them. Last year I chaired a conference on nationwide ancient-village protection. I gathered all the heads of the ancient villages and told them how to protect their villages."

I wondered how the village heads felt about that. Maybe they wanted their towns to be as comfortable and heated as this office, and to live in cement buildings, not wood and adobe ones that let in water, wind, pests, and dust. I could not interrupt Feng, however, who suddenly looked as imperious as the surrounding decor.

When I had met him four years before, *hutong* preservation had been an abstract topic to me. That morning in my courtyard, as the Widow's television set blasted Beijing opera, I had told her where I was heading. Of course she had heard of Feng Jicai: he protected culture. "Ask that guy how he plans to save our neighborhood," the Widow suggested. "Let's hear what ideas he has for us common folk." I passed her question on to Feng.

"At this year's national legislative meetings," he said, "I raised a suggestion, which is that in historic districts like Dazhalan, we should build small-scale museums. Then, the area's native objects could be protected there. Because if these items leave their locale, they cease to have value, they just become old objects.

"When they were tearing down old Tianjin, I told the mayor I wanted a courtyard home, a big one. He said, 'What do you want to do?' and I told him, 'I am going to build an old-city museum. You guys are destroying the old city, all this stuff will be taken away, it will be as if nothing ever took place on this land. You have to allow them to leave behind the things that belong to this place.' He said, 'How can they leave objects behind? If you don't offer money, they won't want to leave anything.'

"So I grabbed tens of thousands of my own cash and bought some items and then organized an event and donated these things to the museum. The residents saw it, and it moved them, and as a result they started donating their own objects. The museum was filled, and now we have an Old City Museum. I inscribed the sign.

"I think Dazhalan's protection requires the same approach. No one is doing this in Beijing. It wasn't easy, our Tianjin Party secretaries and leaders at the time were really against me, they said a sentence then: 'Feng Jicai

A case at Feng Jicai's personal museum, displaying his novel
The Three-Inch Golden Lotus, *and related items.*

is protecting backward culture.' Jiang Zemin's theory of the Three Represents said that the Communist Party is the 'advanced representative of culture.' However, what I was protecting was backward culture. They were really vexed. The residents supported me, and then the government retreated a step. The same could happen in Dazhalan. But in Beijing no one has done this, no one has raised their head, they are afraid that it will not profit themselves. Then, there were people unhappy with me, but what I did was profitable toward people's culture."

His actions also appeared to be a good investment in himself; Feng's status had markedly appreciated. His classroom building included a high-ceilinged gallery whose walls displayed his watercolor paintings. Glass cases held editions of his books, translated into several languages. Five-foot-tall wicker flower baskets sent by well-wishers ringed his plush office, his cell phone whirred with a stream of incoming messages, and reporters waited outside to take his photograph. Feng excused himself. After he cleared the office of these admirers, the haughtiness endemic to officials and intellectuals finally drained out, too. He downshifted from self-promotion to relaxed conversation.

"I often say that on the entire earth, there isn't a nation that could, in the name of the Olympics, destroy its own cities, and its own history. Beijing needs people who love to talk less and love to do more. They are just changing the appearance of Dazhalan, but that's not real, that's just a fake antique. They don't want genuine history, but a pretend history."

Residents should be given a choice whether to move or remain, he said. The government could provide repair stipends to those who chose to stay. "Over a long period, every object becomes dilapidated, just like a person. If someone is sick and you do not aid him, it is your fault, not his. All the homes need repair. They have to have bathrooms installed, first off, and heat and better wiring, and so on. The government will not provide this money. That way, they can claim the house is too run-down. The goal of this talk is to raze the house, certainly not to protect it."

In Tianjin, Feng had faced off with the developers who wanted to demolish the old street he aimed to save. "They weren't happy—they said by protecting this building they would lose tens of thousands of yuan. I was very unhappy. I said, 'There is no such thing as a development company losing tens of thousands by protecting a building. You can say you're not profiting tens of thousands additionally. Earning less does not equal losing money.'"

One of Feng's graduate students led me upstairs and unlocked the doors to the "Jumping Over the Dragon Gate" Folk Art Museum. According to a sign, the two floors of artifacts from all over the country had been culled from "the various important achievements of the Chinese Folk Culture Heritage Salvation Project." I looked through the glass at delicate paper-cut decorations, bright calico, and Spring Festival paintings. They were beautiful, but the time spent gathering them had replaced time spent creating. Feng had transformed from artist to collector, from a writer to an encyclopedist. As someone drawn to him through his books, it seemed an unfortunate trade.

After living in the *hutong*, I grew impatient with inanimate museum displays of "culture." Like Miss Zhu's grandmother, I would rather have been dropped off out front and wandered outside, among the living.

The rooms echoed with my footsteps, then those of the student close behind. "Professor Feng is really great, isn't he?" she said. I leaned over an old wooden chair. "Don't touch," she warned. "Professor Feng collected all of this. Don't touch."

Despite his high profile, Feng was waging a battle against a Hand that could stroke or swat him aside as it pleased. Off campus, I told the cab-driver, a lifelong city resident, to go to the Tianjin Old City Museum that Feng had founded.

"Never heard of it," he said. The other drivers, and people we asked on the street, were also unaware of the museum. I directed the cabby to an old Tianjin neighborhood I remembered of wooden houses on narrow streets shaded by rows of trees. It was gone. The cab looped a big-box Carrefour, the French version of Wal-Mart.

"Let's go to Ancient Culture Street."

The bazaar, built in the nineteenth century, had been replaced by New Ancient Culture Street. Its cement-framed buildings, covered in gray brick-shaped tiles, resembled the old market's outward appearance, but held none of its worn, ragtag charm.

The cab dropped me in Tianjin's former British concession, whose late-nineteenth-century masonry buildings still lined the lanes. A new marble plaque had been fitted on each structure, detailing its former use, its architect, and year of completion. I walked from here through the old Japanese and French concessions, where buildings were also marked, as at the FORMER FRENCH MILITARY BARRACKS. Across the river, in what had been the Italian concession, workers were renovating the distinctive stone buildings into offices and condominiums.

At the neighboring construction site for Hundred Villas town houses, a red-white-and-blue billboard promised in English that its design SELLS THE UNITED STATES OF AMERICA.

Ideally, courtyard homes could add bathrooms and heating systems. The homes' foundations, frames, and roofs are often so dilapidated, however, they cannot support new plumbing or wiring. Ideally, residents could do these repairs themselves. The majority of homes' property rights are held by the state, which reduces residents' willingness to invest their own money on maintenance. Ideally, residents could be given a choice to remain in the neighborhood or move. Who would calculate—let alone fund—resettlement and renovation? Dazhalan has three thousand houses, shared by nearly sixty thousand people.

One model of neighborhood renovation that draws favorable public response is located inside Beijing's east Second Ring Road, where the district government condemned dilapidated courtyards but replaced them with a chain of simple, modern walk-up apartments built to house the former residents. Easements between the buildings retain the old *hutong* names: South Grain Storehouse Lane; Broad Bean Lane. A letter to a person who had lived on Sea Transport Storehouse Lane is still addressed to that place, although with an apartment number substituted for that of a house. The map for that section of the Old City reads as it did in imperial times. When residents say, "I live on South Bow Maker's Lane," their words fan an ember of the city's historic flame. Some of the developments retained a few old cypresses—propped up with metal braces—that had for centuries shaded the *hutong*.

New apartments on South Bow Maker's Lane. Similar projects to resettle courtyard residents in their former neighborhood were limited to a handful of Old City sites.

Residents are given transferable usage rights to their apartment. To curb speculation in subsidized real estate, however, controls include requiring the seller to wait five years, and to pay a hefty fee to recompensate the subsidy. The apartments' owners may rent them to others. As at a subsidized low-rise development amidst courtyard homes on Chrysanthemum Lane, the apartments are favorites with Chinese and foreigners for their proximity to the subway, lakes, and extant *hutong* neighborhoods. Despite the project's good intentions, the market still exerts constant pressure on the community to profit from its buildings and to disperse original tenants.

Though labor and material expenses are low in Beijing, the cost of preserving a century-old building remains high. Restoring a single courtyard home required the same paperwork and approvals as constructing a twenty-story high-rise. In the spring of 2007, an old hotel on the east end of Red Bayberry and Bamboo Slanted Street was being renovated into a backpacker's hostel. Its proprietor said he spent $250,000 just bringing the two-story, brick building up to fire and health codes. That total did not include the "gifts" he was compelled to present to authorities. They decreed the business would be a hostel; because it was a historic structure, he was forbidden to install en suite plumbing or otherwise alter its infrastructure. They also wouldn't tell him the city's plans for the surrounding *hutong*; the Hand could come along and paint 拆 when it pleased. As his business was about to open, the district government announced it was constructing a new upscale hotel directly across the street, in the antique style of the authentic structure he had spent so much to revive.

Replicas replaced architectural heritage across China. "It's becoming more and more like Disneyland," a Canadian millionaire told a reporter. Jeffrey Huang had rescued more than 150 historic buildings from destruction in central and southern China. His efforts had not been supported by a single government official, though some had phoned him later, asking to buy a structure back to decorate a shopping district. "These officials are not interested in preserving old architecture unless they can get money from it," Huang said. "If you develop a site, you can have all this money, you get a car, you can go overseas to see other developments—they get all these benefits."

After Huang purchased the temple, home, bridge, or teahouse, the relic was disassembled and shipped to warehouses near Shanghai. He planned to arrange them in an open-air park or arts district. I had visited a similar site outside Nagoya, Japan, where the Meiji-Mura museum displays buildings a tycoon plucked away from the wrecking ball as Tokyo remade itself to host the 1964 Summer Olympics.

Beijing does not have a courtyard home that was restored as a template for other homes' renovation, as in Hanoi and Luang Prabang, or a residents' museum, as proposed by Feng Jicai. There is no shortage of sites in Dazhalan. Aunty Yang holds full property rights for her courtyard next door to mine. When I returned from Tianjin, the spry seventy-one-year-old was straddling her home's roof, nailing down another patch.

The Widow's television still pumped the squealing opera into the courtyard. A museum exhibit about her would have to include that spine-shivering music, the smell of fried cabbage and cheap cigarette smoke, her single picture frame holding family portraits, the creak her door made when opening, and a mechanized liver-spotted hand that playfully cuffed observers.

"Little Plumblossom, have you eaten?"

I lied.

She brought pork dumplings over, anyway. Her frail body leaned close as she passed the steaming bowl. "Slow down! If you eat that fast—well, no wonder you have problems."

She described how she had bargained down the price of chives, adding that I really ought to watch those chive sellers, because they were crafty. I nodded gamely. As she left with the empty bowl, the Widow said without emotion, "I sold my room. I'm moving out next month."

CHAPTER 19

THE WIDOW'S STORY

Don't worry, Little Plumblossom," said the Widow. "I'll still cook for you. You just have to come to my new house. First I'll be living a few *hutong* north, with my granddaughter and son. Then I'll be moving into a high-rise."

The apartment was located in a development where one hundred thousand people lived, outside the southeast corner of the Old City. "I got a good price for my room," she continued. "It's more than I would receive in compensation when they destroy the neighborhood. If I wait until then, all these other people will be looking for houses, too. This way, I can take the money and give it to my granddaughter. She and my son will use it to buy an apartment and fix it up for me. I'll live with her there. I need someone to take care of me, you know."

She slapped me again on the shoulder. "My health is not good! I'm old and alone. No one is here during the daytime. During this year's Spring Festival, I was really scared. What if I needed help? What if I died? No one would find me for days!"

She closed one eye and took a long drag on a Flying Horse.

"Miss who? Miss me?" She laughed. "I'm not going far away. We'll still see each other. We are friends." She smiled. "Good friends. I like having you as a neighbor. I wasn't worried about having a foreigner move in at all. You keep a clean house, and you don't make trouble or cause a disturbance. If you did, I would hound you out of here, just like that. I'm speaking frankly. Say, you really ought to have a child immediately. You're not so young anymore."

For nearly two years, we had lived within yards of one another and interacted in several minutes-long encounters every day. If pressed to retell each other's biography, the result would have been fragmented and incomplete. The intimacy of the *hutong* was like that—the closer physically, the greater the emotional distance. The first day I moved in, the Widow had preached, "Public is public, private is private!"

She had never told me about her husband, and whether she really was a widow. I knew she moved into the house in 1962, and not much more. I asked if we could talk. She put the teakettle over the coal-fueled flame and invited me across her threshold.

"Now life is good, it's nothing like the old society," the Widow began. She was born near Port Arthur, in a city now called Dalian. Located on the Yellow Sea, the city was a transportation hub. The Widow's father worked as an engineer on the South Manchurian railroad, which ran through China's northeast, then occupied by Japan.

In 1941, when the Widow was fifteen, her father moved the family to Beijing, then named Beiping. He never told her why they came. "When I first got off the train here, I saw the enormous Front Gate," she said. "The only building I had seen like that was a temple. I said, 'Dad, why did you bring me to a temple?' But it was Beijing."

The Widow laughed and took a sip from the spout of a small clay teapot. "There were so many great gates then." She splayed her fingers and counted them off. "We rented a courtyard house off Fresh Fish Junction. Four families shared that house, but it was comfortable. Except when it rained. The *hutong* was all dirt and other things—yellow earth, you know?"

Her father found a bigger house on Big Ear *hutong*, located five lanes north of ours. "I haven't left this neighborhood since then," she said. Several families also shared the family's new courtyard. "During the Japanese occupation, families with money had their own gate and their own yard, they could even rent a car, if they needed it. It was like an opera, the divide between rich and poor. We commoners lived several families to a house and didn't have a stove like this one. At that time, you had to stoke the fire with your hand, and all we had to burn were coal balls; once the fire got going, you had to tend it."

Her memories moved muscles. With a furrowed brow she mimed stoking the fire. When she talked about hunger, she smacked her lips. "White flour was hard to come by then. It was reserved for Japs and top officials. We ate a lot of *woutou*." She frowned at the coarse-grained cakes' phantom taste. "I can't speak for families with money, but at that time, we were alright, because my father worked on the trains. Everywhere he went, he would buy whatever food he could find, bring it back, and set up a table outside our door to sell things like a bowl of tea leaves. The people's workers, you know, they loved and needed to drink tea, so they would stop and spend a few cents."

Her father also collected scrap cloth, to be cut into patches. "Today's kids, they just throw away torn pants. At that time, there was no such phenomenon. You had to patch everything, you couldn't just go and buy more. Children's socks had to be darned!"

The Widow didn't remember seeing Japanese soldiers in the neighborhood. "They didn't dare come down here," she said defiantly. "Most of them lived in the eastern suburbs. The Japs were really bad. Just as bad were the 'dog tails' they used as spies. Those people were evil from their hands to their heads. They would say whose house was trouble and finger them to the Japs, even though they would never have known."

The Widow sipped from the small teapot. Padded sleeves covered the forearms of her sweater, colored the same red as our courtyard's painted beams. The second finger of her left hand wore a gold ring. I asked when she got married. Her mouth puckered sourly.

"When I lived on Tea *hutong*, some people that migrated here from my father's ancestral village asked him for assistance. He found them a house. Back then, shops fronted a courtyard, and you lived in the rooms at the back. They lived behind the Emerald Screen Pavilion printing factory.

"One day, the father was working and he heard a co-worker talking about so-and-so wanted to find a bride. He said the guy came from a really powerful family, one that could afford dancing girls. So this guy says, 'I have a friend whose daughter is young and beautiful.'

"After the guy saw me, he said, 'That girl is really pretty, I'm afraid her father won't give her up.' I didn't want to get married—the age difference between us was too big—ten years. My father had a feudal mind. Never mind that he worked on a train, he wouldn't allow his daughter to find her own match, no way. I was nineteen then.

"My father wanted to meet the guy. He was an officer in the Nationalists'

Ninety-second Army. They went out to a theater together, and that night my father agreed to the marriage. My mother was against it, and so was my big sister. I said, 'No way, military guys have fierce tempers.' My father said I didn't have any freedom.

"He made all the arrangements. That was 1946. In 1947, I gave birth to my daughter. In 1949, I gave birth to my son. My husband left when my son was still in my belly. He said he was going to his hometown in Shandong province and would send for me. I never saw him again. My son never even met his father. I was twenty-three, and my troubles were enormous. I was without his salary. I didn't even know how much money he earned. My father had always controlled me, but now when I looked to him, he wouldn't look at me."

The People's Liberation Army saved her life, she said.

"In 1949, they entered the city on day six of Spring Festival. They counted my household as a military family, and the Communists gave me a hundred and ten pounds of rice, a big sack of noodles, and eleven pounds of flaxseed oil. Then they said they were leaving to liberate Hainan Island. The Nationalists' Ninety-second Army reentered Beijing, but my husband wasn't with them."

His name was Wu Zhendong. He sent her two letters, both bearing a Hong Kong postmark. The first one, from 1949, said he was going to Taiwan. When the second letter arrived in 1958, the Widow was frightened to be holding something that might mention the "renegade province," to where the Nationalists had retreated. She carried the envelope to the neighborhood police station. An officer opened, read, and burned the letter. She never learned what it said.

"When Hong Kong returned to the motherland in 1997, the Red Cross offered to help locate my husband. They found no trace. He may still be alive, but if so, he's really old. I don't want to see him or talk to him, of course not! In all those years, he never provided any money, or a house. I had to rely on these two hands to raise two children. The Communist Party welcomed me with an open door. The Party's great kindness to me is something I can't ever completely express or finish attempting to."

The Communist takeover of Beijing occurred without a large battle. "In 1949, you never heard cannon fire or even one shot. The only explosion was when the People's Liberation Army pointed a cannon toward heaven and fired twice," she said. "That was Liberation."

In 1951, the government certified that she was divorced. "I was introduced to a lot of men, but none were interesting enough."

Following her sister's marriage, the Widow moved into her courtyard on another *hutong*. It was the best house she had ever lived in. "It had two complete courtyards, and we each had our own room. It was on the north side of the courtyard, but it was really big. In 1958 during the Great Leap Forward, the state seized it but let us continue living there as tenants under the Housing Administration Bureau. My parents were allowed to move in, as well."

That year, she was assigned a job as an attendant at a bathhouse, housed in the two-story, gray brick building being renovated into a hostel at the junction of Red Bayberry and Bamboo Slanted Street and Coal Street. The bathhouse had been an underground meeting spot for Communists at a time when capture meant execution. An appointment there carried some cachet.

"My work unit often went to Tian'anmen Square to see the Labor Day celebrations. I remember one year it was really raining hard, and my poncho was soaked through. At nine o'clock, Chairman Mao appeared, and everyone cheered!" She covered her ears from a din only she could hear.

During the Great Leap Forward's campaign of self-reliance, "backyard furnaces" produced steel. The result of melting down cooking implements and whatever else households could forage was often unusable, but the Widow recalled the era with zeal. "I collected all my metal and walked out of the house and gave it to the collectors on the *hutong* myself! And I was willing to do it, too!"

She enrolled in night classes her employer provided, learning arts and crafts. "I'm an optimist. If my kids are sick, I cry, and if they're well, I forget about all other problems. During the day, I worked as a service girl, washing floors and so on, and at night I studied." It was the first time she had been a student. When she was a child, her father refused to enroll her in school.

In 1960, the Three Big Disasters—a pseudonym for the famine induced by the failed policies of the Great Leap Forward, including communal kitchens—affected even the capital. "When the disasters struck, and food was sharply rationed, I went to the work unit and said my children weren't eating well. I had been dividing my rations and giving the food to them, you see. My bosses said, 'You can't rely on your friends and family forever, you have to rely on your job and trust the Party.'

"The bosses organized a planting trip, and we all had to go out to a field in Yellow Village. Every worker was sent out there for two months to plant crops, raise pigs, and tend ducks. I really worked hard, which drew notice, because a lot of people just went through the motions and didn't work at it. But no vegetables ever poked through that sandy soil. When that period was over, I was assigned to live in this house in 1962."

The Widow knew it had been one family's home, though she didn't recognize the names on the register I had photocopied at the archives.

"The rent was fourteen yuan for a month, for six square meters [sixty-five square feet] that three of us lived in. I couldn't afford that, so the bathhouse paid half. I didn't have any choice in the matter, I was just assigned to this place. You might think that seven yuan a month was nothing, but I only earned forty a month. I still had to pay for electricity and water, plus food and school supplies and clothes."

Presently she had sixteen square meters (172 square feet) of space, for which she paid the Housing Administration Bureau twenty-seven yuan monthly.

"I don't own the property rights, only usage rights. When it's razed, they wouldn't count the kitchen that I added on as part of my settlement because it's not 'living area.' So instead of the value of sixteen square meters, I would only receive payment for six. This concept of usage rights is really a historical leftover. Everything in this former mansion used to be privately owned, but not anymore, now only half of it is, and not our half. If I needed more space, I could go to the bureau and tell them, and maybe I could trade with someone else looking to move."

Now, however, it was often more profitable to transfer the rights yourself, and to leverage that money into an apartment. Or, in the case of the man moving into her room with his fiancée, to transfer a demolition settlement into another courtyard. "He is going to convert the kitchen into a living space for his parents," the Widow said. "Their courtyard was torn down, so he took some of that money and put it here. Maybe if this isn't torn down for a while, the compensation will be higher than now, and he'll have increased the living space and earn even more."

In Beijing, there was a market for everything. The latest was speculating on government compensation for housing demolition.

When the Widow moved in, the derelict printing factory next door had been the Number Five Chinese Medicine Factory, a state-owned enterprise that took over the private Tongrentang Chinese medicine plant. "Our *hutong* sold a lot of eye medicine," she said. "Of all the dozens of *hutong* around us, this one has always been comparatively dilapidated. Coal Lane used to have gold shops, banks, and antique stores—I'll tell you, there was no small number of cultured people that lived there. The police station used to be a Buddhist temple. You can still see a hall or two inside. On this street, we just had a bank and printing factories."

None of her neighbors from 1962 remained in the neighborhood. "One man was the assistant manager of the Dazhalan East Gate Prosperous Worker's Stationers," she remembered. "He thought this place was too small, and so his work unit got him another house. Then came a railroad engineer, and his wife. She worked in the beer factory. Their relationship wasn't very good. They were coldhearted neighbors. He went to the bureau and demanded a new place, and they were gone. Your landlord's brother had made a similar demand, so he was moved here. He brought his mother and little brother. She left the earth here in 2004."

"In my room?"

"Of course in your room! She died on your bed!" the Widow said in a tone that suggested I really ought to use my brain once in a while.

In the black-and-white photograph hanging on the wall, she smiles sweetly, wearing a gray dress. After I said her looks must have turned heads on the lane, she swatted my arm. "I'm thirty-one there. I don't have any pictures of me younger than that. They were all confiscated during the Cultural Revolution."

Up to this point, she had told her narrative in waves. A topic such as marriage would rise, then be subsumed by a memory from the Great Leap

Forward, then her tale washed forward to present housing policy, then surged back to her marriage. When she talked about her experience starting in 1966, however, her words settled into a calm, flat recollection of a stormy time.

"'Most beloved great instructor, great leader, great commander, great helmsman, Chairman Mao—forever, forever, forever!' Every day at work for ten minutes in the morning and ten minutes at night, I had to face a poster of Chairman Mao and recite that. They called it 'admitting guilt,' and it was to help me 'rectify my crimes.' It wasn't just me, the bathhouse Party secretary and the human resources director stood beside me and did it, too.

"I wasn't beaten during the Cultural Revolution. You know, at that time I had already been awarded as an 'advanced worker,' and a 'Xuanwu District Skilled Girl.' I had been taking night classes and receiving training from my work unit. They gave me books by Liu Shaoqi."

Liu was president of China and toppled from power during the Cultural Revolution. Branded a counterrevolutionary, he died naked on a cement prison floor.

"I was labeled a spy," the Widow continued. Her marriage to a Nationalist officer painted her with a guilty brush, even though he had abandoned her nearly two decades before. "My workmates, the neighborhood leaders, they gave me a real hard time. I was to be struggled against, and then reformed. The leaders at the bathhouse, from what I understand, branded me a 'rebel element.' I said, 'You're talking about top leaders like Liu Shaoqi and Zhu De. Me? I'm just a blade of grass.' How had I sinned against the people? I didn't have any ghosts in my heart. I trusted the Party, I put faith in Chairman Mao, what did I have to be afraid of? Because I stand straight, I don't fear my slanting shadow. I'm still me."

She nodded defiantly. "Look at me, you know I'm in the optimist's camp. But all my health trouble began at that time." She developed an irregular heartbeat and frayed nerves. "They told me to pay for treatment myself if I wanted it that bad. Since I was a 'secret agent,' they said I could afford it."

Like any survivor, the Widow stressed that things could have been worse. She remembered a former landlord who lived on our lane, named Zhang Yishu. "His mother and mother-in-law were beaten badly by Red Guards. Not his children, because they had 'separated themselves' and turned against him. In the house opposite ours lived a shop proprietor. His father was hauled off and came home dead. On the second floor of that house lived the former physician of the Nationalist general Yan Xishan. He was beaten, and so was his daughter. His granddaughter worked at a department store. She hadn't done anything wrong, but the Red Guards forced her to kneel in front of the house and shaved her head. Then they cut up her cloth shoes and made her eat them."

"They made her eat her shoes?"

"Absolutely!" the Widow grunted. "They were attacking normal workers and their families. They called them rebel factions. They made that girl kneel and eat her shoes."

The Widow kept her head down and muddled through. "You showed your spirit in badges. I used to have so many Chairman Mao badges! People used to give them to each other out of kindness, the way money is given today. Big mirrored ones, small ones, anything I could afford, I would buy and pin them on my kids."

They did not protect her children from being denounced and "sent down" to the countryside. Her daughter was shipped to Qinghai province, a barren region of western China on the Tibetan plateau. "They trained her to be a physician," the Widow said. "I was shipped to the countryside for six months, but my daughter didn't deserve to be sent so far away. I said, 'Whatever evidence you want, I'll give it to you. Whatever information you need, I'll hand it over.' But it was no use. They sent her anyway."

Not until 1990 was the Widow's daughter allowed to move her residence permit back to Beijing. The Widow had not seen her daughter for nearly two decades. "I thought her return was really hopeless. When two people are separated, it's really a difficulty! A nice clerk finally said, 'Grandmother, don't worry, I'll take care of it for you. That was in October of 1990, and by December she was approved to come back. She found a job at the Beijing Chemical Factory Workers' Hospital."

I asked what became of the people who had accused her.

"We all knew who they were, of course. My file was 'rehabilitated,' and I was cleared of all wrongdoing. But I still passed these people on the lane. Misfortune struck the people who criticized me. A guy who beat someone to death had been sent away for his own reeducation, but when he returned, his wife also had lost her mind and taken his children back to her hometown. The man who wanted to become a Party secretary never made it. His wife committed suicide by throwing herself in front of a vehicle. Another saw his kid suffer paralysis on an entire side of his body. Those rebel faction leaders, they never amounted to any good."

She recounted how some of her favorite performers had been beaten, such as Hou Baolin, master of the fast comedic wordplay called cross talk. "When the Red Guards came for him, he didn't struggle, he just laughed, put on a tall hat, and played word games. The opera singer Xiao Bai Yushuang died then. He swallowed a bunch of sleeping pills. I liked his singing. He didn't sing much Beijing opera, however. I like Beijing-style opera the best. That's what I chose to perform when our work unit had events."

The Widow's television was always tuned to the opera channel. She had three favorites, each a tale of righteousness and comeuppance. The first was *Four Successful Candidates of the Imperial Examination*, in which the candidates pledge never to abuse their official powers. Three of them soon attempt to conceal a murder by a family member. Only one man stands firm and brings the killer to justice.

The Orphan of the Zhao Family tells the tale of a six-month-old minister's son whose family is massacred by a traitorous general. A servant saves the boy by swapping him with his own son. After the servant raises the boy to become a warrior, he takes revenge on the general.

The Widow's other favorite opera was *Qingfeng Pavilion*, in which the emperor's wife forbids an infant born to a concubine to live in the palace. A tofu maker finds the boy and raises him. Many years later, the tofu maker returns the boy to the concubine. The boy forever rejects the impoverished couple that raised him. They kill themselves. After arduously studying for years, the boy passes the imperial examination. But before he becomes an official, lightning strikes him dead.

"Those are the good stories," the Widow said.

Although the traditional calendar indicated it was time for the mid-April spell called Grain Rains, the Widow placed a fresh honeycomb coal cake in the lit stove with a pair of iron tongs. "It's not heavy," she said, waving me away. "I can still do it. I'll boil some more water. In early spring you still have to wear a lot of clothes, otherwise you'll catch a cold. I saw you wearing shorts the other day. Idiot!"

It took a year to build Dazhalan's air-raid shelters, she remembered. "I had to move into that cement house across from the Neighborhood Committee for a month when they came to dig mine. Your shelter is under your bed."

The word *bed* conjured an image of my landlord's dying mother. Sometimes you don't want to know too much about your house or neighborhood.

"When the Tangshan earthquake struck in 1976, I grabbed your landlord's mother and told her we had to get out. My God. We didn't take anything with us, just grabbed our grandkids and ran. They moved us all to Tian'anmen Square. We lived there in tents for nearly two months. The entire neighborhood! Tens of thousands of people, at least! We slept and cooked there, because everyone was afraid to go back home, in case there was another earthquake. Really! It wasn't so bad, the tents were well made and there weren't any leaks when it rained. When we returned home, the doors had been unlocked all that time, and not one thing had been stolen. If it were today, there would be nothing left after an hour!"

She remembered the day Chairman Mao died in 1976. "I cried. I wailed. Everyone did. I really was sad. But when [Premier] Zhou Enlai died, I not only cried, I couldn't eat for the entire day. He was really great. The paper didn't report it until the next day, but the day it happened, everyone knew. Who didn't know? Everyone knew, just by word of mouth. That's how much people loved him."

She did not go to Tian'anmen Square to mourn Zhou, as thousands did, ignoring restrictions. She never paid attention to "that business," she said, meaning politics. When I asked what she remembered about the demonstrations on the square in 1989, she stared blankly and said, "That's not my business."

Of the period of "open policy and reform," which began under Deng Xiaoping, she remembered getting her first television, Hong Kong returning to Chinese sovereignty, and raising her granddaughter in this room. Now the girl taught business English at a Beijing college. That was the Widow's proudest achievement.

"What else happened here?" she repeated. "You foreigners started arriving one after another. Now there are so many rickshaw bicycles carting you foreigners around that sometimes I can't cross the lane to use the bathroom! They come through two by two, a row of twenty of them at times! *Ba!* What relics are there worth seeing here? The Eight Big *hutong* have all the good sites."

Again she splayed her fingers and counted off the name of each of the Eight Bigs.

The Widow insisted she wasn't sad about leaving her home after forty-five years. After listening to her stories, I better understood why. Aside from uncomfortable conditions—she had cracked the small room's door so the coal stove wouldn't asphyxiate us—the *hutong* and courtyard held memories. Though, the narrow street grid and traditional architecture was not the reason she had raised her children alone, or was assigned to live here, or did not have any keepsakes from her first thirty-one years of life, or did not see her daughter for over two decades. The Widow could not say the reasons, exactly.

I often heard that the Hand wantonly, and largely unopposedly, razed neighborhood heritage because many residents had lived through the Cultural Revolution, which instructed citizens to destroy the Four Olds: thoughts, culture, customs, and habits. Thus, they recalled destruction as a positive—even fun—collective act. Another, more tenable explanation was simply that Beijing's residents wanted to forget the recent past, instead of remember it. It is said that the cure for nostalgia is to read history. Living through tumultuous times is another remedy.

The opposite of 拆 (*chai;* raze) is 建 (*jian;* construct). The Hand brushed the former in deathly white on old houses and printed the latter in celebratory red on digitized renderings that sheathed new apartments' building sites. It set countdown clocks that steered citizens' gazes forward, not backward. Good-bye, past! Hello, future!

"It's always best to be with your family," the Widow said. That, not the surrounding architecture, was what mattered. Still, she would miss the shopping convenience the *hutong* afforded. "The drawback is that when it rains, buying things isn't so convenient. Also, our lane is too long, the rooms are too small, the courtyard space is too small, and there's no place to shower. It's not convenient for old folks to go out and use the latrine. In the apartment building, there will be central heat. I won't have to burn coal to stay alive." She grunted at the stove, where the kettle boiled.

She poured more water over our green tea leaves. "I'll tell you, the best part of living in a house like this is having your feet always in contact with the earth's energy. It's good for your body. You can bask in the sun, too. Also when you live in a house like this, you can always talk to others and help each other. People who live in apartments stay in their own houses and don't like to go out and mingle."

Her evidence was the attitude of my landlord and his brother, both of whom now lived in apartments. The first day I moved in, she had scolded me for trusting them, though she never explained why. "When I see them on the street, I won't say one word to either of them," she said.

"Before in this neighborhood, people were united. On holidays you would greet each other and share food and always help each other out. We once lived next to a Muslim family, and I said, 'We won't eat pork or hang pig posters up during the Year of the Pig, okay?' Would anyone do that today? Now, nobody cares. There's no community spirit. After Liberation, we could sleep with the doors unlocked without worry. If a kid on the street was sick, we would all bring the parents medicine. People today are slippery, I'm telling you.

"I fed your landlord and his brother and their mother for years, but never took a bite of their food. They always ate mine, no problem. The boys moved away and went off to the army or whatever, and I looked after their mother. I even dressed her for her funeral. Do they care? No. They live in apartments, they're all cadres and have military pensions. They can just happily look forward to the announcement that the house will be razed and collect their bonus money."

The Widow denied having class envy. "My granddaughter is married. That's what's most important to me. Your landlord's son is thirty-three and hasn't even found a girlfriend."

I asked how the government should handle the residents' relocation.

"If I waited here for the house to be destroyed, the money I got wouldn't be enough to buy an apartment nearby. Where would I live then? The state provides subsidized housing, but it's too far away, I'm afraid. People want to live at least within the Third or Fourth Ring Road. If you want common people to accept a move, then at least they have to be provided with a community to move to, including a supermarket and a hospital. Those aren't high demands, that's just convenience. People will be willing to pay their own money for that sort of housing, if the government can be responsible for some of the cost and ensure the quality of construction. Otherwise, who wants to leave the *hutong*?"

She wouldn't miss the older women on the lane. "They're not that interesting to talk to," she admitted. "I usually just go for a walk by myself."

She was *not* afraid of the dark, she said, laughing. Her face suddenly fell. "Little Plumblossom," she said in a low voice, "my new apartment will be on the seventeenth floor. I'll have to ride an elevator to go outside."

"It's perfectly safe, don't worry. You just press a button—"

"I know all that." She swatted my arm. "I'm worried that if I go outside, and the elevator breaks, then—" She paused, waved her hand, and from her lined face came the frightened voice of a little girl. "I can't climb all those stairs. I won't be able to return home. I'll have to spend the night outside."

CHAPTER 20

A BRIEF HISTORY OF 拆 PART FOUR:
The Industrialization of Maoist Beijing

ON OCTOBER 1, 1949, after a four-year civil war in which the Communists defeated the Nationalists, Mao Zedong stood on the rostrum of the Gate of Heavenly Peace (Tian'anmen) and proclaimed the founding of the People's Republic of China. Surrounding Mao were the new caretakers of Beijing, which had its former name restored (from Beiping) after the Communists chose it as the nation's capital. The rostrum faced south, toward a skyline dominated by the Front Gate and the city wall. Beyond these imperial relics lay Dazhalan's dense *hutong* and courtyard homes. The city's appointed mayor pointed at the view and informed an architect present that Chairman Mao expected the sky there to become an ocean of smokestacks.

"I was dumbstruck," the architect recalled decades later. "Mao said we would transform Beijing from a 'consumption' city to a 'production' city. I really could not comprehend. China was so big that industry did not need to rely on Beijing. It should resemble Washington, D.C.'s tranquil, refined administrative center, and protect the existing architecture and city plan . . . At that time I didn't realize that 'every word of Chairman Mao's is the absolute truth,' but even today I still don't get his statement about 'smokestacks everywhere.'"

His name was Liang Sicheng, and for the next twenty years he would wage a lonely, losing battle to save Beijing's architectural heritage. Liang was born in 1901, the son of a renowned scholar who fled to Japan after the Dowager Empress crushed his and other imperial ministers' proposed reforms to liberalize education and politics. After the Manchu court fell, his family returned to Beijing, where Liang grew up.

While his father schooled him in China's ancient traditions, Liang came of age in Republian-era Beijing, when the city modernized. He was a slight, bespectacled man who walked at a tilt after a motorcycle accident near the Forbidden City made one leg shorter than the other. At Tsinghua University—designed and funded by Americans using Boxer indemnity money—Liang learned English and was versed in Western arts, traits that informed a perspective of what was different—and endangered—in his own culture.

In 1924, Liang attended the University of Pennsylvania School of Architecture on a Boxer indemnity scholarship. Penn's curriculum taught not only the practice of the profession, but also its roots. Assignments required Liang to draft the restoration of ancient Greek and Roman ruins, and to complete the designs of unfinished Renaissance cathedrals. He was trained to be an architect, but also an architectural historian.

Liang could not have received a similar education in China, where architecture was not an academic discipline; not a single university had a department, and the most recently published "textbook" was a 1734 collection of structural regulations. While he was at Penn, Liang received from his father a copy of *Building Standards* (*Yingzao Fashi*), a manual that had been lost for centuries but recently rediscovered. The book, thick with technical terms and no illustrations, captivated Liang, who attacked it like a puzzle.

Standards was published in 1103, during the Song dynasty, a time of artistic and scientific flowering and political and military weakness. The embattled empire was losing territory to northern tribes; the threat to Chinese civilization inspired intellectuals to document their culture, which suddenly seemed perishable. Liang lived in a similar era, when the empire fell, the economy lagged, science and technology replaced orthodoxy, and the country was under military threat. "Recent tendencies in China, especially since the founding of the Republic," he wrote at the time, "have not been favorable for the preservation of ancient edifices. After repeated defeats by the modern powers from the middle of the nineteenth century, the Chinese intellectual and governing class lost confidence in everything of its own. Its standard of beauty was totally

confused: the old was thrown away; of the new, or Western, it was ignorant."

In 1928, at age twenty-seven, Liang established China's first academic
architecture department, at Northeastern University in Shenyang (Muk-
den). Three years later, Japan invaded Manchuria. Liang returned to Beijing, where the newly formed Society for Research in Chinese
Architecture hired him to translate *Building Standards* into modern
Chinese.

The society's office was located just inside the Gate of Heavenly Peace,
which led to the Forbidden City. Finding himself unable to decode the
Standards, Liang realized "the only reliable sources of information are the
buildings themselves, and the only available teachers are the craftsmen."
Architecture in China was regarded as a trade, whose traditions were
passed down orally. Liang sought out a pair of imperial-era carpenters and
followed them around the palace, recording descriptions of their construction techniques.

Before returning to China after graduation from Penn, Liang had traveled to Europe on his honeymoon with his wife, the architect Lin Huiyin
(whose niece Maya Lin would design Washington, D.C.'s Vietnam Veterans Memorial), to see firsthand the great buildings he had sketched in
school. Now, with China under threat, he began a similar tour of its un-
written architectural history. Beginning in 1931, Liang completed twenty-
two hundred field studies that to him were not quixotic whims, but a race
to document endangered heritage. Traveling by springless mule cart, carrying sketchbooks and Liang's Leica camera, Liang and Lin located temples,
pagodas, and bridges that rotted, unrecorded, in remote areas. They found
China's oldest extant wood structure—a ninth-century temple near Wutai
Mountain—and he oversaw the restoration of Confucius' ancestral manor
and burial ground, in Qufu.

There had been no tradition of restoration in China: successive dynasties
ordered other emperors' buildings razed or converted to their own designs.
"Since there existed no guides to buildings important in the history of Chinese architecture," Liang wrote in 1940, "we sought out old buildings 'like a
blind man riding a blind horse.' . . . My experience was that local people
were not interested in architecture. When I told them I was interested in
antiquities, they would guide me to their stone stelae inscribed in earlier

times. They were interested in calligraphy, impressed by the written word, not the carpenter's handiwork."

In 1934, after the national capital moved south and Beiping attempted to lure tourists to spark the economy, its mayor engaged Liang to help restore imperial edifices. Liang worked at it until Japan occupied the city in 1937, then moved to China's wartime capital, Chongqing (Chungking), in the country's southwest. There, he continued his translation of *Building Standards* and authored the first illustrated history of China's architecture, written in Chinese and English.

In *A Pictorial History of Chinese Architecture*, completed in 1946, Liang noted that it was not until the 1920s that Chinese intellectuals began to view their country's architecture as an art. Outside influences changed their perspective:

> First, a number of buildings appeared, built by foreigners but in the Chinese style. Next, Western and Japanese scholars published books and articles on Chinese architecture. And, finally, a number of Chinese students who had gone abroad to study Western techniques of building came back with the realization that architecture is something more than brick and timber: it is an art, an expression of the people and their times, and a cultural heritage. The contempt of the educated class for matters of "masonry and carpentry" gradually turned into appreciation and admiration. But it was a long time before this consciousness could be implanted in the minds of the local authorities upon whom the protection of antiquities depends. Meanwhile the process of deterioration and destruction steadily progressed in the hands of the ignorant and the negligent.

In January 1949 during China's civil war, a unit of the People's Liberation Army searched for Liang at Tsinghua University, where he had started its architecture school. The soldiers asked him to identify Beiping's architectural heritage, not to attack it, but to protect it from their munitions.

The Communists took Beiping that month from the Nationalists. In May 1949, the *People's Daily* reported that a committee was drafting plans to "build the people's New Beiping!" The government promised to protect the city's culture and convert "the ancient feudalist city into a modern productive city."

The capital's planning commission enlisted Liang. He was a Beijing native, the son of a famous patriot, and the country's best-known architect—in 1947, he had represented China on the design committee for the United Nations' headquarters and taught at Yale. Yet Liang had spent the previous two decades finding and recording ancient architecture, not drafting and building new structures. When he did draw renderings, they depicted sleek, International-style buildings like Le Corbusier's—who claimed his design was selected for the UN headquarters—not austere utilitarian ones. Liang oiled his black hair back and dressed in dapper suits, making him appear like a dandy next to the crew cuts and shapeless blue serge suits Communist cadres favored. His family background was regal, not proletarian; his education was Western and bourgeois, not Soviet and Marxist. For the rest of his life, Liang would struggle to reconcile these extremes.

One of his first design collaborations—the era of individualism had ended—was for the Monument to the People's Heroes, which commemorated popular uprisings that preceded the Communists' victory. The stone memorial is a combination of a classical Western obelisk with a traditional Chinese stela, planted in Tian'anmen Square and severing the flow of the central axis that ran through the capital. Despite its incongruity, Liang's monument nodded toward tradition; other teams presented Soviet-influenced plans, including a woman holding aloft a star, a broad wall, and a trio of stone smokestacks.

The Communists inherited a city that was not only bankrupt, but understaffed and undertrained; Beijing had only fifteen architects. In 1949, only 4 percent of the capital's 1.4 million residents worked in manufacturing, compared to a quarter of Moscow's population. The Soviet Union dispatched more than a thousand technical advisers to guide Beijing's industrialization.

To protect the walled Old City, Liang lobbied for the government's administrative center to be built in the western suburbs, where the Japanese had planned New Beiping. A Soviet adviser responded, "We also had such suggestions, to turn the old city of Moscow into a museum, and build a new city by its side. We turned them down and reconstructed Moscow. The result is not bad at all. The demolition of old buildings in Beijing is a task that must be done somewhere in time. Rickshaw drivers are now employed as factory hands. What means of transport through the *hutong* can you now rely on?"

The founding of new China was an intensely patriotic and optimistic time. Liang was confident the government would be swayed by his campaign to protect Old Beijing. He suggested that the design of the capital should be left to professionals, not cadres, adding that even Chairman Mao did not understand architecture. The mayor upbraided him, asking if a tank could only be driven by a general.

The turret turned to the ancient city.

The new regime vowed to liberate Beijing from Western influences and historical vices. It expelled missionaries, closed foreign shops, and pulled down the Legation Quarter's gates. The ornate embassies were put to new use. Burma moved into the former Belgian mission; East Germany into Germany's; the municipal government into Japan's. The French and British embassies became guesthouses, while the American mission— where Marine Captain John Seymour Letcher had penned letters home—was turned into the Dalai Lama's Beijing offices. Regular notices in the *People's Daily* listed the addresses of Dazhalan courtyard homes whose landlords were thought to have fled the country, leaving their ownership in dispute.

On November 21, 1949, police sealed the city's brothels, opium dens, and gambling houses. Wearing cloth face masks, they corralled thirteen hundred prostitutes in raids that lasted until five the next morning. Thirty-four madams slipped away from Dazhalan, but were captured after being fingered by residents. Venereal disease infected 95 percent of the sex workers; 40 percent had syphilis. At public trials, the women publicly denounced their former bosses. Two madams were executed, while the rest served "reform through labor" sentences. The freed prostitutes attended eight specially created schools to "study politics and culture, and receive job training." By 1950, nearly six hundred had married, four hundred had returned to their former homes, and seventy worked as nurses in hospitals and hospices. Others performed in patriotic plays.

A former prostitute accuses her madam at a public trial.

In May 1950, the *People's Daily* singled out Red Bayberry and Bamboo Slanted Street as an example of the Old City's "treasure chest of heritage." The unpaved *hutong* became a "piss pool" after even light rain and bred mosquitoes and flies; its rickety courtyard homes leaned toward collapse. Like many intellectuals, the author Lao She returned to China from America to "serve the revolution" and build a new China. His novel *Camel Xiangzi*—about the life of an impoverished Beiping rickshaw puller—had been an international bestseller, and now the Communists put him to work to trumpet the city's improvements.

His first work was based on the cleaning up of a *hutong* neighborhood south of Dazhalan. In act 1 of his play *Dragon Beard Ditch*, a resident sings:

> *There will come a day when the Ditch won't stink,*
> *And the water will be sweet,*

> *Then our land will be great, the people happy,*
> *And the world at peace.*

The play ends after the fetid trench is filled in, and residents praise the Communist Party. Lao She would never write another novel.

In February 1950, Liang and his partner Chen Zhanxiang (Charlie Cheng) submitted their plan to construct the new government center outside the city walls. Soviet advisers countered that the Old City's empty palaces and former administration buildings could be occupied immediately, and at less expense.

The debate would last for three years, during which time China joined the fight against American-led UN forces on the Korean peninsula. The war made Mao reconsider the idea of a centralized administration, which could be susceptible to enemy air raids. He agreed that the main buildings should be in the heart of the Old City, but wanted secondary organs placed to the west of its wall. Invoking Stalin's example in Moscow, Soviet advisers urged China's architects to create a "national style" for the new structures, representing native form and politics and not made with glass and steel, the materials favored by Western imperialists.

The new offices, built in an area named Sanlihe, had squat five-story masonry bases crowned by tiled rooftops with flying eaves, a combination that Liang—perhaps regretting his similar design for the Monument to the People's Heroes—said looked as unseemly as a man dressed in a Western suit and Chinese skullcap. He continued to lobby for the Old City's protection, including its wall, a piece of heritage that he knew to be unrivaled in the world. In April 1951, he unsuccessfully proposed converting the top of the wall into a municipal park and pedestrian promenade.

The destruction of the Outer Wall—enclosing the Temple of Heaven and Dazhalan—began in January 1952. A witness said that an army of manual laborers tore at the structure like ants eating a bone. Over Liang's protests, workers pulled down the gates that arched over the Old City's central boulevard, the Avenue of Eternal Peace. They obstructed traffic and impeded the crowds that came to listen to Chairman Mao speak on the Gate of Heavenly Peace's rostrum, now adorned with his portrait.

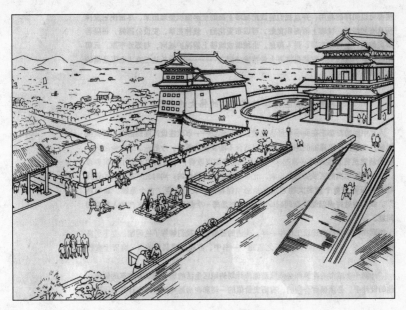

Liang Sicheng's sketch of a park atop Beijing's city wall.

In the spring of 1953, the government adopted the slogan "Learn Everything from the Soviet Union." A cadre warned that "the major danger is an extreme respect for old architecture, such that it constricts our perspective of development." The Outer City wall came down, and gate towers around Beijing soon followed, along with ceremonial arches that spanned streets. An official told Liang, "You are an old conservative, in the future Beijing will construct tall buildings. You and your arches and gates will become bird nests and chicken perches, what cultural value will they have then?" The vanished structures—Di'anmen, Fuchengmen—lent their names to the wide intersections that replaced them.

Some Soviet advisers sided with Liang and urged the preservation of parts of the Inner City wall to retain the former appearance, but it was too late. In August 1953, Mao announced, "The big problem of destroying city walls has already been decided and taken care of." In November, the municipal government declared that the Old City "completely serves feudalism and the imperial era." Liang and Chen's plan was rejected, and industrialization sped up.

In 1955, nine Soviets who oversaw Moscow's rebuilding arrived in Beijing to plan a chemical-industry zone. From this era until 1984, Beijing would become home to 149 of China's 164 types of industry. Fourteen thousand smokestacks punctuated the skyline, like exclamation points proclaiming the city as: The nation's largest petrochemical base! The leading producer of rubber products, plastic, and refrigerators! Second in pig iron and washing machines! Third in power generators, woolen cloth, cars, and color televisions! Fourth in internal combustion engines! Fifth in sewing machines and beer! The city neglected to manufacture what it needed most: housing.

In January 1956, two hundred thousand people massed in front of the Gate of Heavenly Peace to "celebrate Beijing's entry into a socialist society, and the abolition of the private sector of business." After a report titled "Current Information of Privately Owned Houses in Cities and Suggestions on Their Socialist Transformation" was approved by the national government, work units and the municipal Housing Administration Bureau administered urban housing, with rents adjusted to a small percentage of wages.

The government targeted waste in all sectors; for construction, that meant "suitability, thrift, and elegance where possible," putting an end to the "excessive ornamentation" of high-pitched roofs. In May 1956, the central government issued orders for the creation of austere, uniform worker housing that formed self-contained communities. China's urban centers began to look indistinguishable with their north-south facing rows of redbrick facades broken by stairwells and open corridors. The buildings featured shared kitchens fueled by propane tanks, and shared baths with low water pressure.

Yet Beijing's acute housing shortage—formed by the burgeoning bureaucracy and factories—meant that a family fortunate enough to be assigned a new flat had to share it. In new neighborhoods such as Hepingli and Xingfucun, three generations lived in an apartment's single room. Families assigned to subdivided courtyard homes also faced overcrowded conditions, and public latrines. Both old and new housing lacked central heat. Beijing took on an even more uniform appearance as matchbox-shaped, prefabricated concrete apartment blocks were built in rigid rows whose north-south exposure maximized sunlight exposure.

Visiting Beijing in 1955 on an official invitation to see the capital's transformation, Simone de Beauvoir looked out her hotel window at the characterless view and wondered, "When they have demolished the little grey streets, will all of Peking look like this boulevard?"

·HEARTFELT THANKS TO SOVIET PEOPLE FOR HELPING OUR COUNTRY proclaimed a newspaper headline in February 1956. Also published inside, nationwide, was a "self-criticism" by Liang Sicheng, who had been attacked for his objections to the destruction of Beijing's Old City. It said, in part:

> The Party has permitted me to participate in the capital's planning since May 1949. In the past seven years I wholeheartedly supported the political, economic, and cultural policies of the Party and cheered for every improvement in construction under social- ism. However, when it comes to city planning and architectural design, I have always gone against the Party, actively spreading my mistaken theories, blowing an evil wind of formalism and classi- cism across the nation, wasting capital earned by the blood and sweat of workers and peasants.
>
> For a long time I didn't recognize my mistake. That is because I still have a deep reserve for the tastes and aesthetics of the feudal ruling class. Also, I wanted to turn the people's capital into a brand-new "fake antique," and I aimed to force the population to accept my taste, subjecting them to a lifestyle and city that pre- serves the past. Since Liberation, I had many job titles and a lot of social engagements, therefore I did not systematically study Marxist-Leninist thought, and my thoughts were not improved, but mistaken. I only emphasized the artistic side of architecture. I thought I was correct, and that the Party did not understand ar- chitecture, therefore, I lost track of the Party and people, and walked down the wrong road.

Yet Liang continued to voice his objections to the shape his hometown was taking. In 1957, he warned that the widening of the central Avenue of

Eternal Peace to 130 yards would strand elderly pedestrians who could not cross before traffic signals changed.

Of the city wall's demolition, a *People's Daily* editorial said, "It is only the people who love the motherland, love the people, and love the Party" who did not object. "The people all want to use their hands to destroy—you destroy a gray brick, I'll pull down a piece of stone, who can stand by idly? 'A single idiot can move a mountain,' so should citizens of every district help pull down the wall."

In June 1957 during the "Hundred Flowers Movement," when the Party encouraged open criticism, the *People's Daily* published an essay in which Liang declared, "Destroying a gate of Beijing is like cutting off my flesh; stripping Beijing's city wall is like peeling my skin!"

To celebrate the People's Republic's tenth anniversary in 1959, the central government announced plans for the Ten Greats, construction projects that would transform the Old City's orientation and appearance. Workers cleared trees and buildings in front of the Gate of Heavenly Peace to build the world's largest plaza. Fifty open acres in the heart of one of the world's densest cities, Tian'anmen Square could hold six hundred thousand people. Mao was disappointed; he wished it were larger.

The Ten Greats' buildings appear more colossal than they are, with grand (often colonnaded) facades concealing hollow interiors, as wings wrap around courtyards. The Greats are grouped along east-west axes according to their purpose. Buildings related to politics, defense, and transportation—such as the Great Hall of the People, the history museums, train station, and Military Exhibition Hall—were set on the central boulevard, the Avenue of Eternal Peace. Buildings related to culture—such as the National Art Gallery—were placed on the avenue named for the May Fourth Movement, which connected the National Library, Palace Museum, and former Peking University campus. The Agricultural Exhibition Hall, constructed on the eastern end of another axis, was offset by the Soviet-constructed industrial Exhibition Hall on the west. Ten thousand workers completed the Ten Greats in ten months.

The razing of the city's remaining walls continued under the slogans "The Past Serves the Present" and "The Dead Do Not Master the Living."

*The view north from the Front Gate, of the space outside the Gate of Heavenly Peace
before Mao ordered it renovated into the world's largest square. Tian'anmen has since been expanded
to fifty acres, with a capacity of six hundred thousand people.*

The Front Gate's twin towers were spared for posterity by Premier Zhou
Enlai, who struck them from a list of proposed demolition targets. He did
not state whether Liang's lobbying influenced his decision, though Zhou
could admire the elegant structures from the former American embassy,
which became his office after the Dalai Lama fled from Tibet to India in
1957.

A Belgian journalist who had last seen Beijing in 1947 returned in 1962
to find "much of the beauty of ancient imperial Peking was gone, as was almost all its charm." The traffic signals on the Avenue of Eternal Peace
were hand-controlled by policemen sitting in small wooden huts who "always seemed to be picking up their telephones when you drove by. The avenue itself was curiously un-urban. It suggested the middle stretch of an
important highway linking two major hypothetical towns."

The journalist said that the *hutong* were doomed, and "with them whatever remained of individual privacy. But there had been a stay of execution. Building had practically stopped in Peking, and therefore demolition
also. Whole districts, sentenced to death under the 'Great Leap Forward' of

1958, were reprieved when the Leap collapsed; and the *hutong* dwellings might be left for a few more years to crumble of their accord."

In 1966, after the start of the upheaval unleashed by Mao's Great Proletarian Cultural Revolution, factions of college-age Red Guards demanded that Beijing's traffic signals be changed so cars stopped on green and went on red, the color of Communism. The suggestion was ignored, though the city reposted imperial-era streets with names such as People's Avenue and Worker Peasant Soldier Street. Peking Union, built by the Rockefeller Foundation and designed by an American to resemble a traditional Chinese building, was renamed Anti-Imperialist Hospital. Dazhalan's "old famous brands" changed their signboards to such names as Red Flag Clothing Store and the East Is Red Shoe Store. Proposals were floated, unsuccessfully, to raze the Forbidden City, and to change Beijing's name to Hongjing—Red Capital.

Eleven million Red Guards flooded into Beijing. They followed Mao's orders to "destroy the Four Olds." Of the capital's 6,843 cataloged relics, 4,922 were smashed to dust, along with thirty of the eighty remaining historic sites.

Songs such as "Socialism Is Good" blared from loudspeakers, and traditional opera was banned, replaced by militaristic ballets such as *The Red Women's Detachment*, where the dancers' bayonet charges aimed at cowering villains dressed in silk and brocade. The "little red book" of Mao's quotations dominated publishing.

In August 1966—called Bloody August for the death toll of "class enemies"—Red Guards found the famed Beijing novelist Lao She walking on the street and brought him to the Confucian Temple. Lao was sixty-seven and had been released that month from the hospital after a bout of bronchitis. The Red Guards beat him, and other artists, with belts, fists, and boots until strands of his vest cut into his flesh. They called his writing a putrid mess and labeled him a "cow demon." The Red Guards took him home, but said he must appear before them the next morning.

There is no back door to a courtyard. Lao She woke the morning of August 24 and said good-bye to his wife. Later that morning, while at work, she received an anonymous phone call. The voice said her husband had "divorced himself from the people." His folded clothes, spectacles, fountain pen, and walking cane were found beside a pond. He was cremated before a family member could view the body. Nor could they see the papers found on the shore; they were told the writing was just a transcription of Mao's poetry.

The pond where Lao She died was in the northwest corner of the Old City, nearly an hour's walk from his courtyard. After his beating, he would have been hobbled and conspicuous. Was he picked up by Red Guards and drowned there, or did he submerge himself? On his walk, he would have passed a series of lakes before reaching Tranquility Pond. The area was a favorite place, about which he once wrote: "Facing it, with the city wall at my back, sitting atop a stone and watching the tadpoles on the water and the tender dragonflies atop the reeds, I could happily pass a day, my heart is completely at ease, without demands or fears, like a baby sleeping peacefully in a crib."

He described the site, too, at the end of *Camel Xiangzi*, when the rickshaw puller, numb after a betrayal that resulted in a friend's execution, stares blankly at the water, rippled by the backs of breaching fish. "Kingfishers swooped across the surface of the water like arrows," he wrote. "Little fish and big fish were no more to be seen and nothing was left but the duckweed."

The pond where Lao She died was filled in with soil from the razed city wall. Today, the site is a subway station.

In 1969, the last wholly intact gate of the city wall—Xizhimen—came down, revealing the remains of a gate that dated to 1359, built for the Mongol's capital. Liang Sicheng rushed to glimpse the structure before it fell. The rubble was cleared for the Second Ring Road, the beltway being paved on the former footprint of the city wall.

Liang had been labeled a "contemptible pile of dogshit," and reduced to living in a drafty, unheated room at Tsinghua University. Though he was ill, hospitals refused to treat him. Before he died in 1972, Liang said, "I regret that I took up architecture. It would have been better if I had studied mechanics or radio."

During the Cultural Revolution, Beijing's Municipal Planning Bureau was dissolved. For the next decade, construction went unmonitored. Citizens and factories built what they needed, where they wanted, from whatever materials they could scavenge. Shared courtyards resembled rabbit warrens, with kitchens, closets and rooms added in brick, cement, adobe, and wire.

Politics determined urban design. When Beijing's subway opened in 1971, an official said, "At first we had all the lights red to signify that the East is red, but we did not realize that it would make it very dark, so we changed to white light." The two miles of apartment buildings erected along Front Gate East and West avenues in 1979 sat empty, due to what the People's Daily called "Beijing's construction anarchy." It bemoaned the lack of coordination between city agencies, noting that concrete was poured before the water pipes had been laid because the one group of laborers "arrived at the job first [and] just set to work."

The housing situation grew so chaotic that in 1980 the Beijing government arranged a fair that allowed residents to swap homes with one another so they could live closer to work or gain space for a growing family. That year, China's new paramount leader, Deng Xiaoping, removed the portraits of Marx, Engels, Lenin, and Stalin from Tian'anmen Square, and began an era of economic reforms, including the creation of a property market.

When the Communists took over Beijing in 1949, the city's wall had already been pierced for roads and railways, and its gates were in disrepair. Yet only one of the Imperial City's seven gates had been razed. All would be destroyed, save for the Gate of Heavenly Peace, whose original tower was dismantled during the Cultural Revolution and rebuilt with a larger rostrum. Of the nine pairs of towers that permitted entrance to the Inner City, five arrow towers and eight gate towers remained. Today, two arrow towers and one gate tower survive. The Front Gate is the only extant pair, though a wide boulevard runs between them.

In 1970, the historian Nigel Cameron wrote, "It was as if the Europe of the sixteenth century had been suddenly confronted with an alien civilization already developed to twentieth-century standards, and had had to make the attempt to bring itself up to date. Whatever the failures and whatever the successes of the Communist regime in China since 1949, they have to be measured against that simple fact."

The urban-preservation historian Anthony Tung estimated, "The half of Beijing that was destroyed in the three decades from 1950 to 1980 constituted one of the single greatest losses of urban architectural culture in the twentieth century."

In 1990, the municipal government drew up the Old and Dilapidated Housing Renewal program. Neighborhoods that had survived the fall of imperial rule, the republican era's modernizations, Japanese occupation, and Mao's industrialization fell to a faceless foe. The Hand moved through the *hutong* after dark, surreptitiously marking courtyard homes 拆.

Liang Sicheng lobbied for factories to be located outside Beijing, not in its center. He warned municipal officials that they would regret razing the city wall. "In regards to this question," he wrote in 1955, "I am advanced, you are backward. Fifty years later, history will prove that you are mistaken, and I am correct."

After winning the Olympic bid in 2001, the Beijing government announced it would relocate polluting industries. In 2002, workers tore down two thousand homes and sixty businesses to rebuild a mile-long portion of the demolished city wall. The structure was attached to the single remaining corner tower and incorporated two hundred thousand of the original's gray bricks, returned by scavengers following a government appeal.

In 1947, Liang returned to China with the manuscript for his *Pictorial History of Chinese Architecture*, but left the illustrations in the United States with a friend. He sent for them a decade later, providing an address of a student in England who would forward them on to Beijing, where he had fallen out of political favor. The package never arrived. Not until 1980 were the illustrations and the manuscript reunited, and the book published, in English. Liang's son, living in Beijing, translated the text into Chinese in 1991.

In the *Pictorial History*, Liang classified China's historical periods of architectural styles as Vigor, Elegance, and Rigidity. In 2003, I asked his son what his father might label the current era. "Alienation!" he said, laughing.

"I don't recognize Beijing anymore," Liang Congjie continued in fluent English. He founded China's first nongovernmental organization, Friends of Nature. "I am trying to follow my parents' footsteps. Environmental protection was not in their consciousness during their time. The need came after modernization. People call us every day with issues to be investigated. It's getting harder to protect the environment after China entered the World Trade Organization. The economy is growing so fast, and everyone is trying to get rich in the shortest time. If 1.3 billion people want to get rich, just imagine the pressure—it's enormous upon natural resources. Arable land, forest, grassland, water, all divided between 1.3 billion shares. Chinese want to live the life Americans have. The energy consumption of the U.S. is fourteen times that of the per capita consumption of a Chinese person. America has two hundred sixty million people, and one hundred thirty million cars. Chinese see this, they know this. And they want it. But if China wants to reach that way of life, then we need seven earths to support them. This is the darkest side of China. We want to imitate everything from the West. Chairman Mao criticized this mentality of colonialism. That's what it is. A colonialism mentality. That everything not ours is better."

Liang's childhood courtyard home was razed, and the site occupied by "the ugliest hotel, actually a five-story building that houses the staff of the connecting hotel." A museum honoring his grandfather, the reformist imperial minister, was built in Tianjin's former Italian concession. "They moved fifty or sixty families out of their homes to commemorate him. Now it's an empty house. We don't own any of his furniture or papers or calligraphy with which to fill it—all has been lost. For years, my grandfather was branded a counterrevolutionary, and now he is an example of patriotic education."

When plans were announced for the construction of the Oriental Plaza mall near Tian'anmen Square and the Forbidden City, Liang joined preservationists protesting the project's height and bulk, which they said further fractured the Old City's form. "If I were a terrorist," he told me, "I would drive a plane into Oriental Plaza. I would sacrifice my life to destroy it.

"Kant said, 'Because of the subject, so you have the government.' A few years ago, I went to a conference of architects held at Beijing's German embassy. I had been to Berlin and think its planning is beautiful, so I praised it to the ambassador. He said to me, 'The presence of Berlin as a city represents and reflects the taste of its residents.' If that's true, I really feel embarrassed because the presence of Beijing thus also reflects the taste of its residents."

In 2003, 125 students at Beijing Number Four Middle School wrote a letter to the mayor, asking, "If a city does not have its own culture and its own history, what makes it different from any other city? The skyscrapers we build in Beijing are commonplace, while our courtyards and *hutong* are unique in the world. Why, in the name of following a trend, should we destroy this priceless treasure? We do not want to carry the stigma of being known as the people who destroyed Beijing's culture nor the last generation that witnessed its past—but what can we do? What is in our power is so much less than what you can do."

An official with the mayor's office told a reporter that he would pass the letter on.

In 2007, the Geneva-based Centre on Housing Rights and Evictions estimated that since the start of the ODHR program in 1990, 1.25 million Beijing residents had been evicted.

CHAPTER 21

ECHO WALL

O N APRIL 21, 2007, tin sheets went up at both ends of Front Gate Avenue, fencing it in as a construction site. The city's central axis had been broken before, by the Monument to the People's Heroes and Chairman Mao's sarcophagus on Tian'anmen Square. This was the first time, however, that the road between the temples of Heaven and Agriculture and the Forbidden City had been severed from vehicles, be it the emperor's chariot or present-day passenger buses. Traffic was permanently diverted along the new roads through Fresh Fish Junction and Dazhalan.

An architect whose rejected designs for Front Gate Avenue had urged the road to be left open to prevent new streets from piercing the *hutong* told me, "There is no pattern, there is no textbook on how to design a Chinese megacity. City development at such a high speed, not only in Beijing and Shanghai, but Hong Kong, Guangzhou, and other metropolises? There's no example in history. It is a completely new challenge. It's also the most unique and important challenge, because if you imagine Chinese consuming per capita as much energy as Americans, within our life span the world will become a desert. What will come out of this development? No one knows exactly."

Municipal officials, he said, "talk about sustainable development but have no idea what it is. Any measure toward sustainable development is a price increase. It's lip service of the decision makers. And there are twenty bosses making decisions. Not one. That's why Chinese cities look the way they do. Architecture is not sculpture. It's building human-scale quarters. It's really a question of scale."

On May 9, the *Evening News* reported plans to improve Front Gate Avenue so it would combine "the traditional and modern in a newly built pedestrian shopping mall."

The road would still be crowned by its ceremonial arch. It was not the original, but neither was the Front Gate's arrow tower, rebuilt after the Boxer Rebellion with white marble eyebrows over each embrasure. That design had been refurbished in 2006. Front Gate Avenue continues south to its terminus, where workers reconstructed—on a reduced scale—a razed tower that defended the city wall. Now it watches over traffic on the Second Ring Road, running past its base.

"Cities are like people," the architect told me. "They don't learn from other's mistakes, they learn from their own mistakes. I hope Beijing does it quickly."

Safe and Sound Boulevard is neither safe nor sound. The eight-lane road running four miles across the heart of the Old City has only two pedestrian overpasses, neither located where the majority of people attempt to cross its forty yards before the light changes. One of the road's left-hand-turn lanes is located in the far right-hand lane, forming one of several traffic choke points. Listen to the hundreds of horns honking together, smell the exhaust of idling buses and cabs, and see the empty sidewalks that run before shops built to resemble the thirty-three hundred courtyard homes that the road destroyed. I remember them, and the *hutong*, and the promises.

"This project is designed for the next century," the boulevard's chief engineer said in 1998, when it was under construction. "Once completed, traffic jams on the street will be significantly reduced." After the road builders uncovered—then reburied—twelve-hundred-year-old tombs, and bridges and walls from imperial times, another designer said, "I'm not opposed to the conservation of cultural relics, but it should be selective. Only those that have practical value should be protected. The interests of modern human beings should, after all, be placed first."

I remember the warnings. "In comparison, the destruction during the Cultural Revolution is nothing," architect Zhang Yonghe (Yung-Ho Chang) told a reporter in 1998. "This is the destruction of the city itself. The whole notion of widening the streets is so shortsighted; it might be a quick cure for a year or two, but if the growth in the number of cars is not put under control, then all this widening becomes ineffective."

The novelist Lao She's son, Shu Yi, who became a preservation activist, said the *hutong* were the capital's "second city wall," and if razed, the indelible action would later be regretted. "History is being wiped out before our eyes," he told a reporter. "Soon there will be nothing left."

In 1998, as Safe and Sound Boulevard was debated in the Beijing media, a former municipal official was asked to comment on Liang Sicheng's plan to save the city's wall and build the administrative center to its west. "We thought then," the official said, "and still think now, that Liang's plan was not realistic." Yet the official regretted the destruction of the Old City, adding, "What industrialization avoided over the past decades has easily been done by the commercial upsurge in the last few years."

Eight thousand people were evicted to construct Safe and Sound Boulevard. I do not remember them. Although I skated on the lake and wandered the neighborhood's lanes, I only passed through. One day the Hand came along and shunted everyone away.

The Widow left our courtyard in April 2007. As renovations continued at her future high-rise apartment, she stayed with her granddaughter on a *hutong* a few blocks north of Red Bayberry and Bamboo Slanted Street. Her three rooms were part of a former guesthouse and were sunnier than her former dwelling. Jerry-rigged kitchens and coal-honeycomb storage bins crowded the open courtyard, but a poplar grew from the mess. The one drawback was the location of the latrine. Previously, she had to take a few steps out the gate to reach it. Now, the nearest toilet was two *hutong* away.

One night, as the eighty-one-year-old navigated the unlit maze, a man stepped from the shadows. He grabbed her frail arm, yanking the gold ring from her finger. He vanished before she started screaming.

"He laughed while he was doing it," the Widow said. "I was so scared. Nothing like that ever happened in our *hutong*! That was the most valuable thing I owned. I reported it to the police. It was a migrant who did it, a youngster. The police said they would identify him from the security camera."

"I've never seen a security camera in the *hutong*."

"The police said they exist. Who can say? All I know is that they haven't found the thief, or my ring."

Now, everything looked foreign to her. Unfamiliar faces entered the courtyard. People didn't say hello. No one offered to take her to the market. My neighbors, Mr. Han and his wife, began checking on her every other day. I brought her a pack of Flying Horses. She grunted and tossed them on the bureau. Mr. Han laughed and said, "Spoil her." The next time, I brought Chunghwa, the most expensive cigarettes around. The Widow scolded, "What a waste!" but her eyes said I was a good boy.

I never found her husband. Two separate inquiries to Taiwan's Veterans Affairs Commission turned up two men with his name in their records. The only one in the Nationalists' Ninety-second Army, Twenty-first Division, Sixty-first Regiment, with a rank of major, was born in December 1920, not 1917 as the Widow remembered, and in a different county of Shandong province. A friend in Taiwan dialed the number in that man's file. The woman who answered said the man had passed away a while ago. After an uncomfortable pause she said not to call again and hung up.

Where did Mr. Wu Zhendong go when we walked out of the *hutong*? Like most people who lived here, his story remains buried.

Two years before, my offer to volunteer in Beijing was greeted with skepticism from the school, police, and neighborhood. As the number of days on the countdown clock dwindled, volunteering became a trend, then an organized movement. Booths around the city recruited Olympics volunteers. The government bureau that supervised NeighCom announced I would receive a citation for community service. The morning I was to receive the award, I woke with a high fever and cold sweat. I called the office to say this was a case of flu they did not want to catch, so was staying in bed. Five minutes later, NeighCom staff banged on my door. They wiped my face and hair, put tissues in my front pocket—"Use these when you puke"—and said we had better hurry or "we would have no face."

"In America," I protested, "the honor of being a volunteer is to be unrecognized."

"Not in Beijing!" they chorused. "Come come come come come!"

I liked the *hutong* and the school because, even though I could not have been more conspicuous, life felt anonymous. It was the antidote to the other Beijing, where a day out could become a performance. Here, there was no name-dropping (no one knew anyone with a name to drop); no dinner parties (only a few people could fit in a house); no dressing up (expensive clothes were an extravagance and hard to keep clean); and no discussion about the future of China. The present had to be sorted first.

The men from NeighCom held my hands until we reached the award ceremony on Dazhalan West Street, where a microphone and an amplifier stood next to a dais outside on the lane. Two dozen middle-aged women with red armbands indicating their volunteer status waited in lines for their community-service certificate. They chatted and laughed and teased one another. Watching their excitement at participating in a global event—458 days away, they knew—reminded me that this ceremony wasn't about me at all, not any more than anything that happened in the *hutong*. But I wondered what would happen to them after the Olympics' three weeks concluded, and they no longer served a purpose. The banners declaring DAZHALANERS PRIDE IN DAZHALAN CULTURE could be replaced by ones reading HAND IN HAND, NEIGHBORS HAPPILY VACATE THE NEIGHBORHOOD as in other *hutong* slated for renewal.

An official and I signed a banner lauding international friendship. He did not know if Red Bayberry and Bamboo Slanted Street would be razed. He handed me a set of pins, each emblazoned with the image of an Olympics mascot, the *fuwa*.

At Coal Lane Elementary, the teachers were disappointed to learn I wasn't promised Olympic tickets. To get those, you had to apply to a lottery that required either an account at the Bank of China, or a Visa credit card, official sponsors of the games. Like my neighbors, none of the teachers put in a request, due to ticket costs. They would watch on television the games for which their city had remade itself.

Miss Zhu awarded prizes to students whose English had shown the most improvement. They whooped at the pins—*fuwa* were still a very big deal. One winner was a girl whose twin sister had always been better at the language, until the girl asked her to help.

"Their parents won't tell them which one was born a few minutes before the other one," Miss Zhu said. "That way they don't assume the roles of big sister and little sister, with one more responsible for the other. Isn't that great?"

Whenever Miss Zhu talked about parenting, a pall washed over her beautiful face. She had turned twenty-seven and remained childless. She and her husband lived in a single, dim room in a shared courtyard. They often sat side by side at night, each staring at a different computer monitor hooked to the Internet. She watched online movies; he played online video games. Her colleagues found her worries mere trifles to the stuff they put up with at home.

So when, on an early-May afternoon in 2007, Miss Zhu called to say she had good news, the relief in her voice resonated across the line. "I'm pregnant!" She laughed at the sound the words made and repeated them in Chinese.

"Is this the happiest day of your life?"

"I think the happiest day will be when I see my baby for the first time!" she sang.

Her husband wanted a girl. Miss Zhu hoped for a boy. Her grandparents would be delighted with either. She promised not to saddle the child with a name like Plumblossom. That month, the Hand painted a 拆 symbol on their courtyard home. So that she would have help—and central heat and a bathroom—they would move into an apartment next to her parents and grandparents in a high-rise outside the Fourth Ring Road.

"That will be a long commute to work," I said.

"Here's more good news! The school gives six months' maternity leave with nearly my normal salary. Plus, our school isn't going to be demolished, after all. The other elementary school in the neighborhood will be instead, so those teachers and students are moving to Coal Lane. There are two English teachers, so I'm"—she paused to find the new word—"redundant."

She could remain home—unpaid—after her maternity leave expired, until the end of the school year, and return the next autumn if the school was still there. The principal guessed it would be. Following the Education Bureau's directives, the political posters in its hallways had been replaced with framed prints extolling the culture of Dazhalan. The neighborhood was a "treasure chest of Beijing culture and history." I read that and pictured the Hand rummaging through the loot, but the principal was an optimist.

Miss Zhu said the resettlement fee from her grandparents' destroyed house near Wal-Mart would cover her new apartment and expenses.

"Finally, demolition benefits you."

"You said it!" She giggled at her fortune found.

The school played a short documentary for students that depicted China's achievements under the Communist Party. The narrator intoned key terms—*five thousand years of civilization, feudalism, Japanese invaders, Liang Sicheng*. I looked up at the last word to see an image of the architect on-screen as the narrator said Liang protected "the motherland's glorious cultural heritage."

In 2003, a book that reported his struggles with the Soviet and Communist city planners became a Beijing bestseller. In 2005, Liang's rejected plan to save the city wall and build offices outside it was published in a slim volume, found on shelves at bookstores such as the one attached to the novelist Lao She's courtyard on Lamp Market Lane. His widow opened the home as a museum to the writer. His desk is shown with the day calendar turned to the date he drowned. The tiny bookstore was devoted to texts and maps depicting old Beijing, so dear to him. His books enjoyed a renaissance, too. In 2007, an essay topic for the capital's middle school entrance exam asked students to explain why "Lao She is a symbol of Beijing."

Where were today's Liang Sicheng and Lao She? Both men had lived abroad and returned to their hometown with a changed perspective, an appreciation for what was being lost and at what cost. The present, however, was a period of great optimism and a strong economy. It did not feel like the eleventh century, when invasions awakened the Song dynasty's classifiers, who systematically recorded cultural heritage for posterity. Where were today's Song classifiers?

Feng Jicai said that people's improved material lives numbed their memory, their sense of loss. It was a crucial moment for Chinese culture, and yet to most people it did not feel that way. After he stopped writing novels about his hometown to lead a nationwide survey of folk culture, Feng learned to look for one item to gauge a village's cultural erosion: satellite dishes. "They mean that the core value and culture of this village is dissolving, because it has television. Young women find television characters more admirable than anyone they know. Televised life represents the ideal life for these villagers. It's a dreamlike world. The villagers learn to want what city dwellers want, cars and other material products. Average people, unlike intellectuals, have no interest in preserving traditional and immaterial heritage, because they do not understand the values of it."

In spring 2007, Zhang Jinqi, the historian who lived in Dazhalan, continued his building-by-building recording of Beijing's *hutong*. His limp—a physical trait he shared with Liang Sicheng—made his features tilt to one side. When he asked me to read his application for a Ford Foundation grant, I angled in his direction.

His proposed project would conduct surveys, of the sort suggested by Feng Jicai, in seven Chinese cities and villages. Zhang's team would photograph and record oral histories. It would also partner with local governments to restore homes by providing matching funds. An officer at the foundation had worked with him on fourteen revisions of the proposal. Finally, it was approved.

None of the money would be a salary for Zhang. "I've been doing this as an unpaid job for years now," he said at his subdivided courtyard, where his room contained a desk, chair, and bed. "This grant money will all be used for the project. We have so much work to do!" His tone indicated he couldn't wait to begin. Time, after all, was running out.

Inside the Temple of Heaven is a structure called an echo wall. Its gray bricks ring a prayer hall and are topped with an overhanging eave. If a person stands against the wall and whispers a word, the sound will carry around the length of the structure and be heard by someone standing on the opposite end of the circle. The wall's delicate acoustics mean it needs to be maintained. A crack or careless repair can destroy the effect. Only the original resonates. On any given day at the Temple of Heaven, tourists face the echo wall and scream in vain, "Hello! Hello? Hello!"

The "new ancient-culture streets" popular in Beijing and other Chinese cities, which tore down authentic heritage and rebuilt it, often used concrete frames covered with gray brick tile. They were damaged echo walls— pretty, but deadened. The original residents that had enlivened the architecture had been evicted or could no longer afford to stay, leaving uniform-appearing set decorations, not homes and stores altered by their occupants over centuries. The architecture is sculpture.

In 2007, a *hutong* near the Old City's Drum Tower named South Gong and Drum Lane, which mixed courtyard homes with local businesses, was declared "protected" and revamped. The owner of the Pass-By Bar, a neighborhood stalwart, told me he was glad to see facades repainted and the street repaved with gray bricks. However, the former organic appearance had been altered not by a grassroots effort, but a top-down government directive. The lane's new popularity threatened to raise rents, which could put him out of business, as well as force the community to further disperse.

The Hand was selective about grassroots initiatives. A Chinese journalist began a blog campaign to evict Starbucks from inside the Forbidden City, where since 2000 it had operated a one-table outlet. The blogger wanted to end this foreign incursion on a heritage site. He did not mention the multinational corporations and organizations bankrolling the restoration of palace gardens and interpretive plaques, nor did his action spark campaigns to protect the city's dwindling inhabited heritage—courtyard homes. After Starbucks vacated at the end of its lease, a Palace Museum–managed tea and coffee stand opened in its former space.

The Hand was also discriminating about what constituted a blight on the city's appearance. In June 2007, the police informed Recycler Wang that his truck parked on our *hutong* was an eyesore and had to be moved out of the neighborhood. Now he divided his sixteen-hour day between collecting materials, carting them away on a flatbed bicycle to his vehicle—stationed three miles away—and driving them to Trash Village.

Our lane's mah-jongg and "massage parlors" went unmolested.

I assumed that these actions foreshadowed a larger, inevitable alteration of the neighborhood. An architect at Tsinghua University gave me a 2003 plan titled *Renovation and Renewal of the Dazhalan Area*. In it, the Hand wrote:

> Due to the smallness of space and the large amount of makeshift huts, the living environment is rather bad. Even the basic needs of ventilation and daylight utilization are hard to meet. The environment in the lanes is also very bad. Simple and poor public toilets

can be seen everywhere. Foul smell diffuses all over the air. There is not any place in the area where old people and children can rest and play. It is not exaggerating that such an environment is categorically unsuitable for the needs of daily life of present-day people.

On the accompanying blueprint, the Hand had drawn wide roads, bisecting Dazhalan. One cut past the mosque near our school, and through the NeighCom office. Another obliterated the narrow market *hutong* named Prolong Life Street.

Yet, four years later—after Fresh Fish Junction had been wiped clean and rebuilt, after Coal Street had been widened, after Front Gate Avenue had been closed—Red Bayberry and Bamboo Slanted Street remained. Whether that was due to fiat or fate, no one could say. Regardless, I borrowed a GPS and recorded the courtyard and school's coordinates.

As rumors of its demise spread, Dazhalan had become an even more popular destination for domestic and overseas tourists. Hostels and restaurants mushroomed in the lanes, and both National Geographic and the Smithsonian led tour groups through the neighborhood. The American visitors—old enough to have seen their communities add strip malls and parking lots—ranked the walk as a highlight of their trip, over even the Forbidden City and the Great Wall. Perhaps it was a form of noblesse oblige, but they said this was the "real" Beijing, or at least the part that didn't look like Cleveland. The tours increased. NeighCom invited them to the Olympics English class. The elderly students improved steadily and were able to write and speak their own dialogues. A popular topic was "Welcome to our community, foreign friend!"

On the morning of June 24, a typed notice appeared taped to our courtyard wall. I approached it the way I opened the door to the latrine—cautiously urgent, expecting the worst. I looked at it quickly, seeing the bold black characters that meant "dangerous" and "transformation."

My stomach clenched. Then I saw that these words bookended a single, pardoning character that meant "electricity." The letter said that workers would rewire our homes to "ensure safety and protect heritage."

In the two years since I had moved in, the district government had rebuilt Red Bayberry and Bamboo Slanted Street's latrine, laid new sewage pipes, installed individual water meters and high-speed Internet, and was now improving wiring. Although I knew better, that Beijing streets are often repaired and torn up again within months, these expenditures on infrastructure instead of sculpture indicated lives would reverberate in the *hutong*, yet.

"Mocky had a birthday gift for Ken," read Little Liu. She still wore a blue eye patch under thick glasses, and her hair braided up into a single exclamation point. "Ken was surprised because it wasn't his birthday. They went into the house and looked at a calendar. It wasn't Ken's birthday. It wasn't Ann's birthday. It was Mocky's birthday. Mocky forgot his own birthday. He was funny."

Mocky was four. Most of the students had turned eleven. Some would be twelve that year. The change in a child between the beginning of Grade Four and the end of Grade Five is enormous, physically, emotionally, and mentally. Our students traded their Ultraman comic books and yo-yos for novels and Chinese chess. Some mastered sarcasm. Others used their size advantage to bully at will.

In two months, they would be sixth-graders, which meant a year's preparation for the middle school entrance exam that could determine their academic future. Some, such as Little Liu, looked ready for the increased responsibility. Many, such as Wu Wu—the girl who told me she was, in fact, stupid—did not. When she saw me staring at the empty fishbowl on the windowsill, she explained, "We forgot to feed it."

Miss Zhu wore loose clothes to class, and the students guessed she was pregnant. She didn't inform them she wouldn't be back for their final year at Coal Lane Elementary. "If I tell them, their parents will just call the principal and demand that I stay to prepare them for the exam," she said. "I want to be home with my baby."

We went to Soldier Liu's for our last lunch of the school year. The traditional calendar said we had passed the spell of Summer Solstice and were heading into Minor Heat. Beijing was ahead of schedule. At the end of June, the sun was scorching. Still, Miss Zhu wanted to sit outside to watch the lively lane. Soldier Liu made her a bowl of knife-shaved noodles without hot peppers, because he knew pregnant women should not eat too much spicy food. He carefully placed the steaming bowl on the table in front of her and said in English, "A bowl of noodles."

An American tourist stopped on the lane to ask if I would translate. He wanted to speak to the old man sitting next to a perch holding birds tethered on one foot. "That's very inhumane!" the man said. "I will buy the birds from him and set them free."

Miss Zhu pretended not to understand a thing.

"You live here?" the man asked. "It's a good place. I like the whores. They're nice. But those birds, man, that just really pisses me off."

After the man left (without the birds), Miss Zhu said, "Now I know why you tell our students not to approach every foreigner they meet."

That last afternoon in school, I cleared the thick green ivy from a window and leaned out to stare at the gray, scalloped ocean of rooftops. I remained under its spell. The view looked the same as it had when Class Two insisted, daily, that 996 days remained until the Olympics. In the *hutong*, it was easy to believe that time stopped, even as the neighborhood ebbed and flowed.

The afternoon eye-exercise music finished, signaling the end of this half day of announcements instructing how to spend the summer "safe and civilized." My ears pricked up at "Do not pick up syringes." On the walk downstairs to send off the students, whose backpacks sagged with summer homework, a black box caught my eye. Security cameras had been installed on every floor.

I asked Miss Zhu, "What's next?"

"Clocks." Remembering her favorite English expression, she added, "We are off the clock."

Aerial shots of office buildings often appear in Beijing's promotional commercials, evincing its modernity. Look at the Motorola building! See the white boxes of Soho! The camera fails to pan down to the chaos of the surrounding streets, where someone forgot to design a functional crosswalk. Duke, the urban planner from San Francisco whose design for a villa community without cul-de-sacs had been canceled, stared at Beijing's World Trade Center's intersection from his office window, redrawing it in his mind. Then he turned back to his work, drafting a vacation-home development whose English name was Livin' by the Sea.

On a Sunday morning before he left for a job in Los Angeles—"that city will feel familiar"—we took a cab to visit the Olympic Stadium, in Beijing's northern suburbs. The cabdriver listened to the popular radio serial that described a battle against Japan. *"Pow! Pow! Pow!"* the narrator shouted. The view out the window showed cranes, expressways, isolated office buildings, and apartment towers—dots on a shapeless void. Outside the *hutong*, Beijing became an archipelago of detached locales rather than a contiguous neighborhood. The additions are distant; the subtractions personal. A restaurant is gone, a lane has been razed, lives upended. Duke asked if, given the city's transformation, I would be able, one day, to say I missed living in Beijing.

I know that in cities, today's monumental change can turn into tomorrow's status quo. Cities alter with age, just as we do, but they get to repeat the cycle. I am not given to nostalgia. Yet increasingly, whenever I left the *hutong*, I missed Beijing. I missed not its tangible architecture, but the intangible lifestyle that navigated and lived within it. I missed things I didn't know to appreciate at the time, such as commercial streets that invited strolling before the Hand inflated their space. Grandmothers gossiping outside at five in the morning. Men walking to the market wearing silk pajamas. Long meals outside around a steaming hot pot, and an afternoon beer under the locust trees at What? Bar. Receipts with scratch-off panels that may reveal a cash prize. Spray-painted heads. I missed nonstandard English and a pride in being nonstandard, in being weird. Creative curse words. Hockey on the moat. I missed things I saw every day but were already receding. Creeper vines on the school's exterior. Miss Zhu kicking a *jianzi* between class with Cher. Little Liu's father's pigeons, and his wife's protests. Tiled rooftops that needed weeding. I missed celebrations whose start was determined by moon phases, not countdown clocks. The city that long before "New Beijing, New Olympics" branded itself the Capital of Culture, Capital of Civilization, a masterpiece of urban planning to which the world should aspire, and enjoy, and protect. I missed Beijing every day.

The cab dropped us on the edge of a muddy field that would become the Olympic Green. A large artificial lake mirrored the cloudless sky. The surrounding man-made hills were covered with seedlings imported from the countryside. "Migrant trees," Duke said, "planted by migrant workers. I think only one of those will be welcome at the games."

We walked through calf-deep mud toward the "Bird's Nest," the stadium whose exterior was lashed together with ribbons of steel. It was designed in a collaboration between the Swiss firm Herzog & de Meuron—creators of London's Tate Modern art museum—and the Beijing architect Ai Weiwei, whose father, a famed poet, had been exiled to China's remote west and forced to clean latrines during the Cultural Revolution. Ai distanced himself from the stadium being used as a sculpture, an image to be propagandized.

"The joy of design is already there, the rest is rubbish," Ai told the *Guardian* newspaper. "I have no interest in associating with the Olympics or the state. I hate the feeling of stirring up by promotion or propaganda . . . It's the kind of sentiment when you don't stick to the facts, but try to make up something, to mislead people away from a true discussion. It's not good for anyone."

The stadium would host the games' Opening Ceremony, to be choreographed by *Raise the Red Lantern* film director Zhang Yimou, among others. "All the shitty directors in the world are involved," Ai said. "It's disgusting.

The Bird's Nest and extension of the Imperial Way, foreground.

I don't like anyone who shamelessly abuses their profession, who makes no moral judgment. It is mindless . . . Everybody has this tendency not to talk about the past. The only thing left is to try to entertain and celebrate. It's crazy. You cannot walk one hundred meters in Beijing without questioning why you live in this city. Yet they celebrate the Olympics. It is very ironic. Look at the air in the past week. But it is no more disgusting than the political conditions here . . . It is never too late. A person has to do something. We must continuously act by ourselves, to make decisions to participate or resist. We must draw our own lines."

At an entrance to the construction site, the workers, squatting in loafers and sport coats over their rice-filled enamel cups, said hello and turned their attention to lunch. Duke and I walked in without knocking. Workers had completed the stadium's shell and poured the stands' steps. I climbed to the uppermost row. On August 8, 2008, at 8:08:08 P.M., ninety thousand people would be here and a billion more watching on television as China showcased itself to the world.

A year before, on this afternoon: silence. Scaffolding filled the impending playing field. Outside, the vista showed the translucent skin of the "Water Cube" aquatic center, apartment towers, and a courtyard home that had been spared and refurbished on the site, as sculpture.

"I wonder who lived there," Duke said.

Next to its vermilion walls ran an extension of the Imperial Way, the central axis that linked to the Forbidden City and Front Gate Avenue. Made from bone white granite, the new meridian was laid to symbolically unite Beijing's past and future.

I strained my eyes to the present, but couldn't distinguish Dazhalan from up here. Some things are best seen from the ground. I stopped pretending to be a spectator, climbed down, and returned home. It was still there.

Recycler Wang rarely worked outside the gate now, keeping watch over bicycles and relaying neighborhood news. Coming home meant stepping wordlessly through the door, then into a silent courtyard, as Mr. Han and his wife still searched for a storefront or work. They wouldn't see their son all summer, she had admitted, because the train ticket to bring him to Beijing from the northeast was too expensive. The jug-eared policeman and his

parents lived elsewhere, counting the Widow's former rooms as an investment that would mature when the Hand painted 拆 on the house's wall.

I turned to the Missing Person page in the *Evening News*. Unsmiling
faces stared back. Where did they go? The sun arced past my windows, and
as the room grew dark, I thought of the sealed tunnel beneath the bed and
the woman who died upon it. Where did she go?

A popular conception of heaven depicts it as a sparsely decorated white
space peopled with friends and family. Imagine spending eternity in a place
wiped clean of life's settings. Instead of scrubbed newness, I want old, rec-
ognizable backdrops: cornfields, a fishing dock, a baseball diamond, a library, street signs, weather, a pub, the *hutong*, the frozen Forbidden City
moat, neighbors.

Since the Widow had moved, the house felt empty, no matter how many
people came or went. Her presence made it home as much as the bricks and
beams. I missed her walking in without knocking, extending a bowl of
steaming dumplings, giving unsolicited advice, leaving the wake of Flying
Horse smoke and a trail of ash.

The courtyard's dying light turned the shade of black that terrified my
students because it brought out the ghosts. The leaves of the lane's last tree
swayed in the wind. Our wooden gate creaked open. I called, "Hello?" The
echo carried around the walls. The response came back: "It's me. I'm here."

"You're here? I'm here."

Unlocking his door, Mr. Han nodded and said, "We are both here."

We were here.

EPILOGUE

New Beijing, New Olympics

In the early morning darkness of April 25, 2008, the Hand crept past our house and down the lane, pausing at Prolong Life Street to paste white posters on the gray brick walls of courtyards and shops. I saw them there at dawn while walking to the latrine. A crowd gathered around the potsticker stall run by one of my student's parents. "*Chai*," the mother said in greeting, flashing a helpless smile. Men puffed out their chests and insisted that the forthcoming compensation would have to be at least ten times the going rate—still approximately $1,000 per square meter—before they would move. "The Olympics start this summer," the fish-seller said, motioning for the crowd to disperse. "The government will not look for trouble."

I lined up with everyone else, scanning the *hutong* names and addresses of courtyards marked for destruction: Woodblock Lane (eight houses); Cherry Lane (seven houses); Three Wells Lane (one home); Big Ear Lane (one home), and Glazed Tile Factory (Liulichang), the antiques avenue where the city had previously torn down historic structures and replaced them with replicas. There, the destroyed buildings would include eight shops, Beijing's oldest post office, and Songtangzhai, a small museum opened by a hospice administrator that displayed relics he scavenged from the rubble of razed neighborhoods. My eyes scanned down the notice to find Red Bayberry and Bamboo Slanted Street's name, followed by the number of two courtyards. Neither was mine.

Most of the doomed homes were located on Prolong Life Street, slated to be widened into an avenue for car traffic, and a parking lot. The notice

Prolong Life Street

listed each of the one hundred addresses that formed the neighborhood's commercial heart—stores and small businesses that pumped food, goods, and services around the clock into the veins and capillaries formed by the *hutong*.

When I entered Coal Lane Elementary, dumpling breakfast in hand, the principal said she had not heard the news. "We will at least finish the school year," she guessed. Then she added that English classes were cancelled the rest of the year so my students, now in Grade Six, could prepare for their entrance exam to middle school. Before I left, Little Liu intercepted me in the hall. Her eye had strengthened, and the patch was gone. "I have a secret," she said, and I leaned down. "Tomorrow is your birthday!" Little Liu shouted in my ear. "We got you presents!"

I let her tie a Young Pioneer kerchief around my neck and carried home the kids' handmade cards and one-yuan packets of Nescafé. When my cell phone beeped that afternoon, I hoped it was the Widow, calling to wish me a happy thirty-sixth birthday, my third spent in the *hutong*. No one had heard from her for months; when Mr. Han or I dialed her number, the line just rang and rang. Her granddaughter's phone connected to an operator's recorded voice, intoning, "Sorry, the number you are calling does not exist."

Instead, I answered to a genial voice, saying in British-accented English: "I'm a public relations representative for the developer doing the mall outside of Qianmen [Front Gate]. I wonder if we could have a word?"

The man worked for SOHO China, one of the nation's largest developers, which recently had raised a record $1.65 billion in its initial public offering on the Hong Kong stock exchange. Owned by a glamorous, rich-list married couple, the firm was known for hiring star international architects to transform former industrial sites into mixed residential and commercial developments of sleek, modernist design.

After the district government's subsidary developer ran out of funds to remake Front Gate Avenue, it recruited SOHO to do the work, despite the company never having done a conservation project, or a development using traditional Chinese design. Not that it would likely be constrained by regulations—the Hand had already ignored the heritage protection laws covering the area, where Old Zhang's home, Soldier Liu's noodle restaurant, and my neighbor Mr. Han's shop once stood.

Now SOHO determined the ancient neighborhood's fate, and future appearance. I had sought to interview the company beginning three years before, when I moved to Dazhalan, starting with a request for its CEO to further comment on a statement she made that Beijing would have "its own Le Corbusier." I never received a response, until now, after its public relations department heard that I was writing this book, found my number, and called to make the company's perspective clear.

Had I considered, the representative asked, the headaches that the Qianmen project was bringing its developer? Conservationists had prevailed by seeing that the new construction would look traditional, but since then SOHO had been besieged with suggestions on how to remake the area, which had gone through no fewer than thirty-six drafts of blueprints, resulting from quarrels over details as minuscule as what types of trees—plastic or fruit-bearing—should be planted. Even Prince Charles, who had never visited Beijing, disparaged the development, announcing that his Foundation for Architecture and Urbanism would work with Chinese academics and architects to preserve the surrounding lanes of Dazhalan.

"Look," SOHO's representative said, "the company knows the project will exhibit how Beijing treats its past, and as other cities follow the capital's lead, the result may spread nationwide." Did I have any advice, he wondered, on lessening public criticism, on showing that SOHO cared?

I referred the man to Old Zhang, Soldier Liu, Mr. Han and other people displaced by the project, whose high rents would prohibit their return. Beyond that, I suggested that SOHO could preserve a sense of place by at least retaining the original grid of *hutong* and their names, if not the community that once enlivened it. SOHO could remember that working neighborhoods still bordered the area, and include shops and services local people would use, as opposed to souvenir stalls or chain stores selling products available anywhere. SOHO could post interpretive signs detailing the area's history. It could build an ice rink to replace the one shuttered at the Forbidden City moat, and add shaded public spaces useful to all ages of people, instead of the usual manicured lawns decorated with **Keep off the Grass** signs.

Finally, I extended an invitation to SOHO's management to visit Coal Lane Elementary, my courtyard, and *hutong* to meet the people whose lives their design would affect. "That would prove the developer wanted to take a different approach to this neighborhood, which is not a blank-slate indus-

Coal Lane Elementary students at play in front of the school.

trial site, but a unique community." (Internally, I imagined the Widow returning to scold the high-toned executives: *"Listen to my story, you dolts!"*)

The public relations representative said he would pass the suggestions on.

On the morning of April 26, I popped out of the courtyard's narrow door like a cuckoo from a clock, eager to make the latrine. I turned up Prolong Life Street to find that—twenty-four hours after the Hand had passed through—other hands had slashed and peeled the white eviction notices, rendering their commands illegible. The useless action by angry residents created an illusion fostered by the insulated *hutong*, that those who lived there determined its fate.

A few blocks over, garbage gleaners roved the furrows of rubble where Miss Zhu's childhood home once stood: here a sink basin, there a tattered suitcase, here a dismembered dress mannequin. The only notice—looking for a lost dog "60 cm long, 20 cm wide, and an old lady's best friend"—was pasted to the sumac that Miss Zhu climbed as a girl. Formerly, her courtyard shielded the tree, and now it stood alone, looking like an exclamation point atop the landscape of shattered brick.

Some of the backstreet life still lingered at the edges of Wal-Mart, where merchants beside flatbed tricycles sold homemade cakes, in-season fruit, and used clothing. Soon, they would be gone. To where, no one could say. "Out there, like me," Miss Zhu had always guessed, gesturing to the distance where the Hand urged everyone to move.

I saw her only when she bundled up her infant son and took a cab into town from her new apartment, located outside the Fourth Ring Road. Her maternity leave lasted the entire school year, and she used the time away from Coal Lane Elementary to dote on her pudgy newborn and look after her grandparents. Whereas our conversation was formerly dominated by Mocky and *chai*, now we talked about her boy and life in the lonely, if comfortable, suburbs.

Mostly we met at Taoranting (Joyous Pavilion) Park, just inside the South Second Ring Road, near the courtyard home where she formerly lived with her husband. That house—and surrounding *hutong*—had been leveled at the start of 2008, and Miss Zhu did not miss the communal living, coal-burning stove, or public latrine. She did miss the park, however,

A boy practicing wushu *on a lane leading to Wal-Mart.*

and the public gathering space it provided for elderly doing *tai qi* exercises, amateur opera singers, chess players, and grandmothers ogling babies, like Miss Zhu's. "He's so white and fat!" a woman said in highest Chinese praise, and wrested the child from the stroller without asking.

We sat on a park bench, where Miss Zhu complained about the weight she gained from pregnancy. She still looked slim as a scallion to me, and luminous in motherhood. As she talked about her new apartment—long walks to the market, long waits for the bus, and long days inside with her grandparents, who had not made new friends—her gaze wandered over my shoulder to the half-dozen women bouncing and pinching her son. "You two are really lucky!" several women told us, and Miss Zhu did not bother to correct them, squeezing my hand in playful conspiracy.

She handed the giggling boy to me, and I moved to set his bare bottom on the thick green grass around us. "No!" the crowd shouted. A grandmother wiped her hand on the lawn, displaying a palm coated in white powder. "Pesticide!" she scolded. "They really should put a warning sign here."

Miss Zhu frowned and held out her arms. I returned the boy. "I can't even feed him formula," she said. "You can't know if it's fake, or what's been added to it." She flicked her chin toward the smoggy sky. "The environment is so bad for a child. It's so dusty where we live now, I have to keep the windows closed. I rarely paid attention to any of it until he was born."

Likewise, Miss Zhu never thought about the *hutong* until it would be destroyed. "Everyone is like that, right?" she said. "Not just in Beijing, but all over the world. If it doesn't concern you, you don't care. It's like that Chinese saying: "You look but don't see; You hear but don't listen."

We passed through a gauntlet of pawing aunties to the park's northern gate, shadowed by a line of cranes erecting a row of condominiums. Officially, Joyous Pavilion Park was protected from development, but I wondered for how long. What would her son find when he returned one, two, three decades later? "He won't remember what it looked like," Miss Zhu shrugged. "It will all be different, again." She hailed a taxi for the thirty-minute ride to her new home, and life. I waved, but Miss Zhu did not look back.

I was surprised when SOHO's public relations representative called again, even if it was to say that the executives were too busy to visit Coal Lane Elementary, my courtyard, and neighborhood. Instead, he said I would be granted a rare audience with the company's CEO. That morning, I washed my hair under the courtyard's cold-water tap, put on my least-musty shirt, and biked out of the *hutong*, crossing the southern end of Front Gate Avenue, where a veil of green plastic netting covered a restaurant whose owner refused to allow her business to be destroyed to plant a greensward that would border the Olympic cycling and marathon routes. Nearby, workers mortared a ten-foot-tall brick wall around small shops that also had not budged. Inside a cage by one store's door, a starling trained to mimic Chinese squawked lines of a classical poem: "The white sun leans on the mountain, it is gone/The Yellow River enters the sea, it flows on."

Thirty minutes later, I arrived at SOHO's glassy new headquarters in the warren of rising skyscrapers forming Beijing's Central Business District. Typically for New Beijing, there was no place to park a bike, no sidewalk

Our courtyard's interior.

vendors selling water, and no shade. I entered SOHO's office sweaty, parched, and feeling underdressed. A secretary asked if she could bring something fresh-squeezed from the juice bar.

Sitting in her expansive, minimalist-chic office, SOHO's CEO Zhang Xin said, "Qianmen [Front Gate] was part of my old memories." Raised in an apartment in Beijing's university district, Ms. Zhang recalled shopping trips in the city's center as a girl. "But recently," she said in English accented by her Cambridge education, "when I walked through its *hutong*, the neighborhood was terrible, infrastructure-wise. It was an open sewer, with kids peeing outside the doors. I never imagined Qianmen had become that dilapidated. I was surprised how many residents were *waidi*."

My heart sank at hearing the Beijing native's epithet for migrants. Solider Liu was *waidi*; Mr. Han was *waidi*; Recycler Wang was *waidi*; most of my students were *waidi*. Dazhalan and the thriving neighborhood outside the Front Gate had been settled and enriched by *waidi* for centuries.

Ms. Zhang listened to me, then continued in a voice brimming with professional charm. "I said, 'Maybe we can do something.' The area needs development, but it also needs conservation."

But conservation for whom? After partnering with the district government, SOHO hired architects such as Ben Wood—an American who designed Shanghai's Xintiandi mall, which recreates the look of the houses and lanes that it replaced—and Yung-Ho Chang (Zhang Yonghe), a Beijing native whose father designed the national history museum near the project, bordering Tian'anmen Square. Their initial task: to recreate the facades along Front Gate Avenue to resemble a photograph taken in 1950.

"The project is not a replica, as the buildings have to fit into today's functionality, and not resemble a fake movie set," Ms. Zhang said. "It will look respectable as part of our history, and also look respectable as property that can be used today. Old Beijing was a wooden city, unlike European cities. There is a rush to save what's left. There's enough awareness now. We must try. The key here is to inject new energy."

While she did not utter the word *profit*, Ms. Zhang also did not ask how residents viewed their neighborhood, or what intangible elements were worth saving there. I was not surprised; developers raise (and raze) buildings to make money for their investors. But I was dismayed. Given its capital, clout, and culture, SOHO could do something unique in upgrading the area to modern standards. Yet Ms. Zhang and one of her architects intimated they were not making decisions unilaterally.

Yung-Ho Chang, whose firm designed the two traditional-looking new buildings that anchored Front Gate Avenue near its ceremonial arch, said he was more interested in his designs for the neighboring Fresh Fish Junction *hutong*, which would preserve courtyards for art studios, shops, and upscale residences. "The main street does not really have a different approach than other similar projects in Beijing," he wrote via e-mail from MIT, where he heads the Department of Architecture. "It's a political project. Therefore, unfortunately, design does not matter much or is not so desired."

Indeed, my tour SOHO had planned of the new Front Gate Avenue—still sheathed in blue tin preventing public access—was abruptly postponed so

Beijing's mayor could inspect the site. After being turned away, I walked through the remains of Fresh Fish Junction, stopping at the rubble of Soldier Liu's former noodle restaurant. Two years after its destruction, dozens of residents remained in neighboring courtyards, holding out for a higher compensation to move.

At seven o'clock the following morning, a district government chaperone led me silently down the remade Front Gate Avenue. Trolley tracks ran through the center of the gray flagstones, bordered by the vacant storefronts of the newly made "antique" facades. Whatever its planners intended, the street looked to me like the "fake movie set" that SOHO's CEO averred it would not.

Birdcage-shaped streetlamps aside, there were some unique and thoughtful touches. A black-and-white photograph of the original structure hung on each building, alongside a blue tin address plate displaying its former number. Trashcans had been installed, spaced apart from rows of benches shaded by crab apple trees, allowing pedestrians to linger.

Front Gate Avenue (Qianmen Dajie) remade.

I walked to neighboring Dazhalan West Street, which even after a pre-Olympics scrubbing retained its well-worn livelihood, and attracted a mixture of tourists and locals to the *hutong's* hotels, shops, restaurants, bathhouses, and internet cafés. At the historic hostel being renovated at the end of Red Bayberry and Bamboo Slanted Street, owner Kane Kahn exhaled as he scrolled through the digital pictures I had just snapped of the new Front Gate Avenue. Costs to restore his two-story building had reached $375,000—triple his original estimate—and he had taken over much of the remodeling himself, after firing workers who began painting over the structure's wood, dating from its 1850 construction. After Khan paid for the hostel's façade to be restored, a city directive ordered all neighborhood structures look uniform, so laborers showed up to glue gray tiles over its original gray brick.

"In the 1920s, this hotel—Tai Feng Lou—was a secret Communist Party meeting place," he said, pulling on one of his many new gray hairs. "The carved wood screens in the rooms upstairs date to the nineteenth century. It's so difficult to find stories and facts about old architecture. When I signed the lease, it was being used as a dormitory for the Railway Bureau." In the central courtyard, he pointed to a framed collage of black-and-white photos he collected during renovations, showing men posing next to East Is Red diesel engines. "There isn't a plaque out front that describes all of this," Khan said. "Will you write one?"

If developers and officials thought like this *waidi*—Khan had migrated from Inner Mongolia—the neighborhood's built heritage could be preserved. "I figured that visitors would want to see authentic, original Beijing," he said, gesturing at the restored inn that had bankrupted him. "It would have been so much easier to build anew."

As the government had predicted two years before, it did not rain on August 8, 2008, the start of the Olympics. And just as the fish-seller on Prolong Life Street had foreseen, plans to raze the neighborhood before the games began had stalled. Waking one summer morning to the sound of pickaxes striking asphalt, I emerged from the courtyard to see Red Bayberry and Bamboo Slanted Street being sheathed in scaffolding by a gang of laborers. "They're here to paint the houses and patch the lanes before the

Olympics," Recycler Wang said. Teams fanned out across Dazhalan on a beautification campaign, slathering gray and crimson paint on courtyard exteriors and over the shreds of the Hand's remaining posters, announcing the coming destruction.

That evening, I biked past doorways festooned with new national flags, glowing red in the gathering dusk. A crowd spilled from Soldier Liu's, onto the *hutong*. His family's restaurant had become a community gathering place, attracting neighbors with their food and a wall-mounted television. "It's used!" his mother said. "We got it cheap!" Staring at the screen, a group of aunties slapped their bare calves with homemade fans. "It's hot," one told me. "You're hungry," stated another. "He doesn't eat enough," a woman added. As they had for the past year, the three began talking about me as if I weren't there, stopping only when Soldier Liu handed me a bowl of knife-shaved noodles.

Soldier Liu (center) and his parents.

Soldier Liu looked and sounded more urbane every day; his crew-cut had been replaced with styled hair, his army fatigue pants with board shorts, and he now wore the gold wire-rim glasses favored by white-collar workers. The engagement arranged by a matchmaker to a girl from his village had ended after she refused to move to Beijing. He did not want to return to the countryside, and thought of opening an Internet café featuring Apple computers. "That would really attract people here," he said while slicing dough into boiling water. "I just need some investors."

As the Olympics' Opening Ceremony started at 8:08, Soldier Liu and his parents remained in the kitchen or beside the cauldron, steaming on the lane. Customers streamed in, grabbed their own bottles of Yanjing beer from the refrigerator, and lit Red Plumblossom cigarettes. From outside came the passing, percussive thuds of police helicopters, mixed with clanging bike bells and shouts of "Out of the way, bastard!"

Soldier Liu's sister sat beside me to watch the ceremony, as her family worked. She was training to become a math teacher, and manual labor, her parents said, was not for her. The television showed the packed "Bird's Nest" national stadium reverberating from a booming performance of traditional drums. A fat woman wearing pajamas walked in to the restaurant and yelled, "Give me two big bowls!" The television showed soldiers marching with the flags of China and the Olympics. A shirtless man beside us vacuumed his noodles in one loud slurp. The television reminded us that China had five thousand years of history. The shirtless man belched. A woman wearing an "I ♥ China" t-shirt scolded Soldier Liu for the small amount of pork in her bowl. "Don't cheat me! How much do you pay for that meat? I know a guy who can get it for you cheaper!"

An hour after the Opening Ceremony began, the Liu's sat at our table, peeling garlic to fill tomorrow's bowls. Soldier Liu's sister sauntered away, returning with a sausage roasted on a stick. "Yuck," her brother said. "That's not healthy at all."

"It's better than noodles!" she snapped.

At ten o'clock, the Liu's were ready to close; the next workday began at four in the morning. The group of aunties moved to stools on the lane. On television, athletes marched behind their flag, and for the first time all night, Soldier Liu stopped to watch, repeating each nation's name after the announcer, in three languages: "*Xibanya. Spain. Espagne.*" As I pedaled away, I heard him saying *Iran*, then *Iraq*. The aunties agreed that Soldier Liu was a very smart boy.

A police officer prevented me from crossing to Tian'anmen Square, closed at the last minute to curb the crowd gathered there to watch the ceremony on a large screen. I detoured into the *hutong*, and coasted past people sitting in front of televisions carried outside. Red Bayberry and Bamboo Slanted Street glowed with their pulsing blue light. Already the sensation of proud relief that would characterize Beijing during the games was palpable; after seven years, the city could stop preparing, and enjoy the event.

At the renovated What? Bar—same location, larger space, pricier beer— the manager, Qin Xuan, poured a draft of Yanjing and watched marching athletes on the newly-installed TV ("It's used," she explained. "I got it cheap."). After the lighting of the stadium's Olympic flame, fireworks exploded across town. We stepped outside to watch the ones blooming over the Forbidden City next door, and raised a toast to the bar's unexpected survival.

The blue tin shrouding Front Gate Avenue was peeled back that week, opening it to the public. Access to connecting *hutong* remained sealed, however, funneling the crowds down the toilet-less street, snapping photos and dropping trash. The single line of customers formed outside Quanjude roast duck restaurant, one of thirteen famous "old brand names" that the government announced would be allowed to return to the neighborhood.

That was one of what would be many salvos to attract investment to the mostly vacant storefronts as Beijing's sky-high property bubble descended back to earth. By the end of 2008, SOHO's stock would lose 70 percent of its value, and the municipal government would halt the entire Qianmen project for review.

When the redesigned Front Gate Avenue opened, the people who looked happiest were the well-dressed women plucking the potted flowers for souvenirs, and the relieved children lined up against the expensively rebuilt buildings, peeing outside their doors.

For the next three weeks, I mostly watched the Olympics at Soldier Liu's, or at home with the Han's, who had brought back a television—along with their son—from their apartment in the country's northeast. The boy would be a second-grader at Coal Lane Elementary, and a student of Miss Zhu's. His parents looked elated, but the seven-year-old seemed unsure about his new environment, which, unlike his former apartment, lacked a bathroom and space to play. Now, the three of them squeezed into a single room, as Mr. Han continued to repair cell phones at the market, a long bus ride away. He remained optimistic that their fortunes would soon improve. "We're together as a family," he said, "and nothing else matters."

When I noticed a shiny white van parked outside our courtyard's door, Recycler Wang gave a self-effacing laugh and said, "It's used." He had bought it "cheap," of course. Once the Olympics ended, he would use the vehicle to transport goods to Trash Village, but now I saw him only when he cracked his door to surreptitiously accept my empty bottles. All recycling had been banished temporarily from the lanes. "It's to make things look nice for tourists," he said. "Although hardly any tourists have come here."

It was true: Once the games began, the neighborhood—like all of Beijing—was less trafficked, less smoggy, and less ornery, due in part to it

Recycler Wang at his post, prior to the start of the Olympics.

being less crowded, as many residents left town to avoid the masses that failed to arrive.

So most days, the historian himself was the only person attending Zhang Jinqi's small museum, which he set up in an annex of our local police station to display his photographs of Dazhalan's buildings and residents. Zhang still lived in a courtyard a few lanes away and maintained his website that documented China's architectural heritage. His grant from the Ford Foundation allowed him to travel abroad for the first time, observing preservation practices in foreign cities. "I just got back from Kyoto," he said. "I go to Hanoi next." After reading Jane Jacobs, he most wanted to visit New York City. "Greenwich Village is still there, right? Maybe Dazhalan will remain, too."

Who could say for how long? Traces of the eviction posters still clung to Prolong Life Street, where I bought the *Evening News*. The hour of its wandering vendor's arrival, scored by the mournful hum of bamboo whistles attached to pigeons swooping in the air above, remained my favorite time of day. I sat outside the post office and read the paper, whose Missing Person ads had been discontinued during the Olympics. During those three weeks, it seemed that everyone was exactly where they were supposed to be.

Little Liu and her father, atop their courtyard's roof.

I rarely saw my former students now; many had returned to the villages and towns where they had been born, and were required to be educated beyond primary school. Little Liu remained, and I walked to her courtyard to congratulate her for scoring highest in all of Coal Lane Elementary on the middle school entrance exam. She would attend the city's top junior high. Although she was on summer vacation, and although Olympic events were on television around the clock, I found Little Liu inside her family's dark single room, squinting over a workbook of English grammar. "That's not good for your eyes," I said. "Let's go outside." Little Liu climbed up to the coop and cooed over a shoebox filled with newborn pigeons. Her father opened the cages, and we watched the adults fly free over the neighborhood's scalloped-rooftop horizon.

I imagined the Widow looking out an apartment window at a barren sky. Walking home down Woodblock Lane, I dialed her granddaughter and heard the emotionless recording intone: "Sorry, the number you are calling does not exist." I passed the Hand's fresh posters hanging on the gates of the Heavenly Peach farmer's market, and continued down Red Bayberry and Bamboo Slanted Street to our door. As the Widow embodied this courtyard and *hutong*, it was entirely in character that once she left, she ceased to exist outside the memories of people who cared. But still I dialed her number, and listened hopefully to the ring.

February 2009

ACKNOWLEDGMENTS

My thanks go first to the residents of Dazhalan. The students and parents of Coal Lane Elementary made working there my most enjoyable years of teaching, even when narrated by Mocky. In Miss Zhu, I could not have asked for a more engaging and dedicated co-worker and friend. Her son is fortunate to have a mother who remembers the trees. The staff and students at the Neighborhood Committee treated me like their grandson, while Soldier Liu's family, Recycler Wang, Zhang Jinqi, Officer Li, and others made me feel a part of, not apart from, the community. In finding this courtyard, amidst Dazhalan's fifty-seven thousand people and three thousand houses, I won the Neighbor Lottery. The Widow and the Hans were the best companions I could have asked for. May developers and bureaucrats treat them—and the neighborhood—as they deserve, with dignity and respect.

I am grateful for the Blakemore Foundation, which funded a year of language study at the Inter-University Program (IUP) at Beijing's Tsinghua University. Teachers Liu Yu, Peng Li, Wu Haiping, and Wu Jing taught me to read characters and smoothed the edges of Sichuan dialect into Mandarin Chinese that has since been mashed into the slurpy Beijing patois. Director John Thomson and UC-Berkeley professor Tom Gold arranged funding for a research trip to Taiwan to observe preservation practices there, while Blakemore trustee Griffith Way approved an additional summer of study, which allowed me to delve deeper into Beijing's planning history. The Blakemore and Freeman foundations are indispensable sources of aid to researchers in Asia, as is their acceptance and encouragement of freelancers.

A freelance writer in China faces both the challenge of convincing faraway editors that a topic matters, and of persuading locals to talk without formal institutional introductions. I'm grateful to the editors over the years who have been convinced, allowing me to pursue topics related to this book in Cuba, Europe, Japan, Laos, Vietnam, and various Chinese cities: Mary Aikins, David Arnold, Katie Bacon, Keith Bellows, Don Belt, Jeffries Blackerby, Kathleen Burke, Mike Curry, Randy Curwen, Karl Greenfeld,

Catharine Hamm, Laura Helmuth, Chris Hill, Rahul Jacob, Conrad Kiechel, Kaiser Kuo, Richard Lim, Paul Martin, Luke Mitchell, Maureen Murphy, Oliver Payne, and Richard Story. Jonathon Tourtellot, director of the National Geographic Center for Sustainable Destinations, provided the opportunity to participate in UNESCO-led efforts to work with heritage-site managers in China, as well as to try to convince developers to change course in the Wolong Panda Preserve. And I appreciate the patience of the former director of the Peace Corps in China, Bill Speidel, and his wife, Elena. Being a U.S.-China Friendship Volunteer set me on the path to this research.

Beijing is a wonderful place in which to write, not least of all due to the subject matter. I'm fortunate to be able to turn to a large circle of writers and creative types when routes of inquiry lead to dead ends. In addition to people quoted in the text, thanks to writer Leslie Chang, filmmakers Andy and Christene Friend, Jeremy Goldkorn and Luke Mines at danwei.org, the Ford Foundation's He Jin, Susan Jakes at *Time*, lawyer Michael Goettig, photographer Mark Leong, musician/barmaid Qin Xuan, Craig Simons of Cox News, Great Wall historian David Spindler, journalist Wang Jun, anthropologist Matthew Erie, and filmmaker Kai Yang. In America, historian Michael Hunt graciously dusted off old files and maps concerning the American occupation of Beijing after the Boxer Rebellion. Geraldine Kustadter introduced me to architects and scholars. Britt Towery lent insight to Lao She's work. David Douglas tracked down resources. In Hanoi, I was assisted by David Goss, Nguyen Ngoc Dzung, John Reilly, Dana Sachs, and Tran Long.

Jake Hooker of the *New York Times* spent late nights outside at What? Bar, talking about Beijing history and the *hutong*, broadening my research. Aside from providing an insider's look at Beijing's construction, Ted "Duke" Wright contributed photographs. *Time*'s Matt Forney and family—wife Paola, children Roy and Alicia—shared skating and welcomed me into their home for meals. Matt also translated Dong Da Hospital's poetic latrine advertisement.

Literary agent extraordinaire Georges Borchardt e-mailed after reading an article I had written, an inquiry for which I'll always be appreciative. Georges introduced me to publisher George Gibson, who, from an initial call to the completion of the manuscript, has offered unfettered encouragement, ample time, and attentive editing.

I'm grateful to Peter Hessler, Adam Hochschild, and Travis Klingberg for close reading of the manuscript and critical comments. Pete and Travis are also former Peace Corps China volunteers, and I've been lucky to live in the capital with them. Travis was especially helpful in selecting images and trimming excess. Pete clarified structural deficiencies and unresolved arguments. In Adam, I have both a friend and mentor who has never failed to offer patient advice on writing and beyond. I'm happy he and Arlie came to Beijing and Tianjin and walked through neighborhoods before they vanished.

I met Frances Feng in Beijing in 1997. We were both migrants captivated by the city. Our relationship was kindled around Tsinghua's skating pond, over hot pot, and on walks through the *hutong*, many of which are gone. Though we were separated for long stretches as she finished law school in Berkeley and I lived in Beijing, Frances never asked me to stop researching, even when common sense dictated otherwise. As she is an excellent writer and legal scholar in her own right, I look forward to returning the favor. Frances, 我爱你.

Appendix: Gazetteer

As most of Beijing's lanes do not have formal English names, reading accounts of the city in English can be confusing, as authors employ their own translations. *Caochang hutong* becomes Straw Factory Lane in one book, Mat Shed Lane in another. I call it Straw Mill Lane. For clarity's sake, the following is a list of streets identified in English, ranked by the page number where they first appear in the text. Pinyin, the system used to romanize Chinese characters, marks syllables with one of four tone marks: level (ā), rising (á), falling-rising (ǎ), and falling (à). A character can also be toneless, as in the English *upon*. Thus, the characters for lane—胡同—are romanized to *hútòng*.

Page	Name	Romanization with tone marks	Chinese
5	Big Fence	*dàzhàlan**	大栅栏
5	Front Gate	*qiánmén*	前门
7	Red Bayberry and Bamboo Slanted Street	*yángméizhú xiéjiē*	杨梅竹斜街
8	Glazed Tile Factory	*liúlíchǎng*	琉璃厂
8	Coal Lane	*tàn'er hútòng*	碳儿胡同
8	Whisk Broom Lane	*tiáozhou hútòng*	笤帚胡同
27	Vegetable Market Junction	*càishìkǒu*	菜市口

---

*Also called *dàshílàn 'r* in local dialect.

36	Fetching the Lantern Lane	*qǔdēng hútòng*	取灯胡同
36	Cherry Lane	*yīngtáo hútòng*	樱桃胡同
37	Fresh Fish Junction	*xiānyúkǒu*	鲜鱼口
37	Front Gate Avenue	*qiánmén dàjiē*	前门大街
42	Ox Street	*níu jiē*	牛街
43	Flower Market Lane	*huāshì hútòng*	花市胡同
43	Straw Mill Lane	*cǎochǎng hútòng*	草厂胡同
44	West Grindstone Lane	*xī dǎmòchǎng*	西打磨厂胡同
49	"Ghost" Street	*guǐ jiē*	**簋街**
63	Front Lake	*qiánhǎi*	前海
69	Coal Street	*méishì jiē*	煤市街
73	Prolong Life Street	*yánshòu jiē*	延寿街
111	Tobacco Pipe Slanted Street	*yāndài xiéjiē*	烟袋斜街
111	Rear Lake	*hòu hǎi*	**后海**
111	Langfang (Veranda) Second Lane	*lángfáng èrtiáo*	廊坊二条
112	Dazhalan West Street Known locally by its former name: Bodhisattva of Mercy Temple Street	*dàzhàlán xījiē*	大栅栏西街
		guānyīnsì jiē	观音寺街
114	Rice Market Lane	*mǐshì hútòng*	米市胡同
128	Langfang (Veranda) First Lane	*lángfáng tóutiáo*	廊坊头条
140	Source of Law Temple	*fǎyuán sì*	法源寺
154	Temple of Agriculture	*xiānnóng tán*	先农坛
183	Eight Big Lanes	*bādà hútòng*	八大胡同
183	Brick Pagoda Lane	*zhuāntǎ hútòng*	砖塔胡同
213	West Fours	*xīsì*	西四

257	South Grain Storehouse Lane	*náncāng hútòng*	南仓胡同
257	Broad Bean Lane	*dòubàn hútòng*	豆瓣胡同
257	Sea Transport Storehouse Lane	*hǎiyùncāng hútòng*	海运仓胡同
257	South Bow Maker's Lane	*nán gōngjiàngyíng*	南弓匠营
258	Chrysanthemum Lane	*jú'er hútòng*	菊儿胡同
262	Big Ear Lane	*dà'ěr hútòng*	大耳胡同
263	Tea Lane	*chá'er hútòng*	茶儿胡同
295	Safe and Sound Boulevard	*píng'ān dàdào*	平安大道
302	South Gong and Drum Lane	*nán luógǔxiàng*	南锣鼓巷

NOTES

Sources are provided for direct quotations, identified by their beginning words, and for information that cannot easily be found in one—often several—of the most comprehensive books identified at the beginning of the bibliography. If no page number follows a citation, the source is a newspaper article.

CHAPTER 1: THROUGH THE FRONT GATE

7 *Peking's a giant failure, isn't it?*: Stanley quoted by A. B. Freeman-Mitford in *The Attaché at Peking*, 1865, published 1900. Reprinted in Elder, p. 26.

7 *Undoubtedly this Europe*: Kangxi quoted by Attiret, p. 36. The Jesuit also said of eighteenth-century Chinese who looked at prints of Europe's celebrated buildings, "They look upon our Streets, as so many Ways hollowed into terrible Mountains; and upon our Houses, as Rocks pointing up in the Air, and full of Holes like Dens of Bears and other wild Beasts. Above all, our different Stories, piled up so high one above another, seem quite intolerable to them: and they cannot conceive, how we can bear to run the Risk of breaking our Necks, so commonly, in going up such a Number of Steps as is necessary to climb up to the Fourth and Fifth Floors." P. 35.

CHAPTER 2: BECOMING TEACHER PLUMBLOSSOM

16 *A town is a tool*: Le Corbusier, p. xxi. Who would implement his vision? "Here is a fact," he wrote, "which may seem discouraging at first blush, but one which on reflection will encourage and inspire confidence; immense industrial undertakings do not need great men." P. 41.

16 *The Committee for the Preservation*: Ibid., pp. 256–57. Interestingly, Le Corbusier

captioned a map of Beijing's Old City, "Compare this with that of Paris, a little further on. And we Westerners felt called on to invade China in the cause of *civilization*!" P. 88.

Chapter 3: Mocky & Me

32 *I'm afraid we'll have to* detain: Wang Sheng'an, p. 115. I included the dialogues in a "Readings" short I wrote for *Harper's*, "You Can Run But You Can't Hide," September 2003.

33 *Because my family was killed*: Ibid., p. 188.

Chapter 4: "Say Farewell to Dangerous Housing"

35 *is giving way to everything that is new*: Lynn, p. 175.

35 *The loss by vandalism and utter neglect*: Arlington, p. v. The authors continue, "One might, perhaps, pass over minor acts of vandalism, such as converting historic palaces into modern restaurants and tea-houses; famous temples into barracks and police-stations; cutting down ancient cypresses to sell for firewood; defacing age-old walls and tables with political slogans, and so forth. But in many instances historical buildings and monuments have actually been destroyed by official orders. The work of destruction culminated in 1933 with the removal of the entire priceless collection of Palace Treasures to the South, where they are stored in the vaults of banks, the beautiful paintings doomed to be eaten by moths, or destroyed by the damp . . . That the Chinese people, formerly so attached to their own culture and customs, should have acquiesced in this wanton destruction of their ancient works of art, derived from a civilization going back for thousands of years, is not only surprising, but is of serious ill-omen for the artistic and cultural future of the country as a whole." Pp. v–vi. The year was 1934, before Japan and the Communists would control Beijing.

35 *The first thing I did when I arrived in Peking*: Marcuse, p. 19.

39 *Ninety-five percent of the twenty-nine neighborhoods*: Zhang Jie, p. 86.

39 *In April 1990, the municipal government*: Fang Ke, pp. 25–26.

39 *Under the Old and Dilapidated Housing Renewal (ODHR) program*: Ibid., p. 32.

39 *The communities outside the Front Gate*: Ibid., p. 31.

39 *Fiscal deficits of the late 1970s*: Yan Zhang and Fang Ke, p. 290.

39 *In 1988, national policy was changed*: Ibid.

39 *In the late 1990s, the municipal government of Beijing generated*: Ibid., p. 291.

39 *In 1993, the city enlarged the ODHR program*: Fang Ke and Yan Zhang, p. 151.

40 *By 1995, the rights to nearly all*: Yan Zhang and Fang Ke, p. 290.

40 *He did not specify where*: Lü, p. 61.

42 *Cases, such as one filed*: Yan Zhang and Fang Ke, p. 294.

42 *Kickbacks were common*: Ibid., p. 296.

42 *The real estate market is now playing the strongest role*: Lü, p. 67.

42 *City officials said that 500,000*: Ibid., p. 153.

42 *unofficial estimates ran higher*: Jakes.

42 *By the late 1990s*: Fang Ke, p. 30.

46 *The living conditions of the conservation areas*: Beijing Municipal City Planning Commission 1, p. 11. Project statistics are listed in this text.

46 *The Beijing city government is demanding*: Xinhua, quoted in Agence France-Presse 2.

48 *In the locked glass case of the Exhibition Center's gift shop*: Beijing Municipal City Planning Commission 1, p. 10.

48 *Besides demolishing temporarily built houses*: Letter from Dongcheng District Real Estate Operation and Management Centre, "an organ affiliated with the district government in charge of relocation in old streets," quoted in Jia.

48 *This is all a real estate scam*: Nanchizi resident Xie Yuchun, whose family owned their courtyard since 1947, quoted in Saiget 1.

49 *What's intolerable is that our centuries-old houses*: Xie Yuchun, quoted in Jia.

49 *The point of being a world cultural heritage site*: Francesco Bandarin, director of the UNESCO World Heritage Centre, quoted ibid.

49 *We have expressed our concerns*: Quoted in Agence France-Presse 1.

49 *An official said the neighborhood's renovation*: Quoted in Saiget 2.

50 *If Front Gate Avenue forms a mall*: Urban Planning and Design Institute of Tsinghua University 2, p. 28.

51 *Building more roads*: Quoted in Wang Jun, "*Da Malu Zhi Yang*" ["Itching for Big Roads"]. Xinhua, July 5, 2005.

51 *The wider the road*: Huang Hui, quoted ibid.

55 *In order to implement the mighty philosophy*: Zhu Mingde, p. 3.

55 *Standing puddles form*: Ibid., p. 64.

56 *Foreigners absolutely view China*: Ibid., p. 105.

Chapter 5: Wintertime

65 *Skating on natural ice*: Lowe, vol. 2, p. 131.

66 *badger hunting; balancers, flagpole*: Ibid., pp. 230–31.

66   *so cold, even dogs and cats:* Ibid., p. 136.
67   *skating and sledging are a fast vanishing sight:* Ibid., p. 132.

CHAPTER 6: A BRIEF HISTORY OF 拆 PART ONE

76   *First, the land belonged to dragons:* Legend adapted from Jin.
77   *Perhaps they found the remains:* Colonel William W. Ashurst, quoted in Plumb. "The Japanese," Ashurst continued, "had no use for our foods they captured so they just dumped them off the train."
78   *A scaled-down plan was approved:* Broudehoux, pp. 118–19.
78   *It is still a monster:* Luo Zuowen, quoted ibid., p. 121.

CHAPTER 8: HIGH TIMES IN HAPPINESS CITY

95   *The construction industry can make money:* Deng Xiaoping quoted in Lü, Rowe, and Zhang, p. 220.
96   *At the founding of the People's Republic:* Ibid., p. 114. I calculated the percentage; their text reads, "In Beijing, for example, there were 1.2 million houses at the beginning of the republic, with only 280,000 publicly owned houses. The rest were privately owned and half of these were rented houses."
96   *By 1978, 90 percent of China's housing:* Ibid., pp. 114–15. "The proportion of privately owned houses throughout China kept declining and, by 1978, only 9.9 percent of all houses were owned privately."
96   *Though one unofficial estimate:* Fang Ke and Yan Zhang, p. 161.
102 *It used to be a Horizontal City:* Zhang Yonghe, p. 218.
103 *there can be no other possibilities:* Ibid., p. 224.
104 *very practical. The Jianguo was a direct copy:* Zhang Yonghe, quoted in Napack.
105 *You can scarcely imagine the beauty:* Charles Gordon's 1860 letter quoted in Elder, p. 246.
106 *In the late 1980s:* Broudehoux, p. 81. She gives a thorough account of the palace's history.

CHAPTER 9: PRESERVING A SENSE OF PLACE

108 *We were told that it was so overgrown:* Kates, p. 122.
108 *fatigued with a sense:* Ibid., p. 123.

110 *people here don't understand:* Quoted in Steinglass.

110 *People don't differentiate:* Ibid.

111 *for several decades before 2000:* Li Jing. Also in "Beijing spends US$360m on heritage preservation in past 3 years," Dow Jones & Reuters China Business Information Network, February 27, 2003.

113 *The problem in Korea and across Asia:* Peter Bartholomew, quoted in Salmon.

114 *In Russia, elderly tenants were evicted:* Kishkovsky.

114 *Without big companies coming:* St. Petersburg governor Valentina I. Matviyenko, quoted in Myers.

114 *Between the years 1900 and 2000:* Tung, p. 16.

115 *Romans demolished a third:* Ibid.

115 *"Ah, old city, old bitch.":* LaFarge, p. 369.

115 *It is no longer possible, as in Haussmann's day:* Le Corbusier, p. 297.

116 *Many urban historians note:* Rykwert, pp. 90–91.

117 *The historian Tung observes:* Tung, p. 72.

117 *In 1957, Amsterdam founded:* Ibid., pp. 241–43.

117 *Similar city-funded initiatives:* Ibid., pp. 231–36, 313.

117 *two largest works of unified urban artistry:* Ibid., p. 316.

118 *We do not fund the renovation itself:* The speaker is He Jin.

118 *There are twenty thousand:* The speaker is Ding Wen.

119 *We are in many ways:* The speaker is Jeff Morgan.

119 *In the southeast city:* The professor is Daniel Abramson.

121 *The key to restoring the buildings of the Old Quarter:* The speaker is Toulouse native Sebastian Souyri.

122 *They said cyclos obstructed traffic:* The speaker is Do Anh Thu.

123 *The Old Quarter is not easy to explain:* The speaker is composer Cuong Nguyen.

127 *The IOC has become the most influential:* Westendorff, pp. 17–18.

128 *If we continue to discuss urban preservation:* Ding Ai, quoted in UNESCO, pp. 82–83.

129 *We think Las Vegas has special features:* Liu Xingcang, quoted in Wonacott.

Chapter 10: Springtime

133 *Its daily average of suspended particles:* WHO and UNEP dated compiled by Pattinson.

136 *Inside, a red cartoon dinosaur:* Gogo ran on a loop at Book Mansion. My original description of this repeated scene appeared in "The World's Biggest Book Market," which I authored for the *New York Times Book Review*. March 13, 2005.

Chapter 11: A Brief History of 拆 Part Two

143   *After the new rulers evicted thirty thousand households:* Sit, p. 153.

143   *A captive there said:* Li Mingde 3, p. 161. The phrase is 坐井观天
(*zuòjǐng guāntiān*).

144   *When the siege was over:* Aldrich, p. 39.

144   *To legitimize their rule:* Sit, 19.

145   *Heaven and Earth are in perfect accord:* The *Record of Trades,* ibid., p. 25.

145   *When Marco Polo arrived:* Polo, pp. 33–34.

145   *They all live in the suburbs:* Ibid., p. 39.

146   *so broad and straight:* Ibid., p. 38.

146   *One of the first written references:* Li Mingde 3, p.15.

147   *At the time, England's Hampton Court:* Bredon, p. 10.

151   *There is not a more squalid collection of houses:* New York Times 1.

152   *Returning after thirty years, an admiral commented:* Admiral Lord Charles Beresford, quoted in Elder, p. 290.

152   *An American woman visiting in 1900 found:* New York Times 2.

152   *In 1895, a traveler who had heard:* Henry Norman, quoted in Elder, p. 22.

152   *Awful sights were witnessed:* Times of London 1.

153   *Adjoining buildings took fire:* Ibid.

154   *As the first governor of Cuba:* Hunt, p. 505.

155   *In the spring of 1901:* Times of London 2.

155   *It is safe to say that where one real Boxer:* Times of London 3.

155   *presented Chaffee with their signatures:* Hunt, p. 521. New York Times 7 put the number at fifty-six hundred.

155   *We, the people of the American section:* New York Times 7.

155   *An American officer told:* Ibid.

156   *In Chinese, the word for year:* Aldrich, p. 247. I am grateful for his passage on the temple.

Chapter 12: The Unslumming Slum

158   *When people come from around the world:* Beijing Weekend, July 20–22, 2001, pp. 8–9.

161   *Professor Tool had helped correct:* Krich.

164   *It wasn't a slum, he said, but rather a "stable, low-rent area":* Gans quoted in Jacobs, p. 272.

164   *Conventional planning approaches to slums:* Ibid., p. 271.

164   *Razing such a neighborhood that was actually in recovery:* Ibid., pp. 270–71.

164   *Illiterates are transformed into the skilled:* Ibid., p. 288.

165   *Regardless, a neighborhood such as ours was doomed:* Ibid.

165 The Death and Life of Great American Cities *advocated*: Ibid., p. 337. Jacobs quotes a planner named Stanley Tankel, who wrote, "We must learn to cherish the communities we have; they are hard to come by. 'Fix the buildings but leave the people.' 'No relocation outside the neighborhood.'—These must be the slogans if public housing is to be popular."

Chapter 13: Saving the Old Street

174 *One of the letter's authors told a reporter*: Yardley.

Chapter 16: A Brief History of 拆 Part Three

214 *Envoys of Austria-Hungary, Italy, and France*: Moser, p. 95.

214 *The result is interesting, even educative*: Gilbert Collins, from his 1925 book, *Extreme Oriental Mixture*, quoted by Elder, p. 106.

215 *In 1888, one of her ministers had a small train*: Dong 2, p. 35.

217 *one transgression leads to another*: This key notion comes from Tung, p. 302: "Here is a critical point in the psychology of preserving historic cities: When the object is to preserve a unity of ambience, a few violations of that aesthetic harmony can undermine a hundred successful efforts to preserve it. Once such a wholeness is destroyed, it is difficult to argue that the disrupted unity must be saved. One violation leads to another and another."

217 *Peking you simply would not be able to recognize*: Letter from George Morrison to a friend in October 1916, quoted in Pearl, p. 333.

217 *In 1920, a British author described telegraph lines*: Bredon, p. 55.

217 *masses of ugly, foreign-style buildings*: Ibid., p. 22.

217 *we find the new mingling with the old*: Ibid., p. 75.

218 *Beijing was "boring, desiccated, dirty"*: Li Dazhao quoted in Strand, p. 124.

218 *The engineering societies of the world*: Cody, p. 178.

219 *After he was put in charge of modernizing*: Ibid., p. 175.

219 *The streets were cut through the maize [sic]*: Ibid., p. 177.

219 *Murphy designed Peking University's*: Ibid., p. 121.

219 *At Tsinghua, modernizing Chinese*: Ibid., pp. 67–68.

220 *There is no money*: Buck, p. 268.

220 *There was not one touch of sympathy*: Ibid., p. 271.

220 *Why, these streets were made*: Ibid., p. 269.

220 *a great wide sweep of emptiness*: Ibid., p. 274.

220 *Had it taken this road*: Ibid., p. 276.

220 *oil is fragrant, the flour is white*: Constant, p. 21.

221 *A 1926 survey found that a quarter*: Dong 2, p. 215.

221 *The city, the author of a Chinese textbook warned*: Ni Xiying, quoted in Dryburgh, p. 510.

223 *The* New York Times *reported that residents*: Abend.

223 *In October of that year, an estimated twenty-five thousand*: Strand, p. 273.

223 *Grievances were aired in public*: Ibid., pp. 167–78.

223 *We are exhausted, as are our financial resources*: Li Mengji translated in Dong 2, p. 61.

223 *All shops must move as soon as the project begins*: Ibid., p. 61.

224 *Although we are ignorant*: Qi Dekui translated in Ibid., pp. 62–63.

224 *A government representative sent to speak*: Ibid., pp. 63–64.

224 *The media did not report the dissent*: Ibid., p. 64.

224 *Another reporter decried the government's*: Ibid., p. 65.

225 *I cannot too highly commend leisurely*: Kates, p. 171.

225 *The poet Xu Zhimo*: Dong 2, p. 272.

225 *Another writer called it a "phantom city"*: David Der-wei Wang, quoted in Dong 2, p. 301.

225 *Beiping, a writer complained, "after all is only a place"*: Peng Fangcao, quoted in ibid., p. 272.

225 *Osbert Sitwell, another expatriate memoirist, found that the city "has none of the dreadful impersonal quality"*: Sitwell, p. 181.

225 *I dream of the prosperity of Paris*: Dong 2, p. 272.

225 *with the additional disadvantage of slow train services*: R. V. C. Bodley, quoted in Elder, p. 112.

225 *Everyone agreed that Puritanism and Beiping*: Marcuse, p. 19.

225 *Life was an endless string of parties*: Ibid., p. 20.

226 *Of a population of 1.3 million, many are unemployed*: Zhu Qinghua, an industrious bureaucrat, quoted in Dryburgh, p. 517.

226 *there wasn't a single flowering tree*: Lao She 1, p. 162.

226 *Dying must be the easiest, simplest thing*: Ibid., p. 187.

227 *never have I seen such gloom*: Letcher letter dated 8/1/37, quoted in Jeans and Letcher, p. 62.

227 *Peking Dust*: Letcher letter dated 4/13/37, quoted ibid., p. 39.

228 *When the Japanese came, Kates ran an American flag*: Quoted in Bordewich, p. 296. Kates's former courtyard home was razed; it used to be on today's Wax Storehouse Lane (*Lacang hutong*), northeast of the Forbidden City. The plum tree he planted there is said to still be standing.

228 *I don't believe the soldiers are trained*: Letcher letter dated 8/1/37, quoted in Jeans and Letcher, p. 64.

228 *Following the tanks came the infantry*: Letcher quoted ibid., p. 13. This observation comes from his published memoir, *One Marine's Story*.

228 *appears to be quite normal now*: Letcher letter dated 8/31/37, quoted in Jeans and Letcher, p. 69.

228 *to-day in the warm fall sunshine the crowd*: Letcher letter dated 10/10/37, quoted ibid., p. 75.

229 *Engineers punched holes*: Wu Hung, p. 251. The gates were named Chang'anmen (present-day Fuxingmen) and Qimingmen (present-day Jianguomen).

229 *In order to avoid Japanese and Chinese*: Quoted in Wang Jun, pp. 44–47.

229 *These old Manchu families*: Letcher letter dated 9/3/39, quoted in Jeans and Letcher, p. 176.

229 *If a lot of money isn't soon expended*: Letcher letter dated 7/4/39, quoted ibid., p. 166.

229 *Right now the only exercise*: Letcher letter dated 1/25/38, quoted ibid., p. 87.

230 *you see the same people again and again*: Letcher letter dated 6/26/39, quoted ibid., p. 165.

230 *rather ridiculous. Very small frogs*: Letcher letter dated 2/10/39, quoted ibid., p. 28.

230 *I went last year several times*: Letcher letter dated 2/20/39, quoted ibid., p. 151.

230 *told us to look well at the street and the houses*: Letcher letter dated 6/6/39, quoted ibid., pp. 162–3.

230 *If I had to live in a city*: Letcher letter dated 7/4/39, quoted ibid., pp.166–67.

CHAPTER 18: "IF SOMEONE IS SICK AND YOU DO NOT AID HIM, IT IS YOUR FAULT, NOT HIS"

248 *the power of government over the individual*: Kelo v. New London, p. 2678.

249 *Petitioners are not hold-outs*: Ibid., p. 2672.

249 *The beneficiaries are likely*: Ibid., p. 2677.

249 *enables the Court to hold*: Ibid., pp. 2677–78.

249 *In cities across the country*: Ibid., pp. 2686–87. Thomas directly quoted another researcher, Pritchett, "'The Public Menace' of Blight: Urban Renewal and the Private Uses of Eminent Domain, *21 Yale L. & Pol'y Rev. 1*, 47 (2003).

249 *So-called "urban renewal" programs*: Ibid., p. 2686.

249 *We emphasize that nothing in our opinion*: Ibid., p. 2668.

251 *According to the state-run China Daily*: "China mulls property law to secure ownership," October 23, 2004. Uncredited.

258 *Restoring a single courtyard home*: Laurence Brahm, quoted in Marquand.

259 *It's becoming more and more like Disneyland*: Jeffrey Huang, quoted in York.

CHAPTER 20: A BRIEF HISTORY OF 拆 PART FOUR

275   *The city's appointed mayor:* Wang Jun, pp. 67–68.

275   *I was dumbstruck:* Fairbank, p. 182.

275   *Mao said:* Wang Jun, pp. 67–68 and Fairbank, p. 182.

276   *In 1924:* Fairbank, p. 17.

276   *Recent tendencies in China:* Liang 1, p. 152.

277   *the only reliable sources of information are the buildings:* Liang quoted by Wilma
       Fairbank, ibid., p. 40.

277   *Since there existed no guides to buildings:* Fairbank, p. 65.

278   *First, a number of buildings appeared:* Liang 1, pp. 153–54.

279   *In 1949, only 4 percent:* Wang Jun, p. 82.

279   *We also had such suggestions:* Quoted in Sit, p. 245 and Wang Jun, p. 85.

280   *The mayor upbraided him:* Peng Zhen, quoted in Wang Jun, pp. 111–12. Peng,
       who also reported that the chairman wanted to see an ocean of smokestacks, ar-
       gued here that novices could guide experts, just as Mao led the Communists to
       victory in the civil war.

283   *An official told Liang, "You are an old conservative":* Ibid., p. 173.

283   *In August 1953:* Ibid., p. 107.

284   *From this era until 1984:* Sit, p. 157.

284   *Fourteen thousand smokestacks:* Wang Jun, p. 69.

284   *The nation's largest:* Sit, p. 157.

285   *When they have demolished the little grey streets:* Beauvoir, p. 14.

285   *The Party has permitted me:* "Liang Sicheng's Letter." *People's Daily,* February 4,
       1956.

285   *In 1957, he warned:* Quoted in Wang Jun, *"Da Malu Zhi Yang."* Xinhua, July 5,
       2005.

286   *It is only the people who love the motherland:* *People's Daily,* May 27, 1957.

286   *Destroying a gate of Beijing:* "Zhengfeng Yige Yuede Tihui." *People's Daily,* June 8,
       1957. By month's end, the paper ran a Liang essay praising Chairman Mao under
       the headline, "Bravely Luring Rightists from Their Caves for Struggling." Liang,
       baited into this political battle, never recovered his status.

286   *To celebrate the People's Republic's:* Wu Hung, pp. 108–26. Wu notes that the Ten
       Greats are identified differently in various publications. As a result, the term
       "loosely denotes a group of monuments built around the country's tenth an-
       niversary." P. 253.

287   *much of the beauty of ancient:* Marcuse, p. 20.

287   *always seemed to be picking up:* Ibid., p. 21.

287   *with them whatever remained of individual privacy:* Ibid., p. 22.

288   *Of the capital's 6,843 cataloged relics:* Wang Jun, p. 333.

289   *Facing it, with the city wall at my back*: Quoted from *"Xiang Taiping,"* by Shu Yi. *Beijing Evening News*, October 18, 2006.

289   *Kingfishers swooped across the surface*: Lao She 1, p. 244.

289   *a "contemptible pile"*: Fairbank, p. 189.

289   *I regret that I took up*: Ibid., p. 184.

290   *At first we had all the lights red*: Quoted in Topping.

290   *The two miles of apartment buildings*: Butterfield 1.

290   *It was as if the Europe of the sixteenth century*: Cameron, p. 418.

291   *The half of Beijing that was destroyed*: Tung, p. 167.

291   *In regards to this question*: Wang Jun, p. 184.

293   *If a city does not have its own culture and its own history*: Quoted in O'Neill.

293   *In 2007, the Geneva-based*: "Mega-Events, Olympic Games and Housing Rights." COHRE, June 2007.

CHAPTER 21: ECHO WALL

294   *There is no pattern*: The speaker is Johannes Dell of Albert Speer & Partner.

295   *This project is designed for the next century*: Tong Kezheng, quoted in Mickleburgh.

295   *I'm not opposed to the conservation of cultural relics*: Xie Li, quoted in Wei.

295   *In comparison, the destruction*: Zhang Yonghe (Yung-Ho Chang) quoted in Miller.

296   *History is being wiped out before our eyes*: Shu Yi quoted in Higgins.

296   *We thought then*: Gao Han, quoted in Wei.

307   *The joy of design is already there, the rest is rubbish*: Ai Weiwei quoted in Watts.

Bibliography

Using the public latrine in the dead of winter is nothing compared to the challenges one faces in tracking down Beijing's history. This book could not have been written without the tenacious research of a group of scholars whose work both informed and inspired me. The master recorders of the "razing and relocation" policy and its implementation are Fang Ke, Zhang Yan, and Lü Junhua. The latter, with Peter G. Rowe and Zhang Jie, produced the most comprehensive history of modern Chinese urban housing. (For more, see Ian Johnson.) Wang Jun sorted through the papers and drawings that Liang Sicheng's maid spirited away from Red Guards to produce the most thorough—in fact, the only—accounting of his attempts to preserve the Old City. Wilma Fairbank paints a loving portrait of her friend Liang and his wife, Lin Huiyin.

Readers seeking a concise summary of Beijing's development and feng shui should turn to Victor Sit. Wu Hung observes his hometown's symbolic architecture with an art historian's perspective. M. A. Aldrich's city history was my constant companion on bike rides around town. If a building caught my eye, I could usually find its description in Aldrich, who narrates in the relaxed voice of a patient guide. Juliet Bredon penned my favorite expatriate memoir of life in the post-imperial, pre-Communist capital. Marine Captain John Letcher's letters home read like a novel, thanks to their compilation by his daughter, Katie Letcher Lyle, and Roger B. Jeans.

Readers interested in 1920s Beijing should turn first to Madeline Yue Dong, where I found the accounts of the four-year eviction battle between the municipal government and merchants near Dazhalan. David Strand also illuminates this era by detailing the conflict over the city's modernization, primarily between rickshaw pullers and mechanized transport. Jeffrey Cody's telling of Henry Murphy's work in China piqued my interest in his "adaptive architecture," still seen—without explanatory plaques—in Beijing. Li Mingde has produced several texts that, uniquely, use simple language and consistent statistics to guide readers through *hutong* history and neighborhoods. H. Y. Lowe makes it all come alive.

Anthony Tung produced the definitive text on the history of urban preservation. Written in the voice of a detective on a globe-spanning trail, it set me off on my own explorations.

Finally, I am indebted to the *New York Times*, *Times of London*, and *People's Daily* for making their archive accessible via Internet. Long after the Widow had bolted the door, decades-old articles from these papers illuminated my computer screen and Beijing's past. Our courtyard looked different in that light, and I am thankful for the perspective.

PUBLISHED SOURCES

(Note: Where a formal English translation appears on the cover of a Chinese-language text, I have listed it. In other cases, the translation is my own.)

Abend, Hallett. "Old Peking Names and Habits Banned." *New York Times*, August 13, 1928.

Abramson, Daniel Benjamin. "'Marketization' and Institutions in Chinese Inner-City Redevelopment." *Cities* 14, no.2 (April 1997): pp. 71–75.

Agence France-Presse (newspaper articles without a byline).
    1. "UNESCO Raises Concern over Destruction of Beijing Historical Area." February 25, 2003.
    2. "Beijing Rectifies 'Destroy and Relocate' Policy After 1.5 Million Moved." November 6, 2003.

Aldrich, M. A. *The Search for a Vanishing Beijing.* Hong Kong: Hong Kong University Press, 2006.

Arlington, L. C., and William Lewisohn. *In Search of Old Peking.* 1935. Reprint, Hong Kong: Oxford University Press, 1987.

Attiret, Jean-Denis. "A Particular Account of the Emperor of China's Gardens near Peking." A 1743 letter published in *Lettres édifiantes et curieuses écrites des missions étrangères par quelques missionnaires de la compagnie de Jésus,* 27:1–61. Paris: Guérin, 1749. Translated to English by Sir Harry Beamont for *A Letter from F. Attiret.* London: Dodsley, 1752.

Azevedo, Andre, et al. *Beijing Hutong Conservation Study.* Beijing: Broadcasting Institute Press, 2004.

Beauvoir, Simone de. *The Long March.* Cleveland: World Publishing Company, 1958.

Beijing Municipal City Planning Commission, ed.
    1. *Lishi wenhua baohuqu baohu guihua: Beijing jiucheng ershiwu pian* [Conservation Planning of 25 Historic Areas in Beijing Old City]. Beijing: Yanshan, 2002.
    2. *Beijing lishi wenhua mingcheng Beijing huangcheng baohu guihua* [Conservation

Plan for the Historic City of Beijing and Imperial City of Beijing]. Beijing: China Architecture & Building Press, 2004.

    3. *Xuannan, fayuan si* [Xuannan, Source of Law Temple]. Beijing: Beijing Press, 2004.

Beijing Municipal Institute of City Planning & Design, ed.

    1. *Fangxiang ershiyi shijide Beijing* [Beijing Striding Forward to the 21ˢᵗ Century]. 2000 Olympic-bid synopsis of 1991–2010 urban plan. 1992.

    2. *Beijing jiucheng* [The Old City of Beijing]. Beijing: Yanshan Publishing, 2003.

Bordewich, Fergus. *Cathay: A Journey in Search of Old China.* New York: Prentice Hall Press, 1991.

Bredon, Juliet. *Peking.* Shanghai: Kelly & Walsh, Limited, 1920.

Briggs, Chester M. *The United States Marines in North China, 1894–1942.* Jefferson, NC: McFarland and Company, 2003.

Broudehoux, Anne-Marie. *The Making and Selling of Post-Mao Beijing.* New York: Routledge, 2004.

Buck, Pearl S. *The First Wife and Other Stories.* New York: John Day, 1933.

Burgess, John Stewart. *The Guilds of Peking.* New York: AMS Press, 1928.

Butterfield, Fox.

    1. "In Peking, 2 Miles of Botched New Housing." *New York Times*, August 19, 1979.

    2. "In Peking's Housing Crunch, a Chance to Trade Flats." *New York Times*, July 15, 1980.

Cameron, Nigel. *Barbarians and Mandarins.* 1970. Reprint, Hong Kong: Oxford University Press, 1989.

Chao, Julie. "Relics of Beijing's Past in Jeopardy; Building Boom Remakes Capital." *Atlanta Journal-Constitution*, June 6, 2004, p. B1.

Cheung, Ray. "Wall Rebuild Begins with Returned Bricks." *South China Morning Post*, December 24, 2001, p. 5.

Chu-Joe Hsia. "Urban Conservation in Taiwan: Problems and Prospects." *Asian Planning Schools Association* 3 (March 1997): pp. 62–70.

Cody, Jeffrey. *Building in China: Henry K. Murphy's "Adaptive Architecture," 1914–1935.* Hong Kong: Chinese University Press, 2001.

Constant, Samuel Victor. *Calls, Sounds and Merchandise of the Peking Street Peddlers.* 1936 master's thesis. Reprint, Beijing: National Library Press, 2004.

Constitution of the People's Republic of China. Beijing: Foreign Languages Press, 1994.

Cook, Thomas. *Peking and the Overland Route.* London: Thos. Cook & Son, 1917.

Dong, Madeline Yue.

    1. "Defining Beiping: Urban Reconstruction and National Identity, 1928–1936." In Joseph Esherick, ed., *Remaking the Chinese City: Modernity and National Identity, 1900–1950*, pp. 121–38. Honolulu: University of Hawaii Press, 2000.

2. *Republican Beijing: The City and Its Histories, 1911–1937.* Berkeley: University of California Press, 2003.

Dorn, Frank. *Walkout: With General Stilwell in Burma.* New York: Pyramid Books, 1971.

Dryburgh, Marjorie. "National City, Human City: The Reimagining and Revitalization of Beiping, 1928–37." *Urban History* (Cambridge University Press) 32, no. 3 (2005): pp. 500–524.

Elder, Chris. *Old Peking: City of the Ruler of the World.* Hong Kong: Oxford University Press, 1997.

Fairbank, Wilma. *Liang and Lin: Partners in Exploring China's Architectural Past.* Philadelphia: University of Pennsylvania Press, 1994.

Fang Ke. *Dangdai Beijing jiucheng gengxin* [Contemporary Conservation in the Inner City of Beijing: Survey, Analysis, and Investigation]. Beijing: China Architecture Industrial Press, 2000.

Fang Ke and Yan Zhang. "Plan and Market Mismatch: Urban Redevelopment in Beijing During a Period of Transition." *Asia Pacific Viewpoint* 44, no. 2 (August 2003): pp. 149–62. (Author credited as Ke Fang.)

Feng Jicai.

1. *Qiangjiu Laojie* [Saving the Old Street]. Beijing: Xiyuan Publishing House, 2000.

2. *Zhongguo minjian wenhua yichan qiangjiu gongcheng: Diaocha shouce* [The Project to Save Chinese Folk Cultural Heritage: Survey Handbook]. Beijing: Higher Education Press, 2002.

Friedman, John. *China's Urban Transition.* Minneapolis: University of Minnesota Press, 2005.

Han Rongliang. *Five Hundred How's & Why's: Sightseeing in Beijing.* Beijing: Morning Glory Publishers, 2000.

Higgins, Andrew. "Ancient Beijing Survived Mao but Not Money." *Guardian.* Reprint, *Cleveland Plain Dealer*, January 1, 1997, p. 2A.

Hunt, Michael. "The Forgotten Occupation: Peking, 1900–1901." *Pacific Historical Review* 48 (November 1979): pp. 501–29.

Jacobs, Jane. *The Death and Life of Great American Cities.* New York: Vintage, 1961.

Jakes, Susan. "Back-Alley Blues." *Time*, November 11, 2002.

Jeans, Roger B. and Katie Letcher Lyle, eds. *Goodbye to Old Peking: The Wartime Letters of U.S. Marine Captain John Seymour Letcher, 1937–1939.* Athens: Ohio University Press, 1998.

Jia Heping. "Renovation Plan Sparks Heated Debate." *China Daily*, July 10, 2002.

Jin Shoushen. *Beijing Legends.* Beijing: Foreign Languages Press, 2005.

Johnson, Ian. *Wild Grass: Three Stories of Change in Modern China.* New York: Pantheon, 2004.

Kates, George. *The Years That Were Fat: The Last of Old China.* 1952. Reprint, Cambridge: MIT Press, 1967.

Kelo v. New London. 125 S. Ct. 2655. Decided June 23, 2005. (Subsequent rehearing request denied by *Kelo v. New London,* 126 S. Ct. 24.)

Kidd, David. *Peking Story: The Last Days of Old China.* 1961. Reprint, New York: Clarkson N. Potter, 1988.

Kishkovsky, Sophia. "Engels Would Gasp, and Locals Gripe, at a Golden Mile." *New York Times,* December 18, 2006.

Krich, John. "Sign Language: Beijing's Road to the Olympics Comes with English Lessons." *Asian Wall Street Journal,* September 8–10, 2006, p. W12.

LaFarge, Paul. *Haussmann, or The Distinction.* New York: Farrar, Straus and Giroux, 2001.

Lao She.
1. *Rickshaw.* Translated by Jean M. James. Honolulu: University of Hawaii Press, 1979.
2. *Camel Xiangzi.* Translated by Shi Xiaoqing. Beijing: Foreign Languages Press, 1981.
3. *Selected Stories by Lao She.* Beijing: Chinese Literature Press, 1999.
4. *Lao She jiang Beijing* [Lao She on Beijing]. Beijing: Beijing Press, 2005.

Le Corbusier. *The City of To-Morrow and Its Planning.* 1929. Reprint, New York: Dover, 1987.

Liang Sicheng.
1. *Tuxiang Zhonguo jianzhu shi* [A Pictorial History of Chinese Architecture]. Tianjin: Baihua Wenyi Publishers, 2000.
2. *Collected Works of Liang Sicheng.* Vol. 5. Beijing: China Architecture and Building Press, 2001.

Liang Sicheng and Chen Zhanxiang. *Liang Chen fang'an yu Beijing* [Liang-Chen Beijing Plan]. Shenyang: Liaoning Educational Press, 2005.

Li Jing. "Project to Protect Revered Cultural Relics." *China Daily,* January 5, 2004.

Li Mingde.
1. *Beijing hutong luyou shouce* [A Guidebook to Alleys in Beijing]. Beijing: China Tourism Press, 2001.
2. *The Architectural Art of Hutong Gate Buildings.* Beijing: China Architecture and Building Press, 2003.
3. *A Cultural Tour of Beijing's Hutong.* Beijing: China Architecture and Building Press, 2005.

Lin Lina. *The Elegance and Elements of Chinese Architecture.* Translated by Donald Brix. Taipei: National Palace Museum, 2000.

Lin Yan and Fan Wei. *Lao Beijingde miaohui* [The Temple Fair of Old Beijing]. Beijing: Wenwu Press, 2004.

Li Zhang. *Strangers in the City: Reconfigurations of Space, Power, and Social Networks, Within China's Floating Population.* Stanford: Stanford University Press, 2001.

Lowe, H. Y. *The Adventures of Wu: The Life Cycle of a Peking Man.* Vol. 1, 1940; vol. 2, 1941. Reprint, Princeton: Princeton University Press, 1983.

Lü Junhua. "Beijing's Old and Dilapidated Housing Renewal." *Cities* 14, no. 2 (April 1997): pp. 59–69.

Lü Junhua, Peter G. Rowe, and Zhang Jie, eds. *Modern Urban Housing in China, 1840–2000.* Munich: Prestel, 2001.

Lynn, Jermyn Chi-Hung. *Social Life of the Chinese (in Peking).* Peking: China Booksellers, Ltd. 1928.

Ma Bingjian. *Beijing siheyuan jianzhu* [Beijing Quadrangle Architecture]. Tianjin: Tianjin University Press, 1999.

MacCloskey, Monro. *Reilly's Battery.* New York: Richards Rosen Press, 1969.

Marcuse, Jacques. *The Peking Papers.* New York: Dutton & Co., 1967.

Marquand, Robert. "Why Old Beijing's Crumbling Courtyards Face Extinction." *Christian Science Monitor,* March 14, 2001, p. 12.

Methold, Ken.
> 1. *Yingyu* [Primary English], Grade Four. 2 vol. Beijing: McGraw-Hill Education and Beijing Normal University Press, 2000.
> 2. *Yingyu* [Primary English], Grade Five. 2 vol. Beijing: McGraw-Hill Education and Beijing Normal University Press, 2000.

Mickleburgh, Rod. "Beijing Modernization Reduces History to Rubble." *Toronto Globe and Mail,* February 7, 1998, p. A17.

Miller, Rena. "Mixed Feelings as New Road Prepares to Carve Through Beijing." Agence France-Presse, January 11, 1998.

Moser, Michael J., and Yeone Wei-Chih Moser. *Foreigners Within the Gates.* London: Oxford University Press, 1993.

Myers, Steven Lee. "A Russian Skyscraper Plan Divides a Horizontal City." *New York Times,* December 2, 2006.

Napack, Jonathan. "Yung-Ho Chang Tries to Restore an Appreciation for Design." *International Herald Tribune,* April 14, 2001.

New York Times (newspaper articles without a byline).
> 1. "The Interior of Peking." January 15, 1861.
> 2. "Legation Life in Peking." July 14, 1900.
> 3. "Insect and Animal Pests in Peking." November 11, 1900.
> 4. "Praises the Americans." December 27, 1900.
> 5. "Preparing to Leave Peking." March 4, 1901.
> 6. "American Rule in Peking." March 9, 1901.
> 7. "Petition of the Chinese in Peking." May 21, 1901.

    8. "Youth in Peking Fight West's Ways." August 22, 1966.

    9. "Youths in Peking Alter City's Look." September 18, 1966.

O'Neill, Mark. "Home Truths." *South China Morning Post*, January 13, 2003.

Pattinson, Tom. "The Big Smoke." *Time Out Beijing*, December 2005, p. 6.

Pearl, Cyril. *Morrison of Peking*. Sydney: Angus and Robertson, 1967.

Plumb, Robert K. "Peking Man Bones Borne by Marine." *New York Times*, January 5, 1952.

Polo, Marco. *Travels in the Land of Kubilai Khan*. Excerpt from 1958 edition of *Travels*. London: Penguin, 2005.

Rowe, Peter G., and Seng Kuan. *Architectural Encounters with Essence and Form in Modern China*. Cambridge: MIT Press, 2002.

Rybczynski, Witold. *The Perfect House: A Journey with the Renaissance Master Andrea Palladio*. New York: Simon & Schuster, 2002.

Rykwert, Joseph. *The Seduction of Place*. New York: Vintage, 2002.

Saiget, Robert J.

    1. "Destruction of Beijing City Center Escalates with New Plan." Agence France-Presse, March 24, 2003.

    2. "Beijing Defends Destruction of Inner City amid Widespread Dissatisfaction." Agence France-Presse, August 14, 2003.

Salmon, Andrew. "Raise the Roof." *South China Morning Post*, March 25, 2006.

Sit, Victor F. S. *Beijing: The Nature and Planning of a Chinese Capital City*. Chichester: John Wiley & Sons, 1995.

Sitwell, Osbert. *Escape with Me!* 1939. Reprint Hong Kong: Oxford University Press, 1986.

Strand, David. *Rickshaw Beijing: City People and Politics in the 1920s*. Berkeley: University of California Press, 1989.

Steinglass, Matt. "Foreign Growth." *Metropolitan*, February 2005.

Swallow, Robert W. *Sidelights on Peking Life*. Peking: China Booksellers Limited, 1927.

Times of London (newspaper articles without a byline; their Peking correspondent was George Morrison).

    1. "The Siege of the Peking Legations." October 13, 1900, p. 5A.

    2. "America and Chinese Criminals." May 1, 1901, p. 7.

    3. "Report by General Chaffee." June 21, 1901, p. 5.

    4. "Peking." November 5, 1901, p. 5.

Topping, Audrey. "Peking Residents Ride the Subway Just for Fun." *New York Times*, May 9, 1971.

Towery, Britt. *Lao She: China's Master Storyteller*. Waco: Tao Foundation, 1999.

Tung, Anthony M. *Preserving the World's Great Cities*. New York: Three Rivers Press, 2001.

Wang Jun. *Chengji* [City Record]. Beijing: Sanlian, 2003.

Wang Sheng'an, ed. *Aoyun anbao fuwu yingyu* [Olympic Security English]. Beijing: Chinese People's Police University Press, 2002.

Wang Tongzhen. *Shuixiang Beijing* [Watertown Beijing]. Beijing: Tuanjie Publishers, 2004.

Wang Wenbo. *Hutongde jiyi* [Recollections of Hutong]. Beijing: China Nationality Art Photograph Publishing House, 2005.

Watts, Jonathan. "No One in the State Here Would Ever Hire Me for a Project like This." *Guardian*, August 9, 2007.

Wei Bian. "Ping'an Avenue: Conflict of Old Versus New." *Beijing Review*, October 1998.

Weng Li. *Beijingde hutong* [Hutong of Beijing]. Beijing: Beijing Arts and Photography Publishing House, 1993.

Wonacott, Peter. "First Olympic Event: A Pricey Facelift for the Host City." *Asian Wall Street Journal*, July 19, 2001, p. 1.

Wu, Nelson I. *Chinese and Indian Architecture*. London: Prentice Hall, 1963.

Wu Hung. *Remaking Beijing: Tiananmen Square and the Creation of a Political Space*. Chicago: University of Chicago Press, 2005.

Xiao Fuxing. *Bada hutong bazhang* [Eight Chapters of the Eight Big Hutong]. Beijing: Writer's Press, 2007.

Xu Chengbei. *Old Beijing: In the Shadow of the Imperial Throne*. Beijing: Foreign Languages Press, 2001.

Xu Ying. *Jingcheng hutong* [Capital City Hutong]. Beijing: Gongyimeishu Press, 2006.

Yang Dongping. *Chengshi jifeng* [Urban Winds]. Beijing: Xingxing, 2005.

Yang Xin.

    1. *Read Hutong*. Beijing: Jingji Ribao, 2001.

    2. *Da qianmen wai* [Outside the Front Gate]. Beijing: Xinhua, 2003.

Yan Zhang and Fang Ke. "Is History Repeating Itself? From Urban Renewal in the United States to Inner-City Redevelopment in China." *Journal of Planning Education and Research* 23 (2004): pp. 286–98. (Author credited as Ke Fang.)

Yardley, Jim. "Olympics Imperil Historic Beijing Neighborhood." *New York Times*, July 12, 2006.

York, Geoffrey. "Preserving China on His Own Dime." *Toronto Globe and Mail*, January 8, 2007, p. A12.

Yu Runqi. *Gate Piers in Beijing*. Beijing: Arts and Photography Publishing House, 2002.

Zhang Jie. "Informal Construction in Beijing's Old Neighborhoods." *Cities* 14, no. 2 (April 1997): pp. 85–94.

Zhang Jinqi. *Bada hutong lide chenxiang jiushi* [A Carnal History of the Eight Big Hutong]. Zhengzhou: Zhengzhou University Press, 2005.

Zhang Tiewei. *Lao Beijingde miaohui* [The Temple Fair of Old Beijing]. Beijing: Wenwu Press, 2004.

Zhang Yonghe. *Zuo wenben* [Yung-Ho Chang Writes]. Beijing: Sanlian, 2005.

Zhou Zhongzhi, ed. *Fumo Beijing* [Caressing Beijing]. Beijing: Sanlian, 2005.
Zhu Mingde, ed. *Beijing chengqu jiaoluo diaocha* [Investigation of Urban Corners in Beijing]. Beijing: Social Sciences Academic Press, 2005.
Zhu Qixin. *The Sights of Beijing*. Beijing: China Travel & Tourism Press, 2002.

NEWSPAPERS AND PERIODICALS

Agence France-Presse
Asian Wall Street Journal
Beijing Evening News (Beijing wanbao)
Beijing Law Nightly (Beijing fazhi wanbao)
Beijing Review
China Daily
First (Jingbao)
New Capital News (Xinjing bao)
New York Times
People's Daily (Renmin ribao)
Southern Weekend (Nanfang Zhoumo)
That's Beijing
Time Out Beijing
Times of London

UNPUBLISHED AND INTERNALLY CIRCULATED SOURCES

Albert Speer & Partner. "Concept for the Central Axis, Beijing." Design. 2002.
Centre on Housing Rights and Evictions (COHRE). "Mega-Events, Olympic Games and Housings Rights." June 2007.
Dazhalan Subdistrict Government. "Dazhalan Gazetteer." Internally circulated neighborhood history, intended for cadres. 1993.
UNESCO. "Beijing and Beijing." Synopsis of conference. 2005.
Urban Planning and Design Institute of Tsinghua University.
    1. *"Beijing zhongzhouxian chengshi jihua"* [Urban Design of the Central Axis]. Design. 2002.
    2. "Renovation and Renewal of Beijing's Dazhalan Area." Design. 2002.
Westendorff, David. "Beijing's Center City *Hutong*: A Better Future Is Possible." Memo to UNESCO. 2004.

INDEX

A Note on the Author

Michael Meyer first went to China in 1995 with the Peace Corps. A longtime teacher and a Lowell Thomas Award winner for travel writing, Meyer has published stories in *Time*, *Smithsonian*, the *New York Times Book Review*, the *Financial Times*, *Reader's Digest*, the *Los Angeles Times*, and the *Chicago Tribune*. In China, he has represented the National Geographic Society's Center for Sustainable Destinations, training China's UNESCO World Heritage site managers in preservation practices. *The Last Days of Old Beijing* is his first book.